Lost and Found

LOST AND FOUND

Young Fathers in the Age of Unwed Parenthood

Paul Florsheim & David Moore

OXFORD
UNIVERSITY PRESS

Oxford University Press is a department of the University of Oxford. It furthers
the University's objective of excellence in research, scholarship, and education
by publishing worldwide. Oxford is a registered trade mark of Oxford University
Press in the UK and certain other countries.

Published in the United States of America by Oxford University Press
198 Madison Avenue, New York, NY 10016, United States of America.

Library of Congress Control Number: 2019953445
ISBN 978–0–19–086501–6

9 8 7 6 5 4 3 2 1

Printed by Sheridan Books, Inc., United States of America

For Tom and Nancy who have always been with me
For Ben, Nathan, and Sam for being their wonderful selves
For Marcy, my love, who reminds me that life is for living
PF

For Jill, the love of my life
For Aidan and Austin, for helping me learn
firsthand what it means to be a dad
DM

CONTENTS

ACKNOWLEDGMENTS

First and foremost, we want to acknowledge and extend our gratitude to the young men and women who opened up and shared their stories with us over the years and, most particularly, to those who are featured in this book. Over the years, we have relied heavily on a team of skilled and dedicated students and research staff who collected most of the data included in this book. Some of these people we worked with will appear as interviewers— with pseudonyms—in the chapters that follow. We want to give special thanks to Rosemary Adams, Claire McCain Khadakkar, Eugenia Alba, Matt Winstanley, Andy Suth, Mike Voss, Jennifer Briggs, Trina Seefeldt, Chuck Edgerton, Solmaz Shotorbani, Spencer Hall, and Kimberly Fausto, whose research skills were critical to the success of our work.

Like our research participants, our interviewers were racially and ethnically diverse and ranged in age from their 20s to their 60s. There was also a balance of male and female interviewers because we made a point of having young fathers be interviewed by men and young mothers be interviewed by women. These research assistants, who stuck with us over the years, were responsible for helping the young mothers and fathers feel comfortable enough to tell us their stories and then to come back and tell us more as their stories unfolded over time. We think they did their jobs remarkably well. Several students and colleagues also played a critical role in the development of the Young Parenthood Program we describe in Chapter 22. These collaborators include Jason Burrow-Sanchez, Rocio Paredes-Mora, Kellie VanderVeur, Laura McArthur, Sarah Heavin, Tim Fowles, Le Ngu, and Cristina Hudak. A couple of these colleagues appear as counselors in that chapter, with their identity disguised, along with the specifics of their client's identity and circumstances.

Dr. Katie McElligott, who is a pediatrician in Salt Lake City, deserves a special note of appreciation because she played an instrumental role in helping us gain access to the young women and men who participated in our research over many years. Katie ran the Teen Mother and Child Program at the University of Utah Hospital for so long that she provided medical care to the children of the children she had cared for a generation earlier. Katie's patients loved her, and we could tell she loved them too. If not for Katie and her staff, particularly Analee Walton, our work may have never gotten off the ground.

We also want to acknowledge our colleagues who have supported our work and helped us formulate some of the ideas included in this book, including Sheri Johnson, Philip and Carolyn Cowan, Jay Fagan, Alan Hawkins, Michael Lamb, and Jay Belsky. We appreciate the Helen Riaboff Whiteley Center at the University of Washington for providing us with a place to get together, away from it all, to discuss what we wanted to say and how to best say it in this book. That time and space was immensely valuable. We owe a heartfelt thank you to Haley Florsheim for reading and providing valuable feedback on our first complete draft of this book.

Over the years, we have received generous funding from various agencies and foundations to support the work we describe in this book. These include the Office of Populations Affairs, the Robert Wood Johnson Foundation, and the National Institute of Mental Health. Alicia Richmond Scott and Cassandra Chess, at the now-defunct Office of Adolescent Pregnancy Programs, were particularly helpful and supportive of us along the way. We do not want this acknowledgments section to come across as a mere formality because the work we present in this book is the product of a team effort that required tremendous amounts of time, energy, and money. We are grateful to everyone who made this research possible.

CAST OF CHARACTERS

Chapter	Fathers	Mothers	Interviewers
Introduction	Darnel	Cleo	
Chapter 1	Robert	Sarah	Paul & Emma
	Quinton	Shari	Barry & Emma
Chapter 2	Quinton	Shari	Barry & Emma
	Jed	Molly	Keith & Julie
Chapter 3	Carlos		Barry
Chapter 4	Charles	Tasha	Paul & Emma
	Darnel	Cleo	Mike & Lucille
Chapter 5	Tyrone	Sybil	Mike & Lucille
	Steve	Michelle	Dave & Julie
Chapter 6	Steve	Michelle	Dave & Julie
	Tyrone	Sybil	Mike & Lucille
	Robert	Sarah	Paul & Emma
	Darius	Janice	Simon & Lucille
Chapter 7	Theo		Barry
	Kurt		Barry
	Quinton		Barry
	Marcus	Diamond	Mike & Emma
Chapter 9	Ron	Samantha	Barry & Emma
	Jerome	Ebony	Simon & Lucille
Chapter 10	Danny	April	Paul & Julie
	Brian	Brandy	Keith & Julie
Chapter 11	Jack	Nicole	
	William	Phyllis	Barry & Isabella
	Darius	Janice	Simon & Lucille
Chapter 12	Carlos	Monica	Barry & Isabella

Chapter	Fathers	Mothers	Interviewers
Chapter 15	Robert		Paul
	Jed		Keith
	Darnel		Mike
	Steve		Dave
Chapter 16	James	Stephanie	Simon & Emma
	Eddie	LaShawndra	Mike & Lucille
Chapter 17	Robert	Sarah	Paul & Emma
	Tyrone		Mike
	Jed		Keith
	Steve	Michelle	Dave & Julie
Chapter 18	Tyrone		Mike
	Robert		Paul
	Steve		Dave
	Darnel	Cleo	Mike & Emma
Chapter 20	Robert		Paul
	Tyrone		Mike
	Darnel		Mike
	Jed		Keith
Chapter 21	Darnel		Mike
Chapter 22	Tim	Alyssa	Nick & Stacy
	Alberto	Marcella	Eric & Stacy

Introduction

In the mid-1990s, when the soaring numbers of pregnant teenagers and single mothers were hot political topics, we decided to make young fathers the focus of our research. At the time, little was known about young fathers, despite the obvious role they played in teen pregnancy and single motherhood. We figured that a better understanding of these young men could help us develop strategies for keeping families connected. But when we first set out to study young fathers, we discovered that we had a problem: we didn't know where to find them. Unlike pregnant teens and young mothers, there was no place that young fathers received services or congregated. After puzzling over this, we landed on the idea of asking young pregnant women for their help in recruiting their partners, the fathers of their soon-to-arrive children. That decision led to a series of "aha" moments that resulted in the writing of this book.

The first "aha" moment occurred almost immediately. Even though the expectant mothers were not our primary focus, we decided to include them in the research process anyway. What this meant was that we asked the young mothers and fathers to meet with us together, but then we interviewed them separately to ensure that each could speak to us confidentially.[a] This approach gave us the opportunity to see these young

---

a. We anticipated that both expectant parents might censor themselves in the presence of the other, and we wanted to give them the space to speak freely. When we asked our first couple about whether their pregnancy was planned, the father told us it was an accident, and the mother told us that he had wanted a baby but she did not, and so he had sabotaged their condoms. As we put those two pieces of information together, it occurred to us that the story we planned to tell was more complicated—more multidimensional—than we originally thought.

men through the eyes of their girlfriends or, as was sometimes the case, their ex-girlfriends. Occasionally, these young women would tell us things that their partners had covered up, such as their infidelities or illegal activities. But, most of the time, they told us about the softer, tender sides of these young men, such as how he had taken care of her when she was sick or comforted her when she was sad. They often told us about parts of their partner's history that were too painful for them to tell us directly, such as being abandoned or abused as a child. Hearing about these young men from their partners helped us see them more completely and often more compassionately. In addition, by having them come to these research meetings together, we could see how they spoke with and listened to each other, how they looked at and touched their partners. These observations became a vital part of how we came to understand these men and their development as fathers. We realized that what started as a recruitment strategy—asking pregnant women to bring their partners to us—helped us see that fatherhood is an inherently interpersonal process that begins before the baby arrives.

The second insight was that fathers had more to say than anyone could have anticipated, including their partners. At first, the two of us did most of the interviews with the young men, and we hired two young women, both students, to interview the expectant mothers. These were long interviews designed to help our research participants tell their stories fully. Almost invariably, the interviews with the young expectant fathers ran long, often 30 minutes longer than the interviews with their partners. These young expectant mothers could not believe this was happening. Typically, the young woman's interview would last for 70 or 80 minutes, and she often assumed her boyfriend was pacing around outside, waiting for her to finish. When these young women found out that their boyfriend was still talking, they'd often say something like, "What could he be talking about? He never talks!" It dawned on us that, given the right context, these young men are not just willing to talk, they actually enjoyed the opportunity. We were asking questions that no one had ever asked them before; they were saying things they had never articulated. Simple questions like "How do you feel about her?" "How do you feel about becoming a father?" "What sort of father do you hope to become?" and "What could get in the way?" opened doors they did not know were there. Once these young men realized this was not a test, that we just wanted to know, they allowed themselves to get curious.

The third realization was that we often underestimated these young men. This "aha" moment took us much longer to figure out. Here's how it went: we interviewed some pretty rough characters who had been through a lot. Some showed us their bullet wound scars; sometimes we delayed the interview until they got released from jail. Some had dropped out of school to deal drugs; some were doing little other than smoking a lot of marijuana. Sometimes, after the interview was over, we would say to ourselves, and sometimes to each other, "What in the world was this young woman thinking when she hooked up with this guy?" But that was not the "aha" moment. The insight arrived about 2 years later when some of these young fathers who seemed like they were running headlong into serious trouble came back and told us about *their* aha moments and how they were now working 50 hours a week or back in school, or both. To be sure, some of the young men who had very troubled histories continued to have troubled lives, but we found ourselves surprised by how many seemed to turn their lives around or were at least trying the make that turn.

Darnel was one of the young men who surprised us. It's not that Darnel came across as tough or troubled, per se. In fact, when we first met him at a clinic in Chicago, sitting beside his girlfriend Cleo, there was nothing remarkable about the way Darnel looked. He was an 18-year-old African American man, average height and weight, wearing a plain red T-shirt and jeans. He seemed to be without pretention, without any distinguishing style. When he spoke, he seemed to choose his words carefully, sometimes looking off in the distance as if he wanted to see what he was about to say before he said it. Despite this deliberateness, he did not come across as stilted or uncertain. In fact, he was quite articulate, and there was a lyrical quality to his gentle baritone voice. As he recounted recent events in his life, Darnel looked and sounded beleaguered. Over the last few months, he'd been kicked out of school for truancy and fighting, he didn't have a job but admitted he hadn't looked very hard, and his mother had told him to pack up and move out after she caught him dealing marijuana on their front porch. And now Cleo was pregnant. As he shared all this, he seemed to be puzzling over the facts of his life, trying to make sense of his story.

Darnel said things went downhill for him after his father died. He wasn't very close to his father, who would drop by every now and then to say hello. The last time he saw him was about a year ago, and he thought nothing of it at the time. But then, 2 days later, his father died of an illness no one knew he had. He was gone without warning or much explanation. Darnel described this as the worst moment in his life, and it was still hard for him to talk about. At the time, he felt empty, but he started acting angry, getting into fights, and skipping school to get high. After his mother kicked him out, he went to live with his older brother, who was living with Cleo's aunt. This is where he met Cleo, who had run away from her foster home.

Cleo recalls that Darnel seemed to be in shock when they first met, like he had just been jumped or in an accident or something. One day, when

Cleo came back to her aunt's house crying about a fight with her boyfriend, Darnel told her that she was better off without him. It was exactly what she needed to hear. Not long after that, they were spending all their time together. And a couple of months later, Cleo was pregnant. At this point in the story, it's hard to avoid thinking that Darnel is a poor prospect for fatherhood, and it gets worse.

Not long after their first interview with us, Cleo returned to her foster mother's house, and Darnel went to jail after being arrested for possession. He got out in time to be with Cleo when she gave birth to their son, Curtis, but he was back in again before Curtis was a year old. After she turned 18 and was released from foster care, Cleo moved into her own apartment with some financial support from the state. Now that she was a mother, she seemed more grown up and self-assured. Cleo loved Darnel but she told him that if he went to jail one more time she would break up with him. And she meant it. So when Darnel was arrested for the third time, Cleo told him that she knew he could be a good father if he tried and knew that Curtis needed him, but she also knew she couldn't be with him anymore.

If we hadn't told you beforehand, we imagine that many of you would be surprised to learn that, over the next year, Darnel made a rather dramatic turnaround as a father and partner, which we describe in more detail in the pages that follow, beginning in Chapter 4. Improbable success stories like this beg the question: What is it about Darnel or his circumstances or his relationship with Cleo that accounts for his transformation? This is one of the key questions that we attempt to answer in this book, not just for Darnel, but for several other fathers whom we feature in multiple chapters, fathers who defied our initial expectations and surprised us with how well they were doing as fathers when we followed up with them over time.

When we decided to study young fathers, our basic hypotheses were simple and straightforward. We expected that, drawing upon the data that we collected from fathers (which we explain in more detail in the following discussion), we would be able to predict fathers' outcomes based on the number and severity of their risk factors. In other words, we expected poor outcomes for fathers with a lot of risk factors (e.g., psychological problems, substance abuse, criminal history, unemployment) and positive outcomes for fathers who were at comparatively low risk. We predicted that expectant fathers who were doing well to begin with would be doing well as fathers 2 years later, which, as we will discuss, can mean a lot of different things. In contrast, we expected that those who were having more problems to begin with would be functioning quite poorly as fathers, perhaps disengaged or presenting some sort of danger to their children.

When analyzing the data in our various studies, we found that these predictions were pretty accurate for many, but not all, fathers. For the sake of simplicity, we could describe the two main groups of fathers as having generally positive or generally negative trajectories, meaning that their positive or negative outcomes as fathers (2 years after their children's birth) were predictable, based on their respectively low or high levels of risk before they became fathers. Some of the fathers we include in this book were selected because they represent either of these two groups of young fathers.

After identifying fathers who represent the expected trends in the adjustment of young fathers, we looked closely at two other groups of fathers that defied our predictions. These include fathers like Darnel, who ended up doing better than we expected, based on our assessment of their initial risk status. It also included fathers who showed the opposite pattern of unexpected *negative* outcomes as fathers. This process of looking carefully at the outliers in one's data is somewhat unusual among researchers. We did this because it occurred to us that learning more about young men who look like they are heading for big problems but who end up doing quite well might reveal useful information about how to support positive paternal development, particularly among those who are at high risk. These "better than expected" fathers might teach us a lot about resiliency. And, of course, there are also those fathers who appear to be doing quite well when we meet them but who have serious adjustment problems across the transition to parenthood, getting into trouble with the law or using drugs and becoming disruptive to their child's well-being. A careful look at these fathers, and understanding how they become derailed, might provide important clues about how to keep young fathers healthy and on a positive trajectory.

In this book, we try to tell the stories of these different types of young fathers in a way that captures the depth, range, and diversity of their experiences. In large measure, these stories are the backbone of this book, and if there is one thing that has propelled us to write, it is the fact that so many young men and women opened themselves up to us with the understanding that we would use their experiences—their stories—to help other young families.

WHY IS THIS STORY IMPORTANT?

A central premise of this book is that young men in general, and young fathers in particular, warrant more attention than we are currently giving them. One reason for this is that many young fathers are struggling with very difficult circumstances and would benefit from additional support. Another reason is that providing support to young fathers would be beneficial to society because, ultimately, their difficulties become ours too. And so do their successes.

What's the evidence that young men need more of our attention? There is quite a bit. Young men outpace every other age group in their criminal behavior, their substance abuse, their violence toward their romantic partners, and their rates of unemployment. They are the most likely age group to die from injuries due to accidents, and they are also more likely to kill or injure someone else. Ironically, they are less likely to receive mental health services designed to help them manage their emotions, build stable relationships, and stay out of trouble. It's not just that they have less access to mental health services, which is a factor. They are also more averse to receiving help. Even when services are offered, many decline, not wanting to appear weak or hear a lecture about what they are doing wrong and what they ought to do instead.

This is not to say that we think young men, if left to their own devices, will turn into marauding bands of hooligans. We do not think that. After all, we were once young men; we are the fathers of young men; and, as researchers, clinicians, and professors, we have worked with young men almost every day of our entire careers. We know that young men—and young fathers—can be tender-hearted and caring, deeply emotional and conscientious, committed and dependable. Like most people, young men are often more complex than they appear. Nevertheless, young men have always been viewed as a segment of the population that needed to be managed and molded. Some societies, like the Maasai in Kenya and the wealthy in England, sent their adolescent boys away and subjected them to rigorous training, hoping to facilitate their maturation. After teaching young men how to make constructive use of their time and energy, they are encouraged, through our institutions, to get married and become fathers. In some respects, fatherhood, *along with marriage,* has served as a natural antidote to the challenges of being a young man.

What is relatively new in contemporary society is that many young men who are becoming fathers are also foregoing marriage. When we started this work, we were primarily interested in the youngest group of fathers, those who were 18 or younger. But this group shrank over time as the rate of teen pregnancy has drastically and thankfully diminished over the last 20 years. However, as the teen birth rate declined, the rate of unwed parenthood among young adults was climbing steadily. This trend was creating a new set of problems for children and for society at large. And so we began to expand our work to include those young fathers who were a little older.

Readers are probably aware of the statistic that about 4 out of 10 babies are born to unwed parents, up from about 1 in 10 in the mid-20th century. As alarming as this may sound, it's actually an understatement. Among young parents under the age of 25, the figure is closer to 8 in 10. This means that, in a relatively short period of time, one of the most effective ways for societies to formally solidify a man's bond to his family has become far less compelling for a large proportion of the childbearing population. The fact that the trend toward unwed parenthood is greatest among those under 25 suggests that the rate of children born to and raised by unwed parents will continue to grow in subsequent generations.

Later in the book, we address the question of why this shift away from marriage and toward unwed parenthood is happening. However, setting aside for now the "why" question, it is clear that, without marriage, the bond between fathers and mothers and children has become looser, less adhesive. This is evident across most dimensions of fatherhood. Without marriage, fathers are less likely to be living with, spending time with, and providing financially for their children. Based on the percentage of children who are not living with or regularly visiting their fathers, the precariousness of the connection between fathers and their families is greater now than at any point in our history.

As much as it may seem that the bonds that hold families and societies together are deteriorating, deterioration is not the theme of this book, or even a subtheme. Rather, understanding changes in the structure and dynamics of families and how to meet the challenges created by those changes lies at the heart of what this book is about. One of the core questions we address in this book is this: If the old strategies for holding families together are less effective than they once were and if there are risks associated with the breakdown of family bonds, then what else might be done to create more stability and security for children so that the next generation gets off to a good start?

This book is not the first of its kind to focus on fathers, or even young fathers. In fact, there are many fatherhood researchers and authors who helped blaze the "fatherhood trail" that we have followed.[b] One of the

b. Kathryn Edin and Timothy Nelson's 2013 book, entitled *Doing the Best I Can: Fatherhood in the Inner City* (Berkeley, CA: University of California Press) is a good example of a book on fatherhood that is both similar to and different from our book. Like us, Edin and Nelson interviewed fathers (in their case, all from the inner cities of Camden, New Jersey, and Philadelphia) over a period of several years. Like us, they focus on the relationships between fathers and mothers and between fathers and their children. These authors also reflect, as we do, on the dramatic historical changes that have occurred in how these relationships develop and unfold over time. In contrast to our approach, they focus on fathers who are somewhat older and recruit them

things we do differently from previous books on young fathers is make some specific and practical recommendations for strengthening families by supporting the development of young fathers. These recommendations, which appear in the last section of this book, are based on what we've learned from listening to the stories of young fathers and mothers, paying particularly close attention to those parts where they work together to revise and reshape their life trajectories. But before we had any stories to share, we first had to find young fathers and mothers and figure out what information we wanted to gather from them. As you might expect, this process was not so easy—or quick.

FINDING FATHERS

The two of us met at the University of Utah in the Department of Psychology in the mid-1990s. Since we had both recently arrived in Salt Lake City after living and going to school in Chicago, it seemed natural to set up research shops in both cities. Confident that we could recruit young expectant fathers with the help of young expectant mothers, we cultivated the necessary connections, developed a research plan, got lucky enough to secure a grant to fund our plan, and dove headlong into this work, determined and exuberant. By happenstance, it turns out that Chicago and Salt Lake represent two distinct slices of America, which adds balance and depth of perspective to the story that follows.

Chicago is, in many ways, a soulful and vibrant city, and Chicagoans tend to be hearty, determined, and resilient people. But Chicago can also be fractious and tense; its people, divided and divisive. Beyond the glitz of its downtown or the swankiness of its hipper neighborhoods, Chicago has neighborhoods that are intensely poor and hypersegregated. These are

---

later in their development as fathers. Most important, they do not provide specific recommendations for how to support or stabilize at-risk fathers and their families. Moreover, the title of their book, *Doing the Best I Can,* conveys a sentiment that many of the unwed fathers they met seem to share about themselves as fathers. In reflecting on this sentiment, Edin and Nelson acknowledge that many fathers are not living up the expectations of our society or the mothers of their children. They also effectively convey that most of these men are, contrary to stereotypes, wanting to be involved as fathers and to stay connected with their children. Edin and Nelson's message is complex, even philosophical, but ultimately pessimistic. They seem to say that yes, many fathers may not live up to expectations, but given the current constraints on lower-class families in America, they could do worse. If they are doing the best they can, then maybe it's time we take what we can get. We think Edin and Nelson's book is excellent, but we also think readers will find our perspective on fathers and their families to be more optimistic and hopefully pragmatic.

tough places to raise families and grow up. They are also where you are most likely to live if you are young and pregnant and African American or Latina. Everyone in Chicago suffers through summers that are unbearably hot and humid and winters that are even worse, with biting winds that chill your bones. But the heat and cold are harsher for those who are poor. On bad days, going to and from work or school or the doctor or the grocery store can feel like a battle. Families living in Chicago's toughest neighborhoods, like Englewood or the Lower West Side, cannot depend upon their police officers, bankers, doctors, and teachers for the support and protection and care that they need (and that we all need). Many of these families have endured the strain of poverty and discrimination for decades. The social fabric of these neighborhoods has been worn thin by economic and institutional neglect, arguably generated by an underlying racism. The streets are dangerous, the schools are dysfunctional, and decent jobs are nowhere to be found. For young, poor, pregnant women and their partners, just getting by can be a hard and lonely struggle.

The contrast between Chicago and Salt Lake City seemed dramatic to us. Salt Lake City, which is smaller and less dense, has a lighter, breezier vibe. Life is easier for most, the climate is milder, and when you look up, you see mountains. Although Utah is one of the most demographically homogenous states, comprised mostly by members of the Church of Jesus Christ of Latter-day Saints (formerly called Mormons) and mostly white, Salt Lake City is surprisingly diverse. Immigrants have found that it's a good place to settle and raise a family. If you happen to be a young pregnant woman or a young expectant father, Salt Lake City is not a bad place to be. The network of social services is tighter than in most cities, owing to an extra layer of support provided by the Church of Jesus Christ of Latter-day Saints, which we will refer to as the LDS Church. Within the church, there is still a strong stigma against unwed parenthood, but that stigma does not translate into the downgrading of services for pregnant women and young mothers. Salt Lake City is an easier place to be poor than Chicago because the cost of living is lower, neighborhoods are safer, and the economic disparity between rich and poor seems less striking. In fact, Salt Lake City is one of the most upwardly mobile cities in the United States, meaning that a poor person in Salt Lake City stands a better chance of getting out of poverty than a poor person in Chicago.

With a lot of help from our two research teams, composed mostly of graduate students in Salt Lake City and Chicago, we collected data from more than 500 young couples over several years. Like most researchers, we developed a structured and systematic way of gathering these data from the young fathers and mothers who became our research participants.

Throughout, we stuck with a strategy that involved working with the administrators of both prenatal clinics and schools for pregnant teens, who allowed us to recruit young couples into our studies. Over time, all these schools for pregnant teens disappeared, as that model of education fell out of favor. So, we became fully vested in finding fathers in prenatal clinics, by initially recruiting their partners (the mothers of their babies) who were receiving services there.

When we work with a prenatal clinic to recruit expectant couples, we are very deliberate about making contact with every pregnant woman who fits our criteria[c] (often multiple times) and inviting her and the father of her child to be interviewed, after explaining the purpose of our research. Inviting *everyone* who fits our definition of a young expectant mother–father pair is important because we want our sample to be as fully representative as possible. The "science" part of all this—the quality of the data—is made better if the sample is both large and diverse enough to truly represent the population of young fathers and mothers we hope to understand.

The young fathers and mothers in our studies are between the ages of 15 and 24. Most of the young fathers and mothers in Chicago are African American, Mexican American or Puerto Rican, though there are a few young white parents, recruited from the western suburbs. In Salt Lake City, most of the young parents were white or Mexican American, though some were Native American or Pacific Islanders. As a group, the young parents in both cities were economically disadvantaged, but more of the Salt Lake City parents were from middle-class families and more of the Chicago parents were deeply impoverished.

We don't want to give the impression that once we started asking young pregnant women to help us recruit their partners, it was all smooth sailing. Some mothers were not interested in helping us recruit their partners, often because they and the fathers were not on good terms. When this happened, we'd ask if we could check in again, perhaps next month. Sometimes this worked because these young relationships are often on-again, off-again.

c. Our recruitment criteria changed slightly from study to study. But, generally, we recruited young pregnant women between the ages of 14 and 19 who were having their first child and who were willing to be interviewed during their pregnancy along with the father of their child. For most of our studies, we recruited mothers in their second trimester, when they were about 4 or 5 months in their pregnancy. We generally restricted the age of young fathers so that none were more than 5 years older than their partners. We acknowledge that this is a study of mostly heterosexual couples. Due to our focus on young parents, we have never had the opportunity to include a gay or lesbian expectant couple, probably because these couples tend to be older when they decide to have a baby. Our recruitment criteria were not intended to be exclusionary of same-sex couples.

But sometimes, the fathers were just unwilling to talk with us because it wasn't worth the time they'd lose at work or they simply weren't interested for reasons we'll never know. Because we knew that many young men would be reluctant or disinterested, we paid them for their time. We needed to make it worth their while to come to that first interview. If we did not pay couples, we'd be likely to recruit a very small sample of an unusual group of young parents who were willing to be part of a research study just for the fun of it. We wanted to talk to this group, but we wanted to talk to the others too.

Our methods for collecting information have varied somewhat from study to study. But our general approach has been fairly consistent, focusing on gathering information about a broad range of "risk factors" such as psychological problems, school dropout, and economic disadvantage, along with "protective factors," such as strong relationships and well-developed interpersonal skills. In addition to our interviews with young fathers and their partners, we administered a structured diagnostic interview, designed to identify psychological problems that reach the threshold for a diagnosis, so that we could know if either mother or father (or both) was struggling with a substance use disorder, depression, anxiety disorder, or any other psychological condition.

When a couple is willing to meet with us, we work hard to make them feel appreciated. Like all researchers, we have them read and sign consent forms, and we answer their questions about what we are up to and how the data collection process will unfold. Early in our research careers, we learned the importance of building a relationship—a research alliance—with everyone who participates in one of our studies, so that they understand how important they are to the process. We want them to stick with us over the many months or years that we follow up with them, and we want them to recognize that their experiences genuinely do matter to us.

After the introductions and the formalities are out of the way, we take the expectant mother and father into separate rooms for their semistructured interviews,[d] which are designed to help them tell the long version of their story, starting with the basics—school, job, living situation—and getting

---

d. By "semistructured" we mean that we have a standard set of "core" interview questions that we ask participants (this is the structured part), but we also try to make the interview as conversational and personal as possible. This means that we often will ask follow-up questions in response to interviewee's comments to clarify or inquire a little more deeply and/or modify the order of questions somewhat to improve the overall flow of the interview and to follow the interviewee's lead, to the extent that this is possible.

progressively more personal, as you will discover as you read the excerpts from interviews included throughout this book.

We also ask these couples to participate in an interactive task—a communication activity—that allows us to see (and hear) how they communicate with each other while discussing conflicts in their relationship.[e] These data have been crucial to helping us understand the interpersonal dynamics of young expectant couples. Finally, we ask expectant fathers and mothers to independently fill out questionnaires about the quality of their relationship with each other, their parents, their partner's parents, their level of stress, their coping skills, etc.

After all this, we let time go by and then follow up with both fathers and mothers a year after their baby is born and then again a year later, repeating the whole data collection routine. For the follow-ups, we include some questionnaires about co-parenting, defined as how parents work together to raise their child, and parenting, defined as what parents do with and for their children.[f] In addition, we ask each parent to engage in play activities with their child (including putting a puzzle together), which we digitally record and then code (using the coding system described in the footnote below). These activities were designed to help us evaluate the quality of the young fathers' and mothers' parenting skills.

We have collected a mountain of data, which has allowed us to be specific when selecting couples to illustrate different patterns in the adjustment to parenthood and different father types that represent the vast diversity of the fathers we've met. The mix of quantitative and qualitative data was useful in selecting the stories to include in this book. We used the quantitative data—the numbers—to identify specific fatherhood trajectories

e. We digitally record these interactions and later code them using a special coding system called the Structural Analysis of Social Behavior (or SASB for short). This coding system, which we have grown to love over the years (as much as one can love a coding system), focuses on both verbal and nonverbal behavior. In other words, it focuses on both what is said and how it is said, including tone, facial expressions, and body language. The resulting coded data allow us to examine broader dimensions of interpersonal communication, such as overall warmth, hostility, autonomy-giving, and control, as well as more specific behaviors, such as affirmation, nurturing, blame, dismissiveness, or walling-off.

f. In addition to the interviews and communication activities desribed in the text, fathers and mothers are typically also administered a set of measures designed to assess their level of stress and coping capacities; the quality of relations with partner, parents and partner's parents; psychological symptoms (in addition to what we assess using the structured diagnostic interview); and demographic information regarding ethnicity, living arrangement, education, employment status, etc. There is a lot of information that we try to incorporate into this book without getting too technical or tedious.

(i.e., different patterns of negative or positive adjustment during the transition to parenthood), and we used the qualitative data—the interviews—to convey to you (the reader) what these young men are thinking and feeling and, just as important, what their partners are thinking and feeling. From those 500-plus couples, we selected 23 to include in this book. Why these 23?

Well, the answer is fairly simple (though the process itself was very time-consuming). We chose these fathers using a two-stage selection process. First, we looked carefully at our quantitative data to identify fathers that were representative of those four different groups of fathers that we talked about earlier.[g] After having identified possible candidates for inclusion in the book using father risks and outcomes as a guide, we began the second stage of our selection process. This process involved diving deeply into the qualitative interviews for these fathers (and their partners) to identify fathers whose stories could adequately represent the four different trajectories of fatherhood development and illustrate the themes of this book.

WHAT TO EXPECT IN THE CHAPTERS THAT FOLLOW

We have intentionally written this book with a wide audience in mind. Our hope is that the book will be relevant, interesting, and useful not only for academically oriented readers (across a variety of different levels and disciplines) but also nonacademic readers who are interested in fathers and families for professional or personal reasons. There are a total of six different parts or sections, each corresponding to a major theme or a key set of questions related to fathers and their development. Each section of the book contains a number of chapters that fit within that key theme or set of questions. Some chapters draw heavily from the interview data, allowing fathers and their partners to tell their own stories. In these chapters, we orchestrate, edit, and interject to clarify and elaborate the points raised, but

---

g. More specifically, we focused on each father's trajectory of development during the transition to parenthood to identify representative cases that showed either "positive, as expected" or "negative, as expected" outcomes, whereby their level of initial risk factors (at our first prenatal assessment, either low or high) predicted well the quality of their outcomes as fathers (approximately 2 years later after the birth of their child). We then looked at those outliers that we mentioned earlier whose outcomes were notably different from what their prenatal risk level would lead us to believe, resulting in the last two groups of fathers: those whose trajectory of development and adjustment as fathers was "better-than-expected," and, finally, those who were "worse-than-expected."

we do our best to step aside and let the reader connect as directly as possible with these young men and women. Some chapters draw more heavily on the theoretical and research literature on fathers and families. In building our plan for helping fathers, we have worked hard to make the academic part of this endeavor accessible, interesting, and even entertaining. To use a cinematic metaphor, we try to keep the story engaging by balancing the time spent "zooming in" for close-ups (with our focus on a particular father) with the time spent "panning out" to capture the bigger picture.

In Part One, we introduce young fathers, discuss the important problems and challenges that young fatherhood poses (to children, fathers themselves, and society at large), and we illustrate the wide range of outcomes (from very positive to very negative) that we observed during the transition to fatherhood. In this first section of the book, we raise one of the most central questions that we attempt to answer in *Lost and Found*: What causes some young men to thrive as fathers and others to flounder?

In Part Two, we focus on how these young families begin, how young men and women meet, how their romance develops (or not), and how they talk about their feelings for each other. Some of these young couples grew up together, whereas others barely knew each other. Some were in shock and unable to comprehend parenthood; others were excited about becoming parents. Against the backdrop of ongoing debates among scholars and politicians regarding the causes of single-mother, father-absent households, the final chapter in this section raises the question "Are fathers necessary?" Addressing this question is important to understand how big of a problem it is when fathers become lost and disengaged.

Part Three of *Lost and Found* addresses the question "What goes wrong?" when it comes to fathers. This section focuses on major "deal breakers"— including violence, severe substance abuse, and incarceration—which often lead fathers to become disconnected from their families. For each of these major problems, we introduce fathers who lose their connections but also include others with similar problems but who manage to change and remain constructively involved. We also discuss infidelity, which poses less of a danger to the safety of partners and children, but is a common source of serious heartache and can lead to a father's disengagement.

Having discussed what can go wrong with fathers, in the next two sections of the book, we turn our attention to what can go right. In Part Four, we discuss the changing roles and expectations of fathers in contemporary society, and we examine what it means to be a good father in 21st-century America. Underscoring the fact that most fathers have strengths and weaknesses, we suggest that there are many ways for young men to define fatherhood and to construct a positive role in the lives of their children.

A broader, more flexible view of fatherhood can help us move away the tendency to categorize fathers as "good" or "bad" toward an understanding of fatherhood that appreciates fathers who are "good enough."

Part Five describes the developmental processes through which young men *become* good-enough fathers. We explore how fathers connect with partners, bond with children, learn to behave as fathers, and eventually identify with the role of father, as they define that role. We highlight the role of biological factors, including hormonal changes that accompany positive father engagement. We end this section by describing the vital role that relationships play in the development of good-enough fathers. In particular, we discuss the role of a father's relationship with his own father and his capacity to establish and maintain a positive co-parenting relationship with the mother of this child—whether or not the romantic relationship survives.

In Part Six, the final section of the book, we address the question of what can be done to better support young fathers, so that fewer of them are "lost" and more of them remain engaged and connected with their families. We start by discussing what previous interventions have been tried to promote positive father involvement. We then describe a co-parenting counseling intervention that we have developed, which is designed to help couples learn to communicate effectively and develop the interpersonal skills needed to stabilize their relationship so they can provide a more secure environment for their children. Finally, we propose a specific plan for identifying men who are at risk for becoming disengaged or dysfunctional fathers during their partner's pregnancy and providing them (and their partners) with the support they need to become positively engaged as parents and co-parents.

To help readers keep track of the 23 fathers (and their partners) that we feature in *Lost and Found*, we have included a "cast of characters" that follows the table of contents. If you ever forget who's who, please refer to this cast list, which includes the pseudonyms of each father and mother and the interviewers who worked with them. We replaced their actual names and masked some of the identifying information to ensure that everyone's privacy would be protected.

OUR PERSPECTIVE IN WRITING THIS BOOK

We know that it is impossible to tell the stories of young fathers without acknowledging the role of culture, race, and discrimination in shaping their lives. We do our best to convey, for example, that the everyday experiences of a young African American man in Chicago are defined in some measure by the fact that he is African American and that he lives in a nation with a long, ignominious history of racism. By the same token, the experiences of a white father in Salt Lake City are defined in significant ways by the fact that he is part, or at least looks like he's part, of the mainstream, dominant culture. Jobs are easier to find and police officers are more likely to give him a second chance. While recognizing the relevance of race and ethnicity in the lives of the young men who appear in this book, we want to be clear that drawing racial and ethnic distinctions between fathers is not our primary focal point. Our goal is to convey the intricacies of young fathers' individual lives and to draw what we believe to be meaningful parallels and connections that transcend their differences. That said, we want to also explain *why* the obvious demographic differences between the young fathers we interviewed is not our primary focus.

First, we believe that many of the commonly observed distinctions between racial and ethnic groups are often a reflection of the relationship between minority groups and the majority culture. Because of this, we also believe that oversignifying the differences between racial and ethnic groups as representing important features of the minority (or the majority) group can be misplaced and deceptive. For example, the fact that African American men and women are less likely to marry might be more about the oppression of African Americans than the nature of African American culture or relationships. In this regard, we believe that family instability is often a byproduct of social disadvantage, which is sometimes a byproduct of racial or ethnic discrimination. Insofar as family instability is directly linked to social and economic disadvantages (due to discrimination rather than because of race or culture), too much emphasis on the differences between groups of people can falsely reify racial and ethnic stereotypes, mistaking effects of racism for the effects of race.

Second, we are not experts in racism or discrimination and do not want to become imposters in this domain of scholarship. Throughout this book, when we think it is necessary to discuss race, ethnicity, racism, or discrimination, we do so. But we also try to "stay in our lane" as social scientists. For us, that means building the case that the instability of young fathers—their difficulty in remaining connected—is an important human problem to be solved across different racial and ethnic backgrounds. Over the years, we have listened to a lot of stories told by young fathers in different places, with different backgrounds and experiences, across different moments in their lives. Based on all we've heard and learned, we believe we have developed a perspective on why some young men lose their connection with their children and others find themselves through their experiences as fathers. We also think we have something important to say about how to help fathers and families stay connected that is as pertinent to white fathers in Salt Lake City as it is to African American fathers in Chicago. In this book we play to our strengths as researchers by focusing on what we think are the common fundamentals of father development, without ignoring the important individual differences or the social forces that can divide us.

In the chapters that follow, we work hard to situate these young fathers and their families within their social, cultural, historical, and biological contexts. This means that we also try to tell the story of young fatherhood writ large. In the end, we provide a mostly hopeful outlook, complete with a plan for how we can do a better job supporting young fathers and their families. We wholeheartedly believe that what we have learned from the young men and women we have interviewed can be helpful to other young parents (and maybe older parents too). That said, we are sufficiently self-aware to know that earnest beliefs are susceptible to the folly of narrow-mindedness, particularly when it comes to fixing other peoples' problems. It is this professional liability that we'd like to take a moment to address.

Over the years, our children, partners, students, colleagues, patients, and the young people participating in our research have taught us to become more aware of the humbling reality that there is plenty that we do not see, fully understand, or adequately appreciate. So, before you get started on this book, we'd like to acknowledge that we are writing a book about people who have had experiences that are quite different from our own. And, like everyone, our perspective is informed and limited by who we are, personally, politically, and professionally. So who are we? We are middle-aged, liberal-minded, white male college professors and psychologists who grew up with privilege and comfort. The young men and women we write about in this book have had very different experiences. As we learned through our interviews, many of them worry about having enough money for food and shelter, many have feared for their safety or the safety of loved ones, and many won't get the opportunity to pursue the jobs they dreamed about in their youth. Some have been discriminated against in ways that will affect how their lives unfold and even how their children's lives will unfold. In these respects, there is a great distance between us, Dave and Paul, and the fathers and mothers we will introduce to our readers.

Throughout the writing of this book we have tried to acknowledge this distance, hoping to keep ourselves from making incorrect assumptions based on our limited understandings. We also try to bridge that distance by letting the young men and women speak for themselves in their own voices and allowing our readers to know them directly, in a limited sort of way. And, in the last section of this book, we provide some specific and novel suggestions for addressing some of the fatherhood problems we discuss throughout. Knowing how paternalistic this sort of prescription can seem, we try to avoid lapsing into "father knows best" thinking or language. Right or wrong, we have written every word with the utmost sincerity, which is the best we can do.

PART ONE

Fatherhood Begins

CHAPTER 1

A Tale of Two Fathers

ROBERT AND QUINTON

I (Paul) met Robert in an office at a high school for pregnant teenagers in Chicago where Sarah, his 15-year-old pregnant girlfriend, was a student. Sarah escorted him through the school to the office because she was worried other girls would flirt with him. She had given Robert explicit instructions over the phone to wait in the front office. "Do not come upstairs alone," she told him. Males are seldom seen in the halls of schools for pregnant teenagers, and Sarah figured that Robert, who had a winning smile and walked with a self-assured stroll, was likely to draw the attention of other girls. Some of these girls had boyfriends, but some did not, and Sarah was not taking any chances. So she picked him up and escorted him through the halls, hand in hand, and dropped him off with me. With an impish smile, she looked at me and said very clearly, "I'll pick him up here when you're done talking." She wanted to make sure I understood the importance of these instructions. Robert rolled his eyes and smirked.

Robert had come to the school to meet with me and be interviewed about becoming a father. We had just launched a study designed to follow a group of young expectant fathers and their partners from pregnancy to childbirth and through the first couple years of parenting. We had recruited Sarah through this school and she, in turn, had recruited Robert.

Robert and I stepped into our makeshift office, a dreary classroom in a run-down school, just west of one of Chicago's posh neighborhoods. Robert settled into his chair, getting comfortable, as I introduced myself and explained the purpose of the study and the game plan for the day. Robert listened carefully. He had just turned 17 but seemed older and wiser than most adolescents. He was truly intrigued by the idea that he was participating in a research study and that his experience might be useful to others.

Starting with questions about school and future plans, I learned that Robert attended a magnet school for science and technology. Compared to the rest of the Chicago Public Schools, where truancy and dropout rates are high, the school Robert attended boasted that more than 88 percent of its students graduated, and many went on to college. This school, touted as one the system's best, is not easy to get into. Robert had scored high on his SATs, and his assistant principal was encouraging him to study engineering in college. He liked this idea and said that maybe he would go on for a master's degree, clearly proud of his academic success. When I asked what he thought he'd be doing in 5 years, he laughed.

ROBERT: Five years? I'd like to see myself having a nice paying job, probably working in some kind of electrical engineering job. I see myself in a nice house, not really big and fancy, just a nice house that has enough space for me, my wife, and my kids. Nice paid salary, just to live comfortable. I want to be able to have . . . to be able to have money I can give to my family, so whatever they want to have, they can have it. That's all I want.

Pressing him, I asked if he thought anything could get in the way of these plans. He was thoughtful and quiet for a moment.

ROBERT: If I can't keep my mind focused. If I get into college and if I just stay in my work, don't let nothing bother me, don't get into any fraternity, just stay by myself, get what I have to get done. If I just keep going, graduate, and just do what I have to do to get it done, I see myself doing quite well in life. I see myself doing that. If anything could get in the way, it would be me listening to other people. You know how other people try to bring you down. If I don't listen to what other people say, how you can't do this, or you won't ever be able to get that, and just keep focused on what I have to do, then I don't see no problem.

Robert lived with his mother, who was African American, and down the street from his father, who was Puerto Rican. His parents divorced 6 years earlier, but they had remained friends. His mother didn't work and collected public assistance. His father worked as a cab driver and helped support Robert and Robert's younger brother. His family was poor, but Robert was managing to steer clear of the drugs, legal problems, and evictions that plagued many other young fathers in our research studies. He seemed happy and secure.

Robert and Sarah had been together for about a year and, like many of the young men we have spoken with over the years, he was excited about the prospect of parenthood. When I asked how he felt about becoming a father, he smiled and then responded.

> ROBERT: I'm looking forward to it. I was happy when she told me, and I was talking to my friends and they was like, "I don't see how you can be happy, you having a baby, they gonna take all your money." And I'm like, "So?!" I'd be happy to have a son or a daughter just to be there with me. I get along with babies a lot, and I always wanted a baby of my own, just to hold it and take care of it, just like something that is mine and nobody else's. So then, once I found out that she was pregnant, I'm like, *"Oh man,"* and then I started thinking about it. I'm going to have to take care of it, I'm going to have to give it all my attention, and I'm like, OK. And I'm going to go through it.
>
> PAUL: How do you picture your role as a father?
>
> ROBERT: How do I picture it? It's like, I picture it as in case the baby wants something like diapers or something, or the baby needs affection and the mother's not there to give it, in case the mother's not there, I'll be there. That's what I'm for. Or, if the baby needs some extra love and attention, that's what I'm there for. And I just deal with it.

Robert represents an important group of young men who defy the common stereotype of young fathers as deviant or devious. Robert did not look or talk like a "thug" or a "deadbeat" or a "player." He seemed like a good kid who had miscalculated the odds of getting his girlfriend pregnant. Such miscalculations are part and parcel of the adolescent experience, which is why pregnancy prevention is a front-burner issue for those working with adolescents and young adults.

To be clear, we don't mean to say that most young fathers are like Robert. Many young fathers have troubled histories, engage in all sorts of reckless behavior, and are poor bets for becoming positively involved in fathering. However, we have found that even the young fathers who are criminally involved or addicted to drugs have tended to be more thoughtful, more committed, and more sympathetic than one might expect. One of the remarkable things about interviewing young men and their partners is how optimistic many of them feel about their futures, how much they want to be good dads.

As clinicians, we have struggled with how to respond to young men like Robert. Their optimism about the future and their delight at the prospect of fatherhood can easily be viewed as disconcerting and disarming. But while it may seem alarmingly naïve, it is also refreshing. There is part of us that feels like it might be helpful to sober them up to the realities of parenthood. If we allow them to think everything is going to be easy, they may not be properly prepared for the difficulties they will inevitably encounter. But then again, aren't expectant fathers supposed to experience this sort of blissful ignorance about parenthood? Aren't they supposed to feel enthusiastic?

In contrast to Robert, some young men are painfully aware of the challenges they will encounter and are doubtful about their abilities to meet those challenges. These young men seem more anchored—and sometimes mired—in the reality of their circumstances. For example, Quinton was a 16-year-old expectant father who had some serious doubts about his ability to function as a father, knowing that he was much too young to handle the responsibility. We set him up to be interviewed at the same school where we had met Robert.

Quinton wore his hair in a large afro and sported vintage, wire-rim glasses. He had the overall "vibe" of an intellectual artist, cool yet a little offbeat. His girlfriend, Shari, who was 16 years old and 5 months pregnant, brought him in to meet with us but she had told him very little about the research we were doing. At first, he seemed hesitant about being part of our study. But after our standard introduction, which includes signing long consent forms, Quinton settled into talking with Barry, a graduate student from the University of Chicago who we had hired to help interview young fathers. Barry was easy to talk to; he was relaxed but focused, and he has the ability to give others his undivided attention. Quinton, like so many of the fathers we interviewed over the years, seemed to appreciate the opportunity to have someone listen to his story.

Quinton was a good student at school and planned to go far in his career, with dreams of becoming an artist. Like Robert, Quinton's parents were divorced but got along, and he was part Latino and part African American. He too had grown up on Chicago's north side. But Quinton was less self-assured than Robert and less clear about his future relationship with his girlfriend. He was full of self-doubt about becoming a father and was clearly stressed about Shari's pregnancy. Everyone in his family—and Shari's family—was upset with him for getting Shari pregnant. Even his friends were mad at him, saying he had been stupid. He had still not told his grandmother about Shari's pregnancy, fearing it would give her a heart attack. She had high hopes for him, and Quinton was certain that she was going to be very disappointed.

Quinton told Barry that, at one point, he made things even worse by telling his family and Shari that he didn't want to keep the baby, meaning he would prefer adoption or abortion. This did not go over well because it violated a deeply held belief about family responsibility and the sanctity of life. He just kept screwing up, he thought. And he was scared.

In contrast to all the negative things he had to say about himself, Quinton had only positive things to say about Shari. He admired her free spirit and her intelligence. He knew that she would be a great mother because she was caring and loving. He hoped that someday they would get married, but right now, he wanted to finish high school, go to college, and become a commercial artist. With great pride, he told us he had been working with a youth program, run through the mayor's office, painting murals on buildings. He liked the idea that the city was his "canvas" and that he was able to do graffiti without getting into trouble. This program had given him a small taste of success, and he wanted more. Now that Shari was expecting a baby, he was having a hard time seeing how he was going to pursue his dream of going to college.

> QUINTON: It's gonna be really hard, like, raising a child and going to college. Her family doesn't really encourage college or school. If they have a baby, that's the big responsibility, to keep that baby for the rest of their life. You know, that's their major priority, not school, not education, not themselves, but that *baby*. Shari likes photography a lot, but I'm really not seeing college in her future at all. And, in mine, it's really important. I feel very strongly. But now it kinda looks like I can't really grab it anymore. You know, I just can't be, like, "I want to go to college!" Now it's gonna be like, "There goes college." You know what I'm sayin'?

Quinton lived with his mother and her boyfriend. His parents had divorced when he was 11, and his father had remarried and moved to another neighborhood, but they were in frequent contact. He had a good relationship with both of his parents, but he was particularly close to his mother. He had no siblings and seemed to get a lot of attention and supervision. His mother still called to check in with his friends' parents, including Shari's, which did not seem to bother him. He seemed to respect his mother and was proud that she had gone back to college, that she was working to support him and yet was still earning straight As.

He described his father as a Harley biker type. He was big and "macho" and tried to "instill those macho values" in Quinton. Quinton did not see himself as macho and felt that he and his father had little in common. Yet, despite their differences, Quinton loved his father. Whenever there were problems or conflicts in Quinton's life, his father would come over and talk with him. He always ended these talks with the same question: "We cool?"

When Quinton told his father about Shari being pregnant, his father said, "Do the right thing and take care of Shari and this baby even if it means giving up what you want for yourself." Quinton was struggling to make sense of this advice. He knew what was expected from him, but he could not quite comprehend the idea of becoming a father. Did doing the right thing mean not going to college and not being an artist? Barry asked Quinton a series of questions about how he imagined things would change.

BARRY: What do you think a father should be like?
QUINTON: I don't know. I think a father should be there, you know. The normal father role figure, I mean, that's always there for their child. They would do anything for their baby, little boy or girl, or whatever. So, you know, overall a nice guy, understanding parent, level-headed.
BARRY: Level-headed, understanding, and nice. What kind of things could get in the way of you being a father like that?
QUINTON: Me being so young right now, I would probably. . . . It's kinda hard for me to say. I'd probably be like—I don't want to say sick of seein' my child—but I'd probably get really tired of it and, like, pissy 'cause I'd be working all these jobs. You know? I don't wanna be like this huge emotional dent in my child's life.

It is difficult to know what to expect from these young men as they head into fatherhood. Quinton's doubts about being able to manage any of it sounded just as worrisome as Robert's optimism about his ability to manage it all. At this stage of our careers as researchers, our goal was to stay in touch and continue interviewing Quinton and Robert, along with the other young fathers we had recruited. We wanted to gather information about how they managed or failed to manage the transition to parenthood, with a particular focus on their relationships with their partners.

Almost two-and-a-half years later, both Robert and Quinton had beautiful 2-year-old daughters, Carla and Brianna. Both couples had been through some difficult moments in their relationships. Robert and Sarah had broken up for a while, but they reconciled after Sarah found out she was pregnant again. By the time their second child was born, they seemed solid and joked about being like a middle-aged, married couple. Robert was working long hours as an electrician's assistant and complained about being exhausted and sometimes impatient with Sarah and the kids. Despite the strain of parenthood, he told us that he loved being a father.

PAUL: What are your feelings now about being a father?

ROBERT: I love it. Ya know, I wouldn't trade it. I think I would've done it differently. I think I would have waited a little longer than I did, but as far as would I give it up? If I could change it, ya know, I would change the fact that I would have something established first. But I wouldn't give it up.

PAUL: In what ways has it been a hard adjustment?

ROBERT: The fact that you are hardly ever there. I mean, you're there but not like you wanna be. You wanna be more involved. You wanna be home more. You don't wanna worry about, "Oh I'm gonna be gone over here and they all over there by themselves." It's just that you, you just can't have enough time. You just can't get enough. You want to get more and more. That's about it.

PAUL: Can you describe yourself as a father?

ROBERT: Yeah. I think every parent wants their child to have things that they didn't have. Ya know, the only way to do that is to raise them right, bring them up the way that you feel is right. Make sure that they get their education. Make sure they stay healthy. Make sure they eat their vegetables. Make sure they stay reading or keep learning more and more. Like, we get her the ABC toys and the counting toys. Trying to show her what to do and what not to do, tell her the difference between right and wrong. That's the way I feel like a parent should be, ya know. Teach them the right from the wrong, the good from the bad. You know, just teach them how you feel like they should be raised.

PAUL: What do you think is the hardest thing about being a father?

ROBERT: Hardest thing? Worrying about how they gonna be when they grow up. You know, how you want to raise them, you want them to be a certain . . . just like my mother wanted me to be what she wanted me to be. But it turned out different, ya know. And I know it's gonna happen with them, but I'm gonna try to implant what's the right thing to do. When you get to a certain age you can't do that no more. When I got to a certain age I did what I wanted to do. So you want to try to keep that tight little grip on them while you can. You know, keep on adding what you want to add. 'Cause when they get to that certain age, you just can't do no more. They are gonna do what they want.

PAUL: Yeah. What do you think is the best thing about being a father?

ROBERT: Watching them grow. You know, my babies are mine. They aren't nobody else's. That is *something*. I have a chance to raise them and, you know, nobody can tell me, "You have to do this, you have to do that." I don't have to do nothing I don't want to do. This is my child and I raise them how I want them to be raised, ya know. What I think is right, what I think is wrong, not what *you* think. This is something I love. I want to build. I want to raise my kids.

PAUL: Um, how do you help to take care of the babies?

ROBERT: I do everything. Me and Sarah do everything together. It doesn't matter. Change diapers, take baths, cook, clean. Everything we do, we both do together.

Robert was embracing the father role, but he was also very young, and his identity as a father seemed a bit rigid; he had a hard time loosening up with his daughters. Sarah complained that he could be a bit too strict and severe with the kids. Nonetheless, she also gave him a great deal of credit because he was so deeply invested in the well-being of his children and was working so hard to support them.

In sharp contrast to Robert, Quinton's life had gone steeply downhill during the first 2 years of his daughter's life. He dropped out of school to get a job, but he jumped from one fast food restaurant to another because the work wasn't steady, or he didn't like the boss, or it was too far away, or he got fired. When his daughter Brianna was born, Quinton moved in with Shari and her family, but they were constantly arguing, so he moved back to his mother's house. After a few months at his mother's, she kicked him out because he was smoking pot all the time. So, he went to live with his father for a little while, but he did not like his father's neighborhood, so he moved in with one friend and then another. We caught up with him when Brianna was a 1-year-old, and he looked tired and unkempt. He said he was fed up with "couch surfing" and was trying to save up for an apartment. But he also admitted to having just spent all his money on pot.

Quinton's feelings about Shari were mixed. He felt that she didn't care about him anymore, and this infuriated him. He frequently referred to her as a "bitch" and said he didn't "give a shit about her," but he also said he wished he could go back with her. He wished they could work things out. It upset him that Shari and his mother got along with each other, but he could not get along with either of them. He seemed deeply confused about what had happened to his life and distraught about his relationship with Shari.

When Barry asked about their relationship, he became quite agitated—as if the wound was still open—but then settled down.

> BARRY: How do you think her feelings about you have changed since your last interview?
> QUINTON: Like, they just went lower and lower until now. . . . she just doesn't give a shit.
> BARRY: How did that happen?
> QUINTON: I don't know. She's kind of separated from me.
> BARRY: Why did you guys separate?
> QUINTON: Like, we just kind of, you know, really didn't give too much of a shit about each other. We were sick of dealing with each other's stuff.

We ask all young fathers and mothers about how parenthood has changed them. We ask in an open-ended way, giving them the latitude to talk about the positive and the negative impact of parenthood on their lives and relationships. Most fathers focus on the positive effects of parenthood on their own development. They acknowledge the challenges but typically reflect on how becoming a father gave them a sense of purpose and made them more responsible. Some fathers even describe fatherhood as a critical turning point in their lives. By contrast, Quinton knew that he was failing as a father and made no attempt to cover that up. He felt defeated.

> BARRY: Have you changed at all since your daughter was born?
> QUINTON: Yeah. For the worse.
> BARRY: How so, why for the worse?
> QUINTON: Um . . . I've gotten in a lot of trouble, you know.
> BARRY: What kind of trouble have you got?
> QUINTON: Like, trouble with the law, and like, trouble financially, and trouble, like, academically.
> BARRY: How did you get in trouble with the law?
> QUINTON: I got caught stealing and I went to . . . I went to court. Then, like a year later, I came up positive for marijuana in a drug test, and they sent me to detention . . . like a kiddie prison. And, like, I had to stay there for a month and a half. And when I came back, I had a year probation. And I also had to do a rehab program, which I completed. But my mom was still keeping me out of the house. She brought me to, like, a homeless shelter. My mom sent me there, you know what I'm saying?

BARRY: So, you said that things have kind of gone downhill since your daughter was born. What was it like before she was born?

QUINTON: Carefree stage of, like, developing into a teenager. Pretty much your average hormonal shit going on.

BARRY: Why do you think it started going downhill?

QUINTON: Because it did. Like, I dropped out of high school. Like, I got in trouble with the law. It sucks.

Quinton's life illustrates what has been referred to as the cascade theory of risk behavior among adolescents.[1] The theory is simple: when adolescents engage in risky behavior—such as drug use and/or unprotected sex (which commonly go together)—problems begin to accumulate. As problems accumulate, the adolescent's development begins to cascade downward with increasing force and speed. Of course, this is not an inevitable developmental pathway.[a] But the downhill slide tends to happen more quickly for economically disadvantaged groups, such as African American adolescent boys, because they are more likely to get into serious trouble for relatively minor offences (a topic we return to in Part Three), and their families often have fewer resources for catching them before they fall too far.[b]

For some adolescents, when a problem occurs, the world steps in to provide guidance and sometimes a dose of "natural consequences." The response may come from a family member who provides additional support and supervision. Or, if the problem is seen as a cry for help or an adolescent misstep, help may come from the vice principal or even the police officer who gets called. Sometimes, the adolescent has the wisdom and the wherewithal to come to his own rescue. When confronted with a challenge, such as an unplanned pregnancy, some adolescents shift into higher gear, working harder to make the most of a difficult situation and seeking support from previously untapped resources, including their parents.

a. Developmental psychologists think of one's "developmental pathway" as the overall trajectory of an individual's life course, how it is that development in different domains (i.e., physical, cognitive, and social) unfolds over time. When various risk factors accumulate, one's trajectory of development is more likely to be adversely affected. However, this is not inevitable and depends (in part) on the overall balance of risk and protective factors (such as social support, access to mental health services, and economic resources). If there are sufficient protective factors that outweigh risks, this can help "tip the balance" and modify a negative developmental trajectory.

b. Resources is a vague term that can mean a lot of things. In this context, we mean that well-to-do white parents can more easily reassure the assistant principal at their child's school or the police officer at the local station that they will make sure that whatever happened won't happen again. And if that does not work, they can hire a lawyer.

One of the central questions we hope to answer in this book is how to make sense of the difference between those young men who tumble and those who rally when confronted with the challenge of fatherhood. Like other young men whose lives unravel when they encounter a major setback, Quinton seems remarkably unable to make use of the resources available to him, including Shari and his mother. He rejects the support that is offered yet becomes more angry and resentful as the support diminishes over time. As the conversation with Quinton turned to his relationship with his daughter, he seemed more withdrawn, visibly distressed by the pain of loss and failure.

BARRY: So, what are your feelings about being a father?

QUINTON: I don't know. I couldn't really tell you. It's like . . . I don't know. I'm not really . . . I mean, I'm a father but, like, I don't do father things.

BARRY: What do you mean by that? What are you not doing?

QUINTON: Like, spending time with my daughter, seeing her, giving her money, and stuff like that.

BARRY: In what way has being a father been a difficult adjustment for you?

QUINTON: I don't know. I can't answer that. I don't do, like, father things. I don't have, like, father responsibilities. I don't have that shit, you know?

Like many of the young women whose partners withdraw and disengage, Shari was disappointed with Quinton, but she did not write him off. She felt sorry for him and thought her attitude toward him had contributed to him not being around more. She had stopped investing in their relationship, stopped paying much attention to him, and admitted that sometimes she was mean to him. She was caught up in working and going to school, and she was focused on her own adjustment to parenthood. She even recognized that she struggled with some of the same issues that Quinton faced. She told us that she lacked confidence in her abilities as a mother and leaned heavily on her own mother for help with parenting.

Most of what we know about absent fathers comes from their children's mothers. What these young women have to say about their ex-partners is important, but it can only tell us half the story and sometimes it's highly biased. They cannot fully convey what these young men are thinking and feeling, just as the absent fathers cannot fully appreciate how their absence affects their child or their child's mother. A split between parents often leads to a cataclysmic failure of understanding. Many absent fathers feel ashamed of themselves, as Quinton does, but some blame their partners, and some may be too wrapped up in their own concerns to pay much attention to the lives of anyone else.

We know very little about absent fathers because they are so hard to find. Like most of us, they don't want to discuss their inadequacies and failures. Our research assistants worked hard to stay in touch with the fathers who had drifted away from their children, but they were often unsuccessful. Quinton was an exception. He was one of a relatively small handful of absent, disengaged fathers who came in to talk with us because we convinced him that his story mattered.

When a young man is unable to support his child—financially or emotionally—he may experience what Phil Bowman refers to as "role strain." Bowman, who has been studying African American men for decades, came up with this term to describe the psychological experience of fathers who feel inadequate from not meeting their socially prescribed obligations as fathers.[2] Bowman has suggested that role strain can interfere with a young father's capacity to remain engaged with his children if he is unable to live up to his own expectations or the expectations of his significant others.

Quinton appeared to lack the internal resources to manage the chaos of his life and seemed only vaguely aware of how his own behavior contributed to the chaos. Because he lacked the skills to manage his behavior, he was unable to keep jobs, violated his probation, and got kicked out of his mother's house. His pot smoking was almost certainly an effort—conscious or unconscious—to manage his despair, but it only made things worse. He didn't have the fundamental interpersonal skills to maintain relationships with the important people in his life. When asked how he felt about Shari, he seemed confused.

> QUINTON: I don't know. She's nice and I like her. But I really hate her sometimes and I think that she's like a bitch. But like, other than that, I . . . I don't know. She's nice and, like, I love her a lot, but some things that she does makes me real mad.
> BARRY: What are some of the things that you love about her?
> QUINTON: Just that I've known her for almost five years now and she was my girlfriend. I don't know, dude. She's a person you can talk to, makes you feel comfortable. You know?
> BARRY: Uh huh . . . and you said that sometimes you hate her. Why do you hate her sometimes?
> QUINTON: Because she ditched me. She'll, like, hang up the phone on me or, like, just do something that will really fuck me up. Like

really fuck me up and shit. Like um . . . telling me that I can't go by her work. Like, she's ashamed of me, pretty much. That's, like, some real bitch-ass shit.

BARRY: What do you think changed?

QUINTON: Um . . . probably 'cause she's treating me like shit and I've treated her like shit. She doesn't care about me and I don't care about her, really. It's hard to describe. It's like, I don't give a shit about what she does anymore, like, you know what I'm saying? Like, I used to.

When we first met Quinton and Robert, they seemed similar in several important respects. They were about the same age, shared a similar ethnic/racial identity, lived in the same neighborhood, and grew up in similar family structures. One primary difference was that Quinton struggled against the idea of becoming a father while Robert embraced it. Quinton's anxiety about fathering a child was understandable, given his age and his circumstances. His fear of becoming a father needed some attention but is not particularly unusual or inappropriate. Indeed, many young people—like Quinton and Robert—are dealing with the typical adolescent issues of identity and independence. Such concerns, which are characterized by questions like "Who am I?" and statements like "I want to figure things out for myself" can make adolescents and young adults seem too self-oriented. And, of course, their self-focused concerns can sometimes get in the way of their relationships. Under most circumstances, such relationship strain is just part of growing up. For example, when romantic relationships between adolescents feel too constrained, the simple solution it to break up and find a relationship that fits more comfortably. However, for young men and women who are becoming parents together, the stakes are a lot higher, and the simple solution is no longer so simple.

Under these circumstances, having the interpersonal skills necessary to maintain a relationship (despite the push for self-development), is a key determinant of whether a young father rallies or tumbles. For some young men, like Robert, the ability to communicate had a lot to do with how his parents communicated with him; they always expected him to talk about his problems until he found a solution that made sense. We don't know why Quinton lacked the skills to build a relationship with Shari. Compared to Robert, Quinton seems profoundly unpracticed in the art of negotiating what he needs or wants. When he speaks up for himself, he does so in a way that is so offensive to others that it's almost always ineffective. So he almost always feels jilted and deprived.

For a variety of reasons, including his lack of interpersonal skill, Quinton did not receive—or did not accept—much support from adults in his immediate environment. And the pressure was on from all sides. He had gotten Shari pregnant, and he needed to "man up," at least that is how he perceived the situation. And, for him, "manning up" also meant giving up his personal dreams of going to college and becoming a commercial artist. Sadly, the way that the transition to fatherhood played out for him meant that Quinton was neither filling the role of father nor pursuing his educational and vocational dreams. Instead, he was floundering in limbo.

In their follow-up interviews, the differences between Quinton and Robert seem stark. Quinton is in trouble with the law and struggling to just stay afloat, and his bitterness toward Shari is extreme. In contrast, Robert is doing well as a father and as a partner. There are many ways to makes sense of these differences. In the chapters that follow, we will highlight the relationships between young fathers and their partners—including the interpersonal skills needed to maintain a stable relationship as co-parents even if the romantic relationship dissolves—as one particularly critical factor (among others) that helps explain differences between young fathers who tumble (like Quinton) and those that rally (like Robert).

To some extent, the differences we observe between these two fathers and their partners are not all that complex. Robert and Sarah are kind to each other and jointly invested in their relationship. In contrast, Quinton sees his needs as being at odds with Shari's, particularly with respect to parenthood. Shari is understandably frustrated with Quinton's selfishness. Quinton is understandably distraught that he has stumbled haplessly into fatherhood before he is ready. Like many teen couples, it may be that Shari and Quinton are simply not meant to be together. In any other context—if Shari wasn't pregnant—they would probably discover this and just move on. What makes these relationships complex is that, ready or not, they are forever conjoined in their roles as parents and co-parents. Unless one or both decide to forgo a relationship with their child, they will need to figure out how to at least make their co-parenting relationship work, even if their romantic connection erodes (as it already has for Quinton and Shari). This is, of course, easier said than done. Many parents—young and old alike—are unable to rise to this challenge.

It is worth noting that we did not head into this research with a particular interest in the relationships between young fathers and their partners. We began studying female partners somewhat accidently, as they were the only way we could get to young fathers. We knew that young men often acquire the interpersonal skills they need to navigate adulthood within the context of their relationships with their families and later with their peers. But we did not fully appreciate that they also learned—or at least *could* learn—from their relationships with their romantic partners and, eventually, with their children. Men like Robert develop their identities as partners and parents through their participation in these roles and by allowing themselves to become genuinely and constructively engaged in parenting and partnering. Over time, it occurred to us that men like Quinton often fail to find a meaningful place for themselves primarily because they are not as able to draw strength from their relationships, including their relationships with their partner and child.

Over the past few decades, as family structures have become more complex and often more confusing, learning how to engage, connect, care, and commit has become more challenging for young men and women. And yet, learning how to build durable relationships has never been more important *because* families have become more fluid. But how does this happen? How can young people be expected to build strong relationships when the available building materials don't seem particularly sturdy or durable?

Psychologists in the 21st century have embraced the concept of resilience, which is the capacity to bounce back. The idea of resilience is that when something is weakened or damaged, like a broken bone, it can sometimes rejuvenate or repair itself and become stronger than it ever was. Resilience is often used to describe individuals who, when they are confronted with life's great challenges, discover personal resources they never knew they had. They survive and thrive because they are good at adapting to changing circumstances, turning challenges into opportunities. However, recent research that takes a close look at resilient individuals has revealed that the capacity to bounce back often depends upon a person's ability to draw from the strength and support of others.[3]

One of the goals of this book is to unpack the concept of resilience as it applies to fathers. In particular, we address the question of how some young men build strong relationships, as fathers and partners, despite the odds against them. This question is a primary focus of the chapters that follow and, indeed, throughout this book. However, we also address the even tougher question of how to understand and respond to the needs of young fathers, like Quinton, who are overwhelmed and demoralized by their circumstances. When these young people slip and fall, or when they are knocked down, they are less able to get back up again. Moreover, when some young men fall, they end up pulling their partners down with them. Recognizing that there are many people who lack the resources to deal with the challenges they face, another goal of this book is to consider what can be done to help young couples, like Quinton and Shari, who are not particularly resilient but who could perhaps become so, with the right kind of support and help to stabilize them.

CHAPTER 2

The Problem with Young Fatherhood

Given that getting pregnant and having children is a fundamental part of life, the premise that "young fatherhood" is problematic warrants some explanation and perhaps some reflection. In this chapter, we address how and why young fatherhood can be a problem for the fathers themselves, their children, and society at large. We also discuss the history and the current social dynamics of young parenthood, noting that despite the downward trend in teenage childbearing in recent years, the rising rates of unwed parenthood pose new challenges for fathers and their families.

HOW IS YOUNG FATHERHOOD PROBLEMATIC?
The Problem of Lost Opportunities

First, having a child before reaching adulthood often interferes with educational and employment opportunities. Parenting takes time, energy, and resources, and young parents may have to choose between either investing in their own future or taking care of their children. Because it's difficult for young parents to pursue their dreams and support their children, compromises are made. Future doctors and business owners become nursing assistants and assistant managers of fast food restaurants. Robert was able to find a stable job that interested him and supported his family, but he is unlikely to get that master's degree in engineering he talked about before the birth of his daughter. Although Robert reconciled himself to this disappointment by embracing fatherhood, we know it wasn't easy because, a couple of years later, he told us that he had a lot of self-doubt during his first year of fatherhood and would get angry with himself about not living up to his own expectations. With support, he managed to push through this phase. By contrast, Quinton couldn't muster that sort of strength. He succumbed to self-doubt and felt derailed by fatherhood, resentful that he had been robbed of his chance to become a commercial artist. Two years later, when Barry asked him what he would like to be doing in five years, he stumbled over the question.

> QUINTON: I don't know. Working? I don't know, like . . . I really don't have a positive view of my future right now.
> BARRY: Why is that?
> QUINTON: Because of my situation.
> BARRY: What situation do you have?
> QUINTON: Like, not having anywhere to live. Like, a real crappy job, and having a kid I hardly ever see. Having a crazy girlfriend. I don't know . . . this is my whole situation.

Unable to find some way to connect his personal goals and his child's needs, Quinton loses hope and then his self-esteem. Unfortunately, there are many young men like Quinton who are not able to connect with their children, get comfortable with fatherhood, and adjust their personal ambitions accordingly. Beyond the sense of *personal loss* that young fathers sometimes feel about the diminished educational and economic opportunities that often accompany early parenthood, some economists have estimated the *societal* costs of teen childbearing, both in terms of the loss in potential earnings (of the parents) and the burden of supporting their children who are often disadvantaged.[a] In 2008, Rebecca Maynard and Saul Hoffman conducted a series of analyses on the cost of adolescent parenthood; the results indicated that society loses about $28 billion per year in lost income and taxpayer dollars.[1] Decreases in adolescent childbearing have a positive financial impact on society, they concluded, mostly due to the increased earning potential of young men and women and, later, their children. When young women wait to become mothers, the academic achievements and career prospects of their children increase. This last point about the children of young parents segues to the second reason that adolescent childbirth is a problem.

a. It's worth noting that, in our society, a lengthy education is linked to better work opportunity, which is certainly not the case in every society. This is important because some scholars have pointed out that when and where the opportunities for education and jobs are diminished, young parenthood tends to increase because the incentives for waiting are less tangible.

The Problem of Limited Resources for the Children of Young Parents

Maynard and Hoffman (and their colleagues) also found that the children of adolescent parents often tend to suffer psychologically and socially.[1] Some of these difficulties are linked to economic hardship. When parents are poor and undereducated, their children often grow up with inadequate educational resources and few opportunities; this sets up a poverty trap that is difficult to escape. However, in addition to the disruption of early parenthood to the lives and livelihood of parents, young parenthood can be problematic for their children, psychologically. Many young men and women have not yet developed the necessary skills to become patient, attentive, and responsive parents and so lack the emotional resources to be consistently attentive to their children's needs.[2] Put somewhat negatively, they tend to be more self-absorbed and irresponsible than adult parents, which is to be expected because they are, after all, adolescents. Under more typical circumstances, teenagers are preoccupied with their own developmental needs because they are in the throes of exploring whom they hope to become. In this respect, it is their status as adolescents, not their economic status, that can add to the difficulty of providing stable, secure environments for their children. Insensitive or unreliable parenting puts children at increased risk for emotional and behavioral problems.[2] Even among those young parents who feel excited and motivated by the idea of parenthood, many lack the interpersonal maturity to manage the reality of infant and toddler care.

WHY IS YOUNG FATHERHOOD PROBLEMATIC?

The Age Problem

In one of our research reports (yet unpublished), we examined the differences between "younger young" parents and "older young" parents interacting with their 2-year-old children (while engaged in the videotaped puzzle activity that we described in the Introduction). We found that even minor age differences between groups of young parents seem to matter when it comes to a parent's ability to support their toddler's development. The youngest adolescent mothers, a group of 16- to 17-year-olds (when their children were 2), were more controlling and less affirming with their children than a group of older adolescent mothers (18 to 21 years old), presumably because they were less interpersonally skilled. Similarly, we found that fathers who were 16 to 17 years of age were more hostile toward their toddlers than fathers who were 18 to

25 years old.[b] The youngest parents would often get irritated when their children did not put the puzzle together correctly and were more likely to be physically or verbally harsh when their children did not cooperate with the task.

Young adolescents are less interpersonally mature, meaning that many are more preoccupied with themselves and less skilled at finding the right balance between "give and take" in relationships. By contrast, older adolescents are more concerned with creating connections and building relationships, so are more naturally attuned to the needs of others. Readers with teenagers may be nodding your heads because these developmental differences between young and older adolescents are so common and obvious. There is good evidence that this transition from self-absorption to relationship-building has something to do with brain development during this critical period.[3] Nonetheless, biological changes—like brain development—do not fully explain adolescent behavior, especially the differences between adolescents. Some of the differences we see between younger and older adolescents (or young adults) have a lot to do with their social context, including what the grown-up world expects from them. In this respect, it's not that young fatherhood is inherently problematic. Rather, it reflects an "off time" transition in our contemporary society, where adolescents are expected to be working on other developmental issues (such as figuring out their identity). In this sense, young parents are in the position of having to traverse two distinct developmental stages at the same time, which can overtax their personal resources. This raises the question of how to help young fathers grow up a little faster as they face this "double whammy" of figuring out who they are and learning how to establish close connections as a father and a partner.

The Problem of a Troubled Past

Besides the parenting risks specifically linked to age, it is also the case that, for some young men, an unexpected pregnancy occurs within the context of a troubled history. Many are carrying heavy psychological baggage, which makes the transition to parenthood more difficult. At one point, we conducted a comparative study of pregnant and nonpregnant teen couples and found that, in addition to the fact that the pregnant couples were more careless about using birth control (not a big surprise), they were also more likely to report psychological and substance abuse problems, and many also reported poor relationships with their own parents.[4] These risk factors do not bode well for their own success as fathers.

b. In this study, there were 87 young mothers and 20 fathers in the 16 to 17 age group (when their child was 2) and 62 young mothers and 73 fathers in the 18 to 21 age group.

Jed is a good example of one of those young fathers with heavy baggage from a troubled past. When we met Jed and his girlfriend, Molly, at the University of Utah Teen Mother and Child Program, they were still reeling from finding out they were going to have a baby, and they were thinking about putting the baby up for adoption. Jed was a hulking, white 18-year-old, who lived in the town of Farmington, just north of Salt Lake City. Jed described himself as being like the beast in "Beauty and the Beast," big and scary-looking from the outside but soft and kind on the inside. This seemed accurate. He was about 6'4" and maybe 230 pounds, with a scraggly beard and dark piercing eyes. He looked menacing, but he had a gentle and thoughtful manner. Although he seemed uncomfortable in his body, aware that he might scare people, he was remarkably open and chatty. Ironically, he had been the object of bullying at his high school for speaking out against hazing on the football team. In his senior year, with just a few credits to go, he had dropped out to avoid the ridicule of his peers and took a job working full time as a cook at a local diner.

In his first interview, Jed told us that his father had physically abused him and sexually abused his sisters for years, leaving the family in tatters. His two sisters had children as teenagers and were living at home with their kids (his nephews and nieces) because both their boyfriends had been abusive. His younger brother, the focus of his father's most sadistic tendencies, was strung out on drugs, also at home. When Keith asked Jed to describe his father, who he had not seen for several years, he started his description by saying, "Imagine King Kong."

JED: He would walk around all day in his boxers. He was even hairier than I am. All the kids would cross the street when he came out of our house. He was big and gruff. He could scare you. I mean, if you got in a fight with him, you'd wish you were dead. . . . He overpowered our family. What he did to my brother. . . I feel bad for my family. He hurt our family a lot, and it wasn't just our family that he abused. He abused other people too.

KEITH: If you could pick three words for him, which words would you use to describe him?

JED: Mean, overpowering, domineering. He was never, ever wrong, and if he was wrong, he was *still* not wrong. You couldn't argue with him. He'd start screaming and yelling. He had to be right, and we were always wrong. We had to tell him how right he was and how wrong we were. And then we'd get spanked. Not just by his hand, but this stupid stick. It was a big stick, and it wasn't a smooth piece of stick, it was a log with splinters, so it hurt. If we were in trouble, we got our asses whipped, hard core.

Jed told Keith he hated his father, but lately—with Molly's encouragement—he was trying to remember his father's redeeming qualities and the good moments in his childhood. Jed and Molly had been raised in the LDS church but, until recently, Jed had not been religious. Lately, he was going to church with Molly's parents, who had accepted him as a part of their family. Trying to make sense of his own family, Jed told us that his father was probably a normal guy when he was younger but then snapped and lost his mind. But, for as long as Jed could remember, his father couldn't hold a job and was known as the "town nut" who terrorized the neighborhood with his King Kong–like temper.

Haunted by his past, Jed was scared that he would hurt his child, as he had been hurt by his father. He and Molly were considering putting their baby up for adoption because he didn't think he could escape his past.

> JED: I've been scared. People who have been abused have a high chance of abusing. The odds are against you, I mean *me*. People who were abused, a lot of times become the abusers as they grow older. My father had been abused when he was a kid. I've been scared about that. I can say now, "No way," but what happens down the line? The baby comes first, and I believe. . . . I think the baby might have a better life, as far as getting love and nurturing, with an adopted family. But also, I don't want to feel like I'm apart from my child. So, if we are going to give our child up for adoption, I want to do that early so the child has the best chance. I don't know what happens when there's an adoption. Could we still stay together, like see each other? It would make things easier.

Jed and Molly eventually decided to keep their baby, encouraged by Molly's father, who became somewhat of a father figure for Jed. Molly's father reassured Jed that he had control over what kind of father he would become and that he would not wake up one day and become the sort of monster his father had been. This connection with a supportive father figure made a big difference for Jed.

The positive changes that fathers like Jed experience when offered some additional support and assistance raise a couple of important questions. Is it possible to "speed up" the developmental process and mend wounds from the past? Is it possible to help young men like Jed or Quinton grow into fatherhood and become patient, attuned, and warmly engaged with their children? These questions may seem off target. After all, isn't delaying pregnancy the best solution to the problem of young parenthood? Of course, that is correct. Despite our interest in the development of young parents—and in interventions designed to support young fathers in becoming the best fathers they can be—we agree that our resources should be invested in preventing young people from becoming parents before they are mature enough to take on the responsibility of raising a child. And, indeed, public concern about the problems associated with early parenthood led to the development of several highly effective campaigns to prevent adolescent pregnancy, which we discuss in the next section of this chapter. We recognize the importance of doing what we can to prevent young people from becoming parents before they are ready, but we are also realists and recognize that—despite efforts to reduce the rates of early childbearing—many young men will still become fathers. So, for those fathers (and their partners), we think that trying to find answers to the questions of what we can do to support young fathers and their families is a worthy pursuit.

Before we can fully understand young fathers and their families—and before we can wrap our heads around what we might do to support them—we need to discuss young parenthood in its social and historical context. So, after covering some of the ways in which young parenthood is problematic (and why it is so), we now try to situate young fatherhood in terms of relevant trends, particularly the simultaneous decrease in rates of teen pregnancy and the dramatic rise in unwed parenthood. We then end by discussing the implications of these trends for fatherhood and father involvement.

THE DECLINE IN TEEN PREGNANCY AND THE RISE IN UNWED PARENTHOOD

In 1960, about 89 out of every 1,000 young women between the ages of 15 and 19 had a baby. By 2016, the rate had dropped to about 20 per 1,000.[5] As indicated in Figure 2.1, progress toward reducing adolescent childbirth has been slow but fairly steady, with some minor setbacks over the decades.

Public health experts believe that the reduction in adolescent childbirth rates can be attributed primarily to the dissemination of effective birth control and comprehensive sexual education in public schools. It seems that a variety of programs have both successfully discouraged sexual activity among younger adolescents and encouraged the use of effective birth control among those adolescents who are having sex. Consequently, a higher proportion of adolescents are waiting a little longer before having sex for the first time and are using birth control when they do become sexually active.[6,7] About one-third of adolescent girls who get pregnant choose to have an abortion, so it seems that access to abortion contributed to the reduced rate of teen parenthood in the 1970s. But the legalization

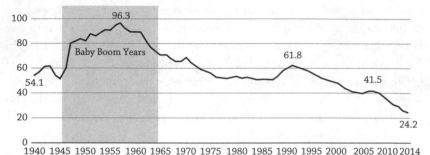

Figure 2.1 US teen birth rate has fallen dramatically over time
From: Pew Research Center. U.S. teen birth rate has fallen dramatically over time. http://www.pewresearch.org/ft_16-04-29_teenbirths_longterm_640/. Published April 29, 2016.

of abortion does not account for the recent declines in adolescent pregnancy (since 2000).ᶜ In fact, the rate of abortion has decreased over the years, from a high of 29 per 1,000 women between the ages of 15 and 44 in 1980 to a low (since *Roe v. Wade*) of 16 per 1,000 women between the ages of 15 and 44 in 2012.[9]

Although the problem of adolescent parenthood hasn't disappeared entirely, the crisis has greatly diminished. However, as the rate of adolescent childbirth was decreasing in the 1970s and 1980s, another interesting demographic shift was occurring. In the 1950s and 1960s, women got married at an average age of about 20, and if a young, single woman got pregnant before she was married, she was likely to get married by the time she gave birth. So, in 1960, only about 1 in 20 babies was born outside of marriage. Today, about 4 out of 10 babies are born out of wedlock. And, as indicated in Figure 2.2, the rate of children born to unwed women under the age of 25 is closer to 7 out of 10.

There are staunch differences of opinion about the root cause of this demographic shift (which we discuss in Chapter 7). But there is little disagreement that this change in family composition has profoundly affected the context of child development, largely because unwed fathers are at greater risk of drifting away from their children than are married fathers. In fact, researchers are just beginning to get a grip on the scope of this problem. A landmark study of mostly disadvantaged fathers, called the

---

c. The recent reductions in adolescent pregnancy and parenthood are good, but there is little doubt that we could do better. The United States is behind most other developed nations with respect to the prevention of adolescent pregnancy. We still have the highest rates of teen pregnancy and childbirth among comparable countries.[8]

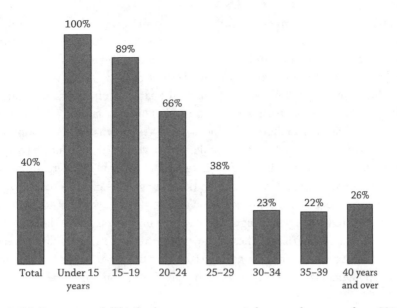

Figure 2.2 Percentage of all births that were to unmarried women, by maternal age: 2016
From: Child Trends. Birth to unmarried women. https://www.childtrends.org/indicators/births-to-unmarried-women. Published September 24, 2018.

Fragile Families Study,[d] found that roughly 50 percent of unwed fathers were no longer regularly engaged in childrearing when the child turned 5.[12,13] This is significantly higher than the rate of disengagement among divorced couples and suggests that when childbirth occurs outside of marriage, fathers have to work harder to stay positively engaged with their child if their romantic relationship ends.

In another study, Jacob Cheadle, Paul Amato, and Valerie King tracked families over 14 years to identify patterns of paternal involvement among nonresident fathers.[14] The fathers were less economically disadvantaged and more likely to have been married than the fathers in the Fragile Families Study. Nonetheless, about 43 percent of the children in this study were not living with their biological fathers for some period of time during the years that they were followed. Cheadle and his colleagues found that about 38 percent of the nonresident fathers they studied were consistently involved in their children's lives, visiting them once a week or more. About

d. We will draw upon publications from the Fragile Families Study throughout this book because, more than any other, it has explored the development of young disadvantaged fathers and their families over an extended period of time. The Fragile Families Study was launched in 1998 and recruited almost 5,000 fathers and mothers in 20 cities across the United States, regularly following up with them and their children over the next 20 years. Interested readers should visit their website at https://fragilefamilies.princeton.edu/.

32 percent of the nonresident fathers were consistently absent or rarely involved. Twenty-two percent of these nonresident fathers became steadily less involved over time, and after 10 years, their involvement was minimal. About 8 percent became more involved over time.

Not surprisingly, we found that the rate of paternal disengagement among the young fathers in our studies was somewhat higher than the rates reported by these other researchers, who focused on a somewhat older group of fathers. Moreover, the rates of paternal disengagement in our studies (ranging from 25 to 40 percent in the first 2 years) are probably underestimates of true paternal disengagement rates in this younger age group because we are unable to report on the paternal involvement of those young men who were not interested in participating in our research in the first place. Knowing that a significant proportion of these nonparticipants were already disconnected from their baby's mother, we assume that that this group of young fathers is at even higher risk for becoming disengaged from their children.[15]

FATHER INVOLVEMENT IN AN AGE OF UNWED PARENTHOOD

Generally, the data from our studies and those of other researchers support what anyone might have guessed: younger, economically disadvantaged, unmarried fathers are more likely to become disengaged over time than married or cohabiting adult fathers. What is somewhat surprising is that the differences between unmarried fathers (including young fathers like Robert and Quinton) are greater than what many people expect, meaning we must be careful about lumping them together. Indeed, researchers have identified several patterns of fathering. Some patterns reflect high levels of father involvement, whereas some reflect consistently low or diminishing involvement. Moreover, if we look across populations, both nationally and internationally, we find that father involvement varies with race, ethnicity, socioeconomic status, and marital status at the time of the child's birth.[16,17] For example, African American couples are more likely than white or Latino couples to have children outside of marriage, but they are *also* more likely to remain in co-parenting relationships over time.[13] This difference suggests that African American couples may have different expectations about their romantic relationships and/or may have developed more adaptive ways to cope with relationship problems that commonly emerge between unwed parents.[18]

We find it difficult to decide if the data on father engagement mean that the glass is half-full or half-empty. Given the sharp rise in unmarried single mothers, the findings that most nonresidential fathers remain at least somewhat connected with their children through the first few years of childrearing might be encouraging. Reinforcing the glass half-full perspective, Julia Goldberg and Marcia Carlson recently reported that when new fathers were asked about their intention to marry, shortly after witnessing the birth of their child, most (71 percent) respond positively.[19] While it may be unwise to make too much of proclamations made in the immediate wake of the excitement and adrenaline rush of childbirth, the good intention is still impressive. Related to this, several research groups have observed that many, if not most, young men have the *desire* (if not the skill) to become good fathers and partners.[16,20,21]

However, it seems that our expectations of fathers—particularly nonresident fathers—have become so diminished that some definitions of father "involvement" are a bit dubious. For example, Cheadle and his colleagues, without a hint of irony, describe nonresidential fathers who see their children *once a week* as "highly involved" in childrearing.[14] Stretching that definition even further, Paul Amato wrote a paper about nonresident fathers in which he described fathers who saw their children *more than once a year* as having "moderate" levels of involvement. Moreover, Amato points out that regular child contact among nonresident fathers has been on the rise over the past 30 to 40 years, and the rates of fathers who have no contact with their children is diminishing (from 35 percent to 22 percent).[22] This is good news, but it's important to remember that the base rate of fathers who are *not* living with their children was also rising during this period, outpacing changes in the levels of father involvement. From this angle, the fatherhood glass looks half-empty.

As we discuss in more detail in Part Four, the evidence clearly demonstrates that some groups of fathers are becoming more engaged in childrearing and other groups are becoming less engaged. Many fathers—particularly those who live with their children—are spending much more time with their children than their fathers spent with them. Frank Furstenberg, a family sociologist at the University of Pennsylvania, observed that we are increasingly becoming a split society with respect to fatherhood.[10] On the one hand, married fathers appear to be more actively involved with their children than fathers in previous generations. On the other hand, fewer fathers are living with their children, so the overall rate of fathers who see their children daily or weekly has decreased in recent decades. In this respect, the fatherhood glass is both *more* than half-full and *less* than half-empty. Another way to put this is that, while there are plenty of engaged dads out there, there are also plenty of disengaged "cads." And, as we discuss in the next chapter (and also Chapter 19), there are important social and biological factors at work that help determine which way it goes for any particular father.

CHAPTER 3

Dads and Cads

The Sociobiological Roots of Fatherhood

In most species, paternal involvement lasts for only a moment. Boiled down to its bare essence, the goal of mating is reproduction, which helps ensure that our genes will survive into the next generation. After conception, a male's job is usually complete, and he moves on to find another mate. A few species are legendary for their lifelong devotion to their mates, such as trumpeter swans and grey wolves, but these are few and far between. Among the 8.7 million (or so) species of animals identified to date, less than one-tenth of 1 percent are thought to be monogamous. Interestingly, about 90 percent of bird species are monogamous or mostly monogamous, but less than 5 percent of mammals are faithful to one mating partner.

Where do human beings fit along the continuum of faithfulness? They seem to occupy both ends of the spectrum and everywhere in between. On the one hand, most humans enter into long-term, committed relationships at some point in their lives, but less than 50 percent remain committed. While they are in committed relationships, many partners (at least 25 percent) profess monogamy but play the field on the sly.[1] As indicated by the high rates of divorce and remarriage, more and more men and women are serially monogamous, committing to one mating partner at a time, but switching partners at some point. Some men (and some women, but fewer) are sexual "opportunists," meaning they are minimally committed to multiple mates.

Among various species, there are also vast differences in how much parents invest in the care of their offspring. Some species invest no time or energy in caring for their young, whereas others invest heavily. Most notably, mammals and birds require some parental care prior to becoming physically capable of fending for themselves, unlike fish or reptiles. How do we make sense of the various levels of parental investment? In 1972, Robert Trivers wrote a paper that became a classic in evolutionary theory that tried to answer this question.[2] Sociobiologists like Trivers seek to understand social behavior in terms of underlying biological processes. Trivers was interested in mating and parenting behavior and used evolutionary theory to make sense of the various permutations of parental investment observed across species. One key component that determines parental investment in childrearing is the amount of time and care required to nurture one's offspring from birth to maturity. In some species, like fish and insects, offspring mature very quickly; once hatched, they can soon take care of themselves. Others take a long time to mature and require significant amounts of parenting. The incredible adaptability of humankind is linked to the fact that we remain dependent for such a long period of time and require extensive nurturing. Our large brains take a long time to develop and, in this respect, the unusual vulnerability of human children is linked to our strength as a species.

In addition to cross-species differences in parental investment, there are also cross-species differences in the parenting behaviors of mothers and fathers. Whereas female mammals tend to be highly involved in childcare for some period of time following childbirth, fewer than 5 percent of male mammals participate at all in raising their children. By contrast, in many bird species, mothers and fathers often share equally in parenting responsibilities. And, in some fish species, the male partner watches over the eggs until they are hatched.

Trivers was also interested in the differential investments made by males and females, and he proposed a theory for predicting whether one or both parents were likely to invest time and energy in raising their young. The basis of his theory is that time invested in childrearing is associated with the amount of effort required in gestation and birth, along with the personal costs of bearing (or hatching) offspring. Mammalian mothers tend to be more invested in childrearing than fathers because the effort that females expend in bearing young is much greater than that of males. This is particularly true for human beings. Women take a significant risk when they have unprotected sex, as pregnancy takes a toll on their bodies, the recovery period takes a significant amount of time, and then there is a baby who needs love and care. Once the child is born, it makes biological sense for its mother to keep investing to get a return on the initial effort. Lactation also requires additional time and expense of energy. In some mammals, the amount of energy required to produce milk is even greater than the energy involved in gestation.

This long-term biological investment of mothers in parenting is supported by the development of a powerful psychological process, often referred to as "bonding." Because human babies and children are so dependent on maternal care, nature conspires to keep mothers and infants psychologically glued together. It's no accident that babies are cute, or at least appear so to their mothers. The babies' emerging capacity for eye contact, sucking, cooing, babbling, and even crying are "designed" (through the process of natural selection) to keep mothers engaged and invested in doing maternal things. Most mothers who are able to calm their fussy infant by feeding or rocking typically feel a mix of relief, satisfaction, connectedness, and competence that is self-reinforcing.[3]

John Bowlby defined much of this infant activity as *attachment* behavior. This attachment behavior helps the infant maintain close proximity to the parent, elicits nurturing behavior, and seeks protection from threats in the environment along with an internal sense of security that results from being close to a caregiver who the child experiences as a "safe base."[4] Reciprocally, parents and other caregivers are also "designed" to respond to infants by providing care and protection. The idea that human beings are hard-wired to both seek and provide care and protection is the basis of attachment theory. The significance of the attachment between mother and child in the evolution of human beings cannot be overstated. Without this sort of "call and response" repertoire of behaviors, most of us would not survive.

The importance of infant attachment was not fully articulated or well-documented until the Second World War when researchers started carefully observing children who had been placed in institutional care, where their basic physical needs were met, but where they were rarely given the opportunity to form a bond with a single caregiver or attachment figure. These infants were physically healthy but often emotionally muted and socially withdrawn. Following up on these observations of socially and emotionally deprived children, researchers began to observe infants whose mothers were particularly well-attuned to their emotional needs. They found that these infants appeared to be securely attached to their mothers, meaning that they seemed more at ease in their mothers' presence and more easily soothed by their mothers when distressed. Most important, these infants were more likely to become well-adjusted children who did well in school, developed few psychological problems, and were less likely to get into trouble as adolescents.[5]

Human biology supports the development of parent–infant attachment by releasing hormones—primarily oxytocin—during childbirth and breastfeeding. Oxytocin has been described as the "love hormone" or "cuddle hormone" because its release is related to feelings of contentment, connection, and euphoria—feelings associated with bonding. The release of oxytocin causes the uterus to contract during labor, so much so that synthetic oxytocin (Pitocin) is used to induce labor. Oxytocin also stimulates the letdown reflex in a nursing woman in response to her infant's need for milk, so that when her baby cries, her milk begins to flow. As soon as that maternal–infant bonding process kicks in, it becomes increasingly difficult for a mother to walk away from her offspring.

Once the long-term benefits of early attachment security for later child development were well-understood, the mother–infant bond became a primary focus of programs designed to support child development. Attachment theory worked its way into parenting books, physician training, and even the design of labor and delivery procedures. Without knowing it, mothers across the United States and Europe have been heavily influenced by Bowlby and attachment theory. It has become part of the cultural lexicon. But what about fathers?

It has been generally assumed that father–child attachments are less automatic than mother–child attachments, largely due to the biology of pregnancy, childbirth, and infant care, which makes it easier—or perhaps just more necessary—for mothers to connect with their infants.[6,7] Bowlby, who had strong sociobiological leanings, was heavily mother-centric. More recently, there has been growing interest in the development of father–infant attachments, and several attachment researchers have demonstrated that children's attachment to their fathers can be as powerful and important to their development as their attachment with their mothers.[8-10] In essence, these findings suggest that infants who are securely attached to their fathers are also more likely to develop into well-adjusted children and functional adults.[11,12] These findings don't diminish the importance of mothers, but they do seem to elevate the relevance of fathers.

Moreover, there is also some evidence that a father's caregiving behavior is also biologically reinforced, similar to mothering behavior. Ruth Feldman at Bar-Ilan University in Israel conducted a study of oxytocin levels in a group of mothers *and fathers*.[13] Feldman and her colleagues visited 112 families shortly after the birth of their first child and again 6 months postdelivery. Mothers' and fathers' oxytocin levels were assessed at both points in time, and both parents were asked to participate in parent–infant interaction activities, which were videotaped and coded. Interestingly, oxytocin levels were similar for mothers and fathers and increased over time at more or less the same rate. Mothers' oxytocin levels corresponded with the amount of time engaged in affectionate parenting behaviors, such as "motherese" vocalizations (baby-talk with exaggerated expressions) and affectionate touch. Fathers' oxytocin levels, on the other hand, corresponded with time spent in "stimulatory parenting behaviors," such as holding the child up and playing with toys. This does not necessarily mean that men are biologically predisposed to engage in more rough-and-tumble play, but it does suggest that in Israeli culture, where this study was conducted (and perhaps many other cultures), biology reinforces this sort of fathering behavior. Remarkably, oxytocin levels between partners were highly correlated at both points in time, which suggests the possibility that fathers and mothers are working synchronously to support their child.

This same group of researchers also identified a genetic marker for oxytocin production, which might help to explain some of the individual variation in both maternal and paternal behavior.[14] While some of us may be more "naturally" loving than others—related in part to naturally varying levels of oxytocin—different levels of investment in childrearing among fathers cannot be simply reduced to variations in hormone production. In fact, there appears to be a reciprocal relationship between a father's investment and his level of oxytocin production. So, fathers who spend more time engaging with their children produce more oxytocin, which then reinforces their desire to spend more time with their children. We say quite a bit more about this in Chapter 19.

Although the mechanisms guiding attachment may be similar across men and women, the vast differences in maternal and paternal engagement suggest that the evolutionary biologists may be right; there might be some deeply rooted, gender-based biological differences in how men and women invest in childrearing. There has been a great deal of debate regarding the essential nature of men and women, namely, whether the differences we observe between fathers and mothers are based on biology, social conditions, or both.[15,16] This debate is not simply a philosophical one, given that it's relevant to the larger issue of how to best support paternal involvement. If there is a distinct male-oriented approach to parenting, anchored in biology, then how do we construct our social institutions to support that approach?

While the issue of gender differences in parenting is interesting, we believe that the question of how to account for the dramatic differences in parenting *among* fathers is more compelling. Some fathers seem predisposed to childrearing; they are playful, nurturing, and patient in ways that seem perfectly matched to the particular needs of their children. Others are remarkably careless, selfish, or destructive in ways that are fundamentally disruptive to their children's development.[17,18]

Louise Silverstein has referred to this distinction as the difference between "cads" and "dads." Some of the young men we've studied have had fathers who fit into the "cad" category, meaning they did not invest much time, money, or love in their children. Many of these young men are quite bitter about their father's absence, but some regard their father's absence as just a fact of life, not worth crying about. For example, Carlos—who was 17 when he became a father—barely knew his own father. Carlos' father was married to someone other than his mother and had another family. So Carlos and his sister were well-kept secrets, and Carlos seemed to accept the distance between himself and his father. In recounting his father's cavalier approach to parenting, Carlos was nonjudgmental:

> He was a guy that usually always had money on him. Kind of a woman's guy, always talking to a woman at a bar, or whatever. So, he was kind of the "go getter." He . . . he would flirt! He was cool. But since I didn't see him that much, he would kind of try and buy me off. You know, here's $50 son, blah, blah, blah. But I didn't mind 'cause, you know, I didn't care. When I was young, it was money, so I'll take it. My sister . . . she kind of has this thing, a grudge against him. Like "you weren't there for me all my life," you know, "I hate your guts." For me, it's like, if I see him, I'm like, "What's up, dad?" I ain't holding nothing against him. When I explain to people about my dad, they may think that he was a bad guy 'cause he wasn't there for me.

As he talked, Carlos took an old picture from his wallet.

> I mean, I've got this picture of him and it's like, man, he looks like *me* right there, but he's my father. You can tell we are related.

The sociobiological explanation for a father's material and emotional investment in his children is that he is motivated to ensure that they not only survive but also have a competitive advantage over other children. By sticking around and helping his child's mother, a father is investing in the "quality" of his offspring. However, the benefit of this investment is balanced against the "cost" of losing one's opportunity to father more children with other available women.

Most men do a better job fathering than Carlos' father, but many—approximately half of young fathers—remain only peripherally involved in parenting, attending to their children's material needs from a distance and periodically engaging in direct childcare activities.[19] We don't know if

Carlos' father was a better father to his other children, but it seems likely that he was, as Carlos suspected. This raises the question of why some of these "caddish" fathers invest in one partner's children but not another's. From Trivers' perspective, the emotional bonds that develop between a father and his children are secondary to the reproductive strategy he employs. Was Carlos' father hedging his bets by using different strategies with different women? In a chapter from the book *Sexual Selection and the Descent of Man*, Trivers explains that, from a sociobiological perspective, paternal disengagement could be a rational strategy.

> In the human species, for example, a copulation costing the male virtually nothing may trigger a nine-month investment by the female that is not trivial, followed, if she wishes, by a fifteen-year investment in the offspring that is considerable. Although the male may often contribute parental care during this period, he need not necessarily do so. After a nine-month pregnancy, a female is more or less free to terminate her investment at any moment but doing so wastes her investment up until then. Given the initial imbalance in investment, the male may maximize his chances of leaving surviving offspring by copulating with and abandoning many females, some of whom, alone or with the aid of others, will raise his offspring.[2p145]

This passage may seem cold, but it helps explain a lot of what many consider "bad" male behavior. This sort of cost/benefit analysis that occurs among men relates to what most people experience as "commitment issues." Romantic partners—perhaps women in particular—are aware of these calculations. Knowing that some men are unfaithful and unreliable, a young woman is motivated to ensure that her child's father will continue to invest in her and their children and not become distracted by competing interests, including the allure of other partners. At the same time, a young woman—even a young mother in a committed relationship—may keep her eye on other possible partners to hedge her bets against the uncertain dependability of her current partner. As such, both young mothers and fathers are motivated to keep the *other* parent engaged in parenting while not ruling out the possibility of attracting other mates. Tension related to this dynamic is common between co-parenting partners, and the emotional strain is often too much for young men and women to manage on their own.

So here's the billion-dollar question: Is it possible to predict whether a particular young man will become positively or negatively engaged as a father or whether he will even stick around? So far in this chapter, we have emphasized the role of biological forces nudging us in one direction or another. We have focused on the role of evolutionary biology because we think it's important to remember that we are biological beings and reproduction is fundamentally a biological process. That said, we do not believe that knowing a man's biological predisposition (e.g., his level of oxytocin) is sufficient to predict his fathering behavior.[a] Whether a father becomes a dad or a cad depends on a complex set of factors.

Let's consider a couple of factors besides biology that predict fathers' behavior. We know that a young man's broader social context, such as the quality of public education and the availability of good jobs in his neighborhood, will likely affect his investment in the future.[20,21] Boys and young men who see few mainstream opportunities for success will tend to divest themselves from mainstream aspirational goals, and it will be hard for the adults in their world to convince them that hard work and good behavior will be rewarded. Without a solid investment in the social order (and a solid demonstration that the social order is invested in them), these boys and young men are prone to become detached.[22,23] Conversely, we know that young men who have access to support and opportunity are more likely to develop the social and cognitive skills necessary to do well in school, find and keep a job, and avoid getting into trouble.[24-26] They are also more likely to invest more time and energy in their children.

However, these large social forces don't explain all the differences we see in the development of young men. For example, it is also the case that how well a young man functions as a father is learned from (or shaped by) his own father.[27] Our experiences of being parented become integrated into our personalities and our behavioral tendencies, so we often habitually say and do things that our parents said and did. Social learning theory, which highlights how we learn through observation in our immediate social settings, helps to explain the consistencies we observe between fathers and sons but fails to explain the discontinuities.[28] As we discuss in more detail in Chapter 20, some young men who had absent or abusive fathers became warmly engaged with their own children, sometimes referring to the negative impact of their own fathers as a source of inverse inspiration.[29] Indeed, we have observed that some young men appear to be at great risk for becoming bad fathers based on their family history, their social context, and their own behavior, but they end up doing much better than anyone could have expected. These fathers, two in particular whom we have selected to illustrate this phenomenon, are the focus of the next chapter. Despite a

a. In Part Five, we dive much deeper into the biology of parenting behavior, which is fascinating, in part, because it is both variable and malleable.

long list of difficult circumstances, these two young men somehow manage to function relatively well as fathers and co-parenting partners. How they do this is one of the core questions that we try to address in this book. This group of young men is particularly important to study and understand because they may be able to teach us something about how to draw strength from unlikely or uncommon sources.

CHAPTER 4
Fathers at the Crossroads

Sometimes when we first meet a young expectant couple, we wonder to ourselves what this young woman was thinking when she decided to get together with this young man. At first glance, Charles and Tasha were that type of couple. Charles was a big, burly, 19-year-old African American man with a diamond earring and baggy pants that hung low. He seemed sharp and articulate, but he had dropped out of high school when he was in ninth grade after getting suspended several times for fighting. He explained that it just seemed like everybody wanted to fight him. At that point in his life, he would take on anyone who challenged him. After he got suspended for the fourth or fifth time, he felt there was no point in going back to school. Four years later, he wasn't working and didn't seem interested in looking for a job. He was tight-lipped about what he was doing on the streets instead of looking for a job, and we didn't pry too much. His criminal involvement came out in later interviews, after he was caught for dealing drugs and went to jail.

Tasha's mother regularly pointed out that Charles looked like bad news, but Tasha paid no attention, convinced that she knew better than her mother. Tasha told Emma, our research assistant, that she could see beneath his tough-guy exterior, that she had seen him cry about the hurt he had suffered as a child. He then made her promise not to tell anyone in his family or any of their friends who might poke fun at his vulnerabilities.

At first, it was difficult to get a clear picture of Charles' life story. This was partly because he was slow to warm up and hesitant to trust us and partly because he had a chaotic, difficult upbringing that was not easy for him to talk about. He bounced back and forth between Chicago and

Mississippi, living with his mother, then his father, then one auntie, and then another. From what little we could gather, his relationships with his parents were complicated, and he had mixed feelings that were hard to reconcile. He paused before answering a lot of our questions, as if considering what to say and what not to say.

He told us he loved his mother but that, when he was still a child, she had a "nervous breakdown" and couldn't take care of him anymore. After that, he never got settled in any one place. Eventually, he came to see himself as his mother's protector because she "couldn't really protect herself against people who tried to take advantage of her," which seemed like an allusion to his father. Charles' earliest memories were dominated by feelings of anger at his father for beating his mother, explaining "My father, he had a violent temper and would just blow up over little things. . . . There was a lot of hate." Charles goes on to say, "My parents, they hated each other. He would just beat her up and stuff. It wasn't a good relationship."

Despite being angry with his father, when we asked him to describe his relationship with him, Charles said it was "pretty good." Pressed for details, he said his father had tried to teach him "values and discipline" and always made sure he was properly dressed before they left the house. When we asked about their current relationship, Charles said they had stopped communicating "a while ago," and he seemed reluctant to say any more on the subject, which is actually quite unusual for the fathers that we have interviewed over the years. We have talked with plenty of young fathers with hard histories and strained family relationships that were willing to open up, appreciative that someone was interested and listening without judging. Charles, however, did not want to go there—at least not initially. It turned out that, in that first interview, he gave us some of the important facts about his early life, but withheld others. It was not until one of our follow-up interviews, when he felt more comfortable with us and more at ease with himself, that Charles told us his father died when he was 7 years old.

When we asked Charles about Tasha, his mood visibly lightened. He told us that he loved Tasha and wanted to marry her someday, that Tasha was the light of his life. Corny as that sounds, it rang true. When they were together in the same room, Tasha leaned against Charles, and, as she settled into him, he seemed to relax. Charles' love for Tasha was evident in how he smiled in response to her larger-than-life persona. Tasha was big and loud, and she exuded warmth. She commanded attention and seemed to fill the hallways with her laughter. Her mile-a-minute speeches and her booming laugh seemed to amuse him. But Charles had learned to be realistic about relationships. And, although he didn't tell us much, he let us know that he and Tasha had their share of problems. When I (Paul) asked him how to describe his relationship with Tasha, he said:

CHARLES: It's very, it's mediocre, I guess. It's like an average relationship. It's pretty good.

PAUL: Mediocre *and* pretty good? What do you mean?

CHARLES: Well, I'm saying that it's like an average relationship. We have our ups and downs, you know. We have our disagreements and arguments, but it's a really good relationship.

In contrast to Charles' reticent, subdued demeanor, Tasha was a totally open book, and she helped clarify what Charles might have meant by "ups and downs." In her first interview with Emma, Tasha readily admitted that she and Charles had cheated on each other in the past, providing all the messy details. She also told Emma that she would sometimes lose her temper and hit Charles. She felt bad when this happened and told Emma that she often asked God to help her find the strength to be calm and in control. She also thanked God for Charles, whose steady presence helped her.

Like many of the young men we talk to, Charles was not worried about fatherhood. He thought he could handle it, just like he handled everything else. He seemed confident that he was going to be a good father. On the other hand, Tasha was plenty concerned about becoming a good mother and looked to Emma for guidance and reassurance. Most of the young men and women in our studies follow our lead during the interview, responding to the questions we ask. Tasha sat down with a lot on her mind. Through much of the interview, Emma was following *Tasha's* lead. Before Emma could get started with our set of questions, Tasha told her that she was afraid of losing her temper and hitting her baby. That was an unusual way to start things off; she just put it right out there.

TASHA: Sometimes I think I'm going to be frustrated with my baby. Like when the baby comes, he'll cry, and I don't want to holler at my baby. I don't want to holler and be like, "Be quiet! Shh! Ugh, stop crying!" You know how babies cry in the middle of the night? They give you no rest all day and then they wake up and cry. So, I've been thinking of how to control myself when my baby wakes up and cries. I'm good with other people's kids, but I don't know, when I have a baby who wakes up every night. I don't know what I'm gonna do.

EMMA: (stepping outside the interviewer role) Um, I think it's pretty natural to get upset at times or get frustrated because you're tired.

TASHA: Some people, they get frustrated, and they hit the baby. I hope I don't ever do that. My boyfriend, he'll be there with the baby and in the middle of the night if I'm tired, he said he'd get up and feed the baby himself. And I hope he keeps his word because he'll be tired too.

EMMA: Yeah, but you're aware of all this and thinking you don't want to hit your child.

TASHA: Yeah, if I feel like hitting my child, I'm going to walk out of the room. I ain't gonna hit my baby, I can't do that, because I don't ever like nobody hittin' me. I get afraid sometimes thinking if I'm gonna do it. I don't think I'm gonna do it though.

A little background helps explain why Tasha was so anxious about motherhood. Tasha's father went to prison when she was a baby and her mother remarried a man who starting raping her when she was 5 years old. He also regularly beat and raped her mother until Tasha's aunt called the police when he tried to rape her too. He was never caught and Tasha was still fearful that he would come back and hurt her. She told Emma that she sometimes thought she saw him out of the corner of her eye or felt his presence in the room. She carried a great deal of trauma with her, and Charles was the only person with whom she felt safe and secure.

TASHA: I ain't really had that much love in my family. Charles is the only person that I feel gives me love because he stands by my side. When I am hurting he always there to cheer me up and he makes me laugh, and I like that. He's the person I been waiting for all my life. That's the only thing I wanted my mother to do and she's still not doing it, still not showing it. She keeps hurting my feelings, she keeps on putting me down and pressuring me, talking about my boyfriend. She says he ain't got no job, never any money, never make a good man. But money don't make a man good. I believe in him and I know he gonna get a job because he is trying.

Despite Tasha's optimism, shortly after their son Jamal was born, Charles was arrested for drug possession, spent a month in jail and another 7 months on house arrest. When we talked with Charles just after Jamal's first birthday, he was much more open with us about the mistakes he had made, admitting that he had been dealing drugs and running around with a gang. When asked about going to jail, he said he had gotten off easy, knowing the charges and the time in jail could have been much worse. He said that being in jail made him appreciate the time he spent with Jamal, and he knew that if he didn't clean up his act, he would end up in jail for a lot longer. Something just clicked and he realized he needed to stop dealing and get a job if he wanted to be around for his son.

When Jamal was 2 years old, Tasha and Charles were living together with Jamal at Charles' aunt's house. They also had a baby girl, Tanya, who was just 1 month old. Life wasn't easy for them, but Tasha seemed much calmer.

EMMA: OK. How would you describe your relationship with Charles?

TASHA: It's good. We do things with each other, we sit down and talk about things when we arguing. . . . Some couples probably would be ready to fight when somebody say something they don't like, but we don't do that. We sit down and talk instead of fighting or walking out. We sit down and talk about our problems.

EMMA: OK. So how do you feel about him?

TASHA: I love him. He the person I want to spend the rest of my life with.

EMMA: How has your relationship changed since the last time you were interviewed?

TASHA: I grew up a little more. 'Cause I got two kids now to raise, and I feel like a whole different person. I feel like a mommy. At the last interview, I couldn't even believe I was a mother. I had to get used to it. And it changed me and Charles' relationship. Because as soon as I had my son, I started changing. I know that I was changing because I stopped arguing with him and cussing him out. When I was pregnant, we was having arguments because he wasn't spending as much time with me, and I wanted to see him. But then I would get mad and tell him to leave, to get out. And I know that he felt like I was pushing him away, like I wanted him to leave. But I didn't. We started changing for each other and for our kids 'cause we want to be together when our kids get older. Now, neither of us is walking out over little stuff or a little argument.

EMMA: What do you like most about Charles?

TASHA: He's been here for me since I was pregnant, before I was pregnant. And he still here, and he still want to be with me. And he still feels the same feelings for me, like he felt when I first met him. And I never known anybody that could feel that strong about me. I never had nobody like that, and I just can't believe that he still feel so strong about me. He still loves me the same, and that's the type of person that I need in my life.

Charles and Tasha were able to get something from each other—or *create* something together—that was missing from their histories. And Charles had straightened himself out. Tasha gave him high marks as a father not only because he was working so hard to support his children, but also because he had become a positive influence. She was proud of the changes he had made. When Paul asked Charles how he felt about being a father, this is what he said:

CHARLES: I ain't had . . . my dad was dead when I was like 7. I love being a dad. I just love being around, and seeing him grow up and just knowing . . . it feels so good just knowing he got a dad. I feel like he is happy I'm his dad.

PAUL: In what ways has becoming a father been a difficult thing for you?

CHARLES: Just being on a mature level, thinking like an adult, not just thinking for yourself. You've got to think about someone else, money issues, you know what I mean? You can't just say, "I want to get this coat," even though it costs six hundred dollars, even though you've got to pay rent and you got to put food in their mouths and clothes on their backs.

PAUL: How did you mature?

CHARLES: What I just said, to come to terms with it. Just becoming a father . . . it really settled me. It made me not think about materialistic things too much no more 'cause you know you ain't supposed to be into that. I got grounded.

PAUL: So how do you think you're doing as a father?

CHARLES: I think I'm doing very good as a father.

PAUL: Why do you say that?

CHARLES: Because I'm working two jobs, and I'm spending time with my kids, and I'm constantly around them. Ain't a time when I ain't around them. When I wake up, they see my face; when they go to sleep, they see my face. So, as long as they see my face then and there, I'm all right. It's like they are a very special part of me and it's just something I can't live without.

There is little in Charles' history that would have allowed anyone (except perhaps Tasha) to guess that this sort of transformation would occur. So, how do we make sense of his turnabout? It is difficult to identify a single factor or a simple explanation. Redemptions of this sort often involve an awakening in which a sense of purpose is discovered, along with the internal strength to pursue that purpose. This seems to be what happened with Charles, who was moved by the deep sense of connection with his infant son. This factor brings us back to John Bowlby, the attachment researcher, who suggested that the psychological bond between parent and child is based on a fundamental biological imperative. Babies need care to survive, so parents (sometimes fathers) need to care for babies. For many young fathers, their infant's dependency persuades them to become more responsible. The transition to parenthood can become a defining developmental moment, as it was for Charles, because as we take care of our babies, we become keenly aware of our role as human beings, the biological imperative to attend to the needs of the next generation.

For some young men and women, the arrival of a baby is enough to jump-start this transformation from being a carefree, self-involved adolescent to becoming a responsible and nurturing parent. Typically, the moment a woman discovers she is pregnant and decides to keep the child, her position in the world shifts, and life becomes oriented around ensuring that this baby survives and thrives. This is not necessarily less true for many young fathers, although the process unfolds quite differently. For women, the relationship with the baby is direct. For many men, the relationship with their child is mediated through their relationship with the child's mother, particularly when a couple is not living together.

This last point is significant, given that the romantic relationships between young parents often don't last. When couples break up, maintaining a positive co-parenting relationship is challenging; many readers are likely to have some first-hand experience confirming the truth of this. In their book about fathers, called *Doing the Best I Can*, Kathy Edin and Timothy Nelson suggest that, for husbands and fathers in traditional families, babies were regarded as part of the package deal, consequential to having a wife. Reflecting on what has changed in recent decades, they suggest that nowadays, many fathers are thinking about "the package" a little differently. More fathers are focused on staying connected with their child, recognizing that keeping things positive with the child's mother is what you do to keep the peace. In this "new package deal" the parent–child relationship is primary and the partnership between parents—especially if they are no longer romantically involved—is like the twine that holds the package together.

If a young couple is able to negotiate a civil co-parenting relationship, the father is much more likely to stay involved with his child. However, if the couple is unable to manage the interpersonal strain of a breakup, a father's relationship with his child often becomes overshadowed by feelings of jealousy, betrayal, and anger toward his partner. The challenge of moving from a romantic liaison to the co-parenting relationship is so difficult that whenever it happens, it seems like a remarkable feat, like a complicated gymnastic routine. Consider the case of Darnel and Cleo.

Like Charles, Darnel (whom we introduced in the Introduction) dropped out of high school and was dealing drugs when his girlfriend Cleo got pregnant with their first child, Curtis. Cleo didn't like what Darnel was doing but put up with it for a long time because she loved him and he loved her. But after Darnel's third time behind bars, Cleo couldn't manage the drama anymore and told him that the romantic part of their relationship was over. That hit Darnel hard, and he finally decided it was time to grow up and clean up his act. He got a real job and quit running the streets. And, remarkably, Cleo and Darnel were able to stay friends despite the turmoil. About 6 months after their break up, when Curtis was 2, Cleo talked with Lucille about their relationship.

CLEO: We're not together, but we get along great. He's a wonderful father. I'm a wonderful mother. Um, we don't have any real disagreements. We get along fine.

LUCILLE: How do you feel about him now?

CLEO: I like him. He wants us to get back together. I just don't see that happening.

LUCILLE: How has your relationship changed?

CLEO: We broke up. We had spent a lot of time away from each other and that made my feelings change.

LUCILLE: How would you say that he's changed?

CLEO: He's changed. He's really stable with the job that he has. Back then, he was kind of shifting in and out of this job, that job, this job, that job. He's pretty stable with this one, I guess. He's matured, and he's really serious about what needs to be done right now.

LUCILLE: Describe him for me. What's he like now?

CLEO: Um, he's very considerate of my feelings. He's . . . um, he's thoughtful, he's there when I need him, and if he doesn't have it, he will get it. . . . He's just perfect, he's a perfect guy. He's considerate about my feelings, like if I'm not feeling so good, or feeling down. He will come and try to spend some time with Curtis and come and try to talk to me. If he can't come here, we'll talk on the phone . . . things like that. He's there for me when I need something for Curtis or for me. I had a lot of bills to pay this week. He lent me a hand. He'll give it to me, you know, but he won't let me borrow it. He'll give it to me. He'll say, "Here you can have this." And, if Curtis need something (clicks fingers), I got it! I think I just like him. His whole personality, it's really nothing wrong with him.

LUCILLE: I'm getting this perfect picture, but you're not together, are you?

CLEO: Because the feelings I have for him aren't the same. I mean, I care for him. He's perfect, but the way that I used to feel for him, it's just not there anymore, and I can't bring that back. If I felt that way for him, we would definitely be together. Not that I don't love him, but I don't love him in that relationship-type way. I love him more as my closest friend, maybe best friend, brother-type thing, not as husband or wanting him to be my boyfriend-type way.

Frankly, it's hard for us to imagine being as open-hearted as Cleo, given the trouble that Darnel caused. Despite the fact that Darnel left her to raise their child on her own for months at a time, Cleo is able to hold on to the positive aspects of their relationship and still protect herself from the disappointment she feels. For his part, Darnel seems to understand that the romantic part of his relationship with Cleo is over, but he is nonetheless committed to developing a friendship and a co-parenting partnership with her. He talked with Mike, another of our research assistants, about his coming to terms with this shift in their relationship.

MIKE: How would you describe your relationship with Cleo?

DARNEL: Cleo? I love her, but we can't be together no more 'cause we grew apart while I was locked up. So, basically we're just the best of friends.

MIKE: How are you guys growing apart?

DARNEL: We don't spend time together like we used to. She do her thing and I do my thing and . . . we hardly ever see each other 'cause she works nights and I work days. And when I come over here to visit Curtis, she be at work, so . . . we barely see each other. We talk on the phone, and we go out sometimes, but we don't spend as much time together.

MIKE: OK. In what ways would you like your relationship with Cleo to be different?

DARNEL: I wish that the time that I spent in jail never happened because that's basically what made us separate, because I wasn't able to be there for her and my son. I was acting irresponsibly, knowing that what I was doing would get me where I ended up [in jail]. If that never happened, we probably would still be together today.

MIKE: What do you think will happen between the two of you?

DARNEL: I don't know. I can't tell what the future holds, but from what is going on now, we probably will be best of friends.

We started our research on fathers by following young men like Darnel and Charles, simply documenting their transition to parenthood. As we gathered more stories, we became more interested in helping these young men manage this transition and "make it" as fathers. A key source of inspiration was getting to know the fathers who surprised us the most. Some young men, despite their own foibles and the cards being stacked against them, are able to stay positively connected with their children and co-parent effectively. Many of these "transformed" young men seemed so similar *and* so different from another group of young men who could not stay out of trouble, could not maintain a bond with their children, could not rise above the heartache and anger that accompany relationship breakups. It occurred to us that to help young men like Quinton (the aspiring artist we introduced in Chapter 1) who "crashed and burned" across the transition to parenthood, we needed to understand young men like Darnel and Charles who "survived and thrived" despite the obstacles. But first, we had to start from the beginning, with how these young couples get together in the first place.

In this first section of the book, we have illustrated how differently young fathers can experience the transition to parenthood, introducing the idea that there is a broad range of possible outcomes for young fathers and their families. We discussed the ways in which young fatherhood can be problematic for themselves and their children without losing sight of the fact that some young fathers function surprisingly well. We also presented some of the relevant social and historical trends that have brought us to where we are today, in an era where the overall rate of teen childbearing has declined but unwed parenthood is on the rise, posing new challenges for keeping fathers positively engaged with their families. Finally, we discussed the sociobiological roots of fatherhood and described how becoming a "dad" (as opposed to a "cad") can be a critical turning point for some fathers, like Charles and Darnel, who grow into fatherhood after an initially bumpy start. Despite the disadvantages they face, these fathers are transformed by the experience of becoming fathers—and by learning how to connect with their partners and children.

In the next section of the book, we take a closer look at the relationships between expectant fathers and their partners at the start. We examine how they met, how they got together, how they feel about each other, and the immediate impact of the pregnancy on their lives and their relationships.

We then move on to discuss how our collective ideas about fatherhood and how the roles of fathers are changing in response to shifting social and economic dynamics. In this era of separated, divorced, and unwed parents and within the context of more fluid family structures, we reflect on the question of whether fathers are really necessary.

PART TWO

Fathers in the Age of Unwed Parenthood

CHAPTER 5
Is This Love?

Since we started doing this research with young couples, we have been asking (and training our assistants to ask) expectant fathers and mothers how they met and got together. If handled well, this line of questioning can help break the ice and create an atmosphere of interest and intimacy between interviewer and participant, without crossing boundaries. Over the years, we have heard it all. Some couples hooked up at parties; some met at psychiatric facilities; some were set up through their gang affiliations. We've been amazed by how many couples met on buses and trains. And, of course, there is Facebook. However, most of these young couples met through school or just lived down the street from each other for years.

We have heard many stories of anguish and heartache, but most of the stories are about falling in love or learning to love, full of hope and longing. We ask young men and women to tell us things that they've never articulated, even to themselves. Simple requests like "Please describe your feelings for her" and open-ended questions like "What do you think will happen in this relationship?" can lead to some remarkably heartfelt responses. And, more important, we gently nudge them along, asking for more details and clarifications, until the story—their story—unfolds.

Before telling these stories, there are two important issues we would like to put on the table. We recognize that teenage pregnancy and childbirth can be dismaying. The general consensus is that adolescents should not be having unprotected sex, and many believe they should not be having sex at all. The fact that they *are* having sex and getting pregnant seems to indicate that something is terribly wrong with our society or the character of these youth. We understand this perspective, but we would like to flip it around and pull biology back into the equation. When thinking about adolescent development, it is important to remember that we are hard-wired to have sex (and procreate) as soon as we come of age, physiologically. Morality aside, adolescents are biologically programmed to have sex and to cast aside concerns about protecting themselves from becoming pregnant. Procreation keeps us going as a species. The problem is that we come of age physiologically before we come of age psychologically or socially. Adolescents are strongly influenced by the biological drive to procreate at the same time that they lack practice in the management of their sexuality.

From this perspective, the question is not "Why are these kids having reckless unprotected sex?" because the answer is that they are adolescents. It's more relevant to ask, "How do we delay a force of nature propelled by millions of years of evolution?" Sexual restraint often requires a great deal of deliberate effort and compelling incentives. This book is about the development of young fathers and their families and not about the prevention of teen pregnancy. That said, the stories of how young couples met and became pregnant contain some important clues about how to prevent teen pregnancy from occurring in the first place.

The second issue we want to put on the table is that the attachment processes described briefly in Chapter 3 compel us—sometimes blindly—to fall in love and try to create that happy family we always wanted, meaning that insecure attachments with our own parents can influence our later relationship choices as we (consciously or unconsciously) try to fulfill previously unmet psychological needs. Attachment theory—the idea that we are psychologically primed to connect—can help us make sense of these adolescent love stories within a broader developmental context. As indicated in Chapter 3, the bond that develops between a parent and child is essential to our survival as a species because human beings require care and protection for such a long period of time. These primary attachments are based on the integration of psychological and physiological processes that set the stage for child development. For example, the experience of love that accompanies the act of caring sets off the release of specific hormones—such as oxytocin—that reinforce caregiving behavior.

The relevance of that primary attachment between parent and child does not end with childhood. We carry our primary attachment relationships with us, such that our experiences of being cared for in childhood set the stage for adolescent and adult relationships. This occurs through the process of internalization, which means that we develop a set of expectations about close relationships based on our early formative experiences, which attachment researchers call "working models." These internalized working models guide our behavior—positively and negatively—as we form new relationships. This is particularly true of our romantic relationships because they serve many of the same functions as our early attachments. We look to our romantic partners to provide care and a sense of security. We look to our partners for comfort when we are anxious or afraid. We are motivated to keep our partners close and connected.

Theoretically, early parent–child bonds create the foundation for our romantic relationships, which set the stage for parenting. Our earliest experiences of love influence how we behave toward our romantic partners. Insecure relationships with our primary caregivers tend to make us more clingy and demanding or aloof and distant with our romantic partners. Conversely, if we felt loved and cared for early in life, we are more likely, as adolescents and adults, to co-create secure relationships with the ones we love. However, whatever our internal relationship template looks like, when we find some degree of security in a romantic relationship, there are strong incentives for hanging on and securing that bond. So, in addition to helping us understand what happens between parents and children, attachment theory is also useful in helping us understand what happens between romantic partners. Although our childhood insecurities tend to get repeated in our romantic relationships, our working models can be transformed through the development of new relationships. In this sense, adolescent love—while increasing the risk of insecurity in some teens—offers others a second chance to achieve a greater sense of security in their relationships. This was certainly true for Sarah, introduced in Chapter 1, who had an insecure attachment with her abusive and neglectful parents but was able to find security in her relationship, due to Roberts' steady, warm presence. It is also true for Tyrone and Sybil, whose early experiences of loss and abandonment played a role in their initial connection with each other and their desire to build a family for themselves.

TYRONE AND SYBIL

Tyrone and Sybil grew up in one of Chicago's poorest neighborhoods, located on the city's South Side near the University of Chicago in Hyde Park, which is an island of wealth and intellectual activity surrounded by a sea of dreary apartment buildings, boarded-up businesses, low-performing schools, and unemployed men hanging out on street corners. Walking a few blocks from Hyde Park to the neighborhood beyond 63rd Street is like moving into another world. There is a clear racial divide, but it's the divide between poverty and wealth that is the most striking. The distinction between the "haves" and the "have nots" is immediately palpable.

When we first met Tyrone and Sybil, they both looked like they had just rolled out of bed, which may have been the case, because Lucille called to remind them about the interview after they failed to show up on time. Tyrone was gracefully lanky, walking with the slightest strut, which seemed more playful than macho. Sybil was small and intense with her hair in corn-rows. She wore a baggy T-shirt that might have been Tyrone's, her pregnancy showing slightly beneath. Like most young fathers, Tyrone had to be coaxed into meeting with us and was unsure what to expect. Nonetheless, he was quick to smile and thank us for the opportunity to be interviewed, as he shook the hand of Mike, one of our graduate student assistants. Once they were fully awake and comfortable with the idea of participating in a research study, Tyrone and Sybil were delightful to be around. They were full of energy and completely entertained by each other. They laughed and teased constantly. And whenever one pretended to be upset or hurt, the other would lean in for a kiss or hug.

Tyrone was the youngest of seven children but was raised without much of a family to hold on to. His mother had left him and his siblings and moved from Chicago to Mississippi after she was reported to the Illinois Department of Children and Family Services for child abuse. Tyrone said his father stayed for a while but could not deal with raising seven children on his own. So, he turned Tyrone over to the foster care system when he was just 2. He grew up as a ward of the state, moving from one placement to another, staying in loose contact with his parents and siblings. Sybil never met her father, and her mother was addicted to drugs for most of her life, leaving Sybil to be raised mostly by her grandmother. Perhaps it's no wonder that this couple looked to each other for love. In separate interviews with Mike and Lucille, they independently told us a remarkably consistent story of love at first sight.

MIKE: So, how did you and Sybil meet?

TYRONE: We were at a bus stop.

MIKE: Can you tell me about that?

TYRONE: I was going with somebody at the time. That's the day me and my girlfriend, we got into an argument, so I left. I went to the mall and I was planning on finding someone else to go with. That's what I did. I went to the mall, you know, and a lot of girls came up to me, carrying on and all that bull crap. I didn't like none of them. But as I was going home, I saw Sybil at the bus stop with her friend. I just approached her, came up to her. And right then, she started talking to me. I got her number, broke up with my girlfriend, called her, and that's how long we've been talking.

Across the hallway, Lucille was interviewing Sybil about how she met Tyrone.

SYBIL: I met him at the bus stop on 63rd, and it was funny 'cause a lot of the girls there were talking to him but he didn't really want to talk to none of them. So, all of a sudden, he saw me, and I had my hair wrapped and I had on a nice little outfit. So he was like, "I'm going to go by her and see what she got to offer." So he moved behind me and I was looking back 'cause he got on some hazel contacts. And I was like, *Ooooh, he is so cute. He is soooo cute.* So I said, *I'm going to talk with him.* I said, "Are those your real eyes?" He said, "Yeah, they mine. I paid for 'em." So, then we got on the bus and exchanged numbers. We was laughing and talking with each other. And he's like, "You going to call me?" And I was like, "Yeah I'm going to call you."

Sybil continued the story, providing more detail than Tyrone.

SYBIL: So, when we got home, he called me soon after. He told me later that he know he was going with me. So, as soon as he got home, he broke up with his girlfriend. Called her and just told her it was over. And didn't even know he was going to get with me, but he just, he just had that thing, like "I'm going to get with her." So he broke up with his girlfriend and he called me about an hour later. And we talked and talked for like three or four hours, and I told him what I expected out of him and what I liked in a boyfriend. He told me the same thing. So we had the same interests in the same things. We was both looking for the same thing out of a boyfriend or girlfriend. I had a boy-friend, but I was like, "I'm going to break up with him." So I said, "You want to go with me?" He said, "Yeah, I'll go with you." And I started screaming. So, then we got together and we have been together ever since then.

LUCILLE: OK, so tell me how you feel about Tyrone.

SYBIL: I love him so much. He is just so nice. And he is just, you know, real sweet. Even though we done, you know, got into a lot of arguments and stuff and, you know, just we done call each other some names sometimes and stuff like that. But I really do love him. . . . I just like to say that he there for me. He ain't going to try to use me, to just have sex with me. It made me glad that he want me and the baby, you know? He don't really put nothing before us.

He let his mother know that I was his girl. I'm just glad he stand up, you know, for me and the baby.

Lucille went on to ask Sybil how she would describe their relationship.

> SYBIL: I hate to let him go places, but I got to break out of that 'cause I can't smother him. But every place he go—he play basketball—I'm going to go play too. If he go over to Seth's house, I want to go. He likes being around me. Ever since the pregnancy, we ain't never been apart, except when he go to work and when I go to school. But he would come straight home and I would come straight home and we would be together the whole day. We just like spending time together and being with each other.

In the room across the hall from Sybil while she was being interviewed, Mike asked Tyrone to describe his and Sybil's relationship. In response to this question, Tyrone became thoughtful.

> TYRONE: Let's see . . . hmmm . . . our relationship. I really don't know how I would describe it. It's, like . . . we love each other to death. We can't leave each other, scared to leave each other. It's like, if I was to lose her, I don't got nobody else to turn to. It's just like, I love that girl so much. I am attached to her and she attached to me.

Tyrone and Sybil seemed to feel some sense of kinship related to the fact that both their parents had abandoned them. Both expressed a great deal of determination to create a family for themselves. And, like the next couple that we introduce, they were able (eventually) to navigate the transition to parenthood successfully and create a family, but not without some notable challenges along the way.

STEVE AND MICHELLE

West Valley City borders the southwest side of Salt Lake City and looks like many working-class suburbs in the United States, with vast, cookie-cutter housing developments near run-down strip malls and bustling superstores. As its name implies, two mountain ranges tower over the sprawling suburb. The majestic Wasatch Mountains rise along the east, and the dry, gray-brown Oquirrh Mountains sit dimly along the west. Like many communities of Utah, most people living in West Valley City belong to the Church of Jesus Christ of Latter-Day Saints (LDS). Despite strict social and religious sanctions against premarital sex, teenagers in West Valley get pregnant at about the same rate as teenagers in other suburban communities across the United States.

Steve and Michelle met at an LDS church dance. Although he was raised LDS, Steve was not very religious. Still, he attended most of the youth events along with his neighborhood friends. It was the thing to do. Michelle was Catholic and had come to the dance with her best friend, who was LDS. Steve asked Michelle to dance, and they quickly realized that they attended the same school. Michelle's friend had a crush on Steve, so Michelle kept her distance, but the two teens continued to talk at school over the next few weeks. They became friends, then started to date, and eventually became sexually active. Michelle was 15 and Steve was 16 when they first had sex. About 18 months later, we met them at the Teen Mother and Child clinic in Salt Lake City, where Michelle was registering for prenatal services. Like many of the young couples we ask to participate in our studies, both were shocked and frightened at the prospect of parenthood, but they were willing to talk about their situation.

Steve had short blond hair and nervous blue eyes. He was initially stiff and uncomfortable with Dave (who was a graduate student at the time when he interviewed him), but he warmed up quickly. Michelle had long red hair, warm brown eyes, and a freckled girl-next-door face. She was more relaxed and open with Julie, an undergraduate research assistant. Dave eased into the personal questions about Steve's relationship with Michelle and the pregnancy.

DAVE: How do you feel about her?
STEVE: I love her. She's the best person in the world, next to my mom. I mean, if I had to put her before anybody, if I had to put *anybody* before anybody, it would be *her*. I mean, I'd cancel my friends for her and everything else. She may not believe that . . . I don't know.
DAVE: How does this compare to other relationships you've had?
STEVE: She's more willing to work things out, where other relationships that I've had . . . they just, you know, one thing went wrong and that was it—kaput, no more—where she would talk about stuff. We'd sit down and talk about it, see what's bugging us and work things out. That's about it. She's just more, like I said, more emotional about things so she's more willing to work things out.

In the next room, Julie asked Michelle about her relationship with Steve.

MICHELLE: It's good. I mean, when I first met him, me and my friend both liked him at the same time. I just let her have him. But then we became really good friends. We knew each other for 2 months before we even started dating. And we were just best of friends. We still are. We did everything together. We still do everything together. So, we were just really really good friends at first. We have our arguments every now and then about certain things, like me doing bad in school and me being pregnant. I mean we fight constantly. We broke up a few times, but I think it's just made us stronger. I love him.

Despite their Leave-It-to-Beaver-like appearances, neither Steve nor Michelle had picture-perfect family histories. Steve recalled his father as a loud, foul-mouthed, alcoholic who had intimidated him throughout his childhood. When Steve was 13 years old, his mother got fed up with his father's behavior and left, moving in with her sister. Steve had always felt much closer to his mother than his father, but he saw his mom much less frequently after she moved out. He stayed with his father for reasons that were never made clear, probably because we didn't think to ask. By the time we met Steve, his father had been sober for at least a year. They were getting along by joking around and talking about sports. Steve was able to value—and see the limitations of—their relationship.

STEVE: Deep down, I know he loves me. He takes good care of me and stuff. Since I've grown up, he's kind of shaped up. When he was an alcoholic, he would yell and scream at us and, I mean, he just didn't like us bugging him. And he constantly sat on the couch and just watched TV and drank beer, all day long. He wouldn't get violent or anything, but he scared the hell out of me. He scared us real bad. I didn't want to be like him, at all. I said, "This is not the kind of person I want to be." So, as far as a role model, I guess I didn't have much to look at, until he kind of shaped up. I just never wanted to talk to him about personal problems because he'd just always scare me. I really haven't become that close to him.

Michelle's mother was 16 years old when Michelle was born. Somewhat disapprovingly, Michelle told Julie that her mother was only 32 years old, but had already married and divorced three times. Her father lived in California with his own mother, unemployed and high most of the day. Michelle had long since written him off as a loser. Michelle felt much closer to her mother, but she was also impatient with all the drama of their lives, created by her mother's poor judgment of men. Michelle also told Julie that her mother would run from one man to the next, dragging her children with her. As such, Michelle took on much of the responsibility for raising her young, half siblings. She felt that her mother's turbulent love life had deprived her of a stable childhood, but she also took some pride in being the most mature member of her family. Michelle liked to think of herself as being on top of things—the responsible one—so it was a tremendous blow to her when she discovered that she was pregnant.

What can we make of these relationships? From the outside, young love often seems supercharged by the thrill of exploration and discovery. It can seem beautifully innocent or worrisomely naïve or dangerously reckless. We know that some young people desperately hope that their partners will fill the empty holes in their hearts, left open by loss or injury. We see some couples get pregnant—and decide to stay pregnant—because they want to create for their child the sort of childhood they lost or never had. Admittedly, we cannot help but look at some of the young couples we study with a mix of nostalgia, amusement, skepticism, and, in some cases, deep concern. However, after having observed so many young relationships unfold over time, we've also learned that we often know less than we think we know about love. We've come to respect that some of these young couples—despite their lack of experience and their rough beginnings—take their love very seriously and work hard at building positive, caring relationships, "brick by brick." We've also come to believe that even when things don't work out, these young relationships are immensely important and not to be trivialized.

CHAPTER 6

Birth Control Anyone?

Researchers are allowed to ask questions that would be intrusive under most circumstances. Because we wanted to understand how pregnant adolescents and their partners think about sex and birth control, we asked a number of questions that could be perceived as inappropriate or rude. To foster a spirit of collaboration, we prefaced these questions with the following words.

> I would like to ask you a few questions about sex and sexuality. Some people don't feel comfortable talking about issues like that, and I don't need to know any specific details about your sex life, but I would like to ask you some general questions about your attitudes about sex and birth control. Are you OK with that?

This approach—asking permission to ask questions—usually helps to disarm even the most defensive adolescent. On the surface, there is no mystery as to how teenagers get pregnant. They are at the peak of their fertility and they have unprotected sex. While a few are just unlucky, claiming to have had unprotected sex only once, most acknowledge being careless, using contraception sporadically. Here is how Steve—clearly embarrassed—responded to our question about using contraception.

> It's a good idea of course. I don't know how she feels about it, but I think it's a good idea. I just never followed through with it, I guess. It's my fault, I guess. We just didn't have it.

Michelle was more adamant when Julie asked if her pregnancy was planned.

> MICHELLE: Heck no, far from planned. My mom always made sure I was educated about sex. And that's what I think bothers me the most. I sit here and I think, *I know better! I knew better!* I don't regret sleeping with Steve; I never will. I wouldn't take it back for probably anything. But I just knew better than to get pregnant.
>
> JULIE: So you didn't really think about the consequences then until . . .
>
> MICHELLE: Until it happened, 'cause I always said, "I'm not going to get pregnant like my mom. I'm never going to be like her." Even when we were, like, having sex, I said that.

Michelle's response mirrors that of many young women and men who "know better" and who sometimes are "determined" to not get pregnant (or not get someone pregnant), but whose actions often contradict their intentions. As adults, we are still prone to doing things that are at odds with our stated values or goals and that threaten to get us in trouble (such as continuing to smoke, drink too much, or eat unhealthily). However, adolescents and young adults are especially prone to this behavior–intention contradiction, often reflecting what has been described by David Elkind as a "personal fable," involving an illusion of invulnerability (e.g. "Other people might get pregnant when engaging in unprotected sex, but not me").[1] This fable is especially likely when it comes to sex, where intentions to take precautions can so easily go out the window when emotions and physiology are really revving up. This is how unexpected pregnancies catch people who "know better" by surprise.

THE NOT-SO-MYSTERIOUS MYSTERY OF UNPLANNED PREGNANCIES

One of the most interesting things about doing research with couples is that the stories of the two partners often fail to converge, and we are left to make sense of the discrepancies. For example, in one of our studies, we found that 40 percent of the couples disagreed about how frequently they used contraception. Among couples that were in agreement regarding the issue, 41 percent reported never using any contraception. This means that less than 20 percent of the couples we interviewed were in agreement about (a) whether they used contraception and (b) how regularly they used it. What is going on here? Our best guess is that when we ask direct questions about how the pregnancy occurred, some young expectant parents feel ashamed about being careless or wanting a baby, recognizing that adults might disapprove.

Why did they choose not to use contraceptives? Again, we've heard it all. Many thought the likelihood of getting pregnant was quite small. Some admitted to "sort of" wanting to get pregnant, leaving it to fate to make that decision for them. Some just weren't thinking, a common trait among adolescents whose cognitive processes are often hijacked by emotions. Here's how Sybil replied when Lucille asked her if this was a planned pregnancy.

SYBIL: We had talked about it and we said we wanted one, but it wasn't like we said, "OK, let's go ahead and just make a baby." But, in a way, you could say it was planned because we kind of both knew what we was doing.

LUCILLE: Were you using any kind of protection?

SYBIL: Yes, I was on the pill. He was wearing condoms. But then he didn't wear them 'cause we knew that we was safe with each other. But I was still taking the pill. I just wouldn't take none some days. I missed. It's like any pill. I got to be better about taking medicine! I do my prenatal pills like that; like, some days I'll miss.

Mike asked Tyrone whether this was an unplanned pregnancy.

TYRONE: It was like this. I said, "Yes, I want to have a baby by you." But when you tell Sybil something, she gonna keep it in her. "I wanna have a baby by you, but not now." But she thought, like, I wanted it now. When she got pregnant, she says, "So you said you don't wanna have a baby?" I mean, I'm not saying that. You know, I just wasn't ready. You know, at that point in time, ya know? I just slipped up and I was scared, like, *wow, baby!* It just hit me, like *bam*. And she just thought I was trying to, like, bail out. But I wasn't trying to do that. I was trying to explain it to her.

MIKE: Were you using protection?

TYRONE: Yeah. We did. It was like an on-and-off thing really. On and off, on and off, on and off. We mostly used condoms, but sometimes we didn't.

MIKE: OK . . . You just told me that you used condoms. Did you use anything else besides condoms, any other spermicides or birth control pills or . . .

TYRONE: No.

MIKE: Just condoms. OK. And how often would you say you guys used them?

TYRONE: Like, one week we might use condoms for the whole week; then one day we might have sex without a condom. It's like, we take 1 day out of, like a whole month, or 2, or maybe 3 days out of the whole month just without, without protection. Like, the rest of it, man, we always used protection.

MIKE: Do you think that she wanted to have a baby, like, right now? What do you think?

TYRONE: Yeah.

MIKE: Do you think that she planned it?

TYRONE: Yeah. I think she planned it.

Such discrepancies and uncertainties about whether a pregnancy was "planned" or not were surprisingly common in our interviews with young fathers and mothers. Relatedly, we sometimes observed discrepancies and ambivalence *within* a given father's or mother's responses, suggesting that they *themselves* were unsure whether the pregnancy was planned or not, whether they did or did not want to have a baby. We think these discrepancies are interesting, and we could probably write another book about the phenomenon of parental ambivalence about *everything*, starting with the issue of *wanting* a baby. In some cases, the discrepant reports may reflect a conflict between conscious and unconscious intentions, whereby someone may consciously not want to have a baby but unconsciously want one, often motivated by the fantasy of having a child who is unconditionally loving. We know of some cases when either a mother or father secretly wants a baby, hoping that it would seal the bond with his or her partner.[2] The upshot is that we've learned to appreciate that these "decisions" are complicated. There are plenty of unplanned babies who are loved and cherished by the time they arrive, but co-parenting a baby that is planned and wanted by both partners is much easier than co-parenting a baby that is wanted by only one or neither, underscoring the need for preconception care—a new area of healthcare—for both fathers and mothers.[3]

Turning back to the issue of the teen pregnancy itself, if adolescents are hard-wired to have sex and make babies, despite the clear disadvantages of adolescent parenthood, the real question is why some adolescents (and young adults) wait. For some young people, the social and religious prohibitions against premarital sex provide powerfully dissuasive arguments. Others are persuaded to practice safe sex by the promise of educational and career opportunities, which might be lost in the event of a pregnancy. Many adolescents feel they are not ready for the emotional demands or financial responsibility of child-rearing, but the arguments for delaying pregnancy are not always sufficiently persuasive. As we noted in Chapter 2, when educational and career opportunities wane and social norms loosen, the rates of unplanned pregnancies increase, particularly among socially and economically disadvantaged populations. For Sybil and others like her, getting pregnant can seem like a hopeful way to escape a difficult past.[4] Given her history, having a baby with Tyrone seemed like her best chance of fulfilling her wish for security and stability. We could argue that Sybil miscalculated her opportunities and misjudged her readiness for motherhood, but Sybil would likely challenge our assumptions. In many inner-city neighborhoods and poor, rural communities, where opportunities are scarce, having a baby provides many young women and men with a sense of purpose.

The Alan Guttmacher Institute has been tracking the sexual attitudes and behavior of American teenagers for 50 years and has produced a rich database that helps contextualize these stories of contraceptive use and nonuse.[5,6] Researchers at the Guttmacher Institute report that about 70 to 80 percent of today's youth are sexually active, having had sex at least once in the last year. Among sexually active men between the ages of 18 and 29, about 37 percent are either never using birth control or using it inconsistently. Among women in that same age range, the rate of inconsistent birth control use or nonuse is 49 percent. So, even though unintended pregnancies have decreased in recent years, it is still the case that about 45 percent of all pregnancies are *still* unintended. The problem, of course, is that that when protection is used inconsistently, accidents happen. According to Lawrence Fine and his colleagues at Guttmacher, when young couples have unprotected sex on a regular basis, they stand about an 85 percent chance of getting pregnant over the course of a year.[7]

More to the point, the rates of unintended pregnancies are highest among couples who are young and economically disadvantaged. In 2010, about 64 percent of babies born to women between the ages of 20 and 24 were reported as unplanned, and even more so for those living in poverty. Among women under 20, the rate was 82 percent.[8] While these percentages are very high, the rate of women in these age groups who are getting pregnant has declined steadily over the last 2 decades. So, even though most pregnancies among young couples are accidental, there are fewer accidents now than ever before. Nonetheless, given the effectiveness of current birth control methods, the sheer number of unplanned babies born to women under 25—about 4.4 million between 2006 and 2010—is a problem because unplanned often means unprepared and less invested.[9,10] It is also puzzling.

The development and dissemination of safe, reliable birth control was one of the great public health achievements of the 20th century.[11] Previous generations of women had little control over their own reproduction and suffered from health problems associated with pregnancies that occurred too early and/or too often (including married women). The advent of accessible birth control has not erased the gender inequities in reproductive health, but women have certainly benefited from increased control over reproduction. So why are there so many unplanned pregnancies? Is this tendency to throw caution to the wind biologically determined, meaning that there's not much we can do about it? Although biology certainly contributes to the drive to be sexually active, the tendency to either use or not use birth control is influenced by a complex mix of cultural and economic factors. For example, European adolescents have sex at roughly the same rate as American adolescents, but there are far fewer pregnancies and births to European teens, largely because sex education and birth control dissemination has been "liberalized" in most of Europe.[a] In the United States, birth control is less acceptable and less accessible.

To better understand why some young men and women forgo birth control, the National Campaign to Prevent Teen and Unplanned Pregnancy conducted a study aptly named The Fog Zone: How Misperceptions, Magical Thinking, and Ambivalence Put Young Adults at Risk for Unplanned Pregnancy.[11] The study asked young women and men about their birth-control beliefs, attitudes, and behaviors. The vast majority of the young people (18–19 years old) interviewed by the Fog Zone researchers believed that avoiding pregnancy *right now* in their lives was very important (74 percent of men and 80 percent of women). However, 49 percent also reported having unprotected sex on a fairly regular basis. How do we make sense of this?

The Fog Zone researchers asked their study participants why they did not use birth control, and the responses were somewhat surprising. For example, 38 percent of men and 44 percent of women reported that "It doesn't matter whether you use birth control or not; when it is your time to get pregnant it will happen." Sixteen percent of 18- to 19-year-olds believed it was either "quite certain" or "extremely likely" that they were infertile and could not get pregnant (or get someone pregnant). More than 30 percent of participants suspected that the government was using

a. This liberalization is revealed in several ways, including much more permissive attitudes toward sex, in general, and toward premarital sex, in particular; widespread, mandatory comprehensive sexual education programs in schools; and widespread access to (and encouragement of) birth control among young people.

contraceptives to control the growth of minority populations. More than 50 percent believed that hormone-based birth control methods posed serious health hazards and that the manufacturers concealed this information from the public. Many young men and women in the Fog Zone study also expressed ambivalence about having a child. For example, 25 percent of those young men who said avoiding a pregnancy was important *also* said they would be happy if their partner was pregnant. The Fog Zone report clearly documents the contradictory feelings that many young men and woman have about pregnancy.

ADOLESCENT RECKLESSNESS IN DEVELOPMENTAL CONTEXT

Adolescents are impulsive, at the mercy of fluctuating hormone levels and often too self-absorbed to fully appreciate the consequences of their behavior. To make matters worse, they are also notorious for regarding themselves as immune to risks.[12-14] While this generalization certainly does not apply to *all* adolescents, it contains more than a grain of truth. Adolescents and young adults are more likely than any other age group to abuse drugs, have unprotected sex, and experience accidental injuries. But why?

One of the reasons that adolescents engage in risk-taking behavior is that their prefrontal cortex—the part of the brain responsible for planning, self-regulation, delay of gratification, and other executive functions—is undergoing rapid growth. It has been hypothesized that this growth disrupts previous patterns of behavior, leading to an apparent regression. Sarah-Jayne Blakemore, a developmental neuropsychologist at University College London, reviewed the research on changes in the prefrontal cortex of the adolescent brain during puberty and the connection with poor decision-making. In essence, findings across several studies indicated that maturational changes in the prefrontal cortex are associated with egocentric behavior and the pursuit of immediate gratification.[14]

In addition to the dramatic physiological changes that adolescents experience, they are also experiencing significant psychological developments. During adolescence, there is a greater emphasis on autonomy, often accompanied by a tendency toward individuation from one's family of origin. Individuation is a psychological process through which the adolescent begins to develop an identity that is distinct from his or her parents. This process is often accompanied by antagonistic behavior, testing the limits of convention, and doubting the legitimacy of authority. Although guidance is often warranted, adolescents tend to resist supervision and seem to dismiss adult input.[b] Simply put, many adolescents want to be left alone to spend time with their friends with little interference from their parents. At the same time, adolescents are suddenly in the position to make important decisions in high-stake situations; they are able to drive, they have easy access to drugs and alcohol, and they are fully capable of having sex and getting pregnant. While the transition is often worrisome, it is part and parcel of the normal developmental process.

As adolescents seek greater autonomy from their parents, romantic relationships intensify. For many young men and women, sex is a powerful way to both express and experience love. Yes, for some, it's just sex, but for most, it expresses something more profound. And for some, having *unprotected* sex is a misguided expression of trust. Adolescents who have suffered from broken attachments are likely to seek a sense of permanence in their romantic relationships. For many young couples, the simple explanation for an "unexpected" pregnancy is *love*. While it's easy to become cynical or outraged by the "foolishness" of these feelings, we have learned to become less judgmental over the years. Indeed, the dangers of adolescent love underscore the importance of taking it seriously. For most adolescents, learning about love is an intensely private affair; they are not looking for consultations with their parents. This conundrum argues for integrating relationship education, including sex education, into the fabric of our society, so that adolescents can learn to manage this part of their lives in spite of themselves. But that is a topic for another book.

NOW WHAT?

Once pregnant, young couples have three options: (a) raise the child, (b) seek an adoption, or (c) have an abortion.[c] Only about 2 to 3 percent of pregnant teens adopt out; about one-third have abortions, about 55 to 60 percent keep their children, and the rest miscarry. Most of the couples

---

b. Despite their strivings for autonomy, many adolescents also report having close relationships with their parents, on whom they still depend for caregiving and guidance.[15] The apparent contradictions of adolescents, who often want both support and autonomy, reflects the ambivalence that characterizes their developmental stage. Resolving the apparent contradiction by learning to both maintain close relationships and manage greater levels of independence is one of the great developmental challenges of adolescence.

c. There is a fourth option—exercised more frequently by men—which is to leave.

recruited into our research studies have already decided to keep their babies, and most hope that their relationship lasts.[d]

Robert (whom we met in Chapter 1) was his mother's golden boy. He was a good student, bright and personable, and never in trouble; she had high hopes for him. When Robert learned that Sarah was pregnant, his first reaction was joy, but his second reaction was fear; he was afraid of what his mother might do to him. Here is Robert's telling of how he found out that Sarah was pregnant.

ROBERT: I was laying in the bed and she's like, "Guess what?" and I'm like, "What?" and she said, "I'm pregnant." And then I thought about it and, like, then a big smile came over my face, and I hugged her, and I'm like, "For real?" And she's like, "Yeah, yeah, they said I am." And I'm like, *Oh, great.* Then I got scared 'cause I told my brother, and my brother says, "Mom gonna kill you. Boy, she gonna tear you up," and I'm like, *Oh boy.* So, I went over to her house to tell her. I said, "Mom, I'm not going to school today." And she's like, "Why?" And I'm like, "I'm going to the hospital. I'm going to run Sarah to the hospital." And she's like, "Why?" And I say, "'Cause she's pregnant." She looked at me and said, "Come into the living room." And I'm like, *Oh no.* Then I walked into the living room with her, and she's like, "You *know* you're going to take care of that baby." And I'm like, "Yeah, I going to take care of it." And she's like, "Why she going to the hospital for?" "To get an ultrasound." And she's like, "Oh, OK." And then we started talking, and she's like, "I'm not worried about it. I'm not going to do nothing, so you might as well just chill out." And I'm like, "OK." And then she just told me, "You just got to take care of it. You just take care of the baby. That's all I want." And I was like "OK, fine." And that was it. That's what she told me. And I felt happy 'cause the only thing I was worried about was my mama, and that was it. And once that obstacle was over, I wasn't worried about nothing else.

PAUL: So how has the pregnancy affected you?

d. Because we recruit expectant fathers though expectant mothers, our sample is restricted to those couples that are willing to come in and be interviewed together, at least at our first meeting. This means that we know little about those fathers who are already disengaged or who are unwilling (or unable) to be interviewed along with the mother of their child. This restriction limits the generalizability of our findings. However, were are able to track those fathers who become disengaged over time.

ROBERT: How? Well, it really hasn't affected me none. I still go over there regularly like I do. Nothing much has changed, really. Just that I'm spending a lot more money than I used to. Buying food 'cause she's hungry. "OK, I go buy you something to eat." Run over there, get her something to eat. Come back and she needs some milk. Just spending a lot more money. That's about it. But other than that, nothing else changed.

In Utah, Steve's reaction to finding out he was a going to be a father was quite different from Robert's reaction. When Dave asked Steve how he responded to finding out that Michelle was pregnant, he paused before answering.

STEVE: It blew my mind. It's like, "Wait a minute here. Are you sure?" And she's like, "Well, yeah." And I just started thinking about what I need to do to help her. So it was just kind of a shock.

DAVE: Did either of you consider abortion?

STEVE: We did. We looked at it as an option. But she said she couldn't do it, and I said I would stick with her, any decision she made. So, I mean, we at least looked at it. I was neutral. I mean, I didn't say to do it, and I didn't say not to do it. She didn't like it at all. To me, it's . . . like, it wasn't as bad as she thought it was. I mean, I could probably live through it. I mean, I could do it. I'm sure I could let her do that. It wouldn't hurt me as much as her.

In the room next door, Michelle elaborated on this with Julie.

MICHELLE: First thing out of his mouth, "What are you going to do? What are we going to do?" And I said, "I don't know." And this is when he said, "Well, this is what I want you to do." And then, when I was really indecisive, that's when he wouldn't talk to me anymore. And I said, "I'm not getting an abortion. There's no way ever that I would do that." And that's when . . . communications just stopped. I don't want me and Steve to separate, and the baby to not know his father. He says he doesn't regret sleeping with me and he will never take it back ever, 'cause he loves me. And I believe him. But he just doesn't want me being pregnant now. He said, "Give it up for adoption." And I couldn't. I just couldn't do that. I don't think there's any other way with me but to keep it. That was a really big issue. That almost broke us up, totally.

JULIE: It's a lot of pressure.

MICHELLE: (sighing) It is. It's a tremendous amount of pressure.

When Dave asked Steve how Michelle's pregnancy affected him, he focused on the embarrassment, shame, and guilt.

STEVE: Um, it's hard to be with my friends 'cause, I mean, a lot of them don't even know yet. Some do, some don't, and the ones that do know have stuck by me. . . . I live in the biggest Mormon neighborhood you've ever seen in your life. And the pressure you would get if they find out, it's all over the place. And so, I just try to keep it as secret as I can.

DAVE: Do you think it has affected your relationship with your friends a lot?

STEVE: Yeah, because it kind of makes me feel almost guilty, because, I mean, they're so . . . they act like they are so, you know, like flawless, and that I did something bad.

DAVE: What are your feelings about becoming a parent?

STEVE: Um, I probably have to get used to it. I bet I'll like it. It just takes a while to adapt to it, I guess.

Like Steve, Tyrone did not want to become a father just yet and was surprised to learn that Sybil was pregnant. When Mike asked him how he felt about becoming a parent, he struggled to find the right words to convey the correct feelings but still sounded like he was in over his head.

TYRONE: Becoming a parent? A parent? Hmmm. Becoming a parent, I feel, man . . . I mean, I feel like I'm ready for it, ya know? Ready to take on that big commitment, that responsibility, ya know? I'm ready for it.

MIKE: How do you picture your role as a father?

TYRONE: Good role, a nice, a steady role. A real role, you know, being there. Being there and taking care of my family. That's all I wanna do, ya know, taking care of my family. Just try to lead my kid, my child, in the right direction. Keep him in school, keep her in school. And teach 'em the right things. Just put 'em in church, stuff like that. Ya know, it's just showing 'em the right way. Tell 'em, "Don't do what we done." You know what I'm saying? Stuff like that. And keep 'em positive. Positive.

MIKE: OK. What kinds of things could get in the way of you becoming the kind of father you'd like to be?

TYRONE: Ain't nothing get in the way with that.

There are, of course, many things that can get in the way. Some of the young fathers we interviewed discussed worries about not being able to get a job or other people "dragging them down" with negativity. Some recognized that if the relationship were to fall apart, it would be difficult to stay connected. They had seen bad things happen when other couples broke up. They didn't want that to happen but acknowledged they could be their own worst enemy and screw things up, confessing that they sometimes acted selfishly and did reckless, stupid things. Ironically, developmental theory tells us that adolescents are focused on themselves for a purpose, as the process of exploration and experimentation helps to ensure that they will be ready to take on adult roles when the time arrives.

In our society, adolescence is first and foremost a period of identity development, which requires personal exploration and experimentation. In the 1960s, Erik Erikson proposed that, although adolescents are highly motivated to develop intense relations with friends and romantic partners, their relationships serve the primary purpose of identity development.[16] They are essentially exploring the interpersonal world, which is why many jump from one relationship to another. According to Erikson, development unfolds in a stepwise fashion, and the capacity for true intimacy and commitment follows the achievement of a coherent and cohesive identity.

Becoming a father during adolescence (or even as a young adult) is challenging because most young men haven't had adequate time to develop a clear sense of where they belong in this world (as mentioned in Chapter 2). Nonetheless, when asked about where they want their relationships to go in the future, many expectant fathers talk about being together, raising a family, and getting married. They may feel pulled in different directions, but there is intense pressure—understandable under the circumstances— to set aside personal goals and be responsible, whatever that means. Steve admitted that he wasn't ready to be a father, but when it became clear that Michelle was going to have a baby, he tried to adjust. Here, he speaks with Dave.

DAVE: What do you think will happen between you and Michelle in the future?

STEVE: I want to get married. I think it will be fun to have a family with her.

DAVE: Did your decision about marrying come easy, or was that a difficult decision?

STEVE: Oh, it's been difficult. Just the commitment, the commitment of being married to her. I don't want to do it so quick, like she does.

She wants to get married as soon as we can. I want to see where I'm going, I mean, before I say "OK, let's do this."

DAVE: How did you make the decision?

STEVE: She asked me one day and I said, "Yeah, I wouldn't mind." It just came to me like that. Yeah, I mean, 'cause we spend so much time together, I'll enjoy it. So, I mean, why not? You know?

DAVE: How do you picture marriage? What will that be like for you?

STEVE: I think it will be hard but it will be fun, 'cause you have your own family. It will be hard to take care of them. I mean, of course there's going to be a lot of troubles—financially, medically, all kinds of little problems. But it's going to be fun because, I mean, there's no one really I'd rather spend my life with than Michelle. I just like being with her, being around her. Um, I think it will be an adventure trying to raise a kid together, I think she's going to teach me a lot. And I'll bet we'll enjoy it.

In contrast with Steve's and Michelle's experiences, not all the stories we hear have happy beginnings or happy endings. In fact, some do not contain an ounce of romance. As indicated at the beginning of this chapter, some of the couples we interviewed hooked up at parties and hardly knew each other before they got pregnant. Sometimes, one partner was far more invested in the relationship than the other, so the other partner (often, but not always the female) ended up feeling "played" and used. Take Darius and Janice, for example.

Darius and Janice

When we met Darius and Janice, they were both upfront about this pregnancy being the consequence of a drunken mistake, but they were trying to make it work, nonetheless. They had met 2 years earlier at a party when Janice was a sophomore in high school. Darius was 3 years older, but they hung around the same crowd and went to the same parties. Like Charles (introduced in Chapter 4), Darius was not a good bet for fatherhood. He had been kicked out of school for "gang stuff," but he was also very handsome and cool, and Janice was drawn into his orbit.

Janice and Darius had dated casually a few times, but it was never serious between them. They had kissed, but Janice had been cautious about jumping into bed with Darius. She liked it when Darius would stop over at her house with flowers and ask if she wanted to go out, but she didn't really trust him. She loved the attention, but then Darius would disappear for a week or longer. After a while, she realized that she was being played and heard that Darius did this with other girls too. She had too much pride for that sort of relationship. She distanced herself from him, and they drifted apart.

A couple years later when Janice was 18, they ran into each other at a New Year's Eve party and ended up sleeping together that night. Because they were both drunk, the question of birth control never came up. Three months later, Janice called Darius to tell him she was pregnant, not yet knowing that he had two other children. This is how she recalled the conversation with Darius.

JANICE: I didn't find out that I was pregnant until I was three months. I was in Minnesota visiting my cousin, and I was just, like, sick all the time. Then I had a change in appetite. So it was like, all the sudden, I hate meat. You know, I just wouldn't eat meat. My cousin was like, "You know you should eat, you need to eat." And I was like, "I'm not eating that, I don't like it." And she is like, "I think you should go to the doctor." So I went and found out I was pregnant. I was, like, about three months.

LUCILLE: What was Darius's response to finding out that he was going to be a father?

JANICE: I don't remember if I got my results that day or another day. But I know the day that I found out, I called him and he was like, "Are you pregnant?" And I was like, "Yes." And he didn't say anything. He didn't say, like, "Oh, boy." He didn't say nothing. He was just asking me, and I told him, "Yes."

LUCILLE: And how was that?

JANICE: It was fine.

LUCILLE: OK, did you, did either of you consider ending the pregnancy, like having an abortion?

JANICE: No, because, I just personally do not believe in it. Even if he would have thought about it, I still just wouldn't have done it. He didn't ever suggest anything like that. And I never even thought about it.

Darius doesn't remember feeling much of anything when he learned Janice was pregnant. Here he talks with Simon, one of our Chicago research assistants:

SIMON When did she tell you she was pregnant, like how far along was she?

DARIUS: Maybe about three or four months, something like that.

SIMON: What was your response?

DARIUS: I really didn't have no response at first. I just asked her if she was sure.

SIMON: So how do you feel about it now?

DARIUS: Well, I already have two kids, so I feel about the same. You know, I really don't have no feelings until they hit.

SIMON: Has her pregnancy affected you at all, had any effect on you?

DARIUS: No.

Darius explained that he didn't see his other children because he had "some little problems" with their mother. He added that he had a hard time picturing himself as a father, but he wanted to be more involved.

SIMON: What kinds of things do you think could get in the way of you being the kind of father you would like to be?

DARIUS: Things could get in the way. Like now, my kids' mama is in the way of me and my kids, you know. So, who knows . . . when you ain't with that person no more, things seem to go wrong. You know, they don't want you to take your kids around your new girl-friend, and all the stuff. It causes problems.

During his interview with Simon, Darius expressed appreciation for Janice's independence and the strength of her character, but he kept his distance from her. When Janice asked Darius to be with her when she delivered, Darius didn't say no, but he told her that he could not commit to anything in the future because he didn't know what the future would bring. One could argue that this response reflects the reality that many young African American men face every day. Exposed to crime, violence, and discrimination on a day-to-day basis, many are truly reticent to engage and commit.[17,18] Darius did not want to be held accountable for making a commitment or promise. He gave the impression that he did not want to cede an ounce of his independence to Janice because it would only lead to more requests and expectations. And, of course, Janice wanted more for herself and her baby.

JANICE: I thought to myself, well maybe we should be together for the sake of the baby. But then I feel, just because I am pregnant, I shouldn't have to put up with his attitude, and if he is not going to change, we will just be friends. So, I feel *just for the sake of the baby* isn't a reason I should be unhappy in a relationship.

A year later, Darius was in jail for dealing drugs. Janice seems to have written him off, telling us that he made some bad decisions. She did not come across as particularly angry or bitter, and she remained connected with Darius's mother, who helped her out with their daughter, Chanté. Janice was receiving public assistance but was about to start working as a housekeeper at a hotel. She seemed comfortable with herself. Lucille asked her about being a mother.

LUCILLE: So what are your feelings about being a mother?

JANICE: Actually, I love being a mother.

LUCILLE: Uh huh, what do you love about it?

JANICE: It's like, sometimes, you know, if she's gone for the weekend, like with my dad, or something, it's like, I'm laying there in the bed, I can't sleep, I can't sleep. I will call my dad, "Bring her back, bring me my baby." You know, sometimes he will bring her all the way back home. Then I can go right to sleep. There's just a bond there, you know? At first, I didn't think I could do it, but now I'm used to it, and I can't live without her! It's fun.

LUCILLE: OK, what's fun about it?

JANICE: I enjoy dressing her with bows in her hair, and stuff like that. And, you know, playing with her, and doing a lot of things, you know? Doing things for her, you know, folding clothes. She folds . . . she helps me fold clothes and things like that, so I enjoy it a lot.

LUCILLE: OK. In what ways has being a mother been a difficult adjustment?

JANICE: Umm, it's been pretty difficult because there are only, like, a few people I really trust keeping her. And if they're tied up, like my father, and I have something really important that has to be done, it's kind of difficult, you know? I can't get it done because I don't want to leave her with anyone. And it's kind of difficult sometimes for me to get important things done.

LUCILLE: Can you describe yourself as a mother?

JANICE: I'm not gonna say I'm the best mother, but I'm nowhere near the worst. I think I'm a good mom. You know, I get things done . . . things that have to be done. Make sure that dinner's cooked, and you know, I spend time with her and do some fun things, you know, rather than just sitting in the house. Make sure that I at least take her to a movie or something. So, I think I'm a pretty good mother.

LUCILLE: OK. So what's the difference between the best mother and a pretty good mother? You said you're not the best mother, but you're a pretty good mother. What do you mean by that?

JANICE: I mean, right now, I can't . . . I give her everything that she needs, you know. I satisfy her, and, you know, things like that. But, I mean, I would like to have . . . to give her the best that I can right now. I feel like I'm not doing that, but I feel like I'm giving her what she needs. Right now, she's getting the proper treatment that she needs. You know, so I cannot wait 'til I get a better job.

Unlike Janice and Darius, most of the couples we met during their pregnancy were romantically involved in the beginning. Even if they were not in love, even if the pregnancy felt like a huge mistake, most of the couples we talked to were trying to work together to make the best of the situation. However, some of the young fathers we met had no real interest in taking care of their children. They appear casually callous, loosely connected, and hard to engage in conversations about parenting. The connection with their child's mother was thin and weak. These fathers raise an important question: Are fathers necessary?

CHAPTER 7

Are Fathers Necessary?

In 1965, Daniel Patrick Moynihan wrote what became a highly controversial report about the rising rate of babies born to unmarried African
American women.[1] As a young member of President Lyndon Johnson's
staff, Moynihan wrote what was intended to be an internal report warning
the Johnson Administration that African Americans were in grave danger
of becoming stuck in a "tangle of pathology" characterized by single
mothers, fatherless children, and unemployable men. Moynihan argued
that centuries of racism and current changes in the economy were the
primary causes of this social crisis but that the "matrilineal" structure of
African American culture was also a factor that warranted some attention.
Moynihan advocated that more should be done to establish racial equity
in employment, housing, and education, and he also suggested that equity needed to occur within the African American family to strengthen the
role of fathers relative to mothers. He referred to the gender imbalance
in African American communities as pathological. Upon its completion,
Moynihan's report was more widely distributed than he had intended, and
the response caused an academic and political firestorm that smoldered for
decades. Several civil rights activists and scholars reacted angrily, arguing
that Moynihan's report "blamed the victim" and unfairly pathologized the
African American family.[2]

Among those who objected to the report, most did not disagree with the
description of the African American family as matriarchal, but a few took
issue with the presumption that families *should* be patriarchal. Challenging
Moynihan's characterization of matriarchy as pathological, Mary
Keyserling, a colleague of his in the US Department of Labor, suggested

that family "leadership" could either be cooperative or given to whichever parent was most qualified for that role. Martin Luther King Jr. had an interesting and subtle objection to the Moynihan Report. King suggested that Moynihan did not give sufficient credit to the current injustices against African Americans, and he gently chided him for failing to acknowledge the resilience of the African American family, which had adapted and endured despite state-sanctioned efforts to destroy it.[2] Of course, the current rates of unwed parenthood are indeed higher, as Moynihan predicted. However, the phenomenon of unwed, single parenthood spread far beyond poor African-American families and has emerged as a significant issue in other racial and socioeconomic status groups, as indicated in Figure 7.1.

Almost 20 years after the Moynihan report was published in 1965, Charles Murray, an unapologetically conservative scholar, wrote a book called *Losing Ground* in which he blamed social programs (primarily welfare) intended to support poor single mothers for the problems facing African Americans.[3] Murray argued that such programs had undermined

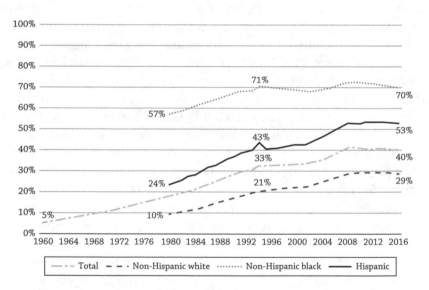

Sources: Data by race and Hispanic origin for 1980–1989: U.S. Department of Health and Human Services, Centers for Disease Control and Prevention, National Center for Health Statistics. (2014). Health, United States, 2013 [Table 5]. Hyattsville, MD: Author. Retrieved from http://www.cdc.gov/nchs/hus/previous.htm#tables. All other data for 1960–1999. Ventura, S.J. & Bachrach, C. A. (2000). Nonmarital childbearing in the United States, 1940–1999 [Table 4]. National Vital Statistics Reports, 48(16). Retrieved from http://www.cdc.gov/nchs/data/nvsr/nvsr48/nvsr48_16.pdf. Data for 2002–2006: U.S. Department of Health and Human Services. Centers for Disease Control and Prevention, National Center for Health Statistics. (2002–2009). Births, Final data for 2000–2006. Hyattsville, MD: Author. Retrieved from http://www.cdc.gov/nchs/products/nvsr.htm. Data for 2007–2016: U.S. Department of Health and Human Services, Centers for Disease Control and Prevention, National Center for Health Statistics. (2018). CDC WONDER [Data tool], Hyattsville, MD: Author Retrieved from http://wonder.cdc.gov/natality-currect.html.

Figure 7.1 Percentage of all births that were to unmarried women by race and Hispanic origin: Selected years, 1960–2016

the traditional role of the father, fostered an unhealthy dependence on the government, and functioned as a disincentive for hard work and sustained commitments. This idea that welfare is a deterrent to marriage illustrates how "the family" had become a hotly contested political issue, with racial undertones. The antipoverty programs were set up to prevent women from participating (i.e., receiving benefits) if they were married or if a man was living with them in the same house. This rule (now defunct) was intended to prevent abuse of the system. It was assumed that a woman who qualified for welfare should not receive the benefit if she was living with a man. The prevailing belief, codified into law, was that if she had a male partner, she should lean on *him* and not the government, regardless of their relationship status or his capacity to support himself, his partner, and their children.

Partly in response to Murray's book *Losing Ground*, William Julius Wilson, a sociologist, who is now at Harvard, wrote *The Truly Disadvantaged*, in which he argued that the rising rates of mother-headed households among African Americans can be traced back to changes in the economy that have left growing numbers of African American men out of work and with poor prospects for marriage.[4] Wilson used data from a variety of sources to meticulously document that changes in the African American family, which he regarded as problematic, were directly linked to the loss of blue-collar jobs and not due to welfare dependency, as Murray had suggested. As the American economy shifted away from manufacturing, so-called unskilled

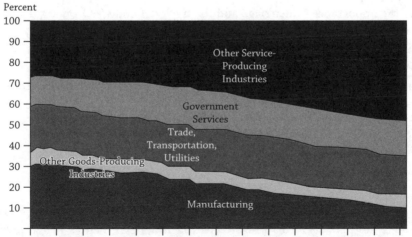

Figure 7.2 Share of nonfarm employment by major industrial sector, 1950 to 2007
From: Lee MA, Mather M. U.S. labor force trends. *Population Bulletin Report.* 2008;63(2).

men (with less than a college education) were no longer able to secure jobs that could support their families. They became essentially "unmarriageable" because they could not fulfill the traditional role of breadwinner.

As indicated in Figure 7.2, which we obtained from a document published by the Bureau of Labor, manufacturing jobs have been declining fairly steadily since the mid-1950s, while growth in the service industry jobs has increased during the same period of time. Many of the new service jobs pay less than the manufacturing jobs they replaced, which contributes to the stress and economic hardship of families.

In *The Truly Disadvantaged* and later in *When Work Disappears*,[5] Wilson paints a complex picture of African American life that acknowledges the role of racial discrimination and "ghetto" culture in the rising rate of single mothers and absent fathers. But he is careful to point out that "black culture" is not driving men away from families. From Wilson's point of view, the elements of culture that we might associate with father absence (i.e., hedonism, distrust between the sexes) are byproducts of poverty and disenfranchisement. Wilson built a compelling case that access to better jobs is the most viable solution to the problems facing African American men and their families. Like Moynihan, he believes that good jobs and good fathers go hand in hand. He also argues that the social and economic problems facing African Americans require significant government intervention, such as training and education programs to help unskilled workers get the sort of jobs that can support a family.

Even though Wilson clearly disagrees with Murray about the root cause of single parenthood, both men seem to be on the same page with respect to the importance of marriage and the nuclear family. Wilson argued persuasively that for African American men to remain psychologically (and physically) connected with their families, they must have decent jobs. When a father is unable to acquire the skills to be employed or when there are no jobs to be found, a man's identity as a father is undermined, his self-confidence is diminished, and he is more likely to drift away from his children.

THE EMERGENCE OF THE SINGLE MOTHER

Up through the 1980s, many scholars discussing fatherless children and single mothers seemed to regard African American men as being at the center of the problem. But, by the 1990s, the percentages of white and Latino children living apart from their fathers rose substantially and the single motherhood problem could no longer be regarded as an "African

American problem." Although the rates of father absence continued to be highest for African American children, the overall rate of children living apart from their fathers more than doubled from 10.7 percent in 1970 to 23.4 percent in 1995.[6] That year, David Blankenhorn wrote a book entitled *Fatherless America* that portrays fatherlessness as the most pressing cultural and social problem for all Americans, not just African Americans.[a] Blankenhorn articulated a vision of family life in which fathers are married to their children's mother, providing for their family, and firmly situated at the head of the household. Moreover, Blankenhorn blamed most of our social problems—violence, drugs, teenage pregnancy—on what he calls the "de-culturation" of fatherhood. His argument is that the father role has been diminished by a liberal view of divorce and unwed parenthood and by fathers themselves, who have lost their sense of direction and purpose. He described a wide variety of ways that a man can fail as a father, but the most common path taken is the decision to not get married to the mother of his children. Blankenhorn gave voice to those who believe that our biggest social problem is our collective unwillingness to make and keep our commitments to family. Despite the fact that Blankenhorn, Wilson, Murray, and Moynihan each proposed different ideas about why so many young men are functioning so poorly as fathers,[b] they all seem to agree that fathers are *essential* to the health and well-being of children. Are they?

ARE FATHERS NECESSARY, DISPOSABLE, OR SOMETHING IN BETWEEN?

In 2010, Joseph Pleck, a psychologist at the University of Illinois and a pioneer in fatherhood research, proposed what he calls the "Important Father Hypothesis."[8] Pleck came up with this hypothesis in response to those who were arguing that fathers are "essential" *and* in response to those who were arguing that fathers are disposable.[9] Pleck anchors his hypothesis in the research literature on fathers and children and takes the middle-of-the-road position, arguing that while fathers play an important role in the

---

a. The rates quoted in Blankenhorn's book (pp. 18–19) are much higher than the previously noted rates, but his rates could not be substantiated.

b. In Part Six, we will address the implication of different perspectives on solving the problem. For the moment, suffice it to say that Wilson has spent the better part of his life working arduously toward developing structural solutions designed to increase opportunity and support the marriageability of African American men, while Blankenhorn (and Popenoe and Murray) have proposed ideological solutions for reclaiming lost values.

development of their children, mothers can fulfill many roles traditionally delegated to fathers. And other people in the child's environment can function as father surrogates. In a chapter of *The Role of the Father in Child Development*, Pleck explains this hypothesis:

> Good fathering is considered one of many influences on positive development. The fact that fathering is not all-determinative does not mean that it is irrelevant. . . . To some, saying that fathers are important rather than saying they are essential is a demotion in our assessment of fathering effects. In my view, it simply represents bringing our understanding of the impact of good fathering in line with the way researchers understand the effects of influences on positive outcomes in most other domains.[8p48]

Pleck is an excellent social scientist and follows the research on fatherhood—his own and others'—to this middle-of-the-road position. His point that father presence is one of several factors that contributes to child well-being and his acknowledgement that some children do just fine without their fathers might seem heretical to fatherhood advocates. Saying that fathers are important but not essential may ring true for many people who have grown up without a father, wished their father had been involved, but who felt good about how their life turned out and about what their mother was able to provide. Some of the young men we've talked with over the years have told us that their mother functioned as both mother *and* father in their lives. Theo, a 20-year-old expectant father, whose own father disappeared from his life when he was 4, explains how his mother made up for the absence of a father figure.

THEO: I can talk to her about anything, any type of problem. We are real close, like a father–son relationship.

BARRY: How involved in your life is she?

THEO: Real involved. She is real close. . . . She's still schooling me, telling me how to manage things, telling me to slow down. She helps me a lot.

BARRY: You said like father and son?

THEO: 'Cause I had to talk to her about something I didn't think I could talk to her about, you know, but she make it easy for me to talk to her.

Many single mothers manage on their own or with the support of their extended families, and many children survive and even thrive without their father's involvement. At the same time, there is an impressive body of research documenting that, as a group, children who live continuously with both their parents are more psychologically secure and more socially and emotionally adept than children whose parents are divorced or separated.[10] Children in two-parent families do better in school; they are less likely to get into trouble with drugs and alcohol, they report fewer psychological problems, and they tend to have more stable relationships with their own partners.[11,12] On the other hand, children in mother-headed households, with absent fathers, are consistently found to be at risk for a long list of psychological and social problems, including depression, substance abuse, and criminality.[13,14] Why is this so? When mothers and fathers are able to work together reasonably well, there are three primary reasons that their children benefit: (a) co-parents provide their children with different types of parenting, balancing each other's weaknesses; (b) co-parents support each other as parents, allowing both to take care of their own needs and refuel; and (c) co-parents help each other out financially, which provides children with a more stable, secure environment.

In the early years, fatherhood researchers focused on what fathers do as parents that mothers do not do. Ross Parke and other researchers observed that fathers tend to bond with their children through "rough and tumble" play, which teaches children to regulate their aggression and balance assertiveness with restraint.[15-17] This more masculine approach to parenting complements mothering, which tends to focus on the development of relationships and the expression of emotion.[18,19] While it is easy to speculate that the "yin and yang" of mothers and fathers is "natural," it's also easy to imagine that these distinct gender roles are largely constructed by social expectations about the "nature" of men and women (rather than anything truly intrinsic to gender). Indeed, there is some evidence that gender differences in parent–child interactions during play (i.e., "rough and tumble" fathers vs. more conversational and gentle mothers) are beginning to decrease, as fathers are becoming increasingly involved in childcare and nurturing activities.[20] This suggests that the differences in father– and mother–child interactions are evolving and are more likely accounted for by socially and culturally prescribed parental roles than by biological sex. Whatever the origin of these differences in style, some role differentiation between parents appears to have a positive influence on child development,[21-23] especially if it is experienced as collaborative. When parents get along and coordinate their caregiving, children's lives tend to be enriched by the differences between parents.[24] Children appear to benefit from the flexibility and diversity of having two role models, regardless of whether those roles are differentiated along traditional gender lines.

Children raised by a single mother (or father) lack the opportunity to see their parents negotiate and compromise or learn from each other. If we believe that any two parents represent different psychological facets of the child's environment, then it makes sense that children growing up with only one parent will find it more difficult to create a coherent sense of self.[c] These children will tend to know less about how to engage in and sustain intimate relationships, which will make it more difficult for them to establish stable environments for their own children when that time arrives.[10] In addition to the yin and yang of parenthood, children benefit from having two parents who cooperatively share parenting roles and responsibilities, providing cover when the other is tired, stressed, sick, or angry.[d] Having two loving parents should result in more love, care, support, structure and supervision, and less stress.[27,28] In this respect, children of two parents are more likely to benefit from more overall parental attention, patience, and energy. When two parents remain constructively involved in parenting, there are clear psychological benefits for both the parents and for their children. Two parents can complement and support each other and more easily provide their children with a sense of cohesion, balance, and security.

The fact that children in two-parent, intact families seem to have clear developmental advantages raises a fundamental question: Does the gender of the second parent really matter? Until very recently, there was almost no research comparing the children of heterosexual and lesbian parenting couples. Theoretically, this research is valuable because it can help disentangle the positive effects of having a second parent figure from the positive effects of having a second parent who is male. In a comprehensive review of the research on single- and two-parent lesbian, gay, and heterosexual families, Timothy Biblarz from the University of Southern California and Judith Stacey from New York University reported that, across most studies, the findings suggest (i) having two parents is better than having only one

---

c. Sarah Hrdy in *Mothers and Others* presents a very interesting counterpoint that, in many societies, women create extended family networks to hedge their bets against father disengagement.[25] From that perspective, which is well-grounded in cross-cultural studies, our notions of psychological wholeness may need to be expanded.

d. Indeed, researchers examining the records of women giving birth in Florida found that that infants born to single mothers were more likely to be premature or have lower birth weights than infants born to two-parent families.[26] Not surprisingly, the stress of fatherlessness can affect the health of a child even before he or she is born.

(which we already knew), and (ii) it does not matter whether or not one parent is male.[29] That is, children raised by two lesbian parents and children of two heterosexual parents function similarly across most domains of development. Digging a little deeper into this research, there is some evidence that the children of lesbian parents may have some advantages over the children of heterosexual parents, demonstrating greater attachment security and fewer behavioral problems. This difference may be due to the fact that lesbian parents are more invested in childrearing than the typical two-parent family, having to jump over mores hurdles to get pregnant or adopt a child.[29,30]

Although some might glibly suggest that Biblarz and Stacey prove that an extra dose of maternal care more than makes up for the absence of a father, the research on gay parenting is not intended to "best" or outdo traditional families. In fact, this research supports the value of the two-parent family structure. Lesbian parents help us think more broadly about what that "second parent" brings to the table. Later in this chapter, we review some of the evidence that fathers can make a unique contribution to child development.[16,17,23,31,32] These father-focused researchers endorse what we referred to earlier as the "yin and yang" theory of family functioning, proposing that fathers and mothers complement each other in important ways and that neither can be easily replaced. The fact that fathers are a different gender than mothers certainly adds *something* to the family dynamic, but it is not clear that what they add is necessarily better than what a second mother might contribute. The research on lesbian couples challenges us to consider that family roles are not so clearly linked to gender. If two mothers can do just as well as a father and mother, then it might be the case that the *number* of parents and the *investment* of those parents matters more than the gender of the parents. This point is not intended to be an aside. We believe breaking down rigid gender roles can help young men think more flexibly about their role as fathers. A broader definition of fatherhood—perhaps better framed as parenthood—may help some young men find a meaningful and attainable way to contribute to their child's development. This is a topic we explore more fully in Part Five of this book.

If two parents are better than one for most, this begs the question: What specifically do fathers (as a second parent) add to this equation? The most obvious answer to this question is that engaged fathers—even nonresident yet still involved fathers—provide resources (time and money) to ensure a child's basic needs are met. Not surprisingly, research findings indicate that when fathers contribute to the financial support to their children, those children are healthier and do better in school largely because more money translates into safer neighborhoods with better schools, access to high-quality medical care, and more opportunities for growth and enrichment, like music lessons, summer camp, and other such things.[33,34] Less obviously, a father's financial support indirectly affects his child's well-being, insofar as it decreases maternal stress, enabling her to be more emotionally available to their children.[35,36] Research looking specifically at mother-headed households finds that nonresident fathers who help cover the costs of raising their children have a powerful impact on their children's development over time. This support contributes in significant ways to the development of children in mother-headed households. In a meta-analysis conducted in the late 1990s, Paul Amato and Joan Gilbreth found that nonresidential fathers' financial contributions were associated with children's academic success and lower levels of externalizing behavior problems.[33] Additionally, several researchers have found that a father's payment of child support had a significantly larger effect on his child's development than other sources of family income, like government assistance or extended family support.[35,37,38] One reason why a father's financial contribution matters so much is that it tends to go hand in hand with other forms of father involvement. In fact, several researchers have found that fathers who provide monetary support also have more contact with their children.[39-41] Of course, the reverse is also true, suggesting that the relationship between paternal engagement and a father's financial contribution to child rearing is reciprocal, one supporting the other.[41]

Early research on fatherhood focused primarily on the *quantity* of paternal engagement, as assessed by the total amount of time that fathers spent in direct interactions with their children. This led to the not-so-shocking discovery that, although the amount of time that fathers spend with their children is important, the *quality* of that time is what matters most.[e] The relative importance of *quality* over quantity is particularly relevant to nonresidential fathers, who spend far less time with their children than fathers who live with their children. In a review paper that compiled the results of 82 studies of nonresident father involvement and child developmental outcomes, Kari Adamsons and Sarah Johnson reported that the quality of father involvement almost always trumps the quantity of his involvement,[42] meaning that how a parent spends time with his or her

e. A couple of caveats are worth mentioning here. When frequency of father–child contact occurs in the context of high-quality interactions, more is expected to be better. In the context of poor quality, however (such as with a hostile father), more contact is likely to be worse—either in the sense of failing to have a positive impact on child development or, more likely, exerting a detrimental effect.

child (e.g., how warm or hostile they are) is a stronger predictor of that child's developmental outcomes than how *much* time a parent spends with his or her child.[f] Of course, we cannot completely discount the importance of quantity. If a father is hardly ever around, the little bit of warmth and support he provides may not be enough to have an impact on his child's development and might be overshadowed by the fact that he should be providing that warmth and support more frequently. We do not know of any research that has tried to discern just how much father involvement is sufficient (assuming the quality of his involvement is positive), perhaps because figuring out the minimum "effective" dose of fathering seems like an impossible task.

If the quality of father–child interactions is more important than sheer quantity, this raises an important question: What specific types of paternal activities (besides involvement in basic childcare) constitute "positive father engagement?" On the face of it, positive engagement involves not only actively playing, reading, teaching, talking to (and with) a child but can also include more passive or noninteractive types of involvement, such as cooking dinner or working on his computer, if that father is "available," should the child need him for something. These types of involvement provide fathers and children with the opportunity to develop an interpersonal rhythm of their own, building a relationship that will become part of the child's emerging sense of self, his or her personality.

More specifically, when fathers are attuned to their children (putting away their cell phones and turning off the TV) and responsive to their child's interactive behavior (babbling, talking, playing), their children demonstrate increased cognitive development during infancy and early childhood and better social functioning in childhood and adolescence. When fathers engage in "scaffolding" behaviors, namely providing help and guidance in a way that also allows for some autonomy and encourages self-reliance, their children tend to demonstrate better problem-solving and interpersonal skills.[43] Along similar lines, children whose fathers regularly read to them are better able to express themselves, attend to others, and absorb information.[44–46]

Generally, there is evidence that fathers' involvement in various types of interactive parent-child activities contribute to their children's cognitive and language development, above and beyond the impact of mothers' involvement.[20,47,48] One explanation for this is that fathers tend to speak to

---

f. What we mean by negative and positive father involvement is something we discuss in more detail in Part Four.

children in ways that challenge their linguistic capabilities.[49] Compared to mothers, for example, fathers are more likely to make requests for clarification, provide more directives, ask more what/where/when/why questions, and refer back to past events.[g] These processes may, in turn, help expand children's language and vocabulary.[11] Again, this likely reveals the important effect of a second parent fulfilling complementary functions, as opposed to necessarily reflecting the influence of biological sex.

All the things that fathers do for and with their children create an overall "affective climate" that envelopes the father–child relationship, for better or worse. What a father does and how a father *is* can make his child feel loved or unloved; his presence can provide comfort or fear.[50] One specific measure of the overall affective climate of the father–child relationship is the degree to which a child experiences acceptance (vs. rejection) from his or her father. It turns out that this variable is an important predictor of several developmental outcomes. For example, children who report higher levels of paternal acceptance tend to score higher on measures of self-reliance, emotional stability, and self-esteem, and they also have a more optimistic overall worldview, compared to children who felt rejected by their fathers.[51]

Somewhat surprisingly, this is true even if fathers do not live with their children. In their meta-analysis of nonresidential father involvement (already mentioned), Adamsons and Johnson found that perceived father–child relationship quality, especially based on mother report but also based on father and child report, emerged as one of the most salient predictors of child well-being, including cognitive, social, behavioral, and emotional domains. These authors noted,

> Our findings suggest that children's well-being is tied less to fathers' general behaviors (spending time or money) and more to the affective climate created by the quality of those behaviors. Fathers matter not when they just spend time with their children, but when they spend time being involved in activities with their children and nurturing the father-child relationship.[42p596]

---

g. Different possible explanations for these findings have been proposed. For example, it could be that these differences between father–child and mother–child interactions are related to gender roles (though not necessarily biological sex) that fathers tend to adopt (e.g., men tend to be socialized to be more directive, which could help explain the increased tendency of fathers to use more directive statements toward their children). Another explanation is that men tend to spend less time with their children compared to mothers. In turn, since they are less "in the know" with their children compared to mothers, this may help explain their tendency to ask more exploratory questions and to seek clarification more than mothers.

Perceived love and acceptance by one's father is no less important than perceived mothers' love and acceptance with respect to predicting children's overall well-being. And it may even be more salient when it comes to lowering the risk for substance abuse, depression, and externalizing behavior problems.[52] Thus, the cumulative evidence suggests that the father–child bond is an important predictor linked with multiple aspects of child well-being.

THE COSTS OF FATHER ABSENCE

Having discussed some of the specific benefits of a father's presence, it is important to also mention the costs of a father's absence, which include psychological as well as economic costs and impact children, mothers, and the fathers themselves.

Psychological Costs of Father Absence

A father's absence, or even his inconsistent or uncommitted presence, can feel like a festering psychological wound, a hole in the heart.[53] Children without fathers see their peers whose fathers are involved and often feel bitter about what they didn't get and don't have. Not all children who grow up without their fathers feel this way, Theo (the young man whose mother also functioned as a father for him) being a case in point. But many—maybe most—do. Take Kurt, a young father who had been raised by his mother and aunt in a working-class white suburban Chicago neighborhood. When we asked Kurt to describe his father, who was long gone, he did not mince words.

> KURT: He's a fucking moron, bottom line.
> BARRY: What do you think a father should be like?
> KURT: Anything's better than my dad.
> BARRY: And what would that be?
> KURT: Just be there. Just to fucking be there. . . . When my parents got divorced he'd be, like, "Yeah I'm coming up, I'll be there in an hour." I'd sit there and wait around, thinking, "All right, he's coming." Doesn't show up. So, you know, the last thing I want to do is be like my dad. He's a dipshit. I just don't get along with him. The thing that pisses me off all the time is I have to teach myself how to do everything. 'Cause, I mean, as soon as my parents got

divorced, my mom gets a job, and I can understand that. We need money. She did her best to see me off to school and all that, right? But she was sort of gone a lot. My dad was never around.

Economic Impacts of Father Absence

Apart from the psychological damage done by fathers who disappear, the economic disadvantages of father absence are profound. Children in mother-headed households are five times more likely to be poor than children growing up in two-parent families.[54,55] The reasons for this are obvious but worth spelling out. First, most children (61 percent) in two-parent families have two working parents bringing home two paychecks, adding up to an average household income of about $87,000 (in 2016). By contrast, most single parents have sole custody and struggle to get by on a single paycheck (76 percent) and/or on public assistance (50 percent), bringing home an average income of $41,000 (in 2016). Second, only about one-third of single mothers receive formal child support from their non-custodial partner, averaging under $4,000. Sometimes this is because fathers either don't have or refuse to provide the money, but it is also because only about half of mothers who could file for child support do so,[14] a topic we return to in Chapter 21.

The upshot of all this is that about 40 percent of children living in single-mother households are living below the poverty line. This might sound bad, but it reflects an improvement over time. Ten years ago, during the great recession, the rate of poverty for children living in single-mother households was 47.1 percent and if we look back as far as the early 1960s, the rate of poverty for children in single-mother households was 68 percent.[55]

In many respects, the prospects for a single mother and her children are better than they've ever been, which might help explain the rise in single motherhood. Indeed, it's somewhat remarkable that poverty rates for single mothers and their children decreased over the same period of time that the rate of children born to unmarried parents *increased*. However, before we get too celebratory about these improvements in the social fabric, it's important to remember that a 40 percent rate of poverty among children in single-parent households is quite high. This number highlights the fact that, despite improvements in services and protections for impoverished families, the rising rate of absent fathers continues to put a great number of children at risk for poverty-related problems. We've mended part of the social fabric, but other parts are more frayed than ever before. Our enthusiasm for the progress made is dampened by the fact that poverty has a profound impact on the health and well-being of so many children who are also disadvantaged by their father's absence. Poor children are less likely to have access to healthy food, safe housing, quality daycare, or adequately performing schools. They are provided with fewer opportunities to develop their innate skills and interests. They spend less time with their parents, who are working long hours. And they are more likely to be exposed to family chaos and instability, neighborhood violence, and environmental health hazards, such as lead in the water and pollution in the air.

Because of their exposure to these social and environmental toxins, poor children are at significant risk for developmental delays, learning disabilities, academic underachievement, and a long list of physical and mental health problems.[56] Much of the research linking child poverty to negative developmental outcomes focuses on the role of family stress and social trauma. This body of research has demonstrated again and again that when our stress response systems are overloaded, normal development is short circuited.[57] In addition, there is evidence that children living in poverty are at significant risk for diminished cognitive development and academic performance because their young minds are insufficiently stimulated and/nourished (with physical nutrition and interpersonal interaction). Digging further into this presumed link between poverty and brain development, Seth Pollack at the University of Wisconsin–Madison led a team of researchers that measured the brain development of 389 children over several years, using magnetic resonance imaging.[58] Their findings indicated that, compared to nonpoor children, children growing up in poverty had significantly less grey matter in the frontal and temporal lobes, which corresponded with lower performance on tests of cognitive and academic functioning. Pollack and his colleagues attributed this diminished growth to a combination of insufficient cognitive stimulation and overwhelming stress. It is disturbing to learn that poor children's brains are being stunted by their environments, but these findings only substantiate what is already well known, especially by those whose lives reflect this reality: poverty can have devastating consequences on child development.

However, there is also good evidence that impoverished parents can protect their children from some of the negative effects of poverty. For example, Jeong-Kyun Choi recently analyzed the effect of nonresidential fathers on the behavioral and cognitive development of young impoverished children participating in the Fragile Families Study.[59] Choi found that the positive influence of nonresident fathers' parenting predicted fewer child behavioral problems and better cognitive performance scores, but he notes an important wrinkle: nonresident paternal influence on child development was indirect, mediated through the mother's parenting behavior. In other words, a nonresident father's positive involvement with his child helps the custodial mother be a more effective parent, thereby diminishing the effect of poverty on behavioral problems and cognitive delays. The bad news is that poverty continues to be a huge problem for children in single-mother households; the good news is that parents—including nonresident fathers—can help ensure their children grow up in a positive nurturing home environment, protecting them from some of poverty's damaging effects.

The Impact of Father Absence on Fathers

There is an interesting line of research indicating that fatherhood is good for men. Men who become fathers earn more, are generally happier and healthier, and live longer than men who never become fathers.[60] Why would this be the case? There are, of course, different ways to make sense of this phenomenon. It might be that men who become fathers are better off in the first place and that fatherhood only fortifies their predisposing health. But it also seems likely that fatherhood has a galvanizing effect on young men, propelling them into adult roles, perhaps protecting some against the risks of being untethered. Whatever the case may be, men typically benefit from the stability and social support that accompanies family life.

Given all that, we cannot help but wonder if fathers who abandon their children suffer the psychological consequences of that lost connection. We know that father absence is bad for children, but is it also bad for fathers? Unfortunately, the research on fathers who disengage and disappear is thin because these fathers are resistant to research or just impossible to find and recruit into studies like ours. While some of these fathers are already absent before their child is born, many become disengaged gradually over time.[61] Because of this, we can begin to piece together a few clues about what makes these disengaging fathers different and what happens to them as they become more absent. In our own research, we found that fathers who reported mental health problems (particularly substance abuse) prior to the birth of their first child are more likely to report a rocky adjustment to parenthood, sometimes leading to disengagement.[62] Intuitively, these findings make sense and highlight the importance of identifying and addressing an expectant father's mental health problems prior to childbirth, if only for the sake of his partner and child. But we also know that some fathers show no signs of trouble *before* their partner's pregnancy and then experience serious problems *after* the baby is born.[63]

Recall Quinton (from Chapter 1) who felt derailed by fatherhood. Although Quinton was unhappy about the prospect of becoming a father when we first interviewed him, he was, by most accounts, doing well. He had some minor symptoms of anxiety and depression, but the results of the diagnostic interview we administered in our first meeting indicated a clean bill of mental health. Indeed, he was feeling good about school and excited about an arts program for teens that was paying him to paint murals on buildings. Almost immediately after his daughter was born, Quinton sank into a deep state of misery and dysfunction. He dropped out, started smoking pot, and got arrested for stealing. Two years later, he was minimally involved in his daughter's life and described parenting as a painfully humiliating experience because he felt so hopelessly ill-equipped to function as a father. He seemed frozen by his inadequacies.

> BARRY: Can you describe yourself as a father?
> QUINTON: Um. . . . I don't know. I'm probably not really that good.
> BARRY: Why do you say that?
> QUINTON: I haven't, like, done it enough.
> BARRY: What do you mean you haven't done it enough?
> QUINTON: I haven't been with her long enough, you know? I hardly ever come to see her. I'm not an actual. . . . I don't know. It's hard to describe. Right now, like, the hardest thing about being a father is how ashamed I am with myself, you know?
> BARRY: Why are you ashamed with yourself?
> QUINTON: Well, like, 'cause I can't take care of myself, and I have a daughter, you know? I'm not a real winner. I don't really have money to take her . . . like, the only time I can see my girl is when I can go and take her somewhere, you know? Like, I can't go outside and take her to the park or something. I mean, I can, but it's not for a lot of time.

When we interviewed Quinton before his daughter was born, he was already worried about his prospects as a parent. Two-and-a-half years later, he is overwhelmed and undone by his failure. Understandably, Quinton's self-pitying tone can easily lead to the wish that he would just "snap out of it" for the sake of his daughter. At the same time, it's important to recognize that this young man was debilitated and paralyzed by his low self-worth. What's more, in addition to his drug use and legal problems, Quinton's anxiety and depression have become much more significant, which is apparent in his narrative. Taking all of these challenges into consideration (and recognizing that Quinton's various risks far outweigh any protective factors, as we discussed in Chapter 1) "snapping out of it" is far easier said than done.

Indeed, Quinton represents an important subgroup of young men who develop serious psychological problems after becoming fathers. In the only published study of this phenomenon that we could find, Sarah Meadows, Sarah McLanahan, and Jeanne Brooks-Gunn reported that among the 389 uninvolved, nonresident fathers they tracked down through the Fragile Families Study, about 25 percent reported significant signs of depression and/or anxiety 3 years following their child's birth.[64] Because Meadows and her colleagues were able to control for earlier indicators of depression and anxiety, their findings suggest that these fathers experienced declines in their mental health as they were becoming disconnected from their children.[h] In an unpublished study based on this same data set, Marcia Carlson and Kim Turner reported that fathers who became less involved with their children also earned less money and became more socially disconnected.[68]

Fathers like Quinton are relevant to the question of whether fathers are necessary in two important respects. First, when a father disengages from his children, he creates feelings of loss and deprivation that are hard to reconcile. As we have already discussed, this will be a heavy burden for their children to bear. Second, when fathers are not contributing to the well-being of their own children, they are doing something else with their time, and some of them are up to no good. While it's possible that some disengaged fathers are making great scientific discoveries (like Albert Einstein) or creating great works of art (like Paul Gaugin), it's more likely that they are smoking weed (like Quinton) or selling it (like Darius), or worse. The void they leave in their absence is only made worse by the roles they choose to occupy instead. Some of these men are culpable for the choices they make, but some cannot be blamed for their failures, as they too bear heavy burdens. Whether a father is at fault or not, the point still

---

h. Of course, it is difficult to know what happens first. If a young man is already experiencing psychological problems at the time of his child's birth, he is at risk for becoming an absent or dysfunctional father.[62] However, a man's mental health status at his child's birth does not fully explain his subsequent health or his functioning as a father. Some young men with significant problems prior to becoming fathers report that the experience of their child's birth helped give them a sense of purpose and motivated them to become healthier.[65] Indeed, there is plenty of evidence that fathers who manage to stay connected are healthier than other men, including fathers who disconnect and men who never become fathers.[60,66,67]

holds. Absent fathers are more likely than present and engaged fathers to become rootless, troublesome men. Fatherhood helps keep men constructively occupied.[60,69]

The Hardship of Single Parenthood

Raising a son or daughter alone, without a partner, can be a hard and lonely struggle. Most single mothers come to terms with the absence of their partner. Some may even feel relieved when the conflict and drama disappear, but that relief does not necessarily minimize the hardship. For example, when Diamond told Marcus she was pregnant, he secretly wondered whether the baby was his, but he didn't say anything to Diamond, figuring he would wait and see, maybe get the baby tested.[i]

After his son, Damien, was born, Marcus never bothered with genetic testing. He just broke up with Diamond and kept his distance. He never told Diamond about his doubts, which may have been more of an excuse than a real concern. More important, he never talked with her about his *self-doubts*, his struggle with trusting others and making commitments. For the first year, he dropped by to see Damien every month or so, but he did little to help with parenting. When Emma asked Diamond what went wrong, what came between her and Marcus, she described the situation but couldn't provide much of an explanation, because she did not know.

> DIAMOND: During the pregnancy, he was like a real father then. I call him and tell him, "I want this," and he'll go to the restaurant by his house and bring it to me. Man, I was completely in love with him. We was always together. I would meet him when he got out of school on his doorstep, 'cause I was staying next to him. If you saw him, you'd see me. If you saw me, you'd see him. We was always together. He was there when I was pregnant but after the baby came, I guess it was like a big burden. And now it's like you can't put us together in the same room. I can't stand to be around him, and he can't stand to be around me. I hate him.

---

i. A conversation Marcus had with another girl when he was in high school nagged at him. He had asked this girl—a friend of his—what she would do if she got pregnant with someone she didn't like. She told him, "I'd just go to another man and make him think it's his. You know, have sex with him, make him think it's his."

Late in her pregnancy, Diamond developed gestational diabetes, which is relatively common and usually transient. But after she delivered, it turned into Type 2 diabetes, and she had to start taking insulin. Her son, Damien, developed asthma, which is increasingly prevalent among African American children and potentially quite serious. Diamond and Damien were living in her friend's apartment, but the cats in that apartment aggravated Damien's asthma. He had to be hospitalized twice in 6 months, so Diamond and Damien moved in with her sister and her family. The asthma was under control, but the pediatrician discovered that Damien had lead poisoning. Alarmed by the levels of lead in Damien, the pediatrician called the health department. They tested and found lead in both her friend's and sister's apartments. It was just one thing after another. And yet, these health problems—diabetes, asthma, lead poisoning—are frighteningly common among people living in the most disadvantaged neighborhoods of Chicago and other highly segregated and impoverished cities throughout America. Diamond was unlucky, but it is likely that many of her neighbors were too.

Diamond was working hard to move forward with her life and take care of her son. She had been on public aid since her pregnancy, but now she was off assistance and working full-time as a certified nursing assistant. She was feeling stronger and more independent, but she was also irritable and angry. She was staying afloat but still confused and angry about Marcus. When Emma asked Diamond to describe her relationship with Marcus, it was easy to feel her anguish.

DIAMOND: We have no relationship, no communication. My son is two years old, he's done nothing for him. He bought him a coat, a thing of Pampers, and some cheap wipes through this whole two years. There's nothing he's done for me to appreciate him. I'm to the point that I hate him and don't want to be around him. I wish nothing bad on him 'cause I still got love for him, but it's not the love I had before. And I don't want to be around him. Just for the simple fact that he can buy himself a car and do all this stuff for himself but not for my child. I put my child before myself. I won't buy myself nothing until he got everything he wants. But Marcus, he won't do nothing, nothing at all.

EMMA: What ways would you like his relationship with your child to be different?

DIAMOND: I want him to be more involved. That's really all I want. If he thinks it's too hard to get a job, fine. I have been doing it for two years. Just be around your child. Take him someplace and do something with him, talk to him, read to him. Something!

Emma changed the topic and asked Diamond how she was feeling about being a mother.

> DIAMOND: It's fine. It's good to have something that's yours. You know, something you can take care of, something you can do for. But it's tiring. It's an all-day job, and I'm not there enough. I got to work *and* make sure he got what he needs. And I just feel like I'm not being there enough. I don't do nothing no more. I don't go out with my friends no more. If they're having a party, I don't go 'cause I don't like leaving Damien with anyone, not even my boyfriend. I can't leave him for too long 'cause I get nervous. If it's something that kids can't come to, I don't go. I got to stay here with Damien.
>
> EMMA: What do you think is the hardest thing about being a mother?
>
> DIAMOND: The responsibility . . . you gotta make sure, you gotta watch. The main thing, I'm serious, you gotta watch who's around your child. You gotta watch what goes on around your child when he's someplace else. You gotta make sure your house is right, little stuff. It's crazy. There is a lot of responsibility, a lot of stress that comes with having a child. Especially when you are young. I didn't know what to do. I was like, I have to get a job, I have to buy Pampers, I have to do this and that. He's not helping. You have to be more grown up. You got a baby, you gotta grow up fast. You gotta be *on* it. You gotta do a complete change for your child 'cause you don't want your child to grow up all screwed up. You gotta watch how you talk. You gotta make sure you don't talk bad. That's one thing I did. I made sure I never talked bad about Marcus around Damien 'cause I don't want him to grow up hating him. There's no cause for all of that.

Diamond clearly articulates the incredible stress of being a poor young single mother. Although Diamond had some support—a friend, a sister, a pediatrician who went to bat for her and her son—she feels alone and wants much more. There are very few things that are more persistently challenging than raising children without a partner. As any single parent will tell you, being "on duty" all the time is physically and psychologically exhausting.[70] The type of stress young single mothers experience is chronic and pervasive, increasing exponentially with each child.[36] The strain of doing it alone can affect a mother's physical and psychological health and, not surprisingly, the quality of her parenting.[71] In this way, her stress can be transmitted to her child so that stressed-out parents tend to have stressed-out children.[72] Indeed, some of the psychological differences observed between children with and without engaged fathers (previously noted) are likely due to the stress associated with being raised by stressed-out single mothers.[36,73]

There are plenty of children who grow up without the benefit of their fathers' involvement and manage to do well for themselves, Barack Obama being perhaps the best example. Nevertheless, President Obama has said—somewhat sardonically—that his father's absence was so psychologically challenging for him that he needed to write a book to figure out his relationship with his father. We all know how that story ends. Despite the hole his father left, Obama became successful because he made such good use of the love and support offered by those who stayed, most notably his mother, his grandparents, and eventually his wife. Things obviously turned out well for Obama despite his father's absence; however, many others are not so fortunate. Indeed, the psychological damage inflicted by absent fathers and absent partners can be severe. Kurt (whose father was unreliable) and Diamond (whose partner disappeared) endured, as many children and mothers do in the wake of a father's departure. But their suffering is palpable. And Quinton's story illustrates the point that father absence can be hard, even for the absent father.

SO, ARE FATHERS NECESSARY?

It may be the case that fathers operate differently than mothers in some respects, but much of what we (and others) think is important about fathers (responsibility, engagement, overall positive emotional climate) is not unique to fathers, or particularly "father-like." A close look at the research on the impact of fathers and mothers on their children reveals that "good parenting" is somewhat generic. It's possible that some parenting qualities may indeed be more common among fathers, such as a greater propensity toward rough-and-tumble play, for example. And it may be that fathers can impact their children in ways that are distinct from that of mothers. But we don't think that proving this is necessary to proving the value of fathers. That said, we think it is important to ask: Does father engagement in childrearing have an impact on child development beyond what mothers provide? Examining all of the available research leads us to the conclusion that, in most cases, having two parents benefits children in many important ways (economically, socially, and cognitively). Responsible and engaged fathers add something important to the parenting equation that goes beyond what mothers, by themselves, are able to provide for their children. Conversely, although children can survive—and sometimes even thrive—without fathers, there is no doubt that father absence tends to take a major toll on children and their mothers, as well as the fathers themselves.

So, where does this leave us? In returning to the question posed by the title of this chapter, we are in agreement with Joseph Pleck that, when considering each particular father, "important" might be a more fitting word than "necessary" or "essential." However, when considering the effects of father absence on our society *as a whole*, keeping fathers connected seems more than just "important." Research on the social and psychological effects of father absence on fathers, mothers, and children puts the question of whether fathers are essential in a somewhat different light. If the trend in father disengagement continues, it seems that child poverty rates will remain high and greater numbers of young men will become more rootless and dysfunctional.

Thus, we would argue that keeping fathers constructively engaged with their children, and their children's mothers, is *important* for building strong families and *necessary* for building a healthy society. This, of course, is easier said than done, which is why we are writing this book. There is a lot that can go wrong between young parents, often leading fathers to become loosely involved or entirely disengaged from their partners and children. Before we turn our attention to what contributes to the development of positively engaged fathers, it is important to first understand what can go wrong.

PART THREE

Fathers Lost

CHAPTER 8

What Goes Wrong?

There are three major problems that get in the way of fathers engaging with, providing for, and committing to their families. These are violence, serious substance abuse, and criminal activity that leads to jail or prison time.[a] Of course, this is not an exhaustive list of problems that disrupt fatherhood, but these problems are distinctively disruptive, having a direct impact on the co-parenting and parenting relationship, often driving a permanent wedge between fathers, their children, and their children's mothers.[1] Other problems, such as mental illness or joblessness, can have a powerful impact on fathers and fatherhood, but the impact of these problems is typically mediated through violence, substance abuse, and/or criminal involvement. Fathers without jobs are more likely to engage in illegal activities to support themselves and their families. A father who is depressed or traumatized may look to drugs and alcohol to ease his mind and escape his angst; then, over time, he may become addicted. This is not to say that problems like joblessness or mental illness don't directly affect fatherhood. These conditions can cause irritability, impatience, and instability, but in our experience these harmful consequences are not typically "deal breakers" for young couples. The distinction we are making is this: some problems, like most mental health problems, do not present a clear and

---

a. There is a distinction between jail and prison in the criminal justice system. Jail, which is usually more local, is where people are held before a trial or where they may be sent after being convicted if the sentence is relatively short (less than a year). Prison is where people are sent, usually further away from their homes, after they receive longer sentences. The term *incarceration* can be used to indicate time in either jail or prison.

immediate physical danger to a young father's loved ones, whereas violence, substance abuse, and criminal behavior often do.

In this section, we draw upon the stories of several young fathers and their partners to illustrate how these problems unfold. For some fathers, the damage they cause is irrevocable. For others, there is damage, but there is also some hope that the problems can be resolved or managed and that their connections can be maintained or recovered. After deciding on our "short list" of what goes wrong between fathers and their families, we had to determine our approach to making sense of these problems. Do we get "up close and personal," defining the problems as belonging to the individual father? Do we delve into their histories and describe how this father fell in with the wrong crowd or how that father learned the wrong lessons from his own father? Do we look outward and examine how cultural and political forces led to these problems? Do we examine how social and economic policies exacerbate individual risk factors, setting some fathers up to fail? It seems foolish to ignore the relevance of any of these approaches, yet equally foolish to try to do it all.

We are not epidemiologists, but our thinking about the problems that divide fathers from their families has been influenced by the work of epidemiologists, who study the patterning of disease. Epidemiologists describe how diseases spread from one person to the next, seeking to identify their root causes. The goal is to curtail, contain, and eradicate. One of the fascinating things about epidemiologists is that they tend to be meticulous in their effort to collect data from each and every person who is affected by a problem. But their primary interest is in determining how problems affect populations and how to stop the spread of problems—from individual to individual—by treating the population as a whole. In their approach to resolving public health problems, they try to understand what is going wrong at multiple levels, sometimes using several strategies.

Like many in public health, we have been inspired by the story of John Snow, who is considered the father of epidemiology. Dr. John Snow was a young physician working in 19th-century London at the height of the Industrial Revolution when living conditions were particularly harsh. An obstetrician and family doctor, Dr. Snow was treating a lot of people with cholera, which, as we now know, is a bacterial infection, usually transmitted through drinking water tainted by human waste. When untreated, cholera causes severe diarrhea and vomiting that can lead to death in a matter of hours. At the time that John Snow was practicing, the cause of cholera was still unknown, but it was surging through some neighborhoods in London, leaving in its wake a great deal of illness and death.

Snow was curious about why cholera was spreading more quickly in some areas of London than in others. As he methodically talked to people in a neighborhood of London that had been hit particularly hard by the epidemic, inquiring about their daily living habits, he learned that many of those infected were drawing their water from the same well. He mapped the spread of infection house by house and became convinced that the source of the illness was well water contaminated by some sort of germ, infecting whoever drank it and killing those who were most vulnerable. With his evidence in hand, he convinced local authorities to remove the handle on the pump that drew water from this suspicious well. The spread of infection was quickly contained.

Unlike most doctors who focused on the internal workings of their patients, Snow looked for patterns in how disease was spreading through neighborhoods to determine its origin. He investigated how the context in which his patients lived—their behavior, their social relations, and physical environment—affected their illness and the way in which it was spreading. This layered approach to understanding illness helped him identify the cause of cholera and eventually stop it at the source. But what made Snow heroic was his commitment to treating not *just* his patients but the *whole community*. In the case of cholera, because the source of the illness was in the water, it could not be effectively treated by only attending to those who were infected. Snow's approach to understanding and treating cholera—at both the individual and the population level—helped others think more broadly about the causes and treatment of other diseases. At the individual level, cholera causes diarrhea; at the population level, contaminated water causes the spread of cholera. There are causes and then there are *causes* of causes.

Like Snow, we try to tack back and forth between the problems of individual fathers while never losing sight of how those individual problems emerge within distinct social contexts, adhering to the idea that each of us is, to some extent, a product of our circumstances. As clinicians (like Snow), we cannot help but see the unique experiences and circumstances of each father and his family. As public health researchers, we cannot help but try to piece together each father's story with the hope of identifying patterns and trends that might help solve the underlying problems that impact fatherhood.[2-4] To be clear, we do not see young fatherhood as a "disease;" and we do not want to make any direct comparison between fathers and cholera! However, we believe that young fatherhood is an important public health issue and father absence is a problem, as are some of the social risks associated with young fatherhood and father absence. As such, we think there are some important lessons to be drawn from Snow's approach to the public health problem that he faced in his day.

In the next three chapters, we focus on the biggest potential "deal breakers" when it comes to fathers' involvement with their partners and children: violence, substance abuse, and criminal involvement that leads to incarceration. Additionally, in Chapter 12, we focus on infidelity, which can also put fathers' relationships with their partners and children in jeopardy although not necessarily to the same degree as these other threats. Throughout these chapters, in the spirit of John Snow, we attempt to highlight individual factors as well as broader contextual factors that contribute to these various problems, with an eye toward identifying the causes of what goes wrong between fathers and their families, as well as the *causes* of those causes.

CHAPTER 9
Love Hurts

The impulse to use violence seems to be a natural part of being human.[1] Not every human is violent but, throughout our history as a species, we have used violence to both protect ourselves and take what we wanted from others. When our ancesters defended our tribe against an attack from a neighboring tribe, violence was the obvious, necessary thing to do. And when those ancestors attacked their neighbors to acquire resources and expand their domain, the use of violence was perhaps less necessary but still regarded as justifiable in some fashion or another. Even today, if survival means looking out for ourselves and our own against potential adversaries, the use of force is often viewed as acceptable and sometimes even glorified. It is more perplexing when violence occurs within families, between people who ostensibly love each other. How do we make sense of this form of violence, especially given that it often leads to the deterioration and destruction of important and valued relationships? In this chapter, we focus on aggression between partners or ex-partners, called intimate partner violence or IPV, that occurs with some frequency among the young fathers and mothers participating in our research.

Although it may not be apparent at first, there is often a logic to the violence that occurs between intimate partners.[a] The most obvious rationale

a. In this section we focus on intimate partner violence and not child abuse, another prevalent form of domestic violence, which can result in the expulsion of the abusive parent from the family or the removal of the abused children from that parent's custody. Although child abuse and neglect have occurred in a small number of the families we've worked with, sometimes leading to disconnection, we chose to highlight intimate partner violence because it occurs more frequently in our samples. That said, we know that many of the parents we work with use physical punishment to discipline

for violence against someone we love is that we expect some advantage will be gained. Consider the man who hits his girlfriend because she has been "disrespectful" and he believes she deserves punishment, which is a disturbingly common scenario. This man is convinced that violence will make it more likely that she will capitulate, that she will follow his direction and not talk back. Further, he may believe that if he doesn't hit her, she will get the upper hand and not obey him. He is likely to measure and track his use of violence carefully, albeit subconsciously, knowing that if he goes too far, he might lose her.[b]

While this sort of violence is offensive and reprehensible because it violates the rights of others and is antithetical to how most of us define a loving, trusting relationship, it happens all the time. Among the 3 million or so women who reported being the victim of a violent crime in 2012, about 26 percent report that they were hurt by an intimate partner (a boyfriend or spouse).[2] Among these women, 43.2 percent suffered minor injuries (cuts and bruises), and 11.1 percent had more serious injuries, like gunshot wounds, knife wounds, internal bleeding, etc.[c] Knowing that only about half of intimate partner violence (IPV) is reported to the police, it's safe to assume that the number of women who have been abused by their partners is higher than what appears in crime statistics, produced by the US Department of Justice.[d]

While it may be tempting to regard such behavior as only characteristic of people who are more barbaric than "us" (whoever the "us" might be), the idea that a woman should obey her husband and that a husband is entitled to enforce a wife's obedience is woven into our nation's cultural

their toddlers. We regard this form of discipline as a problematic form of family violence which sometimes leads to conflict between parents who disagree about how the kids should be punished. Nonetheless, this form of violence seldomly causes father disengagement during the early phases of parenthood.

b. We focus on male-generated domestic violence or intimate partner violence because this form of couple violence tends to be more severe and more dangerous. It is important to acknowledge, though, that more than half the violence that occurs between young couples is bidirectional, an issue we return to later in this chapter.

c. Not surprisingly, the rate of IPV reported to the police by male victims is much lower. Among the 3.5 million or so violent crimes reported by male victims in 2012, about 5 percent were committed by intimate partners and far fewer resulted in physical injury.[3]

d. According to the Centers for Disease Control's (CDC) National Intimate Partner Violence and Sexual Victimization Survey Report (which was published in 2010 and is the most thorough accounting of the problem), the lifetime prevalence rate of women who have been raped, physically attacked, or stalked by an intimate partner (husband, boyfriend/girlfriend, or ex-partner/spouse) was 37.3 percent of the female population, or 44 million women.[3]

and legal history. Although there has never been a US law that expressly *permits* a husband to use violence to discipline his wife, such behavior was not against the law until quite recently. Throughout most of our history, when a wife pressed charges against an abusive husband, the courts tended to favor the husband's position. For example, in 1864, the North Carolina Supreme Court upheld a husband's use of force to punish his wife, provided he does not go overboard.[4] In documenting their decision, the presiding judge wrote:

> The law permits him to use, towards his wife, such a degree of force, as is neces-sary to control an unruly temper, and make her behave herself; and unless some permanent injury be inflicted, or there be an excess of violence, or such a degree of cruelty as shows that it is inflicted to gratify his own bad passions, the law will not invade the domestic forum, or go behind the curtain. It prefers to leave the parties to themselves . . .

While this may seem shocking, the fact that high-ranking judges were put into the position of needing to write such opinions was a step in the right direction. Prior to this point in our history, domestic violence cases did not make it to State Supreme Courts. Despite the unfortunate outcome of this case, a woman's right to file a legal complaint against her husband for behaving violently was finally being taken more seriously. Seven years later, in 1871, the first judicial decision finding a man guilty for beating his wife was filed by the Alabama Supreme Court.[5] The presiding judge, Thomas Peters, wrote that

> the husband's privilege, ancient though it be, to beat her with a stick, to pull her hair, choke her, spit in her face or kick her about the floor, or to inflict upon her like indignities, is not now acknowledged by our law.

Perhaps Judge Peters used such specific language to make his opinion more explicit, knowing that he was the among the first to actively defend a wife's right to her autonomy and safety against her husband's presumed right to maintain his position of dominance. Several other states quickly followed Alabama's lead in protecting women against abusive husbands, but society was slow to respond to this shift in legal opinion. Over the next 150 years, women have achieved progress toward equal rights and equal protection in dribs and drabs. Thousands of years of precedence created a culture of male dominance and female submission that has been difficult to dismantle.

Not all IPV is calculated or deliberately designed to bully and coerce. Some of the time—perhaps most of the time—violence between people who care about each other is emotional and reactive. For some people, the vulnerability that accompanies intimacy can quickly turn to feelings of anger and hurt, particularly when one partner feels betrayed. When tempers flare, violence can occur without warning or clear intent. Intense rage is a fairly common feature of our most intimate relationships, particularly during adolescence and early adulthood when men and women are first learning about love and the vulnerability that being in love entails.[6] The best estimates indicate that between 10 and 30 percent of young people have hit, pushed, or slapped a romantic partner or been hit, pushed, or slapped at least once in the course of their relationship.[7,8] Much of this violence is bidirectional, meaning that young men and women are hitting each other, which highlights the fact that both men and women can be victims of IPV.

To illustrate this point, in 2010, a group of researchers headed by Thomas Simon at the CDC reported the results of a study in which they asked 5,404 sixth graders about the acceptability of IPV.[9] These researchers found that 44 percent of girls thought it would be acceptable to hit a boyfriend under some circumstances. Among those girls who had a boyfriend, the rate of acceptability rose to almost 60 percent. This finding is consistent with what we hear from many young women in our studies, who use minor acts of aggression against their boyfriends as demonstrations of their affection and connection, as if to announce "You belong to me!" In the same study, 22 percent of all boys thought it was acceptable to hit a girlfriend. And, among those boys who had a girlfriend, the rate increased to 32 percent, a rate that is strikingly consistent with actual reported rates of physical violence among married couples. For example, in a recent study of young married couples who were recruited while picking up their marriage licenses, Kenneth Leonard and his colleagues at the University of Minnesota found that 35 percent reported physical violence in their relationship.[10]

When we first ventured into our research with young couples, IPV was not on our agenda. In fact, we are somewhat embarrassed to say how slow we were to appreciate its importance and seriousness.[e] Yet, over time, in

---

e. The variations in the rates of violence across studies are due to differences in how IPV is measured (whom you ask, how you ask it) and the differences in samples being studied.[11,12] For example, if you ask adult women if they have *ever* been physically assaulted by an intimate partner (lifetime prevalence), the answer will be much higher than if you ask adult women if they have been assaulted by their current partner in the last year. Also, there is evidence that more specific questions about the types of IPV will yield high response rates. An adolescent is less likely to say he or she has been *assaulted* by an intimate partner than to say he or she has been hit or punched or choked, largely because the term "assault" can mean such different things to different people.

study after study, we found that about one-third of the young couples we interviewed reported some violence in their relationship, similarly to what Leonard had found. For some couples, the violence occurred only once and then never again, as far as we knew. For others, it occurred more regularly, even weekly. Some of it involved boyfriends hitting girlfriends or girlfriends hitting boyfriends, but much of it involved bidirectional violence. Some of the young women and men we talk to claim that their physical fighting is no big deal, just small outbursts of pent-up anger and frustration that blow through the relationship and clear the air. However, many men and women tell us they are frightened and concerned about where this behavior is headed.[f]

RON

A tall, thin young man with short hair, a clean-shaven face, and light brown eyes, Ron identified himself as being of "mixed-race, a little of everything." He was introduced to us by his girlfriend, Samantha, a senior in high school and 6 months pregnant when we recruited her to participate in one of our studies. Samantha identified herself as "Hispanic" and said that although she's proud of her heritage, she never learned Spanish and being Hispanic hasn't affected the choices she makes, including who she hangs out with. In her first interview with Emma, Samantha was honest when responding to our standard set of questions about physical violence, explaining that, yes, Ron had hit her a few times. She also told Emma she loved Ron, wanted to be with him, and saw herself as partly at fault for their fighting, admitting that she had also hit him and that she enjoyed the drama of their volatile relationship. When Emma asked Samantha to describe her relationship with Ron, she was effusive:

SAMANTHA: The best relationship I think a couple could have!
EMMA: How so?
SAMANTHA: As far as being able to talk, as if we're best friends. We share everything with each other now. We're ready to work our problems out with each other.
EMMA: How do you feel about him?

f. Relevant to this first point, most violence between romantic partners is perpetrated by women.[7,8] Although this violence can be very harmful, in this section we will focus on male violence, including male violence that is in reaction to female violence.

SAMANTHA: I love him to death. I think I would do anything for him. Um, I feel as if he's my best friend, he's my lover, he's my everything.

While Emma was interviewing Samantha, Barry was down the hall interviewing Ron, who was 22 years old at the time. Ron had come to the interview dressed more professionally than most of the young men we meet, wearing a tie. He was very friendly, almost excessively polite. And, within the first few moments of the interview, it became clear that Ron was different. He spoke quietly but with great intensity, sometimes going on for 10 or 15 minutes without pause.

There is a logical flow to how we structure our interviews. We ask open-ended questions and usually our research participants—the young fathers or mothers—respond accordingly, often telling stories that help illustrate what they mean or feel or think. In contrast to this pattern of discourse, Ron's responses to Barry's questions were hard to follow, often tangential and disorganized. Sometimes he seemed to be preaching, as if he wanted to convince us of something. When on a roll, he allowed little room for Barry to interject and was unresponsive to Barry's cues that he would like to speak. He came across as wanting to connect with Barry but impervious to the rules of dialogue.

When Barry asked about arguments or fighting in his relationship with Samantha, Ron explained that he had to maintain a firm grip on Samantha because she had been poorly raised by her parents, and he was having to fix their mistakes. He told Barry he had to teach her how to dress and how to talk to other men. She didn't know what she could and couldn't do, sometimes putting herself in harm's way. He had to protect her from herself. When asked about whether he and Samantha ever got into physical conflicts, Ron gave a convoluted response that was difficult to follow. Eventually, after several minutes of not answering the question, he came to the point:

RON: The physical fighting started . . . I noticed that it started when she first hit me. She had run away from her mother's house and had stayed with me at my mom's house. I had to get up the next morning and take her back to her mother because I didn't want to get in the middle of it. I was telling her, "Come on, let's catch this train" and, you know, she was being a brat about it. She turned around and swung and hit me. And that made me mad.

My reaction was to grab . . . I grabbed her by her neck. I grabbed her by her neck, and I squeezed it so hard. Now this is why I didn't want a relationship, first of all. At that time, I was strong—I am stronger than her. I am a very strong person. I'm not built, but I am strong. I know these techniques to where you can hurt a person. . . . I knew the pressure points. I told her, "Listen here, Samantha," and I'm constantly squeezing her neck and I could feel the—I could feel her chords and things in her neck. And she's sitting there looking me in my eyes like, like I'm gonna throw her onto the expressway or something. And I say, "Samantha, I want you to go home, OK? I do not wanna fight with you, alright?" And I picked her up. I picked her up by her neck and turned her around. And then I said, "Now let's get you on this train, OK? I want you to get on this train. We can talk about this later, OK? It's only until Friday, alright?" I didn't want her to be out there by herself, me caring so much about her.

That was the first time I put my hands on her. Then I noticed that it started to happen frequently . . . when she made me mad. 'Cause she started acting more like a brat. That's 'cause I was allowing her to act like a brat, so that's when she took advantage of me. When she started acting like a brat towards me . . . that's when I got defensive. I started treating her like the people I would treat on the streets. It was messing up the whole relationship. . . . I knew I had to gain control of that relationship . . . that's when I started hitting her. That's how all this mess got started . . . and it just really got outta hand to where I got out of control. I allowed her to get me out of control by pushing my buttons like that. And that's when it all broke down. I told her, before we even start fighting, I told her early in relationship: "Poking comes to pushing. Pushing comes to grabbing, and once you start getting bruises, then it's going to move up. It's gonna keep moving up."

BARRY: What happened then?

RON: What was going in my head was "I wanna hit. I'm going to hit you. I'm going to hit you to where I hurt you too. I'm going to hit you in the eye." Now, I'm not going to tell her I'm gonna hit her in the eye. It's just that's the reaction when you fighting . . . you gonna go for the face. And that's one thing I—I told her before. I said, "Baby, I don't wanna argue with you, I don't wanna fight with you, I don't wanna do none of this stuff. I just wanna love you."

From Ron's perspective, Samantha is responsible for his violence. She makes him lose control, puts him in the position of having to control her. He sees Samantha as the instigator of his attacks. Even more worrisome, his violence seems almost compulsive. Once the idea of hurting Samantha is in his head, the thought takes hold of him and compels him to act.

Samantha's parents, who were divorced, both wanted her to break up with Ron. On several occasions, Samantha came home in tears and told them that Ron had hit and choked her. On several occasions, her father called the police, but Samantha refused to cooperate and eventually the police threatened to charge her father for calling them out to the house for no good reason. At that point in their relationship, Samantha found ways to justify Ron's violence to herself, which is not uncommon. Some young victims of IPV believe they are getting what they deserve because they hold deeply rooted feelings of self-loathing and self-incrimination. Some blame themselves for "starting it." Some believe the violence will end when they learn to love him more, treat him better, get things right. Some feel trapped or dependent, too afraid to extricate themselves.

After her daughter was born, Samantha's father helped her understand that Ron was dangerous, and that she and her baby, Tricia, were at risk for serious harm. So finally, when Tricia was about 10 months old, Samantha called the police herself and pressed charges, which resulted in Ron going to jail for about 5 months. After being released, he was required to complete an anger management class and ordered to stay away from Samantha and Tricia. A year later, Ron was living with his mother, not working or going to school. He had returned to jail for two brief stints after violating the restraining order by going to see Samantha. He was angry with Samantha for sending him to jail but still harbored hope that they would get together, still unwilling to take any responsibility for his behavior.

When Emma followed up with Samantha, she was living with her mother and Tricia, going to school, where she was studying accounting. She was doing well and seemed resolved that her relationship with Ron was over. She reflected on what had happened between them with clarity and remarkable equanimity.

> SAMANTHA: In the very beginning of the relationship it started out very typical, perfect, sweet. Then, we moved in with each other and things changed. A little bit more fighting that turned into physical abuse, and the physical abuse just got worse, more into an everyday thing.
> EMMA: What kind of physical abuse was he doing?
> SAMANTHA: Um, kicking, punching, slapping, strangling. I mean, choking. He used to throw things. I wanted to believe that he was good-hearted, but he was just messed up. He was messed up in the head. And I figured, I don't know, that he just had problems from

his past that bothered him a lot, I guess. For whatever reason, he felt he needed to let it out in anger. He would just go from happy to mad, to hitting, to rage. He would get very jealous. That's when he would strike. That's when he went, went off . . . very easily.

EMMA: You said at times he was nice, or at least in the past he once was?

SAMANTHA: Yeah, everything was, you know, nice, compliments. He did things for me, treated me like a lady, respectful. He was imaginative and very easy to talk to. Usually laid back, you know. You could feel comfortable with him and enjoy your day, your time with him. But, like I said, he just had issues where he got very jealous and angry. I guess he felt that I was *his*. He liked to control. If he seen me talking to another guy, even if it was someone he knew, he would ask me why. Or he would tell me not to do it 'cause he felt that I shared too much, that I was too nice.

EMMA: What has changed in the way you feel about him?

SAMANTHA: I'm not in love with him anymore. I think somewhere down deep I will always love him. Not only being the father of my baby but also being my first love, being the one who helped me through some rough times.

Men like Ron, whose violent behavior comes from a dark and deeply disturbed part of their personality, are relatively rare, at least in our experience. It is more common for men (and women) to become violent toward their partners because they lack the interpersonal skills to manage their emotions during intense arguments; they don't know how to communicate their anger or fear without lashing out aggressively.[8] Jerome, a young African American man, whom we first met at his girlfriend's school in downtown Chicago, seems very different from Ron, though he too had been violent toward Ebony, his girlfriend, on at least two occasions.[h]

g. There are several types of IPV-prone men, underscoring the importance of knowing how, when, and why men become abusive. For example, Kim Bartholomew and her colleagues have identified a subgroup of men who react violently to threats of abandonment, real or imagined. These men tend to be anxiously insecure and use violence (or the threat of violence) to keep their partners from leaving.[13,14] There are also men who are more likely to become violent toward their partners when they are drunk or high. Because these men are much less likely to become violent when sober, treating their substance use is an important step in ending their violence.[15]

h. Most clinicians and researchers who work with young couples will find themselves having to respond to reports of IPV. Whenever violence is reported, it is necessary to appraise the situation and provide the victim (and sometimes the perpetrator) with information about how to ensure safety. Sometimes it is necessary to inform the "authorities," as was the case with Ron and Samantha. Sometimes it can be challenging

Jerome met Ebony when they were kids in a rough, impoverished neighborhood on the South Side of Chicago. In middle school, they were in class together, and Ebony remembers Jerome as the brainy kid who always knew the answers to the teacher's questions. He seemed confident and cool. As the oldest of four children, he was used to taking charge of things and making sure that others were taken care of, getting his brothers to school, making sure they did what his mother said. Jerome and his mom had a good relationship. She was his "rock," always there for him, but she was also always stressed out, so he was there for her too. When we asked Jerome about his relationship with his mom, he said they made a good team; they had each other's back.

Ebony was the class spitfire, but her antagonistic tendencies belied her soft heart and tender feelings. She was the middle child of five, with two younger brothers and two older sisters. From a young age, Ebony learned that she had to fight for whatever she wanted, so she learned to be strong-willed, opinionated, and loud. But there was another side of Ebony too. Sometimes she sank into deep depressions and retreated from the world, folding in on herself. In these dark moments, she thought about suicide and once tried to kill herself. When she first met Jerome, her mood was swinging. Back in seventh grade, she thought Jerome was the cutest, nicest, smartest boy in school, and she had a crush on him from the start, even though he didn't seem to like her.

EBONY: He liked everybody, but he didn't like me. He said I was ugly.
LUCILLE: I don't believe that!
EBONY: He did!
LUCILLE: OK, so what did you do about that?
EBONY: I called his mother a big, tall wildebeest.
LUCILLE: A big what?
EBONY: A tall wildebeest.
LUCILLE: And what happened? What did he do?
EBONY: He smacked me. He looked at me for five minutes straight, and I said, "What you gonna do?" And then he just rolled his eyes

to know whether to call the police or make a report to child protective services or advise a victim to leave and seek shelter in a protected environment. In such cases, we follow a protocol that involves consulting with child protective services and domestic violence professionals before taking action.

and turned back around and smacked me backwards out of the chair. And then after that, he said he was sorry.

LUCILLE: Did you hit him back?

EBONY: Yeah! (Giggling) I hit him with the garbage can, the chair, books, checkerboard. He didn't hit me back after that, though. I guess I just made him so mad. I always used to mess with him. He'd be playing checkers and I'd throw the checkers off the board. After that, I went to the hospital for two months.[i] And then, when I came back, we got together.

LUCILLE: OK, how did you make up? I'm really curious about going from a fist fight into a relationship. How did that happen?

EBONY: He just said he missed me.

LUCILLE: He missed you picking on him?

EBONY: He said he missed me 'cause I was always the goofiest one in the class. No one knew why I was gone, so he thought I transferred to another school. So, when I came back, everybody ran up to me and gave me a hug. And he gave me a hug too. I was like, "Oh my God!" and then I was smiling, and he said, "I missed you." And then, after that, he walked me home, and then we started.

Ebony and Jerome stuck together. Both had strong, high-octane personalities, so they continued to argue and bicker throughout high school, but they also encouraged each other to study and were part of the same friend group. As they got older, they started skipping school together, going to Jerome's house when his mother was at work so that they could fool around. Eventually, Ebony got pregnant.

The pregnancy seemed to intensify their arguments. Jerome was stressed out because he didn't think he could handle the responsibility of becoming a father. When he was stressed, he got irritable. Ebony told Lucille, "It was as if he was the one who was pregnant!" And, from his perspective, that was how it felt. Unlike some of the young expectant fathers we interview, who didn't have a clue about what was coming, Jerome appreciated the weight of parenthood responsibilities, and he knew he wasn't ready.

Ebony was feeling fat and jealous, common feelings among pregnant teens. She was worried that Jerome would lose interest in her and find someone else. For the first time in the years they had been together, they

i. Lucille asked about going to the hospital for 2 months, and Ebony reported that she swallowed three bottles of pills because she was so upset about the recent birth of her younger brother. Years later, this younger brother went to live with Ebony and Jerome, after he was removed from the custody of Ebony's mother.

were struggling as a couple. When Simon asked Jerome about whether he and Ebony had ever gotten into a physical fight, he acknowledged that he had hit Ebony on two occasions. He told Simon about the "wildebeest incident" in middle school but also about a more recent fight when Ebony hit him and he hit her back, hard. In recalling both these incidents, Jerome did not defend or justify his behavior but seemed to regard these moments as important turning points in his own development and his relationship with Ebony. He took these fights as signs that it was time for him to make a change.

JEROME: It was right after a basketball game. Ebony went home and I went to the store. I see this girl I know, so we was talkin' and we was walkin' home, right? Next thing I know, Ebony and her friend are coming up the street going like 200 miles an hour, right? I'm like, "Oh shit, this is gonna be crazy." I'm hoping they don't jump on this girl. So Ebony calls me, and I walk across the street, "What's up?" She says, "What are you doing with this bitch?" I tell her, "Look, it ain't even like that." So, she's like, "I told you, you can't talk to her."

So, she's like, "If you keep talking to her, you aren't gonna see your baby." So I told her straight out, "Fuck you, I'm gonna see my baby regardless." So . . . she had, like, this cup of ice, and she just smacked me with it. So, I'm like, "Whatever." I'm walking away like, "I'm gonna tell your momma you're acting stupid." So, she is hollering at me, "Oh, you are fucking her!" So, I turn around, "Look, stop acting stupid." I'm like, "You need to cool the fuck out, real quick." She just, she just, acting like she gonna beat my ass, right?

SIMON: What did you do? What did she do?

JEROME: She was punching me and everything. Face, chest, everything.

SIMON: What did you do?

JEROME: I told her straight out, I said, "Look, if you hit me again, I'm gonna whoop your ass." So, she punched me again. So, I hit my lady. She fell, but she got back up. I said, "Don't fucking touch me no more." She hit me again. So, the arm that she was using to hit me with, I hit her in the arm. It hurt, so she couldn't hit me again. I walked to her house, and I told her mom, I said, "Look, your daughter's out here acting like a fool; she started beating up on me, so I hit her." I told her just like that. So, she said, "Oh yeah thanks, do what you need." I'm like, "Well, you need to talk to her, because she's too jealous."

When I get back outside, the police is out there. "Are you Jerome Wright?" They do their routine. You know, put my head on the car, whatever. So that night, I get arrested. They give me the story, "Oh, she pressed charges on you, said you kicked her in the stomach. She's pregnant." I spent five days in jail over the Fourth of July weekend. I finally call her from jail, "Why you lyin' and telling the police that story?" "Oh, I didn't tell the police that, somebody else did." So, I said, "Well, in order for me to get locked up, you had to sign a paper, a paper to press charges because no one else could except you."

SIMON: Well what happened?

JEROME: I get out of jail. I finally get home; they put me on house arrest and all this other stuff. So, all my guys are calling our house, "Oh, you know, Ebony and this girl are best friends now." So, the girl called me, like, four hours after I got out of jail. She was like, "Oh yeah, you know Ebony told me that she lied and told the police that you kicked her in the stomach just to have you locked up, just to teach you a lesson about talking with other girls." Totally pissed me off. Come around, I got two years probation and all kinds of other crazy shit. It was just absolutely terrible.

Amazingly, Ebony and Jerome made up almost immediately. To some extent, this attests to the resilience of their relationship and their commitment to each other. Perhaps it also suggests that they just didn't know when to call it quits. Sometimes it's difficult to know the difference between healthy perseverance and foolish co-dependence. The sort of rapid escalation in conflict that we see between Ebony and Jerome is worrisome and dangerous but less so than what we observed between Ron and Samantha. Jerome is not out to dominate or control Ebony. He reacts violently in situations that feel out of control, beyond his capacity to cope. This sort of reactive violence occurs when young men (and women) lack skills to regulate their emotions and talk about their feelings in those hot-temper moments.[16]

Unlike Ron, who didn't take responsibility for the harm he caused Samantha, Jerome immediately understood the seriousness of what just happened. After he hit Ebony, he ran to Ebony's mother, told her what he did and sought her help. Jerome was angry at Ebony for lying to the police about trying to harm their baby, but he accepted the consequences of his behavior. He took the punishment and recognized that he needed to control himself, regardless of what Ebony did to provoke him.

Two years after their daughter Tiffany was born, Jerome and Ebony were still getting into frequent arguments, mostly about how to manage money and about how they communicate. They still hurled insults at each other, and because they had been together so long, they both knew how to make it hurt. But Jerome resolved to never become violent with Ebony again, and he stuck to that, no matter what. If things got too hot, he would just leave. He told Simon about how their arguments sometimes became hurtful, but he had learned to talk it through or let it go or leave the house for a while.

JEROME: She tells me that I'm not a man because I don't make as much money as she does. But I say, "A real woman will understand and not throw it in her man's face." Then she feels bad and apologizes, but she still makes it seem like she's a better parent than I am since she spends more money than I do.

SIMON: And how do you feel about that?

JEROME: I mean, I think it's pretty stupid. 'Cause right now I am in the process of finding another job, but she just don't understand. I'll be like, "Ebony, if I give you my whole check, I'm not gonna have anything." She throws it back and says, "Oh, I give my last for my kid, so why won't you?" And then there is no way I'm gonna argue it.

SIMON: And you also said that you would fight because of the way that you talk to each other?

JEROME: She has a tendency to call me stupid, and I don't like it. I told her, "I'm not gonna deal with it." And one time, I just like, I totally disrespected her on something. We was talking and she was saying something that pissed me off, and I said, "I don't even know why I talk to you sometimes." And she was like, "Why?" And I was like, "Because I don't think you're smart enough to talk to me." She got, like, pissed. I had to leave 'cause she was, like, throwing stuff.

SIMON: What do you mean, throwing stuff?

JEROME: She was throwing everything, throwing hangers. I mean, it was wrong of her to do that, but what I said was kind of off the hook.

SIMON: So, what happens eventually? I mean, how do you resolve it?

JEROME: We break up all the time, like once every month or something.

SIMON: OK, what happens when you guys break up?

JEROME: We get back together. The most recent breakup was about a month ago. I was at my friend's house and got back late. When I got home, she's hollering and screaming and following me around, calling me stupid, and a deadbeat dad, and all this other crazy stuff. So, I just left. I was like, "I don't have time for this. Who are you?" So, I went over to my guy's house, and she's calling me all night. So, I was like, "I don't have time for girls." And she be like, "What you mean?" I was like, "I don't think we should be messing with each other no more." And she was like, "Well, whatever." So then, that was it for like two weeks.

SIMON: What happened when you got back together?

JEROME: I don't know . . . we just started talking and stuff. 'Cause at first, I was like, "I ain't going back over there no more." But of course, I went over there probably like once or twice a week. Then, I started going over there three or four times a week. Then, it was like, "I miss you." She like, "Oh, I love you" and gave me a little kiss. Stuff like that. You know, we got back together.

Jerome and Ebony recognize that this kind of drama is bad for everyone, especially their daughter, but they cannot seem to break their habit of getting into fights and then calling it quits. In their interviews, they complain about each other a lot, but they also readily say they love each other and that someday they'll get married. Unlike Ron, Jerome is capable of self-reflection and taking responsibility for his part of the ongoing conflict; he just does not know how to change it.

JEROME: Sometimes I'm not understanding. When me and Ebony get in an argument, she'll say something and she's right, but I'm not gonna tell her that. Sometimes she's right and I just won't give in. You know what I'm saying? I just won't say, "OK baby, you're right." Sometimes she'll say something, and I really won't take the time to think about what she's saying, her opinion.

SIMON: Why not? Why don't you do that?

JEROME: I do it sometimes but not all the time. I don't do it when it counts. 'Cause I mean, there might be one time where she's, like, totally pissed off at me. She needed that "Yeah baby, you're right," but I don't do it, purposefully, you know? It's just a problem that I have.

Both Ebony and Jerome have a hard time letting the other person have their say, and neither wants to relinquish any ground once a battle begins. If Jerome says, "Don't call me stupid," Ebony says, "Stupid, stupid, stupid." The tendency to push each other's buttons feels automatic. At one point in time, the fury between them invigorated their relationship, but now it just exhausts them. The breakups leave them both feeling guilty and resentful. They both know they are wrong. They both feel wronged.

There is love and warmth in Ebony and Jerome's relationship, but they lack the skills to fight constructively and with civility. Because the hurt feelings accumulate, they must work hard to remember what they like about each other. When Lucille asks Ebony about how Jerome has changed as a partner, she can't quite get there, so she focuses on how he's doing as father:

LUCILLE: Do you feel like he's changed?

EBONY: Yeah, in some way, but not when it comes to hearing me out and, you know, understanding where I'm coming from.

LUCILLE: In a positive way, how would you say he's changed?

EBONY: He's changed when it comes to, like, responsibility. Like before, he wasn't working. He got a job, and he takes care of Tiff. When I go to work, I don't have to get her ready for school. He does it. He takes her to school, he tries to comb her hair, and he cooks her breakfast and stuff. I don't have to do none of that. I just go to work. I'm his back up; he's my back up. When it comes to our problems, you know, it's different.

LUCILLE: OK, so there are some positive things going on in your relationship?

EBONY: It's a lot of them, but there are problems financially-wise, and communication-wise.

LUCILLE: Do you think the two of you will be able to work that out?

EBONY: Yeah, I'm gonna talk to him, today. Tonight.

Even when there is no physical harm, violence between partners is linked to a long list of mental health consequences for victims, most notably depression and posttraumatic stress disorder.[17-19] Within families, the ripple effects of IPV can be significant and enduring. A woman who experiences IPV during her pregnancy and is psychologically traumatized is at heightened risk for birth complications, including premature delivery, which puts the baby at risk for developmental problems.[20] If the violence between parents continues, it can lead to significant and enduring psychological problems for their young children, whose central nervous systems absorb the fear and anger in their surroundings. These children grow up in a state of chronic psychological stress, which disrupts their capacity for processing emotions and exercising self-control. When children live in a state of fear with someone they love—and, by extension, when they fear for their own well-being—their stress response goes into hyperdrive, marked by the overproduction of cortisol, the hormone which tells us to fight or take flight. With their systems in a chronic state of high alert, these children cannot learn to calm themselves down when they are upset or angry. So, not surprisingly, they are more prone to be aggressive toward their siblings, their peers, and eventually their partners.[21–23]

Despite the laws against domestic violence that were first enacted in the 1870s, the rates of IPV in the United States remained extraordinarily high because these laws were often not enforced. The police frequently turned a blind eye to domestic violence, which was widely regarded as a "private" matter. In response to the persistence of domestic violence, the Violence Against Women Act (VAWA) was introduced by Senator Joe Biden.[24] This law did two things. First, it required the police to make an arrest whenever they are called to a house for domestic violence and, second, it required prosecutors to press charges, regardless of whether the victim withdrew the complaint. Of course, this doesn't always happen. The first few times that the police were called on Ron, no arrest was made. Second, the VAWA provided funding to create a system of services that made it easier for women to leave abusive relationships. Communities received federal funding to build and staff emergency shelters for victims of domestic violence, empowering women to escape from—and protect themselves against—violent partners. And new laws were passed that compelled the police to uphold laws against domestic violence.

For the most part, VAWA has been an effective tool for reducing the rate of domestic violence. The yearly incidence rate of IPV—the number of new cases each year—has decreased steadily each year since 1993. Now, the current rate is about 900,000 new cases of domestic violence each year, down from about 2.3 million per year just prior the passage of the VAWA.[2] How did the VAWA have such a dramatic effect on the perpetration of violence? And what does this change tell us about the roots of violence against women? Requiring that suspected perpetrators be arrested clearly disincentivized the use of violence, and some young men cleaned up their act, motivated to avoid jail time. The effectiveness of this approach suggests that some IPV occurs simply because some men think they can get away with it. For these men, a strong legal response is perhaps the only thing that will change their behavior. Did it also change our culture? Joe Biden thinks it did. In 2014, he reflected on the 20th anniversary of the law's passing:

As a consequence of the law, domestic violence rates have dropped 64 percent. . . . And along the way we've changed the culture. Abuse is violent and ugly and today there is rightful public outrage over it. It matters that the American people have sent a clear message: You're a coward for raising a hand to a woman or child—and you're complicit if you fail to condemn it.[25]

Sometimes new laws help shape culture by changing the patterning of our collective behavior. Laws granting women the right to vote, guaranteeing equal pay and civil rights, and protecting against domestic violence have slowly but surely helped to shift gender dynamics, inching toward gender equity. Both laws and cultural norms are a check on human nature, civilizing us. It's possible that the propensity toward violence in human beings remains the same, but society is different because of the VAWA. The VAWA has been a useful, effective way to contain some of the violence against women, but protecting victims and punishing perpetrators will only get us part way to a solution. The enactment of laws that forbid violence are necessary but insufficient because, as can be seen in Figure 9.1, although the rate of IPV has diminished since 1993, it is still a big problem.

It's important to note that protecting women against aggressive men is not the same as teaching men how to behave differently, helping them to tame their aggressive impulses and to use their energy in more constructive ways.[26] If violence is intrinsic to human nature, then we need to teach

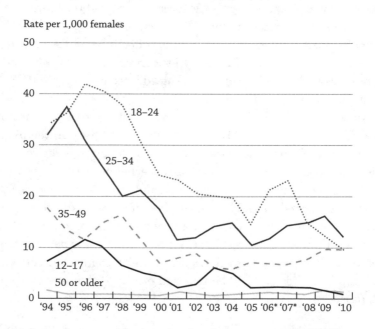

Figure 9.1 Intimate partner violence against females by age group, 1993–2010
From Catalano SM. Intimate partner violence: attributes of victimization, 1993–2011. Bureau of Justice Statistics. NCJ 243300. https://www.bjs.gov/index.cfm?ty=pbdetail&iid=4801. Published November 21, 2013.

nonviolence, again and again, forever and ever. Jerome initially lacked the skills to extract himself from conflicts with Ebony before lashing out in anger. Later, he developed the capacity to walk away and simmer down, though it often took him a week or more to regain his composure. Would it have been possible to help Jerome and Ebony learn to communicate more effectively and reduce the drama and instability?

There is some controversy about whether it's helpful to provide couples who have engaged in IPV with couples counseling designed to reduce hostile conflict and help them learn positive communication skills. Some victim advocates believe couples counseling poses too great a risk for further harm and that the appropriate, therapeutic response is to advise separation to ensure physical and psychological safety. There are two problems with this perspective. First, some couples will choose to stay together regardless of what others think is good for them. For these couples, it may be pragmatic to work with them, to help them identify and diminish their risks for violence and develop counterbalancing strengths. If we can help volatile, aggressive couples change their behavior, we might interrupt the intergenerational cycle of violence from spilling over into their relationship with their child. Second, there is evidence that some men who have been violent with their partners can change and become more positively engaged as partners and fathers.[27,28] Indeed, for several years, many clinical researchers have been developing and testing models to help couples stop being violent. Unfortunately, the efficacy of these programs has yielded mixed results. On average, IPV treatment programs reduce violence among perpetrators by about 33 percent; the most effective programs reduce the occurrence of violence by about 60 percent among those who complete the intervention.[29] This means that most programs can effectively reduce violence for most violent couples, but some violence is likely to persist. Even under the best circumstances, about one-third of men who complete these programs will go on to commit another act of domestic violence.

Offering couples counseling to men like Ron is too risky. Some men are not in control of their own behavior; when they become angry or upset, they are incapable of self-restraint. In Ron's case, the biggest concern is that he took no responsibility for his violent behavior. As Samantha said in her last interview with us, "he was messed up in the head." In contrast to Ron, but no less worrisome, some violent men are deliberate and calculating in their use of aggressive behavior. For these men, IPV is part of a chronic pattern of coercion and control in their relationships. Both of these types of violent men are distinct from men like Jerome, who is reactively violent and appropriately ashamed of his behavior. From our perspective, Jerome (and Ebony) could benefit from couples counseling focused on the development of basic communication skills, if the process can be carefully monitored and quickly interrupted if either partner gets too aggressive. We acknowledge that working with violent couples like Jerome and Ebony entails some risk, but we believe that sometimes the potential benefit of trying to help outweighs the risk of doing nothing, particularly when couples plan to stay together.

There is no question that all forms of IPV pose a threat to the health of women and children, and sometimes men. As we have noted in this chapter, the occurrence of violence—particularly when it's a function of emotional reactivity and limited interpersonal skills, as opposed to an entrenched pattern of violent coercion—does not necessarily doom a father's relationship with his partner and children. Nevertheless, the occurrence of any violence is a potential "deal breaker." Much the same can be said for substance abuse, which is the focus of the next chapter.

CHAPTER 10

Drowning Sorrows

The use of drugs and alcohol, legal and illegal, medicinal and recreational, has been a dominant force in our culture for thousands of years, with both positive and negative consequences. Long before our distant ancestors invented the wheel (about 3500 BCE), they figured out how to ferment fruit juice (about 7000 BCE), and we've been perfecting the process ever since. Wine has been part of Jewish and Christian religious rituals from the beginning, and it has long been regarded as a temporary remedy for many human ailments. Although the broad use of prescription medications to treat psychological problems is a relatively recent phenomenon,[1] doctors and pharmacists have been concocting and cultivating substances to alter our moods and diminish our suffering for centuries.

In America, alcohol has been a staple in our diet since Europeans first settled in the 1500s. Even the Puritans, despite their reputation for stodginess, carried more beer than water with them on their voyage from England to America. Throughout the revolutionary war, George Washington agonized over how to control the alcohol consumption of his men, wanting to provide them with enough to raise their spirits during those frigid nights on the bank of the Charles River but not so much that they would bring disgrace to the Continental Army.

It's easy to understand Washington's dilemma. How much is too much? As a society, we are deeply ambivalent about drug and alcohol use. Current reports indicate that about one-third of American adults drink regularly, about 1 in 10 smoke marijuana, and about one-fifth of Americans take a prescribed psychiatric medication.[2-4] We—meaning most of our society—enthusiastically endorse and promote the use of legitimate substances to lift our spirits or relax, while we bemoan the abuse of drugs and alcohol as a destructive force. Drugs and alcohol are widely marketed as the critical ingredient of any party, yet children and adolescents are told that drinking and smoking pot are off limits until they are old enough to "handle it." This is a difficult position to maintain. And so, even in Salt Lake City, where drug and alcohol use is more strictly forbidden than in other parts of the United States, illicit drug use among adolescents is common. In fact, we found that the rates of substance use disorder (SUD)[a] among young fathers in Salt Lake City was higher than the rates we observed among young fathers in Chicago. For example, in our first study of young expectant couples in Salt Lake City, we found that 40 percent of the young fathers interviewed had at least one official diagnosis of SUD, either abuse or dependency.[5]

Heavy drinking and marijuana use is so common (and so culturally engrained) among adolescents and young adults that it can be difficult for them and their parents to know when they are in trouble. A relatively recent epidemiological study, led by Bridget Grant at the National Institutes of Health, found that 8.3 percent of young adults between the ages of 18 and 29 had a *current* drug use disorder (mild, moderate, or severe) and an additional 5.9 percent of this age group was recovering from a *previous* drug use disorder. These figures do not include the rate of *alcohol use* disorder (AUD), which Grant and her colleagues report as 26.7 percent (mild, moderate, or severe) among 18- to 29-year-olds, with another 10.2 percent in recovery.[6,7] The rate of SUDs has remained mostly the same for 18- to 29-year-olds for the past 15 years, except for marijuana use, which has increased slightly, presumably due to the trend toward legalization. Despite the strain that drug and alcohol abuse cause for families—something that almost everyone understands firsthand—there has been no serious effort to curb the industries that support it, and no comprehensive, equitable effort to provide treatment.

Over the years, we've observed that many, but not all, of the young expectant mothers we've worked with stop drinking or using drugs when they become pregnant. In contrast, most young fathers don't miss a beat. To better understand this pattern of substance use through the course of pregnancy, Julie Bailey and her colleagues at the University of Washington

a. SUD is a clinical diagnosis that covers substance abuse (persistent, reckless use of drugs and alcohol) and substance dependence (the psychological or physiological need for contnued use—or more use—to avoid withdrawal symptoms). Determing the occurrence of SUD involves administering a diagnostic interview designed to ask a patient about the presence or absence of specific symptoms and then check those symptoms against the criteria outlined in the official Diagnostic and Statistical Manual of Mental Disorders (DSM) published by the American Psychiatric Association.

followed a group of about 800 young women and men through their adolescence and into early adulthood, asking about their substance use before, during, and after pregnancy and childbirth, month to month.[8] Bailey found that about half of the young women in their study who became pregnant were either drinking in excess or smoking marijuana or tobacco just prior to the pregnancy. About half of these young women stopped using substances almost immediately after finding out they were pregnant, which means that the others continued to use at some level. Consistent with our anecdotal observations, Bailey also found that expectant fathers were about twice as likely as expectant mothers to be using drugs, and most continued to use across the transition to parenthood at the same rate they were using prior to the pregnancy.

There is a large body of research documenting the impact of SUDs on families.[9–11] Not surprisingly, substance abuse is associated with higher rates of intimate partner violence and higher rates of child abuse and neglect.[12–14] Consequently, children whose parents have SUDs are at greater risk for behavioral and emotional problems.[15] Moreover, the children of parents who abuse drugs are more likely to develop substance abuse problems of their own.[16–18] This pattern is so pervasive (and so obvious to the casual observer) that the intergenerational transmission of substance abuse was noted long before we had a clear understanding of how genetic information is transmitted from parent to child.

There is now a wealth of evidence on the genetics of substance abuse, indicating that inheritance accounts for about 40 to 70 percent of the variance in AUD and about 50 to 60 percent for cannabis use disorder.[19,20] While these statistics are impressive, they also remind us that substance abuse is not determined by genes alone;[b] it is also a learned behavior. Setting aside the issue of genetic heritability, children and adolescents learn to abuse drugs and alcohol, often from their peers and siblings, but sometimes also from their parents.

b. For those who aren't familiar with the terminology of "variance," it is helpful to think of the percentage of a whole "pie" (in this case, the pie is a particular type of substance use disorder) that is accounted for by a given "slice" of the pie, or the key predictor variable of interest (in this case "heritability"). So, having a single piece of pie that accounts for 40 to 70 percent of the whole pie is saying something. That's a big piece of pie.

DANNY

Danny was a quiet, skinny 17-year-old Mexican American kid, with long unkempt hair, dressed in a baggy T-shirt and oversized jeans that made him look even smaller and younger than he was. We had recruited Danny and his girlfriend April, also 17, through the University of Utah's prenatal clinic in Salt Lake City when April was 5 months pregnant. In our first interview, Danny often responded to our questions by saying he was unsure or had never thought about the things we wanted to know. He didn't seem overtly resistant or defensive, but he told us relatively little about his family situation or his current problems with drugs or the law. Sometimes young men seem to have a particularly hard time talking about the most important parts of their lives, so they proclaim profound uncertainty. At times, this seems quite genuine, as if they are not quite sure who they are or how they got there.

With bright brown eyes, a radiant smile, and an outgoing personality, April, who was also Mexican American, seemed like the antithesis of Danny. A natural caretaker, April felt drawn to Danny because he was cute, in a "lost puppy" sort of way, and clearly in need of some care. He showed up late for class, unprepared and looking tired. She had noticed that he hung out with the fringe element, the "druggies" and the "wannabe thugs," but he didn't seem to fit in. She saw him at lunch, but he never had a lunch of his own, accepting whatever other people didn't want and were willing to give to him. She started talking with him in class, tried to help him with his assignments, and shared her lunch when she saw him in the lunchroom. She knew he was smoking a lot of marijuana because he reeked of it, and she gave him a hard time about it, saying it was destroying his ability to concentrate. When he told April that his parents had introduced him to drugs, it broke her heart and made her angry. Over the years, April continued to blame Danny's parents for his problems, at one point telling us "He never had a chance. His whole family did drugs. His parents started giving him pot when he was like 10 or 11."

Eventually, April brought Danny home to meet her mother, who also took him under her wing, insisting that he sit down and eat a proper meal. Danny did not come across as tough or angry, just intensely needy and a bit lost. He liked that April and her mother wanted to take care of him; he was finally getting what he had always craved.

Danny and April had been hanging around together for about 6 months when April found out she was pregnant. April was upset but quickly geared herself up for it. Danny, on the other hand, was completely overwhelmed by the idea of becoming a father. He wanted April to get an abortion, but she wouldn't even consider that possibility because it went against her beliefs. As her pregnancy developed, Danny became more distant, spending more time with his "druggie friends" and getting high more often. Danny had learned to use drugs to escape from whatever was bothering him but—as is almost always the case—the drugs only made things worse. During April's pregnancy, Danny became more strung out as April became more focused on getting ready for motherhood. The gap between them became wider and more difficult to bridge.

After their son Gabriel was born, Danny tried to help April take care of him, but he couldn't get used to the idea that he was a father. He felt jealous of his son and resentful that he was no longer the sole recipient of April's love and care. He tried to make it work for the first 3 months. He held, fed, and diapered Gabe but could not feel attached. It is not uncommon for people who were neglected and deprived as children to be so overwhelmed by their own needs that they feel they have little to give to others. For many young fathers, taking care of their baby is scary and intimidating but also thrilling and life-affirming. For Danny, taking care of Gabe made him feel even more depleted, depressed, and bereft. And it was hard for Danny to see April so totally absorbed with their son. After a while, he gave up trying and dove more deeply into drugs, taking whatever he could get his hands on. When he was high, Danny's mind was elsewhere, not connected to the reality of his circumstances. When he wasn't high, his primary focus was to get high, to stave off the cravings, to avoid the pain of withdrawal. Like many individuals in the throes of addiction, Danny was unable to think clearly or care deeply about anything, including April or Gabe.[c]

When Danny was caught burglarizing houses for drug money, he was sent to a treatment program, and then another, and then another. Getting caught and being court-ordered to treatment can be a blessing in disguise for many who are addicted to drugs, giving them the opportunity to get their lives back on track. For Danny, it did not work out that way. After bombing out of three programs in 3 months, the judge gave up and sent him to jail where he spent his son's first birthday. April had not seen him for 6 months, but she knew where he was being held, so we set up an interview at the jail. Danny was desperately lonely and eager to talk to someone, so he was glad to see Paul. Despite being so reticent during his first interview, Danny was remarkably articulate about the negative impact of becoming a father on his emotional state, expressing feelings that we suspect other

---

c. Bryon Adinoff described addiction as a pathology of motivation and choice in which "the compulsive drive toward drug use is complemented by deficits in impulse control and decision making."[21p305]

absent fathers feel but don't talk about because they feel too ashamed. He told us that his son's birth felt like an intrusion on his relationship with April, drawing her away from him.

> PAUL: How do you think April has changed since Gabe was born?
> DANNY: She is not as caring as she used to be. She is more wrapped up in Gabe and what he needs. She says she still loves me no matter what, but all she talks about is Gabe. Before he was born, everything revolved around me. Now, everything revolves around Gabe.
> PAUL: What is that like for you?
> DANNY: I don't like it.
> PAUL: How has that affected your relationship with her?
> DANNY: I still love her and want to be with her. But it seems like she's got more things to do, things she needs to get done. After he was born, I got depressed; I just felt empty. I wanted more attention from her. Before, she was paying more attention to me. Before he was born, she said she loved me more than him, but now she loves him more than me.

Clearly, Danny's substance abuse problem is layered on top of other problems, as April told us again and again.[d] April's attunement to his deprivation, her sensitivity to his fragile emotions, and her strong protective nature quenched his thirst for nurturance and salved his emotional wounds. So, when April became less available to him, as she invested more of her emotional energy in caring for their son, Danny used drugs to escape from his sense of loss and unhappiness—and the insecurity beneath that loss. Once he disconnected, he became so profoundly depressed that his ability to see beyond his own immediate needs was almost nonexistent.

> DANNY: After he was born, I got very depressed. That was hard for me.
> PAUL: Was your depression related to him being born?

d. When we first met Danny, we administered a formal diagnostic interview as we did with all fathers at that point in our research. These interviews ask a lot of yes-or-no questions about specific symptoms and are designed to determine the presence or absence of disorders as defined by the *Diagnostic and Statistical Manual of Mental Disorders*. Most of the young fathers we interviewed over the years receive no psychiatric diagnoses. Danny was diagnosed with attention deficit/hyperactivity disorder, depression, conduct disorder, and three distinct SUDs (alcohol, marijuana, and amphetamine use disorder). The high level of overlap between SUD and other psychological disorders is a common phenomenon. Grant and her colleagues found that if someone is depressed or suffering from posttraumatic stress disorder (PTSD), they are twice as likely to develop a SUD and three times more likely to develop an AUD.[6]

DANNY: Yes . . . I was overwhelmed. I just felt blank. I didn't care about things. I was so depressed. I would try to escape out of the house, and she would chase after me. But I was just there. The first three months, I *did* help out with Gabe. I got him dressed, fed him, cleaned bottles. But I really haven't been able to help her since. About six months ago, I was hanging out with friends and doing more drugs, and she said she didn't want me around. She thought I cared more about drugs than I did about her. I was so messed up on drugs, mostly meth, that I just said, "Fine." That's how I got into programs and then jail, 'cause of the drugs. I was just going downhill.

About a year later, we met with April again, now with a second child who was almost 3 months old. She and Danny were not back together but after he got out of jail, she had let him stay over now and then because he had nowhere else to go. One of those times, she got pregnant again. She seemed embarrassed to tell us about that incident, saying that she loved her new baby son, Caleb, but knew how stupid it was to sleep with Danny again. April told Julie that she was stressed out by the demands of motherhood, often feeling lonely and not up to the task of raising two small children, becoming tearful as she talked. April, who liked to look on the bright side of things, then regained her composure and said that she was grateful to have her mom around to help and was proud that she had matured a lot in the last year, saying, "Just like kids grow up, parents grow up and I've grown up with my kids!" When Julie asked about Danny, she frowned and said she felt guilty for having "abandoned" him.

APRIL: I just feel bad for him. I don't feel love for him, but I do feel bad for him. I think about him every day. At some point in the day, I think about him. Nobody wants him. Not his mother. Not his aunt. I can't imagine what it would be like, living on the street and not having one person want you. I wish he would get some help. I don't really know how to help him anymore. He's changed so much.

JULIE: How is Danny doing as a father?

APRIL: He's a horrible parent, a waste of human potential. Right now, Danny is homeless; he has nowhere to stay. It breaks my heart. I feel bad for him, but he doesn't help himself. He wants everyone to help him, but he doesn't want to help himself. Since he started doing drugs really *really* bad, it's been downhill. He was staying with his sister, and his sister's boyfriend sells drugs, and Danny would steal them from him. I don't like putting him down but it's true. He doesn't help himself. He doesn't even try. He came here a while ago asking for food, 'cause he hadn't eaten in like three days. But I don't have a lot of money, so I can't really take care of him. He doesn't want to get a job; he just wants to do drugs all day long. He was court-ordered into treatment, but he was there just because he was court-ordered. When I think about it, I should have seen it coming. He was smoking pot since he was a kid. I knew that, but then he started using crank and freaking out. I should have seen it coming.

From April's perspective, the origins of Danny's substance abuse problems are not difficult to understand. She knows firsthand that many young men and women abuse drugs because they are raised in a context where drug abuse is the norm, just part of the landscape. If there is any propensity to use, the opportunities are overwhelming. And once the use evolves into addiction, it takes tremendous strength to stop it. It takes a powerful counterforce—like family, career aspirations, religious conviction, professional help, or sometimes just a burning desire—to overcome the grip of drugs.

One day, April took Danny's small stash of colorful pills off the couch where he was sleeping and hid them in a kitchen cabinet where Gabe couldn't get them. When Danny woke up and couldn't find his drugs, he went ballistic, shouting and threatening. April suddenly realized how bad things were and told Danny to leave and stay away, that she did not want to see him again. Danny took his pills and left for good. On that day, after years of supporting him, April decided that Danny had finally crossed a line because he was putting her child in danger. It seemed obvious to us that she made the right call, but we also know that for many young mothers the decision is less clear and very difficult to make. The distinction between a father who is merely dysfunctional and a father who cannot be trusted to take care of his child can sometimes be difficult to discern.

How often do young men like Danny get treatment for their substance abuse problems? Every year, the Substance Abuse and Mental Health Services Administration (SAMHSA), which is the part of the federal government that helps support and track substance abuse services, produces a "barometer" of mental health in America. This report includes an estimation of service utilization based on a survey conducted with about 68,000 people across the United States.[22] Based on the latest iteration of this survey, they reported that of the 17 million people estimated to have an AUD in 2014, only 7.6 percent had received any treatment. Among the

7 million people estimated to have a drug-related disorder, only 14.6 percent had received treatment. To make matters worse, drug use and abuse appear to be increasing slowly but steadily, particularly among young people. The results of the SAMHSA National Survey (summarized in Figure 10.1) indicated that young people between the ages of 12 and 17 are not particularly concerned about the risks posed by smoking pot and drinking regularly, underscoring that the culture of drug use and alcohol consumption is becoming more deeply entrenched.

Why there has been so little progress in dealing with the drug and alcohol abuse problem is a difficult question to answer. From our perspective, there are a few major obstacles. *First*, some people make big money from the production and sale of drugs and alcohol. For example, the alcoholic beverage industry posted about $219.5 billion in sales in 2016 and marijuana sales—a growth industry—reached about $56 billion, including about $10 billion in legal sales.[23] People who are profiting from the proliferation of a problem will not be inclined to help solve that problem unless compelled to do so. *Second*, although drug and alcohol abuse are not infectious diseases, they seem to function like them in some respects. Drug abuse and excessive drinking often begin as social activities and because drugs and alcohol are ubiquitous, it is difficult for an ex-addict to avoid re-exposure. Because we have been unable to stop the distribution of substances, the best we can

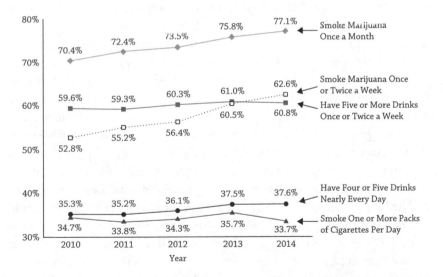

Figure 10.1 Adolescents aged 12–17 in the United States who perceived no great risk from the use of selected substances (2010–2014)

From: Substance Abuse and Mental Health Services Administration. *Behavioral Health Barometer: United States, 2015*. HHS Publication no. SMA–16–Baro–2015. Rockville, MD: Substance Abuse and Mental Health Services Administration, 2015.

do is help young people develop effective strategies to protect themselves from their contagious effects. In some respects, addiction is more insidious than true infectious diseases because our attraction to drugs is embedded in our nature, probably impossible to completely eradicate. *Third*, drugs and alcohol provide us with a remarkably effective means of escape from psychological or physical pain. When we are suffering, a stiff drink or a little pill is perhaps the most reliable way to feel better quickly, albeit temporarily. From the perspective of the drug user, the benefits associated with drug use—especially its numbing effects—are a disincentive for getting into treatment. If a young man checks into a drug treatment program, he cannot go out and drink or smoke, which means he will have to deal with withdrawal and whatever psychological demons are lurking behind the fog of intoxication. The grip of addiction is difficult to unclench.

Related to this third point, it seems clear that to effectively deal with the spread of SUDs, we must become more effective in addressing the mental illnesses that often underlie substance abuse. Based on a recent report from SAMHSA, the rate of co-occurrence between SUDs and serious mental illness was about 29 to 35 percent among 18- to 25-year-olds in 2014. Specifically, among young people in this age group who were found to have a SUD in the last 12 months, about 29.3 percent were also diagnosed with at least one psychiatric disorder, with PTSD and depression being the most frequent co-occurring problems.[6,24,25] Conversely, among 18- to 25-year-olds diagnosed with a serious mental disorder, about 35.3 percent also had a SUD. While it is conceivable that substance abuse precedes the development of a mental illness, most of the evidence indicates that it usually goes the other way. People develop a SUD to cope with an untreated mental illness or psychological trauma, or both. This idea—that people "self-medicate" with alcohol and drugs—is broadly accepted in the world of substance abuse treatment.[26] Obviously, if a psychological problem leads to the development of a SUD, then we must deal with that problem if we want curb or stop the substance abuse that stems from it.

Danny had three strikes against him. He grew up in an extraordinarily dysfunctional family, he developed some significant mental health problems, and he became addicted to drugs. Although substance abuse and addiction can destroy a young father's relationships with his partner and child, as it did for Danny, there are also fathers with SUDs who veer off course but don't crash and burn. It's important to underscore that addiction—even when accompanied by underlying psychological problems—doesn't necessarily doom a father to failure as a partner and parent. In the next section, we introduce Brian, who also had a serious SUD and whose early family life was not much different than Danny's, but who managed nonetheless to recover his footing as a father after being forced by his girlfriend to confront his problems.

We include Brian's story as a counterweight to Danny's, just as we wrote about Jerome and Ron in the previous chapter, to make two points. First, some fathers can get badly derailed and still get back on track again. Second, when this happens, recovery is never simple and never involves a "miracle cure." When people who have trouble controlling their tempers or regulating their temptations finally get their problems under control, it's because they work at it continuously, which is why mental health providers like the term "in recovery." Whether individuals have a "relapse" typically depends on the severity of their problem, the depth of their psychological reserves and whether they are able to get—and receive—the help they need.

BRIAN

When we first met Brian in our research offices at the University of Utah, he showed up late, looking tired and bleary-eyed. He was a burly, white 18-year-old in a dirty sleeveless T-shirt and a knit cap, handsome and athletic despite his disheveled appearance. He presented himself as laid back and carefree. Yet, as we learned more about his history, it seemed clear that his cool pose was an effort to cover over and cope with a lifetime of trauma and neglect. Both his parents had been alcoholics, and when they drank, they would often get into knock-down fistfights with each other. Eventually, his parents split, and his mother got sober by throwing herself into her work, becoming a workaholic, and attending Alcoholics Anonymous meetings every day.

When Keith asked Brian to describe his father during their first interview, all Brian could say was: "He's an alcoholic. A mean drunk. That's all he is." Pressed further, he explained that his father beat him regularly throughout his childhood until Brian got big enough to fight back. "That pretty much ended the relationship," Brian told us. When asked to describe his mother, he sort of shut down: "She's my mom. I can't, I don't know. I can't, I can't, I can't, I can't . . ." When Keith persisted, telling him to take his time, Brian told him, "I don't really have a relationship with her either."

KEITH: Can you tell me anything that helps me understand what she is like? What kind of person she is?
BRIAN: She's involved with her work. You know, a lot. That's about it.
KEITH: OK.

BRIAN: I just don't ever really. . . . I just up and left them and I don't see them anymore.

KEITH: Is there anyone else, another parent figure?

BRIAN: Yeah, my grandfather. He was my dad, pretty much. We did everything together, you know. I liked to stay there with him. We'd go fishing and camping, doing all that fun stuff. He took me to the Harlem Globe Trotters once. We did fun stuff all of the time. We'd rent movies and sit there and watch them, go get ice cream, stuff like that.

After his grandfather passed away, Brian dropped out of high school and started smoking a lot of pot. He rarely went home to his mother's, preferring to stay with friends. It was difficult for Keith to get Brian to talk during their first interview partly because our questions about family stirred up unhappy feelings that Brian was working hard to avoid. But it was also the case that Brian couldn't find the words to convey those feelings. Strange as it may sound, talking about himself—and his family—was an unfamiliar and confusing experience for him. He didn't know what to say.

Although reticent when talking about personal issues, Brian liked to be with other people and was naturally sociable. Even though he wasn't much of a communicator, he had learned to connect with others by being good-natured and easygoing. He was the guy who was always up for an adventure. When he eyed Brandy at a mutual friend's cookout by the Jordan River in West Salt Lake, he introduced himself by inviting her to jump in the river with him, fully clothed. She did, and that was enough to get things going. Brandy was attracted to Brian's fun-loving persona, and that night, they got drunk and slept together. They weren't dating, but they started hanging out together more and more, "hooking up" from time to time. When Brandy got pregnant several weeks later, she was pretty sure it was Brian's kid but she wasn't certain because she had also been sleeping with one of Brian's friends. In his first interview, Brian explained the situation:

You want to hear something funny? Between me and my friend, we don't know if it's me or if it's him. 'Cause stuff happened, and it could have been him or me. But she swears up and down and all around that it's mine, and so I don't know what would happen if it's not. I'm kind of really emotionally involved into it. I'd be pretty sad if it wasn't mine but, at the same time, I'd kind of be like "Whoa, life goes on." There's other people, there's other girls I could see, you know?

When Keith asked Brian how he felt about Brandy, the question seemed to throw him, as if it was the first time he had been asked to consider that dimension of his situation.

KEITH: How do you feel about her?

BRIAN: What do you mean?

KEITH: Um, how do you feel about Brandy, what do you feel about her, what do you feel for her?

BRIAN: Do you mean, like, do I love her or not?

KEITH: Yeah.

BRIAN: Yeah, I love her. I love her a lot and stuff. Before it wasn't, like, love. But now it's love. It was probably lust at first. And then, you know, we got along with each other, we liked being together and stuff. We were having difficulties, like communicating and stuff, but we're doing alright communicating now. I was all stressing about how we had to have conversations with each other. You know, I don't really talk about very much except, you know, what's going on and stuff. I don't think I could sit down and have a straight discussion about a topic.

Like Brian, Brandy had also used a lot of drugs and alcohol throughout her adolescence. But, when she found out she got pregnant, she stopped drinking, stopped using drugs, and stopped hanging out with friends who used drugs. After their daughter Brittany was born and Brian found out that he was indeed her father, he cleaned up his act too. He cut back on partying and got a job at a grocery store. As a couple, they were both trying to grow up and pooled together enough money to rent a small apartment. Happy to have a place of their own where they could become a family, they settled into a routine. To her surprise, Brandy liked being a mom. She liked taking care of Brittany, liked cooking, enjoyed how "boring" life had become.

Brian was having a different experience. After a few months of domestic life, he began to feel that the apartment was too small, and the quiet intimacy of family life felt alien to him. Also, he knew he wasn't living up to Brandy's expectations. She didn't complain about money or his messiness, but she wanted more time with him, to talk and be together. Their biggest argument was about when Brian would be home after work. Brian loved Brandy and Brittany, but he missed his independence, and he began to look for ways to escape for short periods of time. Brandy wanted him to come straight home after work, but Brian had started heading to the bar to meet friends. At first it was every once in a while, but then it was almost every night.

Predictably, Brandy got annoyed, and then she got fed up. She felt lonely in the apartment, especially when she knew that Brian was playing pool and drinking beer at the bar down the road, as if he didn't have a care in the world. She didn't want to fight about it. So, one day while Brian was out with his buddies, she packed up her stuff and moved back in with her mother. When Brian came home and found that Brandy and Brittany were gone, he was upset. It bothered him that she had not warned him or given him a second chance (which was not true, according to Brandy), but he was also annoyed that, without her income to help with the expenses, he could not afford to stay in the apartment on his own. This meant that he had to move back to his mother's house too.

At first, Brandy didn't even want to talk. But, after a couple of days, she agreed to meet with Brian. Brandy explained that his hanging out at the bar all the time was a problem for her. For the first time, he seemed to get what she had been trying to say before. He understood that she needed him to be present. Instead of just getting back together, they decided to start "dating," which was something they had never done. Brian got a new job working the night shift at a gas station, which helped him stay sober because he got off work at 7 AM. He would come over to Brandy's mom's house after work and stay with Brittany while Brandy got ready for work. Then, he'd take Brittany back to his mom's house and crash while his mom took care of Brittany for a few hours. This new arrangement felt better to Brandy. She didn't feel angry all the time, and Brian was spending more time with Brittany than he had when they were living together. When Christina (one of our research assistants) asked Brandy what she thought would happen in the future, she took a few seconds to think about it and said, "Knowing what I know about his past, I have my doubts about whether Brian will be able to stick with it, but I'm willing to give it another shot, to give him a chance."

It is difficult to know exactly why Brian was able to make a comeback and Danny couldn't. Both had serious, diagnosable substance abuse problems, although Danny's were more severe. Both were haunted by the trauma of being raised by dysfunctional parents, who had their own problems. Both entered fatherhood with very few psychological resources.[e] Perhaps the most important distinction between them was that Brian did not have a

---

e. Notably, Brian also had the advantage of having had a supportive grandfather (until he died), who seemed to function as a father surrogate for him. We talk more about the role of fathers and father surrogates in Chapter 20.

significant mental illness underlying his substance use problem, as Danny did. Whenever Danny stopped using drugs, he had to deal with his depression, which felt intolerable. When Brian stopped drinking, he felt better and was able to function more effectively at work and in his relationship with Brandy and Brittany. He also had the support of his mother, who understood recovery.

From our perspective, both Brian and Danny would have benefited from mental health services. The skills that are taught in counseling, such as self-expression, effective communication, and self-management, could have directly addressed what both these young men were missing. Therapy cannot undo past traumas, but it can help young people avoid the intergenerational transmission of bad habits and help them forge new pathways for themselves. In this respect, providing mental health and substance abuse services to Brian and Danny might have prevented at least some of what went wrong in their relationships with Brandy and April. Unfortunately, such services are not integrated into those parts of the healthcare system where men like Danny and Brian are likely to show up, like the clinic where April and Brandy receive their prenatal services and where Gabe and Brittany receive their well-baby checkups. Within these contexts, if the focus of counseling can be linked to their wish to be better partners and fathers, young men might be more persuaded to give counseling a chance. A warm word of encouragement from a prenatal nurse who helps a father understand that his health is connected to his baby's health can sometimes be enough to get him talking to a mental health provider. In the absence of any such supports for young fathers, these young men—especially those who do not have supportive families—are on their own to navigate their challenges.

CHAPTER 11

Bad Seeds or Bad Soil?

For as long as criminal records in America have been tracked, young, economically disadvantaged men—teens and young adults—have been more prone to commit crimes than any other demographic group. By some estimates, about 40 percent of all young men are arrested at least once before they reach the age of 24.[1] Many of these young men regard minor criminal activity as a form of entertainment or a rite of passage, knowing that the risks are minimal. They break the law while trying to impress their friends or just seeing what it feels like to break the rules. However, some men like Danny (from the last chapter) end up in jail because they have serious mental health and substance abuse problems, which can draw them into criminal activity as they become more desperate and less able to think clearly. Others, like Charles (whom we introduced in Chapter 4), see crime as an occupation, a way to pay the rent and buy food and diapers.

Criminologists have made a science out of trying to make meaningful distinctions between types of criminals, based on their reasons for committing crimes, the seriousness of the crimes they commit, the danger they pose to their communities and their families, and their capacity for meaningful relationships. Young men like Danny or Jerome (the father from Chapter 9 who was partnered with Ebony) could be considered dangerous because their reckless impulsivity poses a risk to their families, but these young men find no pleasure or thrill in harming others. In this way, they are distinct from criminals who meet their needs and fulfill their desires by disregarding the rights and feelings of others. This latter group of criminals—often referred to as sociopaths or psychopaths—tend to start young (before they reach adolescence) and continue to engage in increasingly serious criminal behavior until they are put in prison. Criminal behavior becomes a way of life, often leading to disastrous consequences. Some of these men cannot control their aggressive impulses and seem psychologically unable to take responsibility for their behavior, a trait that was evident in Ron (the disturbingly violent father introduced in Chapter 9). But some are more cold and calculating, using violence to get their way, tending to see other people as objects or tools.[2] These men—men like Jack, whom we introduce next—can also be charming, and, unfortunately, their reckless, daring, "take-no-shit" personas can be attractive to some young women.

JACK

Jack grew up in a family that was known to be running much of the drug trade on the west side of Salt Lake City. Jack's father and several of his cousins were in prison, and Jack was already deeply involved in the family business. When we first met him at the university clinic where his girlfriend Nicole was getting her prenatal check-ups, he was still recovering from being shot four times. Jack and Nicole, who were both 18, had met 6 months earlier through a friend of Nicole's who was dating a friend of Jack's. Despite this overlap in their social networks, they came from different worlds, which made their connection more exciting for both of them, like tasting forbidden fruit. Nicole lived on the east side of Salt Lake City with her parents, Spanish teachers who had immigrated to the United States from Argentina before Nicole was born. They lived in a modest matchbox home in a friendly, picturesque neighborhood nestled against the foothills of the Wasatch mountains and close to the university. Jack had the demeanor of a young Marlon Brando. He was tough, mysterious, confident, and charming. Despite his youth, he gave the impression that he and his family ruled the rough, gritty parts of Salt Lake City.

At the time that Jack and Nicole met, and even after she became pregnant, Nicole had no idea what she had gotten herself into. She thought she was in love, so the warning signs were easy to ignore. Jack treated Nicole well, and he seemed more grown up, more exciting than the other boys she knew. Nicole knew a little about Jack's background, but she believed that his family's history—the fact that his father was in prison—should not define him. Yes, he had been shot, but (as she saw it) he was the victim. He had not been arrested. Dating Jack felt like an exotic adventure, a walk on the wild side. She told us she liked the way he blended the "tough" and "charming" parts of his personality. She believed him when he said that he didn't want to end up like his father, that he wanted more for himself and for her.

Two years later, Jack was in prison, serving a 10-year sentence for holding a family hostage after he accidently broke into their house—the wrong house—looking for a drug dealer he and his buddies hoped to rob. By the time they realized they had broken into the wrong house, the cops were already there. Jack tried to bargain for his freedom with the family's lives. Eventually he and his buddies gave themselves up before anyone got hurt or killed. Although things could have gone much worse, that family will probably never forget that harrowing night. Understandably, Jack was given a stiff sentence.

When we talked to Jack in prison, he told us that Nicole had already taken the baby and left him before the botched burglary and then explained why Nicole had left. One evening, he was driving home from dinner at his mother's house, with Nicole and their baby in the backseat, when someone pulled up next to him, took a shot at him, and drove away fast. He said he tried to get out of gangster life, but people kept coming after him, not letting the past go. So, rather than letting this guy get away, Jack pulled a gun out from under the seat and went after him. That was it for Nicole. Frightened and furious, she went home and told her parents. That night, they all decided to pack up and leave town, leaving no information behind. She called Jack to say goodbye, explaining that she just couldn't raise their son this way. And that was the last time Jack heard from her.

Jack belongs to that relatively small group of men who are chronic, hardcore criminals (many, but not all, of whom can be described as socio-pathic). Like Jack, many of these men grow up in "criminogenic" families, where they are often abused and hardened in the sense that they are less able to be empathic or meaningfully considerate of others. They hurt most of the people they encounter, cutting a path through life that is often littered with trauma. These men make interesting characters in movies and television series but are nearly always lousy fathers. The fact that they go to jail or prison is not the primary obstacle to their functioning as parents. Rather, it's their deeply entrenched antisocial tendencies that pose the pri-mary obstacle. If Jack was not in prison, it seems likely that he would try to find Nicole, try to get back together with her or insist that he have access to his son, which is why Nicole and her family left town.

Although Jack is the sort of man that we tend to imagine when we think about who is in prison, the reality is that our prisons are full of men like Danny, who have serious mental health problems, or Jerome, who has trouble controlling his temper but is not a budding sociopath.[3,4] Many of the young men in our studies who commit crimes do so because they need money to feed their children. They steal cars and deal drugs when other ways of earning a living don't work out and the opportunity for quick money presents itself. William, a young African American, jobless and broke, exemplifies this type of young man. William was not born to criminal parents and does not identify himself as a criminal, but he still ends up in jail for engaging in criminal behavior.

WILLIAM

When we met William, he had been dating Phyllis, who was 5 months pregnant, since they graduated together a year earlier from one of Chicago's best high schools. William was a short and stocky young man, 19-years-old, who had a somewhat "preppy" look, wearing a polo shirt and Top-Sider shoes. He was immediately open with us and seemed genuinely interested in what we were researching, curious about what we would do with our data. After working hard throughout high school, William was frustrated when the best job he could find was working the register at a BP gas station. Now he was worrying about making enough to support his soon-to-arrive child. Relatively speaking, he and Phyllis seemed to have a lot going for them. They had a tight, stable relationship, and they consciously avoided the sort of drama that dominated their friends' relationships. They got along well and spent as much time together as they could. Both said they were initially shocked when they discovered they were going to be parents, but they had carefully considered all their options and decided—as a couple— to make it work. Both had supportive parents who could help, but William knew it would not be easy.

In his first interview, when Barry asked about his ambitions, William said he knew exactly what he wanted. He wanted to learn how to become an electrician and to eventually have his own business, but lately he was pessimistic about achieving that goal. When Barry asked him what kinds of things could get in the way, he got right to the point.

WILLIAM: My child, probably.
BARRY: How could having a child stop you from becoming an electrician?
WILLIAM: 'Cause, you need money to go to school, you need money to raise a child. So, you know, it might come to a point where you might have to pay for school tuition. Let's say, in a year's time, you spend six or seven thousand on a child and your school costs eight or nine thousand. And you got to live . . . so you need food,

electricity, all that stuff. That's what's stopping me. 'Cause I probably ain't making but twenty thousand dollars a year, so that's gonna get in the way. Could stop me from being successful. It's a lot of things happening out there nowadays. You know, there's problems, Black people got a lot of problems. And it ain't just Black—it's everybody. You all got a lot of problems too, you know?

Two-and-a-half years later, William and Phyllis have a 2-year-old son and a baby daughter. We tracked William down in Cook County Jail, where he was serving time for drug dealing. Barry was able to set up an interview during visiting hours, and William explained what happened.

BARRY: How long have you been incarcerated?

WILLIAM: Man, I've been incarcerated since June, so about seven-and-a-half months.

BARRY: What happened?

WILLIAM: Well, I was working at the R & R metal factory and I had got laid off 'cause I was too slow. So, I switched to Avis Car Rental and I was thinking, "This is it. This is what I want to do." But I got fired 'cause I was late all the time. I had car troubles. My car broke down and I had to be there at 6 AM. Buses don't start running that early 'cause it takes about two or three hours to get there on public transportation. I was getting there late, and my boss was like, "Why you so late?" I'm telling him and explaining it. "My car broke and this is a long way from where I live." But I couldn't get my car fixed *and* pay bills, so . . . one day he called me in the office and he told me to clean my locker out. I was being terminated.

So, I went back to working at the gas station where I had been before, but it wasn't paying me enough. And then I got a tremendous pay cut, a real bad pay cut . . . so I quit. Then, Phyllis lost her job too, and I was like, "Damn, what am I gonna do now?" I was just really struggling. One day, we had to go my mother's house 'cause we didn't have food at our house. And then, the next day, we go to her mother's house to eat. I was like, "Man, I'm tired of being a burden on other people." I was too stubborn to say, "I need help." So, I invested in the streets, you know. Then one day, I was at the wrong place at the wrong time. And I ended up in here. Got caught selling marijuana . . . and cocaine.

BARRY: How has this affected things with Phyllis?

WILLIAM: About a year ago, it was going good for us. Our life was . . . we weren't hurting or wanting for nothing. Everything was alright. We were happy when we had money, and then our relationship just starting going downhill. Right now . . . we're on bad terms 'cause I'm not there. But the other thing is, like, my attitude. You know, I was . . . we was getting into many arguments and fights, and I guess it was 'cause there wasn't no money. We'd get into it . . . into each other's head, arguing, fussing. And then, neither one of us get no sleep 'cause I can't get my point across—she won't let me talk. And then, I get real frustrated. I'd wake up in the morning wondering, "Man, where am I gonna get my next dollar? How am I gonna feed my kid and get diapers? Man, how am I going pay the bills?" You know, and then it's like our relationship died. I was trying, I was trying to make it better, but I was making it worse. You know, getting mad at her because she couldn't hold no job. I was like, man, *you ain't got no job either*.

William explains just how bad things are between him and Phyllis, yet we know that she has been visiting him regularly. Phyllis held onto her relationship with William partly for the sake of their kids—especially their 2-year-old son, Rasheed—and partly for William's sake, knowing he needed her emotional support. But she also held on and continued to visit William because she loved him and wanted to have a family with him. When Barry asked William how he is feeling about Phyllis, he shifts gears.

WILLIAM: It's getting better, you know. We talk more, we don't argue. It's like, I guess since I came here, I guess she see a change. And she figures like, "Well, I'm either gonna wait on him, or I'm not." She been telling me she gonna wait. She's like, "When you get out, you know, it's gonna be like we had when we first met." So right now, at this current time, it's getting better, you know. We talk more. Right now, at this point in time, I do love her and feel . . . I feel that she, she's the woman that I need to be with 'cause she's one of the most positive things, she is *the* most positive thing. If I'm around a successful woman like her, I might be successful myself.

William resorted to dealing because it seemed like the best—or at least the most accessible—opportunity for supporting himself and his family. Despite William's efforts to do the right thing, he was unable to find and keep a decent job. He was stressed about his desperate financial situation and was too proud to ask for help. When we interviewed Phyllis a few days before we met with William at the county jail, she was clearly stressed out, but she did not seem angry at William for being in jail or even bitter about the challenges she faced. She did not gloss over the problems she and William were having, but she had compassion for William, knowing he was in a bad spot. Phyllis was getting by with a lot of help from her sister and her mother, but she wanted William back home. In the meantime, she wanted William to stay connected with his son, which is why she was willing to take Rasheed along when she visited him in jail.

ISABELLA: How do you think William doing as a father?

PHYLLIS: I think he's doing pretty good. He loves Rasheed. He's not going to win any fatherhood awards, at least not while he's locked up, but he's always trying. I think it's the love that counts. Even when he was making mistakes, he's doing it for the right reasons. Like, sometimes I think that William is too hard on Rasheed, spanks him too hard when he misbehaves. He thinks I spoil Rasheed, and it's true that Rasheed listens to him more than me and behaves when he's around, so I guess he might be right. . . . Rasheed and me got a pretty good relationship. I just want them to have a good relationship too.

ISABELLA: How would you like for things to be different between William and Rasheed?

PHYLLIS: I'd like him to be closer with Rasheed. Rasheed is more comfortable with me. He likes to go places with me, he's sweet with me, gives me lots of hugs and kisses. I'd like for William to be able to take him places, spend more time with him, 'cause he needs that male influence. He needs a man's influence.

ISABELLA: How is your relationship with Rasheed different from his relationship with his father, with William?

PHYLLIS: Well, he's not around him except when I take him to visit, and that's not much. It's been hard on Rasheed, and it's been hard on me. I get really tired, and Rasheed gets upset. I get really tired, like I sit down for a minute, and I feel like I can't get up.

ISABELLA: What do you think will happen between you and William?

PHYLLIS: We're together now. I don't know what will happen in the future. Nobody knows.

How long will Phyllis manage to stay connected with William? A recent paper by Lauren Glaze and Laura Maruschak at the Bureau of Justice Statistics indicates that most incarcerated fathers lose contact with their children over time, as their connection loosens.[5] The longer the sentence, the fewer the visits. For young mothers, visiting a partner in prison, especially with a baby in tow, requires a great deal of effort. It involves taking off from work, and, for many visitors, a long bus ride to the jail and a long bus ride home again. William was at the county jail, just two city bus rides away from where Phyllis lived. If he was sent to the Danville State Prison, which seemed likely, Phyllis would have to travel for about 3 to 4 hours each way. Most fathers in prison are incarcerated in facilities that are more than 100 miles away from their children, and most never see their children.[6]

After getting to know Jack (the young father sentenced to 10 years in prison for the botched robbery), it was hard not to breathe a sigh of relief to know he was off the street and in prison. Strangely, Jack seemed to echo this unspoken sentiment, when at the end of our interview, he said that he felt like he belonged in prison because that's where most of his friends and family were. But, what about men like William, who have no history of violence and are nonetheless kept from taking care of their children? Indeed, the impact of incarceration on families is profound. Recent findings, again from the Fragile Families study, indicate that when a father is sent to jail, even for a short stint, his relationship with his partner is five times more likely to fall apart.[7] Moreover, in a well-executed set of analyses, Amanda Geller and her colleagues at New York University demonstrated that the children of incarcerated fathers were more aggressive and had more attention problems than the children of fathers who were not incarcerated.[8] Of note, these researchers found that children with incarcerated fathers were still more likely be aggressive and inattentive compared to children of fathers who were absent for other reasons.

THE BAD SEEDS VS. BAD SOIL DEBATE

The question of how we, as a society, should respond to criminal behavior has been a point of heated debate for a long time. Starting in ancient Greece, even the philosophers Plato and Aristotle didn't see eye to eye on the issue. While Plato was optimistic about our human capacity for reform through education, Aristotle, his student, was more authoritarian-minded, a strong believer in harsh punishment for the purposes of exacting retribution and deterring others from engaging in crime. In the Middle Ages, when crime was regarded as the work of the devil, punishment tended to be slow and painful despite Christianity's emphasis on forgiveness though confession, penitence, and absolution. In the United States, the criminal justice system seems divided between a law-and-order approach, designed to punish and deter criminal behavior, and a rehabilitative approach, designed to treat, reform, educate, and reintegrate. This divide reflects stark differences in opinion about what causes crime. There are those who believe that criminal tendencies are bred in the bones, mediated by bad genes, and then there are those that believe that crime is primarily caused by misfortune—deprivation, hardship, abuse. This is, of course, the bad seeds versus bad soil debate, whether criminal behavior is best explained by "bad" individuals or by "bad" environments. Those who view criminals as bad seeds tend to endorse tougher sentencing because they are less likely to hold out hope that criminals can reform. Those who believe that social circumstances, such as high poverty and low opportunity, play a role in the generation of crime lean more toward rehabilitation. This highly simplistic way of thinking about human nature and criminal justice does not reflect our personal view of what constitutes a reasonable discussion regarding criminal justice. We present it this way because the criminal justice debate in our nation has been driven by simplistic thinking. To make matters worse, the system often applies this type of thinking to individuals in discriminatory ways, formulaically determining whether a criminal is to be put away or rehabilitated based on factors closely related to his (or her) race.

History tells us that our notions of justice are heavily influenced by our social context and our position in society. For many of us, the debate between these positions occurs internally; we wrestle with what's right and what's effective and how we can best protect our interests and ourselves. To deal with these competing concerns, we typically apply different versions of justice depending on the crime and the criminal, often utilizing different systems for defining crime and meting out punishment. Consider that prior to 1865, it was a crime for an African American man or woman to seek their freedom, invariably leading to swift and harsh punishment, but it was not a crime for a white man to beat a slave for claiming his or her freedom. Viewing this situation from a contemporary perspective, beliefs about who is the victim and who is the criminal can become horribly perverted. And yet, many of our nation's most revered figures, including the founding fathers, not only accepted that twisted system; they built and defended it. With that as our legacy, it has been difficult for us, as a society, to get a handle on what we mean by justice. On the one hand, our nation has a fine-tuned appreciation for human rights. On the other hand, we (as a nation) continue to struggle with the issue of who counts as a full-fledged human. This internal struggle is addressed in Michelle Alexander's book, *The New Jim Crow: Mass Incarceration in the Age of Colorblindness*,[9] which provides a jarring and compelling perspective on both the causes and the effects of mass incarceration in America.

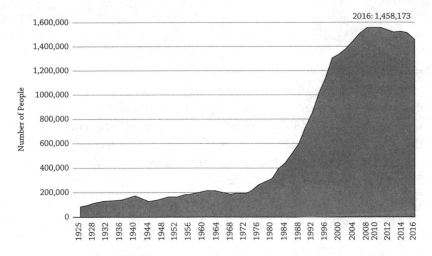

Figure 11.1 US state and federal prison population 1925–2016
From: The Sentencing Project. Fact sheet: trends in U.S. corrections. https://www.sentencingproject.org/publications/trends-in-u-s corrections/. Updated June 22, 2018.

THE TOUGH-ON-CRIME MOVEMENT

Michelle Alexander makes the case that the gains made in protecting the civil rights of disadvantaged groups in the 1960s and 1970s set the stage for the tough-on-crime policies put in place during the 1980s and 1990s, when the US government started sending a lot more people to prison. The growth in the US prison population, depicted in Figure 11.1 conveys the dramatic change that occurred in how we, as a nation, decided to deal with crime. In 1980, the rate of people in prison or jail was 220 per 100,000; 10 years later, in 1990, the rate was 460 per 100,000, and another 20 years later (in 2010), the rate was 730 per 100,000. Although the rate decreased between 2010 and 2016 to 680 per 100,000, that still reflects a *300 percent* increase in incarceration rates over the last 35 years.

Why did this happen? At first glance, it seems to have had something to do with the increased rates of crime during the crack epidemic in the 1980s. Alarmed by the uptick in violent crime associated with drug use and trafficking, state and federal prosecutors began to send people who bought and/or sold drugs to prison for longer sentences. The ostensible hope was that longer sentences would deter them (and others like them) from using and dealing, cutting the demand and curbing the drug trade. As more prison cells were needed to keep up with the increased rate of convictions and lengthy sentences, state and federal governments went on a building spree, and new jails and prisons sprang up across the country.

The cost of running the prison system rose from about $17 billion in 1980 to about $80 billion in 2010, a fourfold increase. Once those prisons were built, there were financial and political pressures to keep them full, which generated tougher sentencing laws and an increased emphasis on law enforcement. This tough-on-crime approach was based on the premise that the best way to reduce crime is to lock up the criminals.

Support for law-and-order policies became a political litmus test in the 1990s. Reagan-era Republicans were the original architects of mass incarceration. However, in the 1990s, Bill Clinton jumped on board, recognizing that the political winds had changed and our nation had become far less generous and forgiving. The Clinton administration engineered the now infamous "three strikes" law, which gave mandatory life sentences to criminals receiving a third felony conviction, some of whom were small-time drug dealers. Clinton also helped bankroll the building of new prisons, which further fueled the dramatic increases in prison populations during the 1990s and early 2000s. These new laws had a chilling effect on the relationships between fathers who had been convicted of a crime and their partners and children, who were consequently saddled with additional social and economic hardships.[10,11]

Harsh sentencing laws seemed to win votes, even in liberal districts, and Clinton's endorsement of tough-on-crime laws made it more acceptable for rank-and-file liberals to follow suit.[12] Meanwhile, on the other side of the political fence, some conservatives began to have second thoughts about what they had started. In the mid-1990s, Patrick Nolan, a former Republican state assemblyman from California, was sent to prison with a 33-month sentence for racketeering. After spending time with some young men swept up by the tough-on-crime movement, he became disturbed by the wastefulness and injustice of what he was seeing. For example, it made no sense to him that crack users (tending to be African American) were given much harsher sentences than cocaine users (tending to be white). Pragmatically, it seemed plain stupid to him that incarcerated men who wanted help with their problems, such as addiction and mental illness, were offered little support but still expected to change their ways. Nolan held onto his conservative beliefs and Republican politics, but he became an outspoken critic of policies that seemed to just warehouse young people who needed a genuine second chance. Over time, Nolan rallied other conservatives to the cause of prison reform by focusing on the ineffectiveness of excessively harsh sentencing rules. Even some tough-on-crime stalwarts, including Newt Gingrich, began to backpedal. In 2011, Gingrich and Nolan coauthored an op-ed piece in the *Washington Post*, outlining the conservative argument against mass incarceration.[13] Their primary argument was rooted in the economics of the problem: we are paying way too much for a system that does not work. Anticipating their conservative colleagues' counterargument that "keeping bad guys in prison will keep crime rates low," they preemptively cited examples of states like Florida that had reduced their prison population *and* simultaneously reduced crime.

The strange juxtaposition of Patrick Nolan and Bill Clinton reflects the debate about how society should respond to bad behavior, never reaching consensus on what's too harsh and what's too soft. When do harsh punishments serve as effective disincentives and when do they only make things worse, either by "hardening" criminals or by undermining the moral legitimacy of our systems? Prison may be necessary to protect the population from dangerous criminals. But when a criminal is not dangerous, wouldn't rehabilitation be a more appropriate form of deterrence than jail or prison time? Obviously, there are no easy answers to these questions, but two points seem clear. First, the United States has been far tougher on crime than on the underlying *causes* of crime. And second, mass incarceration has had a devastating impact on fathers and their families in socially and economically disadvantaged communities.

THE IMPACT OF MASS INCARCERATION ON AFRICAN AMERICAN AND LATINO FAMILIES

It's impossible to discuss the impact of imprisonment on young fathers without also mentioning the role of race and racism in our current justice system that keeps our prisons full. Let's start with the statistics. While African Americans make up 12 percent of the US population, 33 percent of the prison population is African American. Similarly, but less dramatically, Latinos make up 16 percent of the population and 23 percent of the prison population. By comparison, whites make up 64 percent of the US population and 30 percent of the prison population.[14] While it has been proposed that these disproportionate rates of imprisonment are because African American and Latino men are committing more crime, the evidence suggests that this disparity has more to do with a discriminatory criminal justice system.[15] For example, Donna Bishop, at Northeastern University, has carefully documented that minority youth are more likely to be treated more severely than white youth for the same crime at nearly every step in the juvenile justice process, from arrest to prosecution, from sentencing to incarceration.[16,17] More concretely, when white boys in the suburbs get into trouble, their parents typically work things out with the police, with the school, and with the courts. There is a formula for this: the

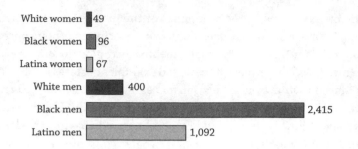

Figure 11.2 Rate of imprisonment per 100,000, by gender, race, and ethnicity, 2016
From: The Sentencing Project. Fact sheet: trends in U.S. corrections. https://www.sentencingproject.org/
publications/trends-in-u-s-corrections/. Updated June 22, 2018.

youthful offender looks appropriately remorseful and frightened, his parents promise to provide extra support and supervision, there is an arrangement to set things right, and the judge goes easy on them, hoping a lesson has been learned. Most of the time, that's the end of it. For young men who are economically disadvantaged and African American or Latino, getting arrested can be like falling into a very deep hole, often because their parents have fewer levers to pull.

Cassia Spohn, at Arizona State University, has found that the same holds true for African American and Latino adults, who are more likely to be sent to jail or prison (rather than given probation) and to receive longer sentences for the same crimes committed by whites.[18] African American men, in particular, are seen (and treated) as more dangerous, more serious criminals by the officers who arrest them, the prosecutors who arraign them, the jailers who lock them up, the juries who convict them, and the judges who sentence them.[19] Figure 11.2 illustrates that Latinos are 3 times more likely than whites to be sent to prison or jail, and African Americans are 6 to 7 times more likely to be incarcerated. This means that an African American child is 6 to 7 times more likely than a white child to have a father who is in jail or prison.[a] More than 150 years after the end of slavery, the rise in discriminatory imprisonment reveals that our beliefs (conscious and unconscious) about who is *more* criminal are still influenced by issues of class and race.

Despite the common-sense political appeal of "lock 'em up" policies and practices, this approach to criminal justice tends to overlook several

a. In 2010, the incarceration rate for white men under local, state, and federal jurisdiction was 678 inmates per 100,000 white US residents. For African American men, it was 4,347. According to the U.S. Bureau of Justice Statistics, African American men were more than 6 times as likely as white men to be incarcerated in 2010.[20]

important higher-level moral issues, including the question of how to deal with racial bias. In this case, racial bias is manifest in the finding that people act as if they know what the most dangerous criminals *look like*.

In the United States, dangerous criminals are *thought* to look brown or black. This is not to say that African American or Latino men *are* more dangerous. Rather, we are saying that the prevailing subterranean belief that these disadvantaged minorities pose a threat to society and ought to be put away has contributed to the phenomenon of mass incarceration. As far-fetched as this may seem to some readers, the proof is in the pudding. Some of this proof comes from the research on sentencing practices, which indicate that racial and ethnic minorities tend to receive harsher sentences than whites for similar crimes after controlling for other factors, such as criminal history.[21,22] Some of the proof comes from research indicating that skin color and facial appearances account for some of this bias, such that defendants who look more "Black" tend to receive harsher sentences than African American defendants who look less "Black."[21,23,24]

But most of the proof comes from careful studies of our criminal justice system's history, which has been unable to shake its tendency toward racial bias. For example, over the years, laws have been passed and judicial decisions have been made to make racism more difficult to practice in the courtroom. In the 1990s, strict sentencing laws were put in place to ensure that judges would be less biased in how they treated criminals convicted in their courtrooms. However, as judges were forced to be less discriminatory, prosecutors became more discriminatory, handing down harsher charges and being less willing to plea bargain with racial and ethnic minorities.[24] The behavior of judges was homogenized, but discrimination did not disappear. Like water running down a stream that gets damned, racism always seems to find an alternative path to follow. When mandatory sentencing laws were struck down as unconstitutional in 2005, again over concerns of discrimination, systematic discrimination continued at the same rate.[23]

The irony of this is that the same sort of discriminatory institutional practices that disproportionately land disadvantaged minority[b] men in detention or jail also play a role in determining why some young men, like William, engage in criminal behavior to begin with. Many of the young

---

b. We sometimes use "minority" to describe African American and Latino men and women, inferring that these groups are marginalized and often discriminated against. Recently, it has been suggested that the term "minoritized" might be more appropriate because it suggests that these groups have been relegated to second-class citizenry by the majority. While we like the term "minorized," we choose not to use it because it will seem unfamiliar and perhaps jargony to some readers.

fathers in our study who went to jail or prison had engaged in criminal behavior to support themselves and their families. These young men live in neighborhoods where the schools are subpar and where unemployment and poverty are high, so they don't graduate from high school and cannot find a decent job.

Believing they could not make the money they needed through legitimate means, these young men are caught in what moral philosophers would describe as a classical moral dilemma: Is it justifiable to commit a crime to feed a baby? Unfortunately for William, as it is for many African American fathers, this was not a philosophical exercise; it was a catch-22, and he could not do right. The consequence of this dilemma—incarceration—has been particularly devastating for African American families, as more than 25 percent of African American children will see their father go to jail or prison before they reach the age of 14.[25]

Given the current inequities in processing crimes and distributing justice, the only way to fight for equal rights before the law (and against systemic discrimination) is to have a good lawyer to argue the case, whatever that case might be. Of course, most African American and Latino men who get caught up in the criminal justice system also lack the economic resources to find a lawyer who will mount an effective defense or bargain for a fair sentence.[22] As such, incarcerated men tend to be more economically disadvantaged, and economically disadvantaged men are more likely to become incarcerated.

Does this mean we should be "soft" on crime or that young men should not be held accountable for their behavior just because they are disadvantaged or have children depending on them? The answer to this question depends on how we define "soft" and how we construe the purpose of our criminal justice system. The dilemma about whether to send a young man to prison or remand him into some type of treatment or rehabilitation program is what judges struggle with every day. Some men—particularly those prone to violence—may need to go to prison to ensure the safety of our communities or to ensure that justice is served. And we cannot deny that, in some cases, putting small-time offenders behind bars for short stints can be an effective wake-up call, as we saw in the cases of Jerome (discussed in Chapter 9) and Charles (introduced in Chapter 4).[26] However, locking up petty criminals for *long* periods of time does little to protect society, particularly if they leave jail or prison with fewer opportunities for legitimate employment than when they went in. Moreover, there is some evidence that our tough-on-crime approach has the unintended effect of hardening small-time criminals, forestalling or precluding the possibility of rehabilitation.[27] For example, Cassia Spohn (cited earlier) and David

Holleran examined the criminal trajectories of men sentenced to prison or released on probation for similar offenses in Kansas City, Missouri, starting in 1993.[28] They found that among those men who were convicted of a drug offense, those sent to prison were 6 times more likely to reoffend once released compared to those who were assigned to probation rather than being incarcerated. So, sometimes providing alternatives to jail or prison is both practical and just. This leads us to a couple of other moral questions that challenge the practical value of the "lock 'em up" approach to justice. First, do we have a responsibility to "rehabilitate" people convicted of a crime? And, relatedly, what is our obligation to prevent crime by addressing some of the underlying social causes of criminal behavior?

PROVIDING ALTERNATIVES

There is some evidence that if we were to rely more heavily on community-based supervision and rehabilitation programs *before* sending people to prison, we could diminish the risk to society posed by convicted criminals in two important respects. *First*, if the system can rehabilitate men who might otherwise become hardened, then they will be less likely to reoffend when they are eventually released. Put somewhat differently, the strain of being in a harsh prison environment for a long time *increases* rather than decreases the likelihood of recidivism.[29-31] *Second*, if these men become con-structively engaged in their communities, then the children growing up in those communities are less likely to grow up fatherless and impoverished. Consequently, they will also be less likely to drop out of school and become engaged in criminal behavior.[32,33] Rehabilitation is not a perfect science and requires great effort, but if applied systematically and persistently, it would almost certainly reduce recidivism and help keep fathers connected with their families.

Setting aside the issue of replacing jail or prison time with community-based rehabilitation, it is inevitable that men like William and Danny will be released from jail, and they will need help staying out of trouble and making it as fathers. During the era of mass incarceration, however, there has been pressure to contain the costs of managing a swelling prison population. One way to accomplish this has been to skimp on rehabilitation services, such as mental health resources, job training, and educational or parenting support services. Politically and practically, state and federal governments could not justify raising taxes to put more people in prison and then raise taxes again to help these prisoners get healthy, develop skills, or go to school. The problem with not providing these services, however, is that when ex-cons are released without the benefit of rehabilitation services, they return to their communities more damaged and more disenfranchised than when they went in.

Research on what happens after convicts are released from jail or prison provides the best evidence that the system as it currently stands is not working. In 2014, the US Department of Justice released a report on recidivism, based on the results of a study that followed 404,638 prisoners in 30 states who were released into their communities in 2005 and then followed over the course of the next 5 years. The authors of this report—Matthew Durose, Alexia Cooper, and Howard Snyder—write that within 3 years, more than two-thirds of these released prisoners were arrested for a new crime and within 5 years, more than three-quarters were arrested.[34] Younger inmates (under 24) and male inmates were more likely than older or female inmates to be rearrested, often within the first 6 months of getting out. Not all rearrests resulted in reconvictions and more time in prison or jail, but that's the way it went for most of these men.

Several researchers who study the ex-offender re-entry process and the prevention of criminal recidivism have suggested that men leaving prison need three basic services: (i) training and/or education that will make it possible for them to find and keep a job; (ii) help developing relationship skills that will enable them to reconnect with family members and provide emotional support for their children; and (iii) help developing self-regulation skills to manage whatever psychological factors put them at risk for recidivating, such as addictive behavior, risk-taking tendencies, and irascible personalities.[31,35] All told, that's a tall order, given that many ex-offenders often have significant deficits in all three areas of need. Although the practice of providing social support services to ex-cons paid for by the taxpayer is not without controversy, criminal justice researchers have demonstrated that effective re-entry programs prevent recidivism, which saves us from the expense of additional prison time and the agony of more crime.[36–38]

HELPING MOTHERS AND CHILDREN STAY CONNECTED WITH INCARCERATED FATHERS

In 2001, Christy Visher and her colleagues at the Urban Institute launched the Returning Home study.[39] This study followed a group of fathers from their time in prison through the process of returning to their communities in Cleveland, Chicago, and Houston, where they may or may not have reconnected with children, partners, and family. In addition to interviewing prisoners, this group of researchers also interviewed their partners, their ex-partners, and their other family members. Given that all the men they interviewed were fathers, it is presumed that each had a partner or an ex-partner out there somewhere. Among those family members that Visher was able to contact, many reported wanting to stay connected with their child's father while he was incarcerated. But many also indicated that the logistical issues, such as transportation and time, made doing so difficult, sometimes too difficult. In addition to the logistical challenges of visiting an incarcerated partner or ex-partner, there were often significant emotional challenges.[40] Children are often frightened by the experience of visiting a parent in prison, intimidated by the guards, the loud metal doors and bleak visiting rooms, where their father, barely knowable, shows up wearing an orange suit. Many young mothers give up trying to stay connected with their child's incarcerated fathers because they find the experience too demoralizing, leaving them emotionally depleted. Fewer than half of fathers in the state prison system *ever* have a face-to-face visit with their children or maintain regular contact (defined as at least once per month) by mail or phone. Sometimes, this is because men in prison have burned their bridges, but it is often because the burden of staying connected, which usually falls on the mother, can be too much to bear.

In Chapter 6, we introduced Darius, who became a father after a one-night stand with Janice on New Year's Eve. Although Darius and Janice tried to become a couple after finding out they were going to be parents, it didn't feel right to either of them. So after their daughter, Chanté, was born, they worked out a plan for raising her as friends. After being laid off from his third job, Darius started dealing drugs. Janice wasn't happy about what Darius was up to, but she appreciated that he could help her out with the expenses and had more time to spend with their daughter. When Darius got arrested by an undercover cop and was sentenced to 3 years, Janice wasn't surprised. She told us that she knew he would get caught because, eventually, everyone gets caught. Janice worked things out with Darius's mother so that Chanté could stay with her when she was at work or school. About a year later, when Lucille asked about her relationship with Darius, Janice explained the situation.

> JANICE: Darius has been in jail for about a year. I think he went when she was about 9 months, and now there's no communication. I speak with his mother, like every day, and she may tell me how he's doing, and, you know, that he asked about Chanté. But otherwise, we don't even communicate.

LUCILLE: Did you stop communicating when he went to jail, or . . . had you been communicating before he went to jail?

JANICE: We had been communicating before, but once he got transferred to prison, we just stopped. Before he got arrested, I would see him just about every day because I was going to night school, and he was picking Chanté up from daycare, from when she was about a month old until she was about 7 months. He was picking her up, bringing her home and stuff while I was in evening school.

LUCILLE: Was he helping you in any other ways at that time before he went to jail?

JANICE: He was paying for stuff. Like, we were taking turns paying the daycare. He would pay one week, I would pay it the next. We did it like that.

LUCILLE: How does he provide for Chanté financially now?

JANICE: Actually, I would say that he doesn't, but I mean . . . his mom takes his place.

LUCILLE: How do you think he's doing as a father?

JANICE: I mean, he's not here with her, and that's the most important part. So, I think he sucks. He's not here with her, and I think being with your child is the most important part. We split up during the pregnancy, but we were still friends, just not involved romantically. We would be together, but there was, you know, just friendship between us. He would take me to the clinic for prenatal appointments and things like that. I wish that he could have been . . . that he was a part of her life. You know? I wish that they could've spent more time together, so that she would at least know who her father is.

LUCILLE: OK. How do you feel about him?

JANICE: He's alright, but there's no more feelings. I mean, we haven't been involved romantically in, like, 2 years. So there's, like, no more feelings or nothing. And I told him I can't deal with the in-and-out-of-jail thing, so the feelings are no more.

LUCILLE: OK. Where do you want your relationship with Darius to go in the future?

JANICE: Maybe friendship. "Hi" and "bye," or something like that, but nothing serious or romantic or anything. I just wish that things could have been better, you know, that he would've been a more serious person and that I had been a more serious person. Then, maybe things could have worked out better for the sake of our child. But . . . it didn't happen, so I really don't think about him anymore.

This passage gives some sense of the chasm between incarcerated fathers and their ex-partners, who are left with the responsibility of raising their children. After a father goes to jail or prison, some mothers move on, not willing to invest in a relationship that offers little in return. Further complicating things, incarcerated fathers often feel ashamed of the mistakes they've made and embarrassed about not being there or providing support. Some don't know how to reach out to their ex-partners and ask for their help with staying connected. Even when a young mother wants to stay connected with her child's incarcerated father, that father may need help managing his feelings about how things turned out before he can respond constructively.

As things stand, the correctional system is not oriented to facilitate family visits between incarcerated fathers and their children. When those visits do occur, correctional facilities are not required or expected to make them more comfortable or less scary for the children. That said, some jails and prisons do offer programs to help inmates stay connected with their families.[40] In 2010, Heath Hoffman and his colleagues conducted a survey of prison programs designed to help incarcerated parents stay engaged with their children, sending requests for information to the wardens of 999 correctional institutions across the United States.[41] Among the 39 percent of the wardens who responded, 10 percent indicated they offered parenting classes that included the opportunity for direct contact between fathers and children; 16 percent offered to audio- or videorecord fathers reading to their children, allowing those recordings to be sent home. In addition, 30 percent of the wardens said they provided some travel assistance to the families of inmates who needed help getting to and from the prison. Although these efforts are encouraging, if we assume that most of those wardens who did not respond to Hoffman's survey *do not have* these sorts of services, the results of this survey indicate that—on the whole—little is being done to keep children connected with their incarcerated fathers.

What more can be done? There have been a small handful of pilot programs designed to help incarcerated fathers stay connected with their children and their partners (or ex-partners).[42] For example, Rachael Barr at Georgetown University and Carole Shauffer at the Youth Law Center in San Francisco developed the Just Beginnings Program designed to help young incarcerated fathers effectively engage with their babies and work collaboratively with their babies' mothers.[43] With the support of juvenile justice administrators in California and Ohio, these researchers arranged for the partners of young fathers to bring their children to juvenile detention centers for a series of father–child visits. Parent coaches worked with the young fathers to help them engage with their children. Over the course of 5 sessions, the fathers became more conversational, warmer, more attentive, and less harsh and controlling. This research demonstrates that, with support, young mothers will bring their children to see their incarcerated fathers, and with some guided instruction, young incarcerated fathers can become more attuned and responsive to their children.[c] Although a few promising pilot programs have been developed to help incarcerated fathers stay connected with their children, these programs are few and far between. Hence, most incarcerated fathers, especially those with longer-term prison sentences, lose touch with their children over time.

Before we conclude this section on what goes wrong between young fathers and their families, there is one additional threat to discuss: infidelity. This threat is different from the others, in that it is purely emotional, leading to profound feelings of betrayal and loss. When discovered, infidelity leaves the betrayed partner wrestling with questions like "Can I heal from this wound?" "Can we rebuild trust?" and "Do I want to have anything to do with this lying cheat?" How couples deal with these questions will determine the impact of infidelity on their children.

c. There are also some programs that help incarcerated fathers learn how to parent their children without the necessity of direct contact. For example, J. Mark Eddy and his colleagues at the Oregon Social Learning Center conducted a well-designed study to test the effects of a curriculum for incarcerated fathers with children between the ages of 3 and 11 who were scheduled to be released. Eddy and his colleagues tested the effects their program, which was designed to teach incarcerated parents how to effectively engage with their children and work collaboratively with their children's primary caregiver. One of the challenges of parenting programs like this one is that, unlike the Just Beginnings Program (which involves in vivo parent–child practice and instruction), this program relies on role play and discussion to create some sense of how this might work on the outside. Nonetheless, Eddy reported some positive findings. Following up with fathers 1 year after they were released, these researchers found that, compared to the control group fathers, those fathers who participated reported less parenting stress, lower rates of depression (suggesting a more positive re-entry experience), and more positive parenting behavior, based on their own report.[44]

CHAPTER 12

Betrayal and Forgiveness

In addition to violence, substance abuse, and criminal behavior, infidelity is another problem that can wreak havoc on relationships, sometimes leading to father disengagement. When a young parent discovers that his or her partner has cheated, it can feel like a knife to the heart. Most young people experience their first significant romantic relationship as something akin to a sacred bond, a haven where they feel shielded from the tumultuous world "out there." When infidelity occurs, this security is threatened in two ways. On an emotional level, infidelity usually undermines the trust and caring aspects of the relationship. On a more practical level, infidelity often means that one partner is divesting some of his or her resources from one relationship and investing those resources in another.

We feel compelled to include a chapter on infidelity in this section on "what goes wrong" even though we see it as belonging to a class of problems separate from crime, violence, and substance abuse. Infidelity does not present a physical danger to either partner (like violence and substance abuse) and it does not inevitably impose a separation (like jail). Yet, it can be just as emotionally devastating. Early on in our research, we were surprised by how much and how often young mothers and fathers expressed concerns about their partner's infidelity. They were expecting a child together, so we assumed that cheating was out of the question, off the table. We quickly learned that the reason young people worry about infidelity is that it is happens fairly frequently, even when expecting a child. We were even more surprised to discover that it's not just men who cheat on their pregnant girlfriends; pregnant women and young mothers cheat too.

The estimates of how frequently infidelity occurs among young couples who are dating range between 20 percent and 50 percent.[1,2] Of course, the prevalence of infidelity depends on how it's defined and how we go about asking whether it has occurred. In the minds and hearts of most people, there is a hierarchy of cheating behavior based on several variables: (a) Was it done in secrecy? (b) Did it violate the agreed-upon terms of the relationship? (c) How far did it go? (d) Was it just about lust and sex or was there an emotional involvement? and (e) How long did it last? When cheating is defined narrowly as sexual contact, the rates of cheating hover around the 20 percent mark for young couples; if we define infidelity loosely to include flirting and kissing, the rate increases tremendously.

In addition to being surprised by how much cheating occurs among young expectant couples, we were also surprised by how many couples manage to work things out after one or the other cheats. When cheating is revealed, about 25 percent or so break up entirely, losing both their romantic and their co-parenting relationship. They don't communicate, and the father becomes loosely involved or entirely disconnected. More frequently, approximately 50 percent of the time, couples end their romantic relationship (often acrimoniously), but they continue to work together as co-parents. Over time, they separate the business of parenting from the disappointment they feel about the failed romance. Old wounds might fester, but many young parents—particularly young mothers—compartmentalize their disappointment and move on. Some young mothers and fathers (about 30 percent of those who break up) will find new partners with whom they will have more babies, further dividing their time and resources and often leading to greater economic hardship for themselves and their children.[3-5] And some couples—about 25 percent—stay together and try to work things out.

CARLOS

Carlos, first introduced in Chapter 3, was the product of a secret romance between his mother, whom he lived with, and his father, who had another family. When we met Carlos, the romance between his mother and father had been over for years, but it was still a well-kept secret. When Carlos and his father ran into each other on the street, his father acknowledged him with a nod (and usually a few bucks) but Carlos' existence was unknown to his father's other family. Carlos seemed to admire his father's reputation for being a "lady's man," despite the fact that he had gotten the short end of that stick. There was little substance to the father–son relationship, outside of the money his father slipped him every now and then. They did not talk.

When Monica started dating Carlos, she knew that he was flirtatious and that he liked the attention of other girls. She loved him and felt reasonably sure he would settle down. During her interview, when Isabella asked Monica where she thought her relationship with Carlos was heading, she responded—somewhat presciently—with this statement:

MONICA: I told him, "No matter what happens between us, or whatever, I will never stop you from seeing your son, unless you commit murder or something serious like that. Then, I would think twice about letting you see him." I grew up without a father and so did Carlos, and I wouldn't do that to our son.

Eighteen months later, Monica was living with Carlos when she found out that he had another son, about the same age as their son, little Carlos. She tried to reconcile herself to this new reality—that her boyfriend was a "cheat." But after a couple weeks, she packed her things and moved into her sister's apartment, taking little Carlos with her.

MONICA: He had been lying to me for, like, two years. He has another child, who just turned a year old. I found out about it and said, "OK, I can deal with this." But then I moved out.
ISABELLA: So how did you find out that he was lying to you?
MONICA: I mean, I had my suspicions. I knew about her and everything. One day, I guess I sort of had a nervous breakdown and just started crying. I was like, going crazy, and he walked in and I was like, "I can't do this anymore. I am miserable." Finally I say, "I just need the truth. All I need is the truth. All you had to do was tell me the truth from the beginning." So, he sat me down and told me *half* the truth. And then he told me about the baby, said he wasn't sure if it was his. She says so, but he is not sure. So I was like, "OK, I can deal with this." And I went with him to get his paternity test, which was kind of awkward. But, you know, I did it. And that test said that he was the father. We tried to work it out, but it was just not good. Like, every time he was with me, she texted me fifteen, twenty times.
ISABELLA: The other girl texted *him*?
MONICA: Texted *me*, looking for him. She is like, psycho. She is really just *out there*. Then, I told him that I was breaking up. I said, "You know, you would be better off staying with her." This girl is like,

psycho. He tried to break up with her, and she stabbed herself in the leg and said she would kill herself if he left her. Just crazy. And I'm, like, "You know, this way, you stay with her. She doesn't go crazy on you, she has your son. This way, you know little Carlos is in good hands. I'm not going to flip out on you 'cause you leave me." That's it. You know, guys come and go. Your child is there forever. I go, "All I'm asking from you is just please don't forget about my son, 'cause that little boy loves you more than anything in this world. And no matter what happens between me and you, you're always going to be his father."

ISABELLA: So you guys aren't really together now?

MONICA: No.

Despite her initial feelings of betrayal and loss, Monica got practical about her situation. Carlos was a warm, loving father but he was also an untrustworthy partner. Monica wanted to hold on to Carlos as a father to her son, but she knew she could not spend her life worrying about those other women. Some young mothers will end the relationship completely when they find out their partners are cheating, but these are relatively few and far between. Most mothers either try to work things out with their partner or decide to end the romantic relationship but remain together as co-parents. Some couples are eventually able to step around their failed romantic relationship and forge a reasonable co-parenting relationship with whatever remains.

ISABELLA: So how would you describe your current relationship with Carlos?

MONICA: I think we are better now that we are not together. But, that is my opinion. When we were together, he would never call. He would take off for three or four days at a time. After a while, you know, you stop getting compliments. He stopped saying "I love you." Those things are something you need to hear all the time if you really care about somebody. When he stopped doing that and all that stuff started happening, I had the feeling that he was cheating or whatever. You kind of find out little things here and there, then the evidence started building. We are more open towards each other now than when I was living with him. We are better now than I think we were when we were together.

ISABELLA: So how do you feel about him?

MONICA: I don't know. I would really like him to just be my friend, but he pushes the sex issue. Even now, I want to be with him. If I could,

I would. But I can't. I am just not built that way. I would have given him anything. And—even to this day—I feel like I would do anything for him. But he did the worst possible thing that any man could do to a woman that loves you. There were points where I would just cry and be like, "Why did you do this to me?" I mean, I would have married him in a minute. But it went from that to "I hate you"' and then "I want to be with you but you got another girl and her baby." And now it's just, like, I came to an understanding that "You know, I want to be with you, but I can't because I can't deal with your issues."

Why do young fathers and mothers cheat on each other? Previous researchers have found that the best predictor of infidelity is relationship dissatisfaction, which often occurs when one or both partners believe they are not a good match. Many of the young people in our research studies stumbled into parenthood unwittingly and are understandably uncertain about whether *this* partner is the right partner. In Carlos' case, it's easy to draw parallels between his behavior and his father's behavior, who cheated with Carlos' mother and then all but abandoned Carlos and his sister. Perhaps Carlos, who seemed to long for his father's acceptance, cheated on Monica in an unfortunate attempt to identify with his father. He opted for the role model that was most psychologically present, despite his physical absence. On the other hand, we may be oversignifying this connection. Like many young men, loaded up with testosterone, Carlos may have cheated on Monica for the simple thrill of having sex with someone new and different, not thinking through how that behavior might affect Monica or how it might compromise his relationship with his son. We know that sociobiologists (such as Robert Trivers, whom we talked about in Chapter 3) believe that infidelity is a normal, expectable part of the reproductive process. Some men choose to have multiple children with multiple partners to increase the chances that their genetic material will survive. From that angle, Carlos might be implementing a biological strategy that men have been using, with some regularity, since the beginning.

Whatever his reasons for cheating, there is no getting around the fact that Carlos irreparably damaged his relationship with Monica. When Monica found out that she had been duped into thinking that what she had with Carlos was special and unique, the beginning of a life together, she became sick with loss. When infidelity occurs and the trust between two young romantic partners is broken, the suffering that follows is often heart-wrenching to observe. As it was for Monica, it often happens in slow motion. Bits of information emerge, accusations are made and denied. And then, the truth leaks out, followed by tears and outrage. When infidelity results in the birth of a baby with another partner, as it did with Carlos and Monica, the feelings of betrayal are amplified because the unfaithful father has not only cheated on his partner; he has also cheated on his child. Nonetheless, when Lucille asked Monica how Carlos was doing as a father, she was remarkably generous.

ISABELLA: How do you think Carlos is doing as a father?

MONICA: With my son, he's . . . I'm sure he wants to do more, but he's doing as much as he can. And I guess that he's a great father when he's around. You know, he plays with him. He's a great father, he really is. But you know, if he could do more he would, but he can't. So I don't, like, knock him down for not doing more.

ISABELLA: Uh huh, what more could he do?

MONICA: I mean, I really wish he would come around more 'cause, you know, it's better for the baby. I don't know, like family outings. We used to go out as a family. Went to the zoo or whatever, and we just don't do that anymore. . . . Yeah, more time would be nice. I wish he would do more father–son things, like take him to baseball games and swimming and whatever. . . . He comes by my house, that's about it.

In my son's room, you see pictures of me and Carlos, like from prom and from his birthday party, and just tons of pictures of us in my son's room. I feel like my son needs to know that he was created in love, not in hate. I need him to know that mommy and poppy are not together, but we still care about each other. "We're still your parents, and you were created in love."

The English language lacks words to describe the emotions that couples experience as they struggle with the complexities of their relationships. There are few words that adequately convey the internal effort required to maintain a functional, constructive, reasonably civil relationship with an ex-partner who is a cheater and a liar but a good parent and an important part of their child's life. In Russian, there is a word, *razbliuto*, which we are told describes the sentimental feelings we have toward someone we once loved but no longer do. But that word doesn't seem right, because it lacks reference to betrayal and disappointment. We imagine that Monica is feeling something more complex, more like a mix of intense sadness for what might have been and profound anger. To deal with these feelings, she must temper her outrage and find the strength to be supportive and even respectful of Carlos for the sake of her son.

When young couples decide to split amidst the complications that accompany infidelity, the process is often extremely painful. Fathers and
mothers are angry with each other or disappointed with themselves, or
they are sad for their children, or all that and more. Even when there is
some sense of relief, there are still feelings of loss for what might have
been. Arguments about what went wrong can simmer for years, occasionally erupting with volcanic force. A young father may feel stressed out
whenever he tries to coordinate parent responsibilities with his ex-partner,
knowing he can never quite get it right. A young mother may feel frustrated with her child's father, who she knows is trying to be helpful and
make up for his past mistakes but nonetheless keeps showing up a day
late and a dollar short. With time, ex-partners move on and form new romantic relationships, which adds another layer of complications, as family
structures become more complex. Children form relationships with their
parent's new partners and possibly a few step- and/or half-siblings. These
new relationships are not unusual or necessarily a problem but maintaining
a stable sense of "family" can become difficult when loyalties are divided,
and resources—emotional and financial—are stretched thin. Tension and
conflict between split parents often become the backdrop of a child's life
when resentments continue to simmer.

FORGIVENESS

Kristina Gordon, Donald Baucom, and Douglas Snyder are marriage and
family counselors that have made infidelity and forgiveness a major focus
of their clinical work and research. While they have worked mostly with
married and divorcing couples, what they have to say about forgiveness is
quite relevant to younger unwed couples too. The concept of forgiveness
was rediscovered and appropriated by the positive psychology movement
beginning in the 1990s and, more recently, by the mindfulness movement,
which has a strong emphasis on the process of "letting go" of negative
emotions. The primary difference between these approaches to forgiveness
and the approach proposed by Gordon, Baucom, and Snyder is the end goal.
Most couples—and perhaps most therapists—see the end goal of forgiveness as reconciliation. However, Gordon, Baucom, and Snyder see it differently. In their chapter in the Handbook of Forgiveness, Gordon, Baucom, and
Snyder distinguish their work from their colleagues as follows:

> We define forgiveness as a process whereby partners pursue increased un-
> derstanding of themselves, each other, and their relationship in order to free

themselves from being dominated by negative thoughts, feelings, and behaviors after experiencing a major interpersonal betrayal. This process is distinguished from a view of forgiveness as excusing or forgetting that a relationship injury or betrayal has occurred, or as requiring a decision to reconcile the couple's relationship. An important aspect of our conceptualization of forgiveness is that it does not stipulate that partners must reconcile in order for forgiveness to occur. Partners can decide to terminate the relationship and still fulfill the conditions of forgiveness.[6p407]

We like this definition of forgiveness because it allows for the fact that forgiveness does not always lead to a happy ending. Sometimes, the best a couple can do is minimize the negativity between them and make peace with their disdain and disappointment.

Gordon, Baucom, and Snyder make the important point that the process of forgiving others—particularly others who are still behaving harmfully—should include an element of self-protection. They propose that forgiveness consists of three components. The *first component* is "a realistic, non-distorted, balanced view of the relationship," which underscores the point that forgiveness should not be mistaken with open-hearted foolishness. The *second component* is "a release from being controlled by negative affect toward the . . . partner," which can be emotionally freeing in two respects. First, it is personally unhealthy to remain steeped in hate and rage. It's bad for our physical and mental health, and for the health of everyone around us. It quite literally eats away at us from the inside.[7] Second, letting go of sustained anger can promote some form of repair or rapprochement, which can protect the children from being stuck in the middle of ongoing strife. The *third component* of forgiveness is "a lessened desire to punish." This last component is interesting because it seems to deliberately set a low bar for what couples might hope to accomplish. The goal of having fewer revenge fantasies seems far more attainable than building a new foundation for trust, which might be unrealistic for many couples.

In this model, "forgiveness" is a process for establishing a manageable space between staying connected and maintaining a safe distance, somewhere that is not quite fully open and accepting but not entirely closed and distrustful. The model could be helpful for young mothers (and fathers) who, when confronted with their partner's bad behavior, must struggle with feelings of loss and betrayal. Consistent with our experience of what happens when cheating occurs, Gordon, Baucom, and Snyder regard infidelity as an interpersonal trauma. Their model of forgiveness is about helping both partners (a) accept their emotional response to the injury and loss; (b) develop a personally meaningful understanding of what happened;

(c) redraw relationship boundaries to re-establish safety and stability; and (d) move forward with the relationship, however it gets defined. We believe this framework for understanding and "treating" infidelity is useful because it provides a road map for helping young couples respond constructively and realistically to the occurrence of interpersonal injuries caused by flawed partners and/or damaged relationships.

More broadly, we believe that forgiveness—as described by Gordon, Baucom, and Snyder—belongs to a set of emotional skills that also include compassion and acceptance. These skills enable couples to build bridges across ruptures in their relationship. Each of these words—forgiveness, compassion, and acceptance—implies that something unfortunate has happened and that, because of this, some form of reaching out is needed. Compassion is called for when we see suffering in others. Acceptance is called for when we are impatient with others (or ourselves). And forgiveness is needed when we have been hurt by someone we love. We like how Gordon, Baucom, and Snyder have defined forgiveness as a process to be learned and practiced. Their down-to-earth definition might make forgiveness more attainable for young fathers and mothers who want to stay meaningfully connected with each other but need to protect themselves from future harm.

CHAPTER 13

The Epidemiology of Heartbreak

Some of what goes wrong between young fathers and their families will be familiar to our readers. Many of us have gone through phases of being selfish, irresponsible, and/or reckless. Some may have flirted with delinquency or overindulged in drugs or alcohol, perhaps becoming addicted. Most of us have lost our tempers and said hurtful things to loved ones, and some of us may have violently lashed out. These problems are common because growing up and sustaining intimate relationships is difficult, and young people are not always psychologically equipped for the challenges they encounter as adults. Many of us also know from personal experience that how we manage ourselves *after* we make mistakes will often determine whether things get better or worse. Both Jerome and Ron (introduced in Chapter 9) were convicted of a domestic violence charge that included endangering their unborn child, and both were sent to jail. But each responded differently to that experience. Whereas Jerome focused on taking responsibility for his part and changing the way that he dealt with conflict, Ron invested his energy in denying that he had done anything wrong. Two years later, Jerome was still struggling to manage a volatile relationship with Ebony but no longer getting into physical brawls, and their relationship remained intact, more or less. By contrast, Ron was completely cut off from Samantha and his daughter partly because he did not take responsibility for his behavior. Without acceptance of some personal responsibility for destructive behavior, change is unlikely to occur.

The importance of "taking responsibility" raises an important question: Who is responsible for what goes wrong between fathers and their families? Most people regard these problems—substance abuse, violence, criminal behavior, and infidelity—as matters of personal responsibility. However, the sheer number of fathers who are failing to stay constructively engaged with their children suggests that our institutions are not effectively supporting the development of men into fathers. In each of the preceding chapters, we have made the case that social, cultural, and economic factors sometimes contribute to the occurrence of what goes wrong. Sometimes our institutions—such as our criminal justice system—operate in ways that make a young man's problems worse or unnecessarily cut him off from his family.

At the beginning of this section on what goes wrong, we introduced John Snow, the English doctor who is credited with being the first epidemiologist. Snow was not satisfied with only treating the cholera that was making his patients ill. Rather, he realized that it was necessary to determine what was causing the spread of cholera through London's neighborhoods and then cut it off at the source. He felt certain that if he could isolate the germ that was infecting his patients, he could end the epidemic. There is much to be admired in Snow's careful clinical observations, his methods for tracking his patients' behavior, and his capacity for deductive reasoning. Snow's story is like a real-life Sherlock Holmes adventure. But, truth be told, his success in stopping the spread of cholera was not as easy as we made it seem at the beginning of this section.

After collecting data and determining that an infected water supply was the cause of the cholera epidemic, John Snow ran into some major political and scientific obstacles that prevented him from getting the Broad Street Pump shut down for several years. The medical establishment believed that cholera was caused by clouds of bad air, called a "miasma," that contained poisons and infected people who lived in its vicinity. Given the abysmal air quality of London in the 1850s (during the Industrial Revolution), miasma theory seemed plausible. After all, you could see that bad air hanging over London. Plausible as the bad air theory seemed, it was inconsistent with the data that Snow had collected from his patients. But, because miasma theory was endorsed by several prominent physicians, Snow's germ-water theory was not taken seriously, and his plea to shut down the Broad Street pump went unheeded.

Snow was persistent, and the debate about the cause of cholera became a hot political issue in mid-19th-century London. The House of Commons passed several laws to regulate businesses that were poisoning the air. Snow was adamant that air pollution—bad as it was—did not cause cholera. He took his concerns to the House of Commons, but his testimony was dismissed and even rebuked in an editorial published by *The Lancet*.

To make matters worse, it wasn't just the scientific community that was against him.

One of Snow's most ardent opponents was a local clergyman, Reverend Henry Whitehead, who believed that cholera was a form of divine punishment inflicted on those who had sinned. Whitehead was so determined to prove Snow's theory wrong that he started collecting his own data on the spread of cholera, interviewing afflicted people in his community. Commendably, as Whitehead listened and took notes, he was swayed by the facts. Apparently, not all the people dying of cholera were as sinful as Whitehead anticipated them to be. In fact, Reverend Whitehead found the same pattern of infection that Snow had detected, and to his credit, Whitehead became an ardent supporter of Dr. Snow. He helped Snow gather more data and present the evidence that cholera was a water-borne infection and that the Broad Street Pump was the likely source of the epidemic. Together, they were finally able to convince city officials to remove the pump handle and see what happened. If Snow was right, the spread of disease would abate. Of course, he was, and the epidemic ended. Snow first proposed his hypothesis about the cause and spread of Cholera in 1849. The Broad Street pump handle wasn't removed until 1855.

Perhaps the most important part of this story is that, despite the tremendous opposition facing him, Snow continued to collect data, present the evidence, and keep the argument alive. In this endeavor, it was not enough for Snow to be a good scientist, imagining a cause he could not see with the naked eye, based on patterns in his data. Snow realized that even though the cause of the disease afflicting his patients was a germ, the problem could not be solved without addressing larger factors. These factors included how people organized themselves in neighborhoods (the sharing of water), individual human behavior (the disposal of waste that infected the well), different beliefs about the cause of the problem (germs vs. poisonous air), and, most important, the political wrangling about what to do about all of it. In some respects, Snow's most important trait was his political stamina.

If Snow were alive today and inclined to address the "fatherhood problem," he would almost certainly first focus on the personal histories of young fathers. In this section on "what goes wrong" we have honed in on the immediate causes of father disengagement. But, like John Snow, we have tried to give some consideration to the *causes* of these causes. Drawing from the example of John Snow, we have come to regard father disengagement as *both* a psychological problem and a public health problem, requiring both psychological and public health solutions. Moreover, we know that the hardest part of solving the father disengagement problem will not be identifying causes or even the causes of causes. The hardest part will be determining who is responsible for addressing those underlying causes and convincing—whoever they might be—to do something.

Of course, some of the responsibility belongs to the fathers themselves. But it's only practical to consider that we—as a collective—may bear some of the responsibility for fixing the problem, even if we are not personally responsible for creating it. More to the point, the question of what should be done to help young men become (and remain) positively engaged fathers is a matter of fierce debate, because there is no simple solution. Do we hold men accountable by enforcing rules and punishing their bad behavior? Do we fund substance-abuse treatment programs for addicted fathers? Do we help young men build good lives for themselves by helping them develop positive relationship skills and their capacity for supporting their families?

Each of these approaches suggests a somewhat different philosophy about maintaining the stability of the family. As we discussed earlier, as a nation we vacillate between two different solutions to the disruptions that occur between young fathers and their families, even those disruptions that don't involve criminal behavior. The first approach seeks to regulate and restrict reckless, destructive behavior that often upends the development of young men and harms the people closest to them. This approach involves passing laws that impose stiff penalties on those who commit crimes or fail to behave responsibly. For example, Bill Clinton, who signed the 1994 Crime Bill into law, probably thought that stiff penalties for minor crimes would deter young people—young men in particular—from acting upon on their harmful desires and impulses.

The second approach is to empower young people by creating educational, occupational, and psychological opportunities that motivate them to engage in healthy behavior, which includes being a good partner and father. The premise of this approach is that if we ensure access to high-quality education and provide adequate support for positive development, young fathers will become and remain constructively engaged with their families. For example, the Workforce Investment Act, also signed into law by Bill Clinton, was designed to provide young, disadvantaged men with decent job opportunities so they could support themselves and their families. The fact that Bill Clinton advocated for strong social supports and harsh anticrime laws may seem contradictory, but it's not. Most politicians see both approaches as necessary functions of the government. When based on good science and solid principles of justice, these approaches can work in tandem to ensure the health and safety of our society and create the conditions for stable family relationships. Both approaches help young men stay dutifully and constructively invested in school, work, and family.

However, neither of these approaches is sufficient to help fathers remain constructively connected to their families when personal or interpersonal problems emerge and interfere. Under some circumstances, fathers need something besides a carrot or a stick. In this section of the book, we have introduced a few fathers who were not able to stay connected with their families because they were derailed by problems they encountered in themselves. We also introduced some fathers who were able to stay connected with their families, despite the occurrence of similar problems. The contrast between these two sets of fathers suggests that connected fathers have something that the disconnected fathers lost, or perhaps never had. This binding force enabled Brian (one of the fathers from Chapter 10 with problematic substance use) to seize the opportunity—precipitated by Brandy walking out on him—to change his behavior and rebuild their relationship on more solid ground. It helped Jerome (the reactively aggressive father from Chapter 9) maintain his composure and self-control within the context of his tumultuous relationship with Ebony. It helped William (from Chapter 11)—while still stuck in jail—to stay constructively focused on his relationship with Phyllis and Rasheed, despite feeling defeated. Something enabled these men to learn from their mistakes and deal with their unfortunate circumstances. In the remaining chapters of this book, we examine the nature of this capacity to bond and stay bonded, and we propose a plan for creating institutional supports to help fathers learn to make their connections stick, particularly when social, personal, and interpersonal problems interfere.

PART FOUR

The Good-Enough Father

CHAPTER 14
Families Redefined

In Part Three, we discussed how fathers become disengaged from parenthood, sometimes on their own accord, sometimes because they are removed from their children by the state, and sometimes because they are expelled by their partner. In this section, we discuss how fathers connect or bond with their families, how our thinking about the father–child connection has changed over the years, and what those changes might mean as we move forward. In our culture—and in many cultures—a mother's bond to her children is regarded as biologically driven, built into our make-up as a species. It's been said in many different ways that "mother and child" are integrally connected, that they function as a unit, that babies cannot survive—physically or psychologically—without their mothers, or at least a mother substitute.

What about fathers? Fathers, we are told, have played the role of provider for thousands of years, first as hunters and now as laborers on the farm or in the factory or at the office. The bond between father and child has been underplayed in our cultural lexicon of myths and symbols. Looking back, there are no statues or portraits of Joseph and Baby Jesus, no iconic images of fathers carrying children on their backs or fathers comforting babies in distress. Those images, rendered as testimony to the strength of the human bond, are all about mothers and motherhood. Until recently, fathers were often portrayed separately or peripherally, if at all. In addition to being the providers, they were also viewed as protectors and sometimes commanders, but they were always depicted as standing apart from the intimacy of the mother–child bond. This does not mean that fathers were not bonded to their children, just that the father–child bond has been portrayed as an uncertain, unstable entity, more susceptible than the mother–child bond to weakening or breaking. Historically, this might be justified by the fact that a father could never (until recently) be sure that a child was indeed *his*, but that fact alone does not fully explain why we came to regard the father–child connection as so different from—and inferior to—the mother–child connection. Whether or not human beings invented marriage to keep families intact and ensure that fathers would stick around and continue to help out is impossible to know for sure. However, for a long time, it seemed to serve that function.

For thousands of years, marriage has been an effective strategy for ensuring that children will be cared for by their parents, particularly their fathers. Over many generations, we developed systems and infrastructure—laws, religious doctrines, and social organizations—to make sure people get married and stay married for as long as possible. Religious beliefs and social norms compelled, enticed, and cajoled young men and women to agree to a legal (and often spiritual) arrangement that would ensure that their children have the resources they needed to become healthy adults. Marriage stabilized the family by keeping men bound to their wives and by keeping women focused on producing and taking care of their children.[a] Setting aside all notions of love and romance, traditional marriage asked men to restrain their tendency to wander away from their families and asked women to subjugate themselves in the interest of keeping men invested in breadwinning. From this perspective, marriage can be viewed as a great compromise that domesticated men and women into distinct, complementary roles.[1-3] This is, of course, an oversimplification of what marriage is about or how marital relationships actually transpired, and there are probably millions of examples of how marriage is far more egalitarian than what we just suggested. However, in several of the major religious traditions—Jewish, Christian, and Muslim—women were expected to "obey" their husbands, who were expected to be the heads of the household.

Because the world (with very few exceptions) was fundamentally patriarchal, marriage favored the fortunes of men over women. Husbands were given extensive legal control over their wives' property and social control over their wives' behavior. Married women were largely prevented from exercising their autonomy or realizing their talents. This is not to say that

---

a. Anthropologists and historians might point out that women in many societies, including our own, have always done much more than tend to the children. Women have always worked in the fields and the factories and the home, and their husbands benefited from that sort of labor too.

marriage was entirely bad for women, but one could easily make the case that the balance of power between husband and wife was not fair, and many women's rights advocates have made that case over the years, to good effect. Remarkably, the institution has worked, more or less. The research indicates that married people, on average, are better able to manage the interpersonal challenges of raising children; they also tend to be healthier and are more likely to live longer than unmarried people.[4-6] Children with married parents tend to function better and are more likely to be securely attached than children in unmarried households.[7] Even when couples divorce, marriage helps, as the legal nature of the break-up tends to keep fathers more regularly engaged with the children, relative to fathers who were never married.[8]

Why does marriage have this bonding influence? Those who are religious might say that the strength of the marital bond comes from God. But, for those who regard marriage purely as a social institution, the source of its power is more puzzling. Marriage advocates believe that the institution of marriage works because it formally and officially entwines us in a social context, which helps us feel secure and work toward stability. The institution of marriage seems to have weight, and in this respect, it acts like the ballast used to help wobbly ships stay upright in choppy waters. We are, after all, fundamentally social creatures and much of our success as a species can be attributed to our ability to come together and form packs and pacts. For many people, marriage is seen as fundamental to being human. The fact that so many couples are opting out of marriage in contemporary society is thus regarded as an ominous sign that humanity is in trouble.

Although it's difficult to know why people began to have more liberal views regarding marriage and divorce, it is certainly the case that the rate of divorce increased dramatically after divorce laws were liberalized in the 1970s. And, as divorce rates increased, marriage rates decreased.[9-11] As people understood they had choices—to marry or not, to divorce or not—they began to make use of these choices. In a nation built on principles of equity and individual rights, it is possible to see much of American history as a slow steady march toward the realization of those principles and the subsequent liberalization of social mores. Despite our nation's track record of discriminatory policies and practices, there is little doubt that the women's rights movement made substantial gains in the last 100 years. Over time, it became apparent that women's roles across multiple institutions, including marriage, were too restrictive, thwarting ambition and wasting intelligence. Something had to give.

While the issue of women's rights may seem tangential to the development of young fathers, we think it has played an important, catalytic role in the rise of unwed parenthood and the displacement of some fathers in the workforce, forcing young men to redefine their roles as men and as parents. Such a statement might suggest that we are about to bemoan the women's rights movement, but that is not the case. Hopefully, this will be apparent by the end of this chapter.

WOMEN'S RIGHTS AND THE EVOLUTION OF FAMILY

Starting in the 19th century, a relatively small group of women began to push hard for more rights, more opportunity, and more autonomy.[12] In 1900, women were given the right to be financially independent from their husbands, and, in 1920, they were given the right to vote. In the early 1900s, upper-middle-class white women had access to higher education, but their educational opportunities were restricted to those domains regarded as acceptable for women, namely teaching and home economics (which meant cooking and child development). It took a long time before women had equal access to *all* the educational opportunities available to men in the United States, and some would argue that access is still being denied. Nonetheless, education has been a bridge to equal rights, and it was within the context of colleges and universities that women could push the boundaries of what was considered proper for women to do and think.

Relative to higher education, equity in the workplace has been a tougher nut to crack. While the fight for equal rights began in the early 20th century, it was not until 1963 that women were granted—at least in principle—the right to receive equal pay for equal work. And it was not until 1964 that women were assured access to employment opportunities previously reserved for men. As women gained access to better jobs, they achieved much more autonomy and control over their own lives. Prior to the 1960s, many women worked but most had low-paying jobs that allowed for relatively little advancement. With the passage of the Equal Pay Act and the Civil Rights Act, this began to change. The percentage of women entering the workforce rose from about 38 percent in 1960 to about 58 percent in 2014.[13,14] But, even more important, starting in the mid-1990s, more women began graduating from college than men. Currently, women are 21 percent more likely than men to graduate from college and 48 percent more likely to attend graduate school.[15] In 2018, half of the students enrolled in medical school and 53 percent enrolled in law school were women.[16,17]

Even in a growing economy, the number of available jobs (particularly high-paying jobs that can sustain a family) will depend on the percentage

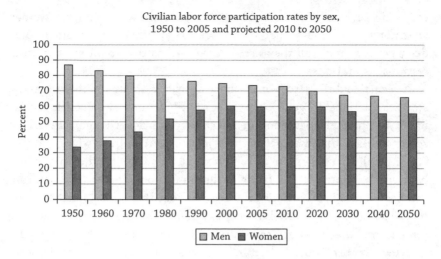

Civilian labor force participation rates by sex,
1950 to 2005 and projected 2010 to 2050

Figure 14.1 Changing trends in labor force participation by men and women
From: Bureau of Labor Statistics. Changes in men's and women's labor force participation rates. https://
www.bls.gov/opub/ted/2007/jan/wk2/art03.htm. Published January 10, 2007.

of the population in the workforce. As long as gender roles remained divided and men had an advantage in the labor market, they did not need to compete with women for the same jobs.[b] Not surprisingly, increased equality for women was tightly correlated with diminished economic security for men, particularly undereducated and unskilled men. As more women entered the workforce, expecting equity, the competition for attractive jobs stiffened. And, as women became more vested and competitive, some men were edged out of the workforce or into different types of jobs.[13,14,18,19] Figure 14.1, taken from the Bureau of Labor Statistics, illustrates this trend in broad strokes. In 1950, 32 percent of women were employed, compared to 87 percent of men. In 2010, 60 percent of women were employed compared to 72 percent of men. These changes in the rates of employed women and men are not independent. As the workplace became less restrictive for women, it became more challenging for men, who were suddenly competing with their wives and their sisters.

During this same time period, new forms of birth control were developed that put women in charge of their own reproductive powers. The invention and distribution of the birth control pill and the intrauterine device (IUD) gave women a measure of sexual and reproductive self-determination hitherto unknown. Prior to this, condoms (and coitus interruptus) were the

b. And of course, women are still fighting to achieve equal pay for equal work in a world in which men are often still given an unfair advantage.

only widely available form of contraception, which meant that many women were not able to choose whether or when to have children. If women could delay getting pregnant, they were in a better position to pursue their professional aspirations.

It seems doubtful that women make decisions about whether to marry, stay in a relationship, get a job, or have a baby just to make a political statement. Yet, personal decisions are affected by political change. Similarly, it seems unlikely that men get married just to control their wives, but in a "traditional" marriage, a man could expect to be the head of his household and in control of his family. A husband's position of assumed control helped him deal with his insecurities about the world "out there" and maybe some of his internal insecurities too. As women began to achieve more rights, the "marriage compromise" began to unravel because its underlying premise (what is "natural" for men and women) became obsolete. The women's rights movement was not anti-male or anti-marriage, but its emphasis on equal access to opportunity challenged some implicit assumptions about the role of men and women in our society and the nature of masculinity and femininity.

This does not mean that marriage is moot, obsolete, or even fading. There are plenty of indicators that marriage is alive and holding its ground, at least in some respects. Many of the men and women in our studies say they hope to get married someday. Illustrating this point, in a recent nationally representative survey about marriage, 66 percent of young men and women under the age of 30 said they valued marriage, and 58 percent said they hoped to get married someday.[20] These statistics would suggest that the "marriage glass" is still at least half-full. It seems likely—almost certain—that some people will continue to marry and stay married. But it is also the case that young men and women no longer feel that getting married is *necessary* and are prone to take a "let's wait and see what happens" approach, even after discovering an unplanned pregnancy. Perhaps this reflects prudent judgment, based on their age and lack of experience with relationships.

Fifty years ago, the decision facing young men and women was *whom* to marry. In the 21st century, young people face the additional question of *whether* to marry. What was once regarded as a social and cultural expectation is now seen as a personal choice. Marriage still looks pretty good to most young men and women, but in the same previously cited Pew survey, 34 percent of those surveyed said that marriage is an "obsolete institution" and 48 percent said marriage was probably not right for them, not their first choice. While 71 percent believed that children needed to be raised by both parents, 54 percent believed that cohabitation without marriage is an acceptable arrangement for raising children.

In their book, *Promises I Can Keep*, Kathryn Edin and Maria Kefalas interviewed young unwed mothers and asked why they did not get married before having a child.[21] The most frequent answer given was that they were not ready to make that kind of commitment to their child's father. For these young women, having a child out of wedlock feels less risky than marrying a man they aren't quite sure about, even if they love him. This response rings true to anyone who has spent time talking with young unwed parents, and it says a great deal about how the fabric of our society is woven differently than the fabric of our grandparents' generation. For one thing, the era of the "shotgun marriage" is long gone; accidental pregnancies are no longer morally compelling events, requiring a couple to get married. It's also true that some men and women are reluctant to make long-term commitments because the marriages they have observed have not been particularly inspiring.

THE TRANSFORMATION OF FAMILY

If marriage has become less compelling (and therefore less "adhesive"), then the question arises: Are there other viable ways to create stable and secure families? In her book *Mothers and Others*, Sarah Hrdy proposed that human beings have always utilized a collaborative approach to child-rearing to help ensure that babies are not left to depend solely on their mothers, who, in turn, are not left to depend solely on their partners.[22] Drawing parallels to primate societies, where mother monkeys routinely receive help from other members of their community, Hrdy believes that human mothers are designed to enlist the support of others, including other father figures. She does not discount the central role of fathers, noting that most mothers also rely on their support, but she suggests that mothers throughout history and across cultures have long recognized that the "nuclear family" is not always the safest bet. Although Hrdy's human research focuses on far away cultures, such as the Yanomamo in Venezuela and the Ache of Paraguay, she is clearly addressing a Western audience and making an important point about family life in the 21st century. Indeed, Hrdy describes how women in other cultures use a variety of strategies for managing and responding to the uncertainties that threaten their children's survival. This may involve flirtations with other men, designed to keep them interested as potential father replacements, and looking to extended family members for support.

Hrdy's work challenges us to consider how traditional family roles and structures may be impeding our ability to adapt to changing social and economic circumstances. Without marriage, how can we create stable and secure families that produce psychologically healthy children? The dynamics of family life—including the fundamental structure of relationships between mothers, fathers, and children—have changed quite dramatically over the past several decades, concretely evident in the widening diversity of family types. This diversity is celebrated by some who see the traditional family as too constrictive and protested by others who worry that some of this diversity is dysfunctional, doing a disservice to children.

Although our definitions of family continue to change, the fundamental goals of co-parenting and parenting have remained relatively constant over time because children's essential emotional needs have not changed. The problem is that meeting those goals is more complicated because family relationships are more fluid and complex in 21st-century America than they were in the mid-20th century. Young men and women today are confronted with relationship challenges that require a level of interpersonal understanding and skill that many don't have. Not yet.

Frank Furstenberg, a sociologist at the University of Pennsylvania who spent much of his long career studying young mothers and fathers, recently pointed out that the family is always evolving and adapting to rapidly changing social, cultural, and economic forces.[23] Somewhat surprisingly, Furstenberg seems nonplussed about the current changes that are occurring between men and women, recognizing that there may be hidden value in more flexible definitions of father, mother, and family.

> I see this process of uncoupling and recoupling of discrete elements of marriage, family, and kinship as inevitable as the family system in different social strata adapts to changing economic, cultural, and social conditions. Whether this means that the institution of marriage and family is "declining" in importance . . . is in my view still an open and unsettled question.[23p206]

As Furstenberg suggests, families can—and will—change to meet new challenges and opportunities, including dramatic changes to our economy. Fortunately, the capacity to be flexible is built into our DNA. A father's ability to adequately support his child's development may depend on how flexible we (as a society) can be about defining *and supporting* a wider range of father roles. Without necessarily rejecting the idea of father as provider and protector, we can still support viable alternatives. The gradual changes in social roles for men and women (subsequent to women achieving more rights) raised new questions about the nature of masculinity and the essence of fathering in our collective consciousness. It is hard to know if our perception that fathering—for most of history and in most cultures—has been about breadwinning and protecting is an accurate reflection of reality or just perception. Whatever the case may be, it wasn't until the 1960s that scholars began to seriously question and study the nature of fatherhood at all.

CHAPTER 15

Discovering Fatherhood

Prior to the 1960s, there was not much interest in fathers within the scientific community, except among anthropologists who, in the early part of the 20th century, conducted research on cultural differences in family structure.[a] It was not that fathers were regarded as irrelevant. Rather, the role of fathers in society was so obvious, so fixed, and so dominant that they were taken for granted by the scientific community. After all, prior to the 1960s, they *were* the scientific community. And, from their perspective, it didn't seem that that there was much to study; there was no problem to solve. That fatherhood became a problem worth studying had much to do with the gradually increasing consciousness of gender roles and inequities, as women began to exercise their newly acquired rights and take advantage of new opportunities. Researchers began to ask some very basic, angst-ridden questions about the purpose that fathers played in the lives of their children, by comparing families with and without fathers. In the beginning, this research on fathers was mostly about confirming that fathers were relevant, often by focusing on the effects of father absence. Some of this early research on fathering was designed to understand how fathers help boys become *men,* in line with current norms of masculinity, and the risk that father absence posed to the formation of gender roles.

For example, Joan McCord was a well-regarded developmental psychologist who conducted several landmark studies of family development. In the

---

a. For an example, see the book by Bronislaw Malinowski (an early 20th-century anthropologist) entitled *The Father in Primitive Psychology.*[1] In that book, among other things, Malinowski highlights that, although the role of fathers varied across cultures, some notion of "father" seemed ubiquitous.

late 1950s and early 1960s, McCord tested the popular theory at the time that children in father-absent homes would become more feminine and veer in the direction of homosexuality compared to boys in father-present households.[2] In contrast to boys from father-absent homes, she theorized that boys from father-present homes would be more aggressive and less dependent (e.g., more *independent* in an era when this was regarded as a masculine trait). In a now obscured study of boys from intact and "broken" homes, McCord found that the boys without fathers were actually *more* "aggressive" and *not* more dependent or feminine, defying expectations. However, McCord concluded that these father-deprived boys were more "feminine aggressive," which was purportedly aggression intended to cover over an underlying femininity.[2] If this seems confusing, we would agree. In the 1950s and 1960s when terms like "feminine" were used to describe men, or when "masculine" was used to describe a woman—in typically un-flattering or disapproving ways—the underlying logic was more than a little convoluted. The most interesting aspect of this research is the ap-parent angst about slippage in the gender identity of boys in father-absent homes, linked to a foreboding (that seemed to be circulating "in the air") that the traditional position of fathers in the lives of their children was precarious.

Following McCord, in the 1970s, Thomas Power and Ross Parke began studying the gender socialization of boys and girls by their mothers and fathers. Specifically, Power and Parke conducted a series of observational studies indicating that fathers and mothers shape the gender of their children throughout infancy and childhood.[3–5] This process, they found, begins even before birth, as they imagine what their sons or daughters will be like and as they begin to characterize their respective parent–child relationships. In large measure, Power and Parke can be credited with put-ting fatherhood research on the map, as they were among the first to doc-ument fathers' distinct contribution to the development of children. Their findings indicated that children whose fathers engaged in warm, reciprocal, give-and-take play tend to have better social relationships with their peers, smoother transitions to school, and overall higher levels of social compe-tence. Parke and Power's research on fathers' play and the importance of balancing warm, autonomy-giving behavior with gentle guidance (when needed) has been replicated many times over. They were also among the first to suggest that how we shape our children's gender identity is a de-liberate and somewhat contrived process, heavily influenced by cultural beliefs about what is appropriate or acceptable. In making us more aware of how we impose stereotypic gender roles on our sons and daughters very early in their lives, these researchers also introduced a measure of uncertainty about *why* we were doing that.

DIFFERENT MODELS OF FATHERHOOD

In the early 1980s, after Ross Parke and Thomas Power laid the groundwork for the objective analysis of fathering behavior, Michael Lamb, Joseph Pleck, Eric Charnov, and James Levine developed the first full-fledged model of fatherhood designed to describe the social and psychological functions of fathers.[6] What came to be known as the Lamb–Pleck model described fatherhood in terms of three components: *engagement, availability,* and *responsibility.*[6,7]

These researchers defined "father engagement" as direct contact with the child through caretaking and shared activities. This term refers to the many ways that a father spends time with his child and, presumably, the quality of those interactions. "Availability" was defined as the *potential* for engaging with his child or supporting the child's mother. This concept reflects the fact that when fathers are not directly engaged in child-rearing they are often lurking on the periphery and available to help, if needed. "Responsibility" was defined as either providing necessary resources, like food and shelter, or arranging for the provision of such resources, like medical care. This component of fatherhood involves the "behind the scenes" work that ensures a child's needs are met. Responsibility is often interpreted to mean financial support, but it also involves role-modeling adult male behavior, so that a child understands what it means to be a responsible, respectable man. This framework provided a broader view of fatherhood in that it does not specify exactly how fathers are supposed to engage with their children, make themselves available, or be responsible, just that these broadly defined constructs are important to understand the role of fathers in child development.

This broader framework, as reflected in the Lamb–Pleck fatherhood model, also seemed to reflect the reality that fathers' roles were changing and that fathers were becoming more directly involved in childcare and child-rearing. Indeed, research examining the amount of time that fathers spend with their children over the last several decades reveals substantial increases in paternal involvement on many different indexes, at least among fathers who live with their children. For example, among married fathers in the United States (for whom we have much more data than unmarried and nonresident fathers), the average number of hours per week spent in routine childcare activities more than doubled between 1965 and

2000, from roughly 3 hours per week to 7 hours. And, fathers' involvement in interactive or "enrichment" activities, including helping/teaching, reading/talking, and playing, was 94 percent higher in 2000, compared to the 1965 level of 1.3 hours per week.[8,b]

An important point here is that the various social and economic changes that have led to the transformation of family (as discussed in the previous chapter) entail notable shifts in the division of labor as well as gender roles of mothers and fathers. In turn, these changes have led to significant changes in the ideals and standards for fathers. So, as mothers' educational and occupational roles have expanded, the role of fathers has also expanded beyond simply that of "breadwinner" to that of "caregiver" and "nurturing co-parent."[9-11] Thus, contemporary norms of fatherhood as reflected by fatherhood models (such as the Lamb–Pleck model and others that followed it) entail increased expectations of involvement in the care of children, in addition to the traditional role of financial provider.[12-14]

Over the next 25 years, Lamb and Pleck continuously updated their model of fatherhood, clarifying what they meant by father engagement, underscoring that *how* fathers help their children get dressed, use a spoon, play make-believe, or settle down before going to sleep matters as much as *whether* they engage in these activities. These sorts of activities are important to a child's development, but they also provide fathers with the opportunity to bond with their children and to help their children feel cared for by them. It's also important to note that attunement and responsivity do not always mean providing a child with whatever he or she wants. Sometimes, it can mean saying "No more ice cream," "Stop hitting the dog," or "It's time to quiet down and go to sleep." In other words, positive father engagement often involves providing structure and setting limits.

While researchers like Parke, Lamb, and Pleck were building a theoretical foundation for the study of fatherhood as a legitimate focus of scientific research, other researchers and policymakers took a more advocacy-oriented approach, organized around fatherhood promotion. This later group, led by William Doherty at the University of Minnesota (and later the Doherty Relationship Institute), zeroed in on the notion of "responsibility" and defined the "responsible father" as being emotionally and financially

b. Some researchers have noted that changes in women's behavior have also contributed to the narrowing of the gender gap between mothers and fathers. In fact, the rate of change in women's behavior has been greater than the change in men's behavior. Fathers are doing a little more of what mothers once did, while mothers are doing much more of what fathers once did. Nonetheless, we don't want to diminish the findings that, on average, fathers have become more engaged in childcare.

prepared to support a child, willing to establish legal paternity, and able to participate actively in childcare.[15] Concerned about the growing numbers of young unwed fathers, Doherty and other responsible fatherhood advocates, acknowledging the moral undertones of this perspective, extorted men to not have children before they were ready and then to fully embrace their role as fathers when the time arrived. With a primary focus on financial responsibility, Doherty's model of fatherhood recognized that if fathers are to become responsible, they need help and resources. This means employment opportunities and social supports, including support from their co-parenting partner. When such opportunities and supports weren't readily available, fathers would need to be more self-reliant and determined. The Doherty model spawned a generation of "responsible fatherhood" programs that emphasized fathers as breadwinners, husbands, and role models, the very type of programs that have been continuously funded by the federal US government since the mid-1990s. Whether or not this is a good use of funding is a point we come back to in Part Six.

Doherty and his colleagues point out that the research on father involvement has tended to focus on fathers' in-person interactions with children rather than the provision of economic support.[15] While these authors do not dismiss the importance of fathers' direct interactions with children, they assert that the quality of a father's interactions with his child is associated with the "father's success, real or perceived, as a breadwinner."[15p283] In support of this, Doherty cites evidence that unemployment, as well as self-reported inadequacies in providing for one's family, is associated with adverse impacts on fathers' parenting behaviors, over and above the impact on mothering.

As society grappled with shifting gender roles and the increasing complexity of family structures, fatherhood scholars were split into two main camps. Some fatherhood scholars emphasized traditional fatherhood roles and quantitative measures of father engagement, such as how much time and money fathers spend taking care of their children. Other researchers were interested in discovering what could be described as the "softer" side of fathering and focused on the quality of fathers' caregiving. Interestingly, Lamb and Pleck revised the *responsibility* component their model to be more explicit that, from their perspective, responsibility is much more than breadwinning.[7] In their revised model, they explained that father responsibility involves a wide range of *indirect* activities to ensure a child's material and social needs are met and requires a proactive approach, anticipating their child's needs before they become urgent. This might include buying and/or arranging for childcare, healthcare, and education, managing their child's peer relations, or advocating for their child at school.

In a deliberate effort to change the fatherhood conversation, William Marsiglio and Kevin Roy published *Nurturing Dads* in 2012.[16] In describing the purpose of this book, Marsiglio and Roy note that they are shifting the view of what it means to be a good father from a focus on "material contributions and a presumption of marriage" to a focus on "relationships that include a close father–child bond, as well as a new style of co-parenting in which fathers and mothers negotiate how care is to be provided for their children."[16p3] As is clear from the title of this book, nurturance is regarded as the central feature of good fathering, which includes hands-on caregiving, developmentally appropriate responsiveness, and an underlying commitment to fatherhood, regardless of the status of any romantic involvement with the mother of one's child. Furthermore, these aspects of fathering are seen as much more important than one's biological or legal status as a father. Just as Doherty's responsible fathering model does not dismiss the importance of fathers' positive emotional involvement, Marsiglio's nurturing model does not devalue the importance of fathers' financial contributions to their children. However, Marsiglio and Roy do criticize policies and programs that maintain what they describe as a "father-as-wallet" mentality and prioritize fathers' payment of child support *over* the development of a positive, emotional bond with their children. In fact, Marsiglio and Roy argue that nurturance is more likely to lead to economic support for one's child than the other way around. In other words, a father who develops a strong bond with his child is more likely to be motivated to provide financially for his child's needs, whereas a father whose connection to his child is primarily financial (particularly if the economic support is forced) is not necessarily likely to forge a positive father–child bond.

MODELS OF FATHERHOOD AND SOCIOCULTURAL CONTEXT

We have already alluded to the fact that fatherhood scholars regard fathers as being embedded in time, place, and circumstance. For example, none of the models we just reviewed assume that fathers are necessarily living under the same roof as their children or involved in a romantic relationship with their child's mother. Indeed, these researchers recognize that concepts like "responsibility" or "engagement" should be loose fitting, so they can be usefully applied to understanding and supporting fathers in different circumstances. Because the role of fathers can vary across culture and context, several fatherhood scholars, most notably Natasha Cabrera, have proposed models for understanding fathering that are explicit about the social embeddedness of fathers and fatherhood.[17] These scholars emphasize the dynamic interplay between a father's history and personal characteristics, his relationships with his family and partner, his culture and cultural identity, and his position in society, which can help enhance or seriously impede his ability to function as a father.

This perspective, emphasizing the interplay between a father's own personal experiences and other social and cultural influences, is consistent with our own studies of young fathers. Perhaps nowhere is this more evident than in the responses of young fathers to our interviews, which reveal their own personal "models" of fatherhood.

FATHERS' OWN "MODELS" OF FATHERHOOD

In our research interviews, we ask expectant fathers a few questions intended to elicit their own theories of fatherhood, such as "What do you think a father should be like?" and "How do you picture yourself as a father?" These questions draw responses based on a young men's own experiences of having been fathered and on their culturally informed beliefs about fatherhood. And their responses suggest that what they expect from themselves as fathers and how they define a "good father" extends beyond being a good breadwinner. For example, when asked about their biggest priority as a father, "being there" for their children is the most common response among the fathers (and fathers-to-be) in our studies, which is consistent with what other father researchers are reporting.[11] When Robert, the young father from Chicago whom we introduced in Chapter 1, was asked "What should a father be like?" he responded with a calm certainty:

> To be there. Whatever the baby . . . whatever the baby needs of you, the father has to be there. No matter what, I will be there if the baby needs me; I will be there no matter what it is. I won't let nothing stop me from being there for my baby.

Robert's father was divorced from his mother, but he was still quite involved in Robert's upbringing, and there isn't a single note of bitterness in Robert's description of the ideal father. By contrast, we often hear a young man's emphasis on the importance of "being there" against the backdrop of a childhood marked by an absent or abusive father. Some of the young men in our studies are painfully explicit about how a father should *not* behave. Jed, the burly Salt Lake City father who had been abused by his father, was impressively reflective as he conveyed his views of fatherhood to Keith, who interviewed him.

JED: I don't think the father should be head of the household. It should be the mother and the father together. All the fathers that I've seen will not accept anything other than what they say is right. All the fathers I've seen either don't care or they don't love enough. If my father would have loved us enough, then he would have never abused us. He would not have felt the urge to hurt us if he loved us like he said he did. He always told us he loved us, and it was very confusing because, even when I was young, I realized if that was true, he would've never done what he did. It was very confusing. I think a father should love his children. He should be firm, and he should set an example, and he should provide for the family. You know, I think providing is nurturing not just the financial needs, but being there for the family to care for them. Even a simple thing . . . like, I would value more than anything, more than all the money in the world, I would like to be able to say, "Dad, come help me fix my car." A father should be loving with his family.

KEITH: Any other specific qualities stick out in your mind as far as what a father should be like?

JED: There's an interesting country song that I really like, it's, uh, "You got to be strong enough to bend." Only the trees that are strong enough to bend survive. If you're not strong enough to accept looking at the other person's point of view, you're just going to break, you won't bend. You won't survive the storm. I really believe that's an important part of being a father.

When it comes to traditional views of fatherhood, of course, two mainstays of the father's role in the family have been that of provider as well as that of "moral compass" or role model. With regard to these two issues, our interviews with young fathers are interesting in that the responses are yet again consistent with a pattern of shifting and broadening standards of fatherhood. First, when describing what it means to be a good father, any mention of providing or being a role model (and/or the primary disciplinarian in the family) is conspicuously absent from many of the young fathers' responses. Second, when either or both of these characteristics are mentioned, which they were by several fathers in our studies, these roles were nearly always mentioned together with an emphasis on involvement or nurturing, in addition to providing or being a good role model. For example, when we asked Darnel (the father who was an active co-parent with Cleo, despite no longer staying together) what he thought a father should be like, he said:

I basically think that [a father] should . . . try his best to provide for his family and give 'em a place to live, and food to eat . . . as well as spend time with his family—know what I'm sayin'? He can't be basically about working, working, working, and not home with his family, with his kids.

So, while some expectant fathers emphasize the "provider" role and/or the role of "moral compass," many underscore that the "softer" aspects of fathering also matter, and many believe that those aspects matters most. Take Steve, for example, the Salt Lake City father we introduced in Chapter 5, who, like Darnel, speaks directly to the importance of paternal warmth without disregarding more "traditional" father roles.

DAVE: What should a father be like?
STEVE: Nice, understanding, always there. Um, ready to deal with problems, help their wife any way they can, um, just loving.
DAVE: How do you picture your role as a father?
STEVE: I picture myself. . . . I'm going to have fun with my kids, but I also want to make sure they're taught right. Make sure they don't make the same mistakes I did. I'll try to make them better than I am. That's probably my goal right there, just to make them better than me in every way I can.

SUMMARY OF FATHERHOOD MODELS

There is still disagreement about how exactly to define fatherhood or what to expect from fathers. Yet, there is a general consensus that our notions of what it means to be a good father have become more complex, more varied, perhaps more flexible. Although most family researchers would probably agree that fathers and mothers still tend to occupy different roles, we can no longer think of these roles as distinctively feminine or masculine, emerging from some biologically innate skill or trait. When examining all the different models of fatherhood together, along with the corresponding research on predictors of child developmental outcomes, we would argue that four major dimensions of fatherhood emerge as particularly important.

(1) *Positive engagement in caregiving*, which includes involvement in various aspects of caregiving (e.g., basic childcare activities, playing) including those activities that have been described as enriching activities (e.g., conversing, reading, and teaching). As previously discussed,

there should be an emphasis on the word "positive," indicating that the quality of how a father engages with his children is more important than quantity of time he spends engaged. Nevertheless, quantity is not trivial, and spending at least a minimum amount of time is necessary to establish and maintain a positive relationship with one's child.

(2) *Providing a stable, consistent, and secure environment* by helping to provide routines, setting up comforting structures, and gently reinforcing expectations that support development. This dimension is characterized by a balanced combination of warmth/responsiveness and structured guidance, which might include calm but firm limit-setting.

(3) *Nurturing*, which includes patience or allowing children to go at their own pace, a demonstrated desire to be involved and engaged as a parent (even if there are external barriers to that involvement), and explicit caring behaviors, like giving a warm hug or preparing a healthy meal. Generally, nurturance involves taking the lead in establishing a positive, reciprocal bond with a child so that he or she feels loved and accepted.

(4) *Responsibility*, which entails ensuring that a child's various needs are met, with whatever resources are available (economic and otherwise). When it comes to young fathers (who typically have limited economic resources and do not yet have established careers or work histories), we would argue that paternal responsibility is sometimes demonstrated by *future-oriented* choices and behaviors that result in short-term sacrifices to achieve long-term benefits. For example, a young father who works fewer hours to earn his high school diploma or GED, with the goal of being able to provide more for his family in the future, could be judged to be demonstrating responsibility. The same could be said for a father who joins the military to provide for his family, even though that may result in a short-term decrease in caregiving while he is away for basic training.

If we were to try to construct a grand theory of fatherhood based on the sum total of all these various models, the ideal father would be working and providing financial support for his children, actively involved in the routines of childcare, warmly engaged in teaching and playing with his children, helping to monitor his children's activities and provide guidance and discipline when necessary, and functioning as a role model by holding himself to a high level of integrity. This seems like an impossible set-up. The image of an *ideal* father who does it all may not be helpful for fathers, particularly young fathers, with limited employment opportunities, unsupportive family members, and/or the lack of any positive role models of what it means to be a father. The ideal father will seem like an impossible proposition, perhaps more demoralizing than inspirational.

Even if we were to apply any *one* of these models of fatherhood to the young fathers we've worked with, most would not stack up. For example, the idea of being responsible, accessible, and engaged (as specified by the Lamb–Pleck model) seems like a reasonable place to begin defining basic standards of fatherhood, but most of the fathers we have studied and worked with over the past 20 years would not rate very highly when it comes to being responsible, accessible, *and* engaged. So, what do we make of a father who is nurturing but unable to provide financial support for his child? What about a father who is a good provider but spends little time with his child? Many fathers we've worked with would probably score in the positive range on being responsible, accessible, *or* engaged. Is that good enough?

These are not easy questions to answer. At the same time, we believe that these are important questions to ask. And we think that attempting to answer them will lead us to a more nuanced and diverse understanding of the role that fathers can occupy in the lives of their children, highlighted by the different emphases of these formal models of fatherhood, as well as fathers' own ideas about what it means to be a good father.

CHAPTER 16

A Tale of (Another) Two Fathers

I t's relatively easy to define good and bad fathers at the outside margins. Bad fathers are absent, neglectful, or abusive. Good fathers are present, nurturing, and responsible. However, the fact is that many fathers operate in the middle, often changing over time, depending on several factors, including their relationship with their partner (and possibly other partners), how well they are managing their lives, how well the world is treating them, and often the characteristics of the child.

JAMES AND EDDIE

James was only 15 years old when he found out he was going to be a father. As a white kid in in Melrose Park, Illinois, a mostly white middle-class suburban community to the west of Chicago, he felt like an outlier. When we caught up with him about two-and-a-half years later, he was living with his girlfriend Stephanie, his son Cody, and Stephanie's mother in the middle-class neighborhood of Naperville. James was working for a company that delivers office supplies, and he proudly told us that, in the last 18 months, he had been promoted from "just being a dock guy to a dock supervisor, to driving supervisor, and now the manager." He was working about 70 hours per week, starting work at 3 AM and finishing up around 5 PM. Recently, he started attending high school classes in the evenings, hoping to graduate soon. After receiving multiple raises from his promotions—especially his most recent promotion to manager—James tells us that his financial situation at home is "comfortable." They have enough money to pay the bills, with a little left over for "fun stuff" and extra things. In a couple of years,

James anticipates being able to afford a new pick-up truck, maybe even a pair of jet skis.

When Simon asked James to describe himself as a father, he said:

> I'm the supporter . . . I'm getting' the money for 'em so he's got what he wants and he's got what he needs. He's pretty well off. I mean, honestly, Steph does a lot of the work and I just kinda come home and play with him a little bit. I'm kinda the good guy. I just come home and play with him a little bit. You know, give 'em a bath every once in a while. I mean, I'm lucky if I see him an hour or two during the week, 'cause most of the time I come home, I'm just dead tired or gotta go to school. So, it's like, "Bye, buddy, Daddy's gotta get dressed, daddy's gotta take a shower."

When Emma interviewed Stephanie, she echoed what James reported:

> He works crazy hours—he really is hell-bent on providing for his son, and Cody has everything a kid could want. Financially, he's in complete control. His pay-check pays for everything. I haven't had a real income for quite a while—about two years.

Emma followed up and asked, "How else does he help you with the baby?" Steph responded,

> Um, he hangs out with Cody a lot during the weekend. He likes to roughhouse with Cody and bathes him every so often. He changes diapers sometimes on the weekend. And he plays with the baby just fine when he has the time.

One of the questions that we ask young fathers (and their partners) at our follow-up interviews is "In what ways would you like your relationship with your child to be different?" Without hesitation, James said, "I'd like to spend more time with him. Spend time with him, play with him, you know, share the responsibility of bathin' him, changin' his diaper, and workin', supportin' him, you know."

As we've mentioned earlier, in addition to conducting in-depth interviews with young fathers and their partners before, during, and after the transition to parenthood, we also collect data by using standardized tests and questionnaires and video recordings of parent–child play activities. Our review of James' data revealed a mix of positive and negative parenting practices. On a self-report measure that asks about specific parenting behaviors, James indicated that he regularly used physical punishment and firm (sometimes harsh) control to discipline Cody. Although his scores indicated that he was at low risk of child abuse, his gruff parenting style, which is not uncommon among young fathers, probably undermines his desire to develop a stronger bond with Cody. For example, while engaging with Cody in a puzzle activity (the same used with all of the parents in our study), James was highly controlling and used critical comments ("That's not right!") to direct his son's efforts to put the puzzles together. Although this approach is likely to undermine Cody's developing problem-solving skills and self-confidence, James also provided Cody with encouragement ("You can do it!") and guidance ("See if that piece fits over there").

Taking all the data into account, James demonstrates both strengths and weaknesses as a father. He is financially responsible and is doing a very good job at providing for his child—no small feat for an 18-year-old who hasn't yet earned a high school diploma. However, he is minimally involved in day-to-day caregiving because he is working so hard to provide for his family. Because he doesn't regularly play with Cody, James is unpracticed in the art of playing in way that can support development and be fun. Overfocused on getting the job done right, James gets too controlling. When Emma asked Stephanie how James is doing overall as a father, she describes him as a good dad who connects with his child but who sometimes seems uncertain of himself as a father, not sure how to help out.

In contrast to James, Eddie had been unemployed for over a year when we did our last follow-up interview just after his son Marcus turned 2. Like many young African American fathers in the poorest parts of Chicago, Eddie couldn't find stable employment and eventually sort of gave up. When we asked about his financial situation, Eddie told us that the "pickins are slim" and that he and LaShawndra (his girlfriend) were struggling to make ends meet. When we asked LaShawndra about money, she confirmed that the family financial situation was indeed difficult. They were primarily supported by a combination of public assistance, help from her grandfather (with whom they were living), and her minimum-wage job checking coats at the art museum in downtown Chicago. When asked if Eddie contributed financially she said: "He don't. He tries, but he can't right now." Nevertheless, LaShawndra told us that when they get really desperate for something for the baby—diapers or a winter coat—Eddie finds a way to come up with the needed item.

Although Eddie is not providing for his child financially, he spends a great deal of time with his son and is, by all reports, positively involved in taking care of him. When Mike asked Eddie how he was feeling about being a father, Eddie described his relationship with his son.

EDDIE: It's a big responsibility, you know, you got to do your job. You know, take care of that responsibility, be patient . . . that's all you have to have is patience. 'Cause, man, you got to have patience. I try to be patient and kind and very understanding 'cause that's how you have to be.

MIKE: What is the best thing about being a father?

EDDIE: To have somebody that I can truly relate to. He's mine and whatever I teach him, he's growing up to be that. You gotta be cautious around him 'cause he'll definitely pick up on my bad habits. And I do have a couple bad habits that I don't want him to pick up. He's growing up and he's going to be a smart . . . something! I'm gonna try my best, though. I'm going to do my best.

MIKE: How do you help take care of Marcus?

EDDIE: Oh, I watch him, change his diapers, make his food . . . wash him up. I dress him, comb his hair, take him outside, play with him . . . go to the store. Everything. I do everything.

MIKE: What are some of the things that you like to do with Marcus?

EDDIE: He will give me hugs and he'll be like, "Give me a hug." We'll just be walkin' down the street so, I'll just give him a hug . . . or a high five. He understand that one already.

When Lucille asked LaShawndra how Eddie helps her with Marcus, this is what she had to say:

LASHAWNDRA: Well, I go to work, so he'll take care of him, get him dressed, feed him, dress him, give him a bath, take him to the park, look at TV, put him to sleep . . . all those things.

LUCILLE: Is that every day that you're working, he'll do those things?

LASHAWNDRA: Yeah.

LUCILLE: How do you think he's doing as a father?

LASHAWNDRA: I think he doing fine. He doesn't hit his child . . . he'll babysit, he'll talk to him—he's very good about that . . . he doesn't tease his child or teach him gang things or anything like that. He talks to him right, he doesn't yell at him . . . he washes him, takes care of him, changes him, whatever need to be done.

In the video-recorded puzzle activity with Marcus, Eddie's behavior corroborated LaShawndra's descriptions. He demonstrated a high degree of warmth, encouraging and affirming Marcus rather than trying to control how his son put the puzzle together. When Marcus got stuck getting a piece to fit, Eddie gently guided his son, patiently helping him find the solution. And in his responses to our questionnaire about his parenting, Eddie scored high on nurturing and low on physical punishment and harsh control.

We think Eddie and James highlight the fact that men can fulfill their roles as fathers in very different ways. James occupies the provider role remarkably well but spends little time with Cody, leaving almost all the day-to-day caregiving to Stephanie. Eddie gets high marks as a skilled caregiver, comfortable in the role of teaching and playing, but is unable to provide for his child financially. Whether we deem Eddie or James to be a "good" father depends on how we define fatherhood.

As we noted at the beginning of this chapter, it's relatively easy to define what it means to be a "good" or "bad" father at the margins. Bad fathers are disengaged and irresponsible. Good fathers contribute to their child's material needs, actively participate in caregiving, and help build a warm, nurturing home for their child, whether the father lives there or not. In the first half of this book, we have introduced several fathers who operate at or near these margins, at least as far as their partners are concerned. But most fathers—including us—operate somewhere in the middle; they (and we) are good at some aspects of fathering and not so good at other aspects. Some fathers are mostly good at fulfilling their particular roles most of the time but make occasional mistakes, sometimes serious mistakes. Some fathers are trying hard but are still deeply flawed. Some fathers fluctuate over time, becoming better or worse, sometimes as their children grow from being infants to toddlers, to preschoolers, and so forth. Some fathers change their roles when confronted with life's challenges, such as when they lose their job or when their relationship with the child's mother goes sour, and they split up.

To further complicate the matter of what it means to be a "good" father, the standards and criteria that we use to evaluate fathers (like Eddie and James) are far from static. In fact, the role and function of fathers is thought to be more contextually bound (and therefore more dynamic) than the role and function of mothers.[1] As such, fatherhood is a moving target, as our understanding of fathers change and their roles shift over time. Indeed, in recent years, fatherhood—and the criteria used to evaluate the roles of fathers—has been a particularly *fast*-moving target, as we discussed in Chapter 7.

Much of the research and theory on fatherhood follows a particular thread of parenting and child development. And sometimes the way that fatherhood research is presented makes it seem like the authors of this or that study have discovered the essence of good fathering. In fact, fatherhood is part of a complex tapestry. Although a tapestry is clearly made up of individual threads, it is a mistake to conclude that we have identified the "essence" of fathering by garnering a collection of threads that comprise the overall tapestry. In this book, we attempt to move beyond a focus on the individual threads to shed light on the complex and intricate way in which the multiple threads are woven together.

Fathers play multiple and varied roles in their children's lives. In light of this, it is important to view fatherhood as multifaceted rather than narrowly defined.[2] Additionally, acceptable paternal roles can vary greatly from family to family and from culture to culture, which means that fathers need to be viewed as part of a broader familial and sociocultural context. As noted by Michael Lamb, "fathers and children need to be viewed as part of complex social systems (notably, the family), in which each person affects the others reciprocally, directly, and indirectly."[2p9]

Our experience in studying and working with young fathers and their families has revealed many examples of fathers who are imperfect and make mistakes but who are nevertheless faring pretty well as fathers. They hit enough of the right notes to make up for their limitations. That said, there is very little research on how a father's strength in one area of fathering compensates for his weakness in another, with respect to his child's development. We have a long way to go before we have a clear understanding of how to help men do their best as fathers, given their strengths and weaknesses. Nonetheless, we know that thinking about fathers as simply "good" or "bad" (or setting up idealistic expectations for fathers) is unlikely to be useful.

GOOD-ENOUGH FATHERING

Donald Winnicott was a British pediatrician who wrote extensively about mothering and child development. In a series of lectures that were broadcast over the BBC in the late 1940s, Winnicott coined the phrase "good enough" to describe the tension between perfect attunement and interpersonal slippage that describes a great deal of mothering within normal, healthy limits. Winnicott used the term "good enough" rather than "good" for a reason. He knew that most mothers could not possibly live up to expectations of their infants and toddlers, who want them to be perfectly attuned and completely available all the time. Indeed, Winnicott believed that the natural gap that occurs between what infants *want* and what mothers *do* actually helps to facilitate growth. The little "failures" of the mother and the little frustrations and adjustments of the child are important components of the developmental process.[3,4]

This is not to say that Winnicott had low expectations of mothers. Good-enough mothers were indeed expected to be attuned to their infants and to learn how to make thoughtful and hopefully accurate inferences about the child's inner world based on their behavioral cues. They were also expected to develop a "working model" of their child's emotional well-being, anticipate his or her needs, and assist in the regulation of their child's emotional states. What this means depends on the child's age, personality, and circumstances. Mothering involves a lot of decisions about whether to do something to calm and sooth, structure and guide, or leave alone and allow the child to develop skills on his or her own.

The good-enough mother, however, is, by definition, imperfect. The mother's primary role is to help the child adapt and engage with his or her environment, recognizing that *she* is the most important part of her child's environment. Ironically, part of the mother's role is to help her child adapt to *her as a mother*, which means that good-enough mothering requires a great deal of self-understanding and playfulness, which Winnicott defined as "spontaneous reflection."[3,4] This comes naturally to many parents, including young parents. But some parents are too immature to see the world through their children's eyes. They misinterpret normal, developmentally appropriate children's behaviors, such as crying, asking repetitive questions, or pulling the dog's tail, as signs of stubbornness, defiance, or malice. They get so absorbed in their own concerns that they cannot see or understand their children's needs.

Winnicott had little to say about fathers, except that they were there to support the mother in her efforts to hold, contain, and nurture the child. In fact, he was among the first developmentalists to consider fathers at all, commenting that as children grow up, the father's role is to help the child adjust to the world outside the safety of environment created by the mother. To be fair, Winnicott lived in an era and social context wherein fathers were regarded as "support staff" for mothers, less directly involved in child-rearing activities. While it's still true that fathers play a different and often secondary role in the lives of their children, contemporary views of fathers have changed. And, as previously discussed, we now have several theoretical models for thinking about what characterizes "good enough" and what factors are likely to support (or hinder) good-enough fathering.

Although Winnicott himself only applied his concept of "good enough" to mothers, we believe that the application of this framework to fathers is quite useful, particularly in combination with contemporary models of fatherhood. When we examine the real (vs. ideal) fathers participating in our research, Winnicott's framework helps remind us that that being a good-enough father means "being there" in some capacity, but it also allows for natural slippage and imperfections. Additionally, being a good-enough father entails learning to compensate for one's own personal liabilities and weaknesses as a father.

Having sketched out some general guidelines for identifying or describing good-enough fathers, the next logical question to ask is how do fathers *become* good enough? Assuming that there is some process of development by which fathers become good enough, what are the key ingredients in this process? What factors help distinguish fathers who are "good enough" from those that flounder?

PART FIVE

Fathers Found

CHAPTER 17

The Father–Child Bond

When we compare and contrast fathers who were able to navigate the transition to parenthood successfully with those who flailed, there are a few primary distinguishing features. *First*, the former group demonstrates that they have been able to make the shift from a more self-focused (or egocentric) stance to one that is more oriented toward caring for others and attending to their needs. Fathers like Tyrone (introduced in Chapter 5), who are initially shocked by their partner's pregnancies, demonstrate how this transformation works. As their perspectives shift from focusing on themselves to putting their children's needs first, by caring and providing for them (financially and emotionally), they begin to really feel like fathers, which, of course, can mean different things to different men. Given that adolescents tend to be rather egocentric in many ways, making this shift is a challenge for young fathers, relative to most fathers who are well into adulthood. Being able to overcome this challenge is critical to the development of good-enough fatherhood. A *second* distinguishing feature of these "good-enough" fathers is the ability to reorient their personal identities around the role of father, a process we discuss in detail in Chapter 18. Related to this, these fathers describe their paternal identity as their greatest priority, having moved "up the ranks" relative to other roles that they might fill, such as the role of son, brother, student, boyfriend, worker, and so on. A *third* feature of these young men, who seem to discover something admirable about themselves in their roles as fathers, is the capacity to form a bond with their children, defined as a deep emotional connection that inspires one to take care of another.

PATERNAL BONDING

The father-to-child bond is the "flip side" of infant-to-parent attachment, which research has found to be extremely important for children throughout life.[a] In fact, many researchers who have examined parental bonding have used the term "parent-to-child attachment" to refer to this process,[1,2] while others have preferred to use the term parental "bonding" or "emotional connection."[3] Whichever term is used, our studies with young fathers over the years attest to the importance of this paternal connection/bonding/attachment process for engaged fathers.

As suggested in Chapter 7, the quality of the father–child relationship seems to be important—perhaps vital—for the father's positive involvement over time. In turn, the father's positive involvement in parenting is linked with a wide array of child developmental outcomes, from cognitive and emotional development to school achievement. Consistent with this emphasis on the father–child bond, William Marsiglio's and Kevin Roy's "nurturing" model of fatherhood (discussed in Chapter 15) describes the father–child relationship as the single most important factor in positive fathering. Hence, this model posits that promoting a strong, positive connection between fathers and their children—regardless of the fathers' marital or residential status—is the most important target of intervention programs designed to improve fatherhood outcomes, especially for at-risk or disadvantaged fathers.

What does it mean to say that a father is bonded with his child? Although the research on parent–child bonding originally focused on mothers only, fatherhood researchers have found that four characteristics of a strong parent–child bond apply to fathers too (just as it applies to mothers):[2]

(1) Bonded fathers express *pleasure about just being with their children;* they desire the experience of physical proximity and experience a sense of satisfaction from spending time with their sons and daughters.
(2) They learn to *accept or at least tolerate child behaviors,* such as whining and throwing tantrums, that might frustrate or irritate them in the absence of their attachment/bond. Most parents struggle to remain patient with screaming children, and many experience a sort of developmental breakthrough when they are finally able to see the connection between their patience and their child's ability to manage the

---

a. Theoretically, children who become securely attached to their parents as children develop the sort of relationship building skills, like the capacity to form close, enduring bonds with others, that help prepare them for becoming loving and attentive parents.

emotions underlying those annoying behaviors. When this happens, fathers derive a sense of purposeful pride from keeping their cool.

(3) A father's bond with his child is also manifested by his *desire to meet the child's physical and emotional needs*, to care for the child, to protect the child from harm. This includes a willingness to put his child's needs above his own. Bonded fathers derive personal satisfaction from the daily sacrifices of parenthood, partly because meeting their child's physical and emotional needs feels like an achievement, feeding their self-esteem.

(4) Last, but not least, a father–child bond is indicated by *a desire to acquire more knowledge* about their child and how to effectively parent him or her. Strongly bonded fathers become curious about their children, wanting to understand what they want, how they learn, and who they are becoming. Paying attention to their child's uniqueness helps them be more effective as a parent. In turn, their ability to empathize with the child's experience and be attuned to their child's needs usually feeds a father's sense of competence as a parent, which further strengthens that bond.

THE INSIDE SCOOP

When we ask the young fathers in our studies who or what helped them learn about fatherhood, the most consistent answer that we get is "my son," or "my daughter." For Robert, the driving force for him to be a good father was his daughter, Carla. When we caught up with Robert and Sarah a year after Carla was born, they were married and Sarah was pregnant with their second child. When Paul asked Robert to describe Carla to us, his face lit up.

PAUL: Can you describe Carla to me? What's she like?
ROBERT: A little bundle of joy (laughs). She's a playful little animal, she just loves to play, that's all, that's it, that's everything about her.
PAUL: What do you like most about her?
ROBERT: The way she'll just sit back and be with me, we'll play with each other, or we'll sit back, sometimes we'll sit back and watch TV . . . and she'll just look at the TV and just put her head on me and lay down. That's all the joy in the world.
PAUL: What are your feelings about being a father?
ROBERT: I love it (laughs) . . . I love every minute of it.

PAUL: What do you love about it?

ROBERT: The fact that this is my child. This is someone that I am raising, not nobody else. Nobody can say how I'm gonna raise her; it's my decision, me and Sarah's decision, how we raise our daughter.

PAUL: Uh huh. Can you describe what you are like as a father?

ROBERT: Playful . . . I'm very proud of my daughter, it's like I want to show her off to everybody. I take her out and they're, like, "Is that your daughter?" And I'm, like, "Yes, that's my daughter!" I'm very proud of her . . . I'm, like, it's almost like we just go out there and we . . . we just be a showboat out there. We be goofy, we're goofy together, we just . . . we have fun. That's it, we have fun.

PAUL: What's been good about being a father?

ROBERT: Watchin' my daughter grow up. It's like, that's your child . . . and it's a chance for me to, to mold her into a type of person that you, that you wanted. It's like, it's almost like a puzzle, that you want to see the end result, and you want it to be good and so you put all this into her, to make her to the person that you want.

PAUL: Uh huh.

ROBERT: It's just watchin' her crawl, watchin' her grow her first teeth, feeding her, changing her diaper. I mean (laughs) . . . it's just, it's like, it's beautiful. There's nothin' I would rather do. I, I wouldn't take that back for the world, ya know, nothin' would ever . . . I wouldn't ever take it back . . . I'm happy I did it.

When we interviewed Sarah, she elaborated on Robert's dedication as a father (and partner), which she said began long before the delivery. Here, Sarah shares with Emma her perspective on Robert as a father to their daughter:

SARAH: He was always there when I had to come to the hospital, or when I had doctor's visits. He was there when I had the baby. He cried afterwards (laughs)!

EMMA: How does Robert help you with the baby?

SARAH: Oh, he could be a mother if I wasn't there.

EMMA: Like, what does he do?

SARAH: Everything. There isn't nothing that he hasn't done. He's taken her bath, he's always been. . . . He calls himself a "versatile father." He says, "I'm versatile," I think he's proud of that, because he never had a father that does for him like that. And I know a lot of guys don't like changing diapers, and don't like taking baths, and stuff like that.

EMMA: Uh huh.

SARAH: But he, I think he gets a kick out of it. He likes feeding her, and he likes taking care of her . . . he'll get up in the middle of the night sometimes, and give Carla her pacifier. He'll get her dressed, he'll do her hair.

EMMA: How do you think Robert is doing as a father?

SARAH: Oh, I think he's doing a great job. I tell him all the time that I wish I had a father like him.

Like Robert, Tyrone (the young father we introduced in Chapter 5 who met Sybil at a bus stop) told us it was the relationship with his son, Isaiah, that motivated him to "step up" to his "responsibilities" as a father. When we followed up with Tyrone 2 years after Isaiah was born, he and Sybil were still together, and they had another baby boy. When Mike asked him about being a father, Tyrone was visibly enthused.

MIKE: So, what are your feelings about being a father?

TYRONE: Aw, man, I love being a father. For me, fatherhood . . . I just like having the responsibility to take care of my own, you know, my own "seed," you could say. It makes me proud, as far as having my son, you know. In the future, I always think about future stuff, barbecuing and stuff like that, fatherly stuff. 'Cause we got two boys now. You know, that's the best thing to ever have. I'm not going to try to eliminate no females, 'cause I always wanted a little girl. But we had little boys, and I like that too. I like to go play basketball with 'em, wrestle with 'em, watch football with 'em. I'm still young, so I have a lot of energy in me, you know. I like to do a lot of stuff and think about a lot of stuff I want to do with 'em in the future. Take 'em places and stuff.

MIKE: What kind of father are you like?

TYRONE: A perfect father.

MIKE: Could you explain?

TYRONE: Yeah, a perfect father . . . a father who loves his kids first. You know, take time, be patient. I'm patient with 'em. I play with 'em a lot, always playing with 'em. You know, this is a father who spends a lot of time with his family, not just the kids but his whole family. I don't mind spending a lot of time doing it . . . that's what I want to do. I get a kick out of doing it. I want to take family trips and just do little stuff for kids, games and stuff like that . . . fatherly stuff.

MIKE: So, how do you help take care of your child, besides . . . I know that you provide financially and support your family and you play with him and you change diapers, but what other ways to you take care of your child?

TYRONE: Umm, teaching him his ABCs and 123s and looking at shows, *Sesame Street* and stuff like that. You know, there's a lot of ways I take care of him. Boy, I provide everything he needs, for one. Teaching him about new things, you know, always on top of teaching him new stuff. If I feel like he learns something, like if he's trying to do something, I push him, you know, as far as teaching him more than what he learned.

Jed, who was initially afraid to become a father, knowing that he was at risk for abusing his own child because of his experience of having been abused by his father, recalled the moment he met his baby daughter, Alyssa, immediately after she was born.

JED: I grew up quickly . . . had to grow up quickly. She changed my life so much! I can remember when she was born. I was looking at her when she was born, and it seemed like she was looking at me too. We were just staring into each other's eyes and I was realizing that THIS WAS MY BABY. This was *my daughter*. I am her *father*.

KEITH: What does it feel like to be a father now?

JED: It means a lot to me. Being a good father and husband are the most important things to me. Now when Alyssa looks at me, I know she's thinking, "You're my dad and you're the greatest." And that makes me very happy. Knowing that she has a father, someone to be there for her. That's the most rewarding thing for me, that I can give to her what I didn't have. The best thing about being father is that she knows that I will take care of her.

While Robert and Tyrone are both enthusiastic about being fathers, this transition was far from easy. Consistently, fathers shared the challenges they experienced from once being able to do whatever they wanted to do (when they wanted to do it), to now being responsible for someone other than themselves. Here's how Robert described the ways in which adjusting to being a father was difficult:

PAUL: How are things different for you since becoming a father?

ROBERT: Oh man, more responsibilities! It's like . . . I can't do the things that I used to do. At the same time, I don't want to, because

I want to spend time with my daughter and I want to spend time with my wife. I mean, we still go out—me and Sarah still go out—but I'd rather stay at home with my child and my wife.

PAUL: What's been hard about that? What's been hard about the situation—having a family?

ROBERT: You don't have time to yourself anymore. I mean, a lot of times you want to go out. Like, I want to hang out with my friends, I want to do this, go to a party or something, but you know . . . that's the sacrifice you have to make. 'Cause you decide . . . you have a baby now, and you have to spend time with your baby and your wife, and you have your family. You don't have time to yourself anymore. But, the situation . . . I adjusted to it. I said, it really didn't matter spending time with my friends anymore, 'cause, you know, I told 'em I have a daughter. If they don't want to be my friends, oh well. I have my family . . . I have my child and my wife to deal with . . . they're the only ones I need. I still call and talk to my friends, but I didn't . . . It was a big adjustment, but at the same time, I wanted to do it. That's why I think it went so well . . . why it affected me well. I wanted it.

Robert proudly concludes this thought by saying, "I said that I have to make sacrifices and I have to do it . . . I'm gonna do it."

Whereas Robert was excited about becoming a father from the moment he found out that Sarah was pregnant, Steve, the Salt Lake City father we introduced in Chapter 5, was scared, embarrassed, and wanted his girlfriend to either put the baby up for adoption or get an abortion. Two-and-a-half years later, now married, working as a forklift operator and in the Marine reserves, he spoke with Dave about his adjustment to fatherhood.

DAVE: What are your feelings about being a father, just in general?

STEVE: For me, being a father, it's hard work. You know, it's harder than I thought it would be. But, then again, you know . . . it's fun. You don't get a lot of free time. I mean, it's a twenty-four-hour job. You know, you gotta cater to your wife, and your son. Or my son, anyway. I gotta make sure their needs are fulfilled.

DAVE: In what ways is it harder than you thought?

STEVE: Um . . . just some of the stuff. Like, I never really grew up around babies, so I didn't know some of the stuff they do. So when I'm like, "What the heck is he doing?" I had a hard time dealing with it. When he was first born, I had a hard time adjusting to getting up. You know, a kid who has needs twenty-four hours.

Getting up at night . . . and keeping him fed, and changed, and quiet. I mean, you've gotta be there for him, you know, when he needs you . . . I had a hard time adjusting to that.

Steve is less exuberant about fatherhood than Robert or Tyrone, or even Jed, but he's able to bond with his son, Caleb, through the more traditional route of going to work all day and helping out when possible.

> STEVE: My job right now is being the man of the house. I bring in most of the dough. That's basically my job. I help Michelle, you know, keep the house clean, do the dishes, help her make the dinner, take care of Caleb when I'm there. We work good as a team together. We take care of each other. Like, when she has to go to work, and I have to go to work. I have to watch Caleb while she's working, or I have to go to work when she watches him. Or, we take turns, you know, changing his diaper, giving him a bath. You know, if she don't feel good, I'll take him. And, if I don't feel good, she'll take him. I mean, we just kind of interact with each other like that. I spend as much time with him as I can. And like I said, I'm always catering to his needs, like taking him to the doctor if he needs it. Gettin' his check-ups if he needs it.

Despite being less emotive about his relationship with his son, which may not convey anything about the strength of his underlying "bond," Steve gets high marks as a father—and partner—from Michelle, who reflects on their inauspicious start as parents-to-be.

> MICHELLE: He's a wonderful father. He is very good with Caleb. At first, he never wanted a baby. When I was pregnant and he's like, "Have an abortion." I'm like, "No." "Give it up for adoption." I'm like, "No!" (laughs) "You don't want it? Fine, but that's just not what I want." So, like, from the first day he saw Caleb, he was the proudest papa ever. And he's really good with him. Caleb loves him, and he's just a wonderful father. He does everything with Caleb. They are like two kids together. . . . They play football in the house . . . and basketball . . . all around the living room. Steve is dribbling the ball all around the living room! And Caleb's, like, chasing him. And they wrestle for, like, two hours a day. It's just chaos in my house, so I put everything breakable away. He is a really good father. And . . . I don't know if there's a word to describe it, but he . . . knows me. He knows every part of me. He knows

when I'm sick, what I need . . . even though he thinks that I'm a wimp when I'm sick, you know. He can predict what I'm going to do, even before I do it. And I think to know a person that much takes a lot of effort. And I love it. Because when I have a hard day . . . I can just have this look on my face, and he's like, "You need a hug?" I'm like, "Yeah, I need a hug." So, he knows . . . he knows me. And I think that's what I love most about him.

Like Steve, Tyrone's description of his transition to fatherhood (which he shared with Mike) also emphasized that the initial adjustment was difficult. At the same time, this challenge seems to be an important part of the bonding process, a part of getting to know the baby but also getting to know oneself as a father.

TYRONE: When he was first born, we came home, and it was kind of awkward.

MIKE: How? In what way?

TYRONE: Like, man, I gotta get up early in the morning, changing Pampers. I wasn't used to getting up that early to change somebody's diapers. But this was my child. I'm, like, *man, this is my child!* Sitting there sleeping, looking at him, saying *this is my child.* I keep thinking, *this is my kid, so I gotta take care of him. I gotta take care of him for the rest of my life.* For the rest of, 'til he's eighteen or whatever, however old he gets 'til he don't need us no more. I ain't gonna try to limit, you know, say, like, let's give him a time limit, eighteen years old. I don't feel that's right. But, just 'til he continue needing me.

MIKE: So, how did you cope with that?

TYRONE: Spent more time with him, as far as, you know, learning, reading the books. I mean, I got two or three father books at home.

We admit that despite our efforts to remain as "objective researchers," it is gratifying to witness young fathers connecting with their children. In these narratives, we see evidence that the emotional connection between father and child is a driving force behind their motivation to be good dads. This bond fuels their positive attitudes about fathering, despite the challenges they face. For some fathers, the love of fathering flows naturally from the love they feel for their children and the love they *receive* as fathers, from their children and their partners. Regardless of whether a father's prenatal adjustment is quick and exuberant (like Robert and Tyrone) or whether it is initially hesitant and slower (as with Jed and Steve), the love these fathers feel and the accompanying bond they develop with their children buoys them, helping to keep them afloat, especially through the doldrums of parenthood. As important as the father–child bond is, many fathers struggle with not feeling bonded and not knowing how to connect. In other words, the experience of feeling bonded does not always just magically happen. Sometimes—perhaps often—it requires learning and adjusting to one's child and one's own sense of how to be a father to that child.

We have already discussed how positive father *engagement* is associated with various aspects of positive child development. This hints at the relevance of the father–child bond for better parenting (and child) outcomes, since engaged fathers are more likely to be "bonded" fathers (and vice versa). However, the question remains: Does all this paternal bonding predict better parenting and more positive child outcomes? We know that the feelings of love and connection a father has for his children do not necessarily translate directly into being a good-enough father. It is often more complicated than that. What is the hard evidence that the father–child bond matters when it comes to actual child outcomes?

As usual, most of the research that directly addresses the links between bonding and child outcomes has focused on mothers. Similar to the longitudinal design of our own research, most of these studies assess the specific impact of the parent–child bond at several different time points: prenatally (usually in the third trimester) and then again after the baby is born (usually at 6 and 24 months postpartum). The strength of the parent-to-child bond is typically measured using one or more parent-report instruments that have been developed by researchers,[1,2] which focus on the different indicators of the parent–child bond that we previously discussed (pleasure in proximity with one's child, acceptance and tolerance of child behaviors, prioritizing the child's needs, etc.). The overall conclusions of this research are that the parent–child bond is strongly related to the quality of parent–child interactions.[4–6] For example, in their study of mothers, Anver Siddiqui and Bruno Hägglöf observed that mothers with higher levels of prenatal bonding displayed more positively engaged and attuned behaviors when interacting with their infants (assessed 12 weeks postpartum).[6] Generally, this research with mothers strongly suggests that mother–child bonding increases the likelihood of certain positive parenting behaviors, such as attunement, sensitivity, and more stimulating parent–infant interactions.

Over the last few years, researchers have begun to examine the role and impact of the father–child bond. For example, in 2016, and again in 2017, Evi de Cock and her colleagues published the results of research with expectant mothers and their male partners indicating that prenatal mother and father bonding with the child-to-be was strongly predictive of postnatal bonding, which suggests that developing an emotional connection during the pregnancy may be an important part of *preparing* for fatherhood (as is the case for motherhood).[4,7] That said, it's not always that simple or straightforward. For example, like Jed, Steve initially wanted his girlfriend to put their baby up for adoption or get an abortion because he was convinced that he couldn't handle fatherhood yet. These examples suggest that prenatal bonding is not automatic for young fathers who do not feel ready, and the absence of a strong *prenatal* father-to-child bond does not necessarily preclude the development of a strong bond after a child is born.[b]

With regard to the importance of the paternal bond for child development, recent research has begun to reveal that the quality of the father–child bond is associated with important child outcomes, such as emotional functioning (including the child's sense of security) and cognitive development.[4,8,9] For example, in another study conducted by Evi de Cock and her colleagues,[7] parental bonding was assessed for both mothers and fathers in the third trimester and then again at 6- and 24-months postpartum. A couple of findings from this study are worth noting. First, these researchers found that fathers and mothers with higher-quality prenatal bonds reported having lower levels of parenting stress at both follow-up assessments. Parenting stress is defined as stress that is directly related to the challenges of child-rearing, including not only personal doubts about one's ability as a parent, but also having to attend to a temperamental infant or an angry toddler. This impact on parenting stress is important, given that heightened parenting stress (for both mothers and fathers) tends to predict a host of negative parenting behaviors.[c] Second, de Cock found that the level of parenting stress was associated with children's "executive

b. Since the results of this cited study were correlational, that means that although a strong prenatal bond was highly predictive of a strong postnatal bond, we can't conclude that a prenatal bond inevitably *determines* the strength of the postnatal bond. Thus, it's possible for an initially strong prenatal bond to weaken over time for some fathers, just like it's possible for a weak prenatal bond to strengthen over time. Similarly, it's possible for weak or strong prenatal bonds to remain stable over time.

c. Recall that specific indicators of strong parent–child bonds include acceptance and tolerance of child behaviors that would otherwise be frustrating and irritating (which includes patience with the child and embracing parental responsibilities without experiencing these as burdensome). In light of this, it makes sense how the generally "positive" frame of a close parent–child connection could indeed buffer a parent from levels of parenting stress that would otherwise be much higher if it were not for the close bond and the corresponding positive interpretations of one's role as a parent.

functioning" when these children were 2 years old. This latter finding, and its importance, warrants a bit more explanation.

"Executive functioning" involves a range of higher-order mental processes that enable us to monitor and regulate our emotions, thoughts, and behavior. As such, executive functioning is critical for all sorts of important abilities, such as maintaining self-control, focusing attention, and considering consequences of our actions. It might come as no surprise, then, that the level of executive functioning in childhood is predictive of later school achievement, and poor executive control predicts later internalizing and externalizing behavior problems. The part of our brain primarily responsible for our executive functioning is the prefrontal cortex (located at the very front of our brain right behind the forehead). Although not fully developed until young adulthood (as we mentioned in Chapter 6), this prefrontal region of the brain undergoes significant and rapid growth in the first 2 years of life.[d]

This latter point helps explain why this group of researchers decided to focus on children's executive functioning at the *age of 2*: the status of these toddlers' brains—how much growth and activation in the prefrontal cortex has taken place by this time—is an important "marker" or predictor of *later* functioning and development. Putting all the findings of this study together, de Cock and her colleagues found that there was an indirect link between the quality of the parental bond and executive functioning of children at the age of 2, which was mediated by parenting stress. In other words, just as is the case with mothers, a strong (high-quality) father-to-child bond predicts lower parenting stress, which, in turn, predicts better executive functioning of children at a particularly important time for brain development. Other researchers have found that good executive functioning at toddlerhood is an important predictor of later functioning for children, cognitively, socially, and emotionally.[10–13]

Because de Cock and her colleagues did not directly observe or measure parenting behaviors, we aren't able to conclude from this evidence what specific *parenting behaviors* or *parent–child interactions* are related to the quality of the parent–child bond and/or parenting stress, which likely account for these findings. However, when we look at all the available research on parental bonding, the picture that is emerging (so far) is that the quality

---

d. The fact that the prefrontal cortex does not fully mature until young adulthood helps explain the risk-taking and immaturity that we tend to see in adolescents. Moreover, the relative lag in development of males (relative to females) helps to explain the common gender differences in risk-taking and immaturity that tend to be seen in young adult men (relative to their female counterparts).

of the father–child bond (as with the mother–child bond) tends to increase the likelihood of certain positive parenting behaviors (such as attunement, sensitivity, and more stimulating parent–infant interactions)—perhaps, in part, by buffering the parent from increased levels of parenting stress. This combination of factors, in turn, can have measurable impacts on children's brain development and functioning (as assessed by early executive functioning).

In summary, a growing body of research indicates that the father–child bond matters when it comes to the development of good-enough fathers. This research is also consistent with the "inside scoop" from fathers themselves when we ask them to explain the process of their own development as fathers. And it helps us make sense of the fathers like Jed and Tyrone who frankly surprised us in the way that they were able to "beat the odds" and navigate the transition to fatherhood as well as they did. Yet, while a strong father–child bond may be important—maybe even essential—to the development of good fathers, it alone is not sufficient. There is more to the story.

CHAPTER 18
Redefining the Self as Father

Developing a Paternal Identity

It is interesting to us that the term "paternalistic" is often used pejoratively, as if fathers who strongly identify with that role are inclined to think they "know best" and don't have any compunctions about telling others what's good for them. Anyone who gets called paternalistic knows it's not intended as a compliment. Perhaps paternalism got its bad reputation from those very powerful white men—father figures—who, over the course of many generations, tended to see the world of women and nonwhite men as needing their governance and guidance. Conscious of this entomological history, we hope to reset our notions about what it means to identify oneself as a father, to be paternal.

Many of the fathers who we see as good examples of "good-enough" fathers—like Robert and Tyrone, as well as Jed and Steve—developed a strong internalized sense of a paternal identity, a full-fledged commitment to their role as fathers. Sometimes, it seems a bit like they have become card-carrying members of the "fatherhood club," a club that they *say* they really wanted to join. For example, when we asked Tyrone what a father should be like, he gave this advice:

> First, you have to want to do it, you have to want to be a father. You know, you have to want to sacrifice a lot of stuff to be a father, giving up this and giving up that. Spending time with your son or daughter, you know. It's just a lot of patience. You have to be patient with your family.

In describing his adjustment to fatherhood, Robert tells us, "I wanted it . . . I made the choice . . . I'm gonna do it." He goes on to say,

> I know that some guys have babies unexpectedly and they don't want it, and they didn't want to make the change, so that's why they don't adjust to it well. I wanted to, and I made the change. I adjusted to it . . . It was something that I wanted, and when I wanted it, I was gonna have it.

Robert's commitment to the role of father was further revealed when we asked him how he balances fatherhood with working 50 to 60 hours per week in his job as an electrician. Here, Paul asks how he manages being a parent plus working all these hours:

ROBERT: Well, through the daily basis, I'll be up at four o'clock in the morning and I don't get off work 'til four or six o'clock in the evening. . . . And then I have my daughter, which I, I just play with her no matter what, even if she comes and I'm working . . . then I'll still play with her, still have time to play with her.

PAUL: Uh huh.

ROBERT: It's not easy but it's something that I dedicated myself to, and I'm gonna do it. . . . And that's just it. But you don't get that much sleep. I mean, I catch up on my sleep on the weekends, and Sarah gets mad at me 'cause I'm always tired (laughs) . . . but it's something that I chose to do and, I explain that to her and she's willing to go through it with me. But you have to put all of your time into it. There's no time when you say, "I don't want to do this or I don't want to do that." You have to do it no matter what. There's no if, and, or buts. You do it. You have the baby. It's your responsibility and you're gonna do it.

PAUL: How do you help her with the baby?

ROBERT: I do everything she does . . . I change diapers, I go to the store. I mean, I even do laundry. I cook, I clean, I do everything that she does. She does everything that I do.

PAUL: Uh huh. And financially, you're able to provide for the baby?

ROBERT: Um hm [yes], both of us work, both of us have jobs, we both do everything.

Psychological theories and research on identity development highlight how our roles shape our self-perceptions as well as our perceptions of how other people in our lives (like our children and partners) view *us*.[1] The latter are sometimes described as "reflected appraisals," and they can have an important impact on our identity.[2,3] In fact, theories of how our sense of self develops in the first place emphasize the messages communicated by important figures in our life (especially parents or parental surrogates), which are "reflected" to us, starting in early childhood.[2] These appraisals by others (whether they are good, bad, or somewhere in between) tend to be internalized (taken in), and they function over time to shape our emerging sense of self. In other words, our perceptions of how other significant people in our lives view *us* influences how we come to view *ourselves*. Although our childhood experiences and relationships—including the reflected appraisals that we internalize—set the stage for identity development, adolescence is the period of the lifespan when identity development is the "prime-time" developmental achievement. This is the time of life when, if things go well, the different rudimentary elements of identity coalesce, leading us to develop a coherent, stable sense of who we are.[4,5]

As anyone who has survived adolescence can attest, the teenage years are not the "finish line" when it comes to identity development. In fact, it's probably more accurate to describe what typically happens in adolescence as feeling like you are at least "in the race"; you have a sense of which direction you are heading in, and you have a growing sense that you'll figure out how to get to the finish line, even though you can't yet see where it is. In other words, successful identity development in adolescence provides a stable *foundation* for identity, but our identity continues to develop and shift throughout our lives, particularly as we incorporate new or shifting roles into our sense of self. For example, many people experience the shift from being a "student" to being a "worker" when they leave school and get a job. For those who get married or who enter a serious cohabiting relationship, the role of "romantic partner," "husband," or "wife" is incorporated as a new, and often salient, role. And then, there's the role of being a "parent," which, for most people, can lead to a fundamental shift in identity. And, for some, this life event can be quite destabilizing.

The ongoing process of identity development (extending into adulthood) involves collecting or adopting new roles (e.g., we might add the role of "partner" to that of "worker"); however, some of our different roles can conflict with each other. For example, the new role of *father* (especially for a young father) may present a significant conflict with the role of *student* or *son*, leading to some hard choices and often some sacrifices. These identity conflicts must be resolved to re-establish a stable sense of self. As we have seen, some young men resolve their identity conflicts by adjusting themselves to their new roles, convincing themselves that they *really wanted this*. On the surface of things, it could appear that being willing to make sacrifices as a father and accepting these sacrifices without resentment is the key to the success of fathers like Robert and Tyrone. For example, Robert put his aspirations to get a master's degree on hold, and he embraced the role of father, fully committing to that role. For both these fathers, it seems clear that, in their personal hierarchy of roles that comprise their identity, fatherhood is now "topping the charts." A closer look, however, reveals a more nuanced picture.

For example, after the first year of fatherhood, Robert does, in fact, continue his education by taking evening college classes after work. And, in the face of recurring conflict with his girlfriend over the issue, Tyrone defends his need to play basketball with friends. Eventually, he negotiates a compromise with Sybil that allows him to carve out time for this activity that he says he needs to do for himself (in part, so that he can be more present as a father and partner when he's at home). It's clear that both these fathers derive self-esteem from fatherhood, but they also clearly derive self-esteem from their jobs, continued education (in the case of Robert), and outside interests (in the case of Tyrone). In this light, Robert and Tyrone seemed to have reached an effective compromise solution, a *partial* sacrifice of their personal ambitions and roles, as opposed to a *complete* sacrifice. They have figured out a way to balance their full commitment to fatherhood while still getting their personal needs met. They have struck a balance between "self-sacrifice" and "self-preservation." And, perhaps that is one important key to their success.

We think that another key to the success of fathers—like Robert, Tyrone, Steve, and Jed—lies in the way that they seem to have molded their personal ambitions and goals to more closely line up with fatherhood. Another way of saying this is that they have reframed fatherhood as actually being *integral* to their own personal ambitions, something that they have convinced themselves they want, something that lines up with their ideals. This type of "cognitive shift" has been repeatedly demonstrated in research on romantic relationships, which reveals that, when people are in a stable and satisfying relationship with someone that they love, descriptions of their "ideal partner" tend to morph over time to more closely align with the characteristics of the *person they are with*.[6] We could think of this as an example of the adage: "If you can't be with the one you love, love the one you're with." But, there's a twist. Perhaps it's more accurate to say that, under the right conditions, the one we're with *becomes* the one we love, as our image of the "ideal partner" begins to look more and more like our real partner. The same type of process may apply equally well with fathers who describe what they "want" in ways that reflect what life has given them. They begin to describe really "wanting" to be a father and being glad that it happened when it did (even though they might have waited, if they were to do it again). It is a case of *wanting what you have* versus being focused on *having what you want*. As a result, they are happier, more satisfied. And their perspective on fatherhood is much rosier than we ever would have predicted.

Perhaps not surprisingly, seeing the glass half-full rather than half-empty when it comes to the role of fatherhood turns out to be an important predictor of positive fathering outcomes. For example, the degree of value placed in the fatherhood role (i.e., how high the role of "father" sits in one's identity hierarchy) is a strong predictor of overall involvement with one's children and involvement in childcare, specifically.[7,8] Likewise, positive attitudes toward their role as fathers predicts father involvement, both in terms of time spent with children and the degree of responsibility for their care (relative to one's partner or other caregivers).[9,10]

Alan Hawkins, the BYU professor whose research plays a prominent role in Chapter 21, has proposed that one important process that promotes fathers' generativity, or the capacity to care for others (especially children), is the father's striving to be as much like his vision of the "ideal father" as possible.[11] From this perspective, a father's motivation to be a good dad involves trying to align his parental behavior with his expectations of what a father "should be like." These internalized ideals or standards may be intrinsic, or they may be influenced by external cultural values that stress the importance of father involvement (or both). Whatever the source(s) of the standards, the degree to which a father perceives alignment between his expectations of the "ideal father" and his perceptions of how he is *actually doing* is an important predictor of his adjustment and functioning as a father.[12] According to this theory, if there is enough overlap between a father's perception of himself and his image of the ideal father, then he is more likely to stay involved. If the perceptions of the "real father" and the "ideal father" are too discrepant, the father is more likely to abandon the ideal and disengage.[11] This relates to what Philip Bowman described as "role strain" among disadvantaged fathers who disengage because they feel like they are failing,[13,14] as Quinton (the father featured in Chapter 1 who became undone with fatherhood) probably feels beneath his resentment.

When we asked many of the fathers in our studies who were functioning well, "What do you think a father should be like?" it was striking how much their responses lined up with their own description of themselves as fathers. Take Robert's response to this question, for example:

> An ideal father, you know, is to be there for your child. You can never be around your child enough. You always want to be around your child, always want to teach your child more. You know, teach her right from wrong, the good from

bad . . . be there, try to give the child everything they need. Not everything they *want*, because everything they want is not right, but everything that they need, as far as to grow, to survive in this type of world.

This description of the ideal is remarkably similar to how Robert described himself (as indicated in the previous chapter). If a father feels like he is doing a good job—and if he receives positive feedback to this effect from his child, the mother of the baby, and other significant people in his life— then this is likely to reinforce active involvement with his child, which then further reinforces his positive perceptions as a father. This process is illustrated in the way Steve describes his own personal transformation as a father, from initially tentative to increasingly confident.

DAVE: How have you changed since Caleb was born?

STEVE: More patience with my son. When I first got around little kids, I just really didn't know how to act. And, I think being with him just changed me into a father . . . a father-type person. And I've learned . . . I've learned so much from him, what kids are like and what they do. And, it just kind of, you know, added to me.

DAVE: How did those changes come about?

STEVE: Just taking care of him. Having to tend him. You know, you learn stuff. You'll find him . . . you'll turn your back and he'll be playing in the garbage or something. And you're like, "Hey, what are you doing?" You have to go see what he's playing with, so . . . you know, just stuff like that. Like, you know, just playing peek-a-boo . . . doing things I never would have thought of. You know, you've got to understand him. I've learned how to actually take care of him. I've learned how to be a father and spend time with him, and . . . and, encourage him and stuff. In a way, I learned it from him 'cause he expects it or just pulls it out of me.

DAVE: How do you think that you're doing as a father?

STEVE: I think I'm a pretty good father. I think I'm a pretty caring, pretty loving father. I . . . I take care of him. You know, when Michelle's gone, I take care of him. I give him what he needs, you know . . . feed him, dress him, bathe him, change his diaper. You know, watch movies with him. Stuff like that.

As is the case with the parent–child bond, parental identity (for both fathers and mothers) also involves multiple dimensions. These include *role satisfaction* (the degree of enjoyment that one experiences in one's role as a parent), *perceived competence* as a parent, *investment* (which involves the desire to learn more about parenting), and *role salience* (the relative rank of the parenting role in one's identity hierarchy).[15] The research on paternal identity suggests that all these dimensions are important for a thorough understanding of what paternal identity entails. At the same time, different dimensions of paternal identity may be more or less important for father involvement among different groups or types of fathers (e.g., divorced vs. nondivorced).

For example, Carmelle Minton and Kay Pasley found that father investment was predictive of involvement among nondivorced fathers but not divorced fathers, whereas role competence and role satisfaction predicted continued involvement among divorced fathers.[16] In their sample of residential and nonresidential fathers, Carol Bruce and Greer Litton Fox found that paternal identity salience—how personally important it feels to be a father—was associated with father involvement, regardless of residential status, suggesting that fathers who have strong father identities are more involved (i.e., spend more time with their children),[17] though it seems possible the reverse could be equally true.[a] Interestingly, another set of researchers found that it was the *mothers'* perceptions of the importance of the paternal role to their partners that was significantly and positively correlated with fathers' involvement and paternal responsibility, as opposed to the fathers' own ratings on these different dimensions of paternal identity.[18] This reinforces the notion that, besides fathers' own perceptions of themselves, their *partners' perceptions* of them as fathers is also an important predictor of the fathers' involvement.[b]

In addition to defining father identity in terms of these four dimensions, it is also the case that the father role is often comprised of several "subroles," including one or more of the following: breadwinner/provider, caregiver, nurturer, "support staff" to mother, playmate, teacher, "coach," disciplinarian, and so on. As is typical of most fathers, Jed, Steve, Tyrone, and Robert each have multiple father identities or subroles; the contents of their "father identity portfolio" is diversified. Some, like Robert and Tyrone,

---

a. In their analysis, these researchers statistically controlled for residential status (to eliminate differences in father involvement that were accounted for by this variable). After doing so, they found that paternal identity salience was the strongest predictor of father involvement across both groups.

b. Of course, there could be several explanations for this. It could be that simply having an additional source of information (an "outsider's" perspective besides just the father) helps to increase our ability to predict a complex phenomenon like father involvement. It could also be that fathers, like anyone else, are prone to present themselves in the best possible light, so that the mother's perspective on the father may provide a perspective that is less influenced by this self-serving bias.

have a profile of fatherly roles that is broader than others, like Steve. Based on their own and their partners' descriptions, both Robert and Tyrone function as providers, playmates, caregivers, teachers, and disciplinarians (and perhaps other roles that are less obvious). Although Robert is the primary breadwinner, Sarah works part-time and contributes to the household income. Even though Sarah is the primary caregiver, they both are involved directly in all aspects of caregiving. Recall Sarah's statements that Robert "could be a mother" if she weren't there, and "There isn't nothing he hasn't done." Consistent with Robert's self-description as a "versatile father," Robert and Sarah pitch in and work together on most parenting tasks, in most parenting roles. And Robert tells us, "Me and Sarah do everything together," including feeding their child, changing diapers, bathing, combing their daughter's hair. When we asked Robert how his relationship with their daughter Carla was different from Sarah's relationship with her, he tells us,

> I don't really see it being different, 'cause we both love her and there's nothing that we both wouldn't do for her . . . sometimes she [Carla] wants to be held by me, sometimes she wants to be held by Sarah, but there's nothing really different.

Like Robert and Sarah, Tyrone and Sybil also seem to have a lot of overlap in their parental roles, in that both appear to be actively involved in multiple aspects of child-rearing. However, Tyrone and Steve seem to fold their gender identity into their paternal identity, describing some of the differences in how they interact with their sons as gender-based, perhaps even gender-determined (from their perspective). For example, in response to how his relationship with Isaiah is different from his son's relationship with his mother, Tyrone responds as follows:

> Oh, see, I'm more rough with him. Sybil, she won't get into him, you know. I'm more rough with him, as far as I wanna do more things with him, and see, she don't know what to do with him but baby him and kiss and stuff like that. It's a difference because, you know, I'm a man and she's a woman.

Whether this interactional difference that Tyrone describes is actually a function of biological sex differences—as opposed to complementing each other's styles, which have been influenced by gender-role socialization—is not clear. Regardless, we think it's safe to say that, for the most part, couples negotiate a way of co-parenting that seems to work well for them, until it doesn't, and then, hopefully, it gets renegotiated. Some of the couples in our studies have settled into arrangements where the father is the primary (or sole) breadwinner, like James, the hardworking father we introduced Chapter 16. And, in other couples, the father is unemployed but fully engaged in caregiving, like Eddie (also introduced in Chapter 16). In this respect, it seems that the specific subroles each partner occupies may be less important than whether the configuration of *combined roles* covers the bases of what their children need and what works from both parents' perspectives. Having said that, we've also observed that a pretty high level of active involvement in caregiving and nurturance among fathers is rather consistently seen in the young men who have developed into good-enough fathers.

Our observation of the relative importance of paternal nurturance and involvement in caregiving is consistent with the changing standards of fatherhood that we described in Part Four. As more mothers have needed (and often wanted) to enter the workforce, this has resulted in an increased need, and opportunity, for fathers to take more active roles in childcare and nurturing. It has meant that mothers can be less exclusively relied upon for these components of parenting, just as it has meant that fathers can be less exclusively relied upon to be breadwinners. Accompanying these changes, expectations have increased—by fathers themselves and their female partners—for fathers to be willing and able to fill other roles besides breadwinning, especially nurturance and caregiving.

There are some real advantages of having diversified paternal roles. We would predict that fathers like Robert who are "versatile" would be much more likely to develop into good-enough fathers, compared to those whose "fatherly portfolio" is narrow or rigid. This is not only because such fathers are more likely to develop a positive emotional bond with their children but also because this is more aligned with current views and expectations of the "ideal father." This means that there is likely to be greater overlap between their self-perceptions as a father and their perceptions of how a father "should be," not to mention their partner's perceptions. It is also the case that such diversified fathers will be more likely to establish a collaborative co-parenting arrangement with their female partner, given that it places less of a burden on the mother to compensate for any major component of parenting that the father cannot or will not do. In other words, a father whose portfolio is missing nurturance and caregiving places a greater burden on the mother's "parenting portfolio" to make up for this. A father whose paternal role is limited to that of breadwinner could potentially be viewed as a good-enough father, but if we think in terms of the overall configuration of mother–father roles, this would require his partner to be the sole nurturer/caregiver in the household. And, if the mother works (either by choice or necessity), that means that she is more likely to experience the stress of role strain as she tries to balance breadwinning with the other roles of parenting that her partner lacks. Given the shifting standards of what it means to be a father, there are fewer and fewer female partners— and fewer and fewer fathers themselves—who are likely to think that this is "good enough."

THE CONNECTION BETWEEN PATERNAL IDENTITY AND THE FATHER–CHILD BOND

There is a close connection between the quality of the father–child bond and a strong paternal identity in the lives of young fathers who successfully navigate the transition to parenthood. Our observations of paternal bonding and identity development among the young fathers in our studies have been consistent with research conducted by Cherine Habib and Sandra Lancaster.[19] In their sample of 115 Australian soon-to-be-dads (mostly adult fathers), these researchers found a significant positive correlation between the strength of the father–child bond and the salience of their paternal identity. In addition to providing evidence that the father–child bond is closely linked with paternal identity, this finding also suggests that the emotional connection to the child *before birth* may indeed be important. If these two processes (paternal identity and bonding) are closely connected, a logical question to ask is, "Which comes first?" Does developing a strong paternal bond (perhaps starting during the pregnancy) help lead to the development of a strong paternal identity and commitment to the father role? Or does the development of a strong identity as a father (perhaps a prebirth determination to be a good father) help to promote a strong paternal bond with one's child? These questions are not simply academic, since if one of these processes precedes the other (and is therefore more foundational), that has important implications for intervention, in terms of figuring out how best to direct resources for promoting father involvement.

One of the advantages of the longitudinal nature of our data is that we get to ask some of the same questions relevant to fatherhood *before the baby is born* (which allow us to get a glimpse into the expectant fathers' attitudes and the presence or absence of a strong prebirth paternal identity). Then, we get to hear how the fathers answer these questions after they've had the opportunity to develop a relationship with their child. Beyond the quantitative data that we collect from our fathers during the transition to parenthood, the in-depth qualitative responses to our questions shed some light on which of these processes comes first and for which fathers.

Many of the fathers that we would describe as good enough (especially those with better-than-expected outcomes) describe the *relationship with the child* as instrumental to the development of their identity and commitment as a father. This would suggest that the paternal bond *leads* and that paternal identity/commitment *follows*. Then again, other fathers in this group describe what seems like an a priori, personal, ethical commitment to a paternal identity after they find out that they are going to become a father, often long before the new baby has arrived. For these fathers, it seems that paternal identity/commitment comes first, followed by the developing relationship/bond with the child. Some illustrations might help elucidate what's going on here.

Some of the young fathers in our studies describe fatherhood as a genuine "turning point" in their lives. Darnel is a prime example of one such father. When we caught up with Darnel at our 2-year follow-up interview after the birth of his son Curtis, Darnel had been released from jail, and he had moved from the South Side of Chicago to the North Side, where he was living in an apartment with his mother. Darnel discloses that his primary motivation for moving was to distance himself from his cousins and other people in the neighborhood that had been connected with his previous gang involvement and drug trafficking. At the outset of the interview, when Mike asked Darnel how he is doing, he tells us, "I got a better look on life this time."

> MIKE: So, how is your outlook different?
> DARNEL: At first, I wasn't really too much concerned and, I was just lettin' things go. And then I see that I got to step up and make things happen. That's basically how I changed.
> MIKE: What do you think brought about that change?
> DARNEL: Well, I let things happen for too long, and I got into the wrong situation, doin' time in jail, and then I got out and knew I had to change . . . and I made the change.
> MIKE: So, I mean, was it the experience of going to jail, or what?
> DARNEL: In some ways that helped, but what really made me change was that, when they took me to jail, I couldn't spend no time with my son. That was what really made me change, the fact that I didn't want to go back, and if I make more mistakes then my son is the one who would suffer, not me. So that's basically what made me change.
> MIKE: How has having a baby changed your life?

DARNEL: It has made me more responsible obviously, 'cause at first I really didn't have no responsibilities. I just did what I wanted to do when I wanted to do it. But now—since I have my son—it's my responsibility to make sure his priorities come first, what he need. And as him needin' stuff, then I have to work and be able to be there when she [Cleo] call me sayin' he need somethin'. I got to have the money for what he need, so . . . he basically make me more responsible. And . . . I think he just brightened up my life. There is somethin' about being around him that make me happy.

These responses from Darnel suggest that the bond that he developed with his son—and the threat of potentially losing that bond if he didn't turn things around—was instrumental in his developing a postbirth commitment to a paternal identity. For him, it seems that the primacy of the relationship with his child motivated him to make the shift from a focus on self (as reflected by "doing whatever I wanted when I wanted to do it") to becoming more concerned about others. This is accompanied by a reorientation of his identity around the father role and a shift in the salience of his paternal identity, so that being a father now seems to be at the top of the ranks in his personal "identity hierarchy."

At our last follow-up interview, Darnel is doing remarkably well as a father, which Cleo confirms.

EMMA: How does Darnel help take care of your son in other ways, beside the financial help he gives you?
CLEO: He spends a lot of quality time with him. Every Sunday, he comes over here, or he'll take him over to his house to visit his other grandmother [Darnel's mother]. And um, he tries to spend as much time as he can with him.
EMMA: How is his relationship with your son different than yours?
CLEO: Um, I don't know. I think Curtis loves his parents equally, and we love him equally. I don't think there is a difference in our relationships . . . we relate to him pretty much the same. He reads to him sometimes, I read to him sometimes. We both play with him, both talk to him and try to get him to talk to us.

It seems that a father's capacity and willingness to both reorient his personal identity around fatherhood and develop a strong emotional connection with his child are central elements in his development as a good-enough father. As with the age-old "chicken or the egg" question, it may be that it's impossible to decipher which comes first, the bond with the child or the paternal identity and commitment. Our studies with young fathers—as illustrated in the cases of Robert, Tyrone, Jed, Darnel, and Steve—suggest that which comes first may differ across fathers. When it comes to establishing a strong paternal identity and commitment to fatherhood, some fathers (like Robert and Tyrone) may begin strong, right out of the gate. Others (like Darnel, Jed, and Steve) may take a while to get going and then build momentum over time. The critical thing is for both a strong paternal identity and relational bond to emerge. And, it's likely that these two processes tend to co-evolve. After all, what good is merely a mental commitment to being a father without a strong bond with your child? And, it's hard to imagine developing and maintaining a close relationship with your child without an emergent identity as a father and an accompanying commitment to that role.

As we mentioned in the previous chapter, there is some research evidence that the father's bond with his child postnatally is strongly associated with a developing bond before birth, which suggests that a budding sense of connection to one's child prenatally may be important in the process of reorienting one's identity around fatherhood. However, our observations of fathers who are slow to adjust to fatherhood but eventually make it work—like Steve, Jed, and Darnel—suggest that both father–child bonds and paternal identities can emerge and evolve later in the game, perhaps with some assistance and perhaps with experience. Indeed, the developing relationship with the child can jumpstart the process for fathers that don't initially "take" to fatherhood. In this respect, the teacher is the child, as Steve seems to suggest. Perhaps helping fathers envision and articulate the kind of relationship and interactions they would like to have with their child may also facilitate this process, supporting the development of their identities and their commitments. The big question is: How do we do this? Is it possible to teach fathers to bond or to see themselves as responsible caregivers in the making? And is this just a social process, or are their biological processes and mechanisms involved in the development of the father–child bond and one's commitment to the role of father?

CHAPTER 19

On Becoming a Dad

The Biology of Good-Enough Fathering

Before there is even a child to parent—and certainly after the child is born—it turns out that there are underlying physiological mechanisms at work that can play an important role in whether a father becomes good enough. In trying to explain why some fathers become dads versus cads, our story would not be complete without addressing the biological changes that lie outside of conscious awareness but nevertheless appear to play a significant role in paternal behavior, including engagement in child-rearing and commitment to parenthood. In this chapter, we discuss two hormones, testosterone and oxytocin, that have received the most research attention and whose roles in fathering are most clearly understood. These hormones—and their vicissitudes—not only support (if not determine) some of the differences in father involvement across species, they also help account for differences in parental behavior within species.

THE ROLE OF TESTOSTERONE IN FATHERING

Whether we are talking about humans, chimpanzees, or any number of other species, males with higher levels of testosterone tend to experience an advantage when it comes to mating success. As nearly everyone knows, higher testosterone (which is often referred to by researchers simply as "T") is associated with increased libido, while lower levels of T are linked with lower sexual desire. High T is also associated with increased musculature, social dominance, and increased aggression—particularly increased competition with other males for access to mating partners.[1,2] And while males with higher T tend to be more focused on *attracting* mating partners, research with married couples reveals that higher T predicts poorer relationship quality, infidelity, and divorce.[3] This suggests that higher T tends to go hand in hand with a focus on mating, as opposed to pair bonding. Compared to males with lower T, males with higher T tend to be more focused on *getting mates*, as opposed to *staying* with them. In turn, males that don't stay with their partners are subsequently much less likely to participate in parenting, once they have produced offspring with a given mate. This last point underscores the fact that, both within and across various species, there is often a trade-off between mating and parenting (and co-parenting).

We can think of this as the age-old trade-off between quantity versus quality that we mention in Chapter 3, namely whether there is a focus on reproducing as much as possible (with multiple mates) or investing substantially more time and energy in a smaller number of offspring, with a focus on helping ensure the survival of that offspring. Our body's adjustment of T levels appears to be an important physiological mechanism mediating the trade-off between mating and parenting.[4,5] Among humans, single, nonpartnered men tend to have the highest baseline levels of T, followed by partnered nonfathers, with partnered fathers having the lowest levels of T among these three groups.[6,7] Furthermore, fathers who are actively involved in caregiving tend to have the lowest levels of T, relative to fathers who are uninvolved, partnered nonfathers, or single men.[8,9]

Of note, differences in T levels between fathers and nonfathers vary somewhat across different cultures, at least in part as a function of the overall degree of expected paternal involvement within a given cultural group. In North America, where a relatively high level of father involvement is the norm, researchers have consistently found significant differences in T levels between fathers (especially engaged fathers) and nonfathers.[10] By comparison, Martin Muller and his colleagues conducted a study of T levels among men from two neighboring tribes in Tanzania.[11] Among the Hadza, where paternal involvement is high, Muller found the same pattern as in North America, with significantly lower T levels for fathers, compared to nonfathers. This pattern was not found among the neighboring Datoga tribe, however, where paternal involvement is low and where polygyny is common; for this group, T levels did not differ between fathers and nonfathers. This suggests that the *degree of paternal involvement* appears to be particularly important, as opposed to merely fatherhood status, when it comes to levels of T.

Experimental research with nonhuman animals provides stronger evidence that T does indeed mediate the trade-off between mating and parenting. Much of this research has been conducted with monogamous species of birds, whereby male fathers are experimentally administered extra T (through special T implants applied under the skin). Compared with controls (who either receive no implants or are given empty implants that contain no T), male birds with the boosted T levels do indeed show decreased parenting effort and increased mating effort, as indicated by visiting their nests less frequently and being more likely to engage in extra-pair copulations.[12]

With humans, one of the best ways to infer that there may be a cause-and-effect relationship between changes in T levels and changes in partnering and fathering behavior is through well-designed longitudinal studies that examine changes in T levels over time. This allows us to see how T levels correspond to the onset of fatherhood as well as the degree and quality of paternal involvement. One of the best examples of just such a study was conducted by anthropologist Lee Gettler and his colleagues who studied a large representative sample of Filipino men over a period of 4.5 years.[a] Focusing on a subsample of 465 men who were who were all single nonfathers at the start of the study, the researchers measured both morning and evening T levels at baseline and then again at the follow-up assessment 4.5 years later. This allowed them to assess changes in T levels for those men who became fathers over the course of the study compared to men who remained single and/or childless. And, since Gettler and his colleagues also collected data on paternal involvement, they could test whether T levels varied as a function of how involved fathers were with their children. If T does, in fact, mediate the trade-off between mating and parenting, we would expect that single men with higher T at the start of the study would be more likely to experience mating success, as indicated by being partnered and having a child at the follow-up assessment. At the same time, if the downregulation of T contributes to a focus on parenting among fathers, then we would expect to see a steep reduction in T levels *after men become fathers*—particularly in comparison with their nonfather counterparts.

Consistent with these hypotheses, the results showed that single nonfathers with higher baseline T levels were significantly more likely to have become partnered and they were more likely to have become fathers

a. The study specifically focused on men living in or around Cebu City, Philippines, where paternal involvement in caregiving tends to be high. This was one major reason for choosing this particular sample.

by the 4.5-year follow-up. While having initially higher T levels, those men who had become fathers showed *steep declines* in both AM and PM T levels (median decreases of 26 and 34 percent, respectively), which were significantly greater than the modest (and typical) age-related declines observed for the comparison group of single nonfathers at follow-up (median declines for this group were 12 and 14 percent, respectively).[b,c]

It turns out that T levels among fathers are not just associated with their overall level of involvement in caregiving, but also with observed father–child interactions and responsiveness. In one of the first studies to examine the link between hormones and paternal behaviors, Anne Storey and her colleagues found that lower levels of T were associated with greater responsiveness to recordings of infant cries (as indicated by feeling concerned and wanting to comfort the baby).[15] These researchers found that the responsive fathers had a reduction in T levels that was greater than unconcerned fathers or expectant fathers. Using a similar research design, Alison Fleming and her colleagues found that men with lower T levels exhibited more sympathy and motivation to respond to infant cries, compared to fathers or nonfathers with higher T.[d] The emerging picture from this research is that declines in T are closely linked with fathers' empathy and responsive caregiving, a conclusion that is further supported by the fact that experimentally administering T leads to lower empathy (and related psychological measures).[18] Interestingly, there seems to be an *interaction* between paternal caregiving and T levels, such that lowered T facilitates (and may set the stage for) paternal involvement. At the same time, the experience of affectionate, responsive fathering appears to suppress T levels.[16] This suggests a two-way, mutually reinforcing dynamic between T and paternal behavior.

Up to this point in the story, we have discussed how *lower* T levels, as well as *decreases in* T, are associated with responsive paternal caregiving. For example, men who are more responsive to infant cries tend to have lower T

---

b. The conclusion that becoming a father *leads to* a suppression in T levels is further supported by the fact that the researchers statistically controlled for other variables besides fatherhood status that could account for decreases in T, such as stress and sleep quality. And they observed that the differences in T levels between fathers and nonfathers were not accounted for by these other possible influences.

c. This finding of decreases in T coinciding with the onset of fatherhood is consistent with multiple other studies, both with human fathers, as well as other species in which fathers routinely participate in caregiving (including birds and some mammals).[4,5,13,14]

d. More recent research by Ilanit Gordon and her colleagues has confirmed this same basic pattern of findings, demonstrating that fathers who were more positively responsive to their infants' cues had significantly lower T levels than fathers who lacked positive attunement or "synchrony" with their infants.[16]

than fathers (or nonfathers) who have higher T levels. However, there is a wrinkle in this tale. Several studies have found that, in some situations, exposure to infant cries can actually *increase* T levels.[15,17,19] How do we account for this apparent contradiction? How can it be that certain fatherhood measures can be associated with both *increases* and *decreases* in T?

The key to resolving this apparent contradiction lies in recognizing that the relationship between T and paternal behavior depends on the specific *context* in which caregiving is (or is not) expressed. The researchers who helped elucidate this point were Sari van Anders, Richard Tolman, and Brenda Volling from the University of Michigan.[19] In a clever application of technology, these researchers used a RealCare infant simulator, which is a high-tech computerized doll that is designed to be as much like a real baby as possible without being a real baby. The life-like doll emits a full range of infant sounds that have been recorded from real human babies, including cries, coughs, sighs, moans, feeding sounds, and even burps. The doll can be preprogrammed and can respond to external stimuli, meaning that it can simulate the need to figure out what a baby needs (feeding? diaper change? cuddling?), followed by the need to respond appropriately. The simulator also responds—with a particularly loud, shrieking cry—when mishandled or when its head is not supported. Because of these features, the RealCare Baby® simulator has not only been used by researchers; it has also been used for teen pregnancy prevention programs, sex education, parent skill training, and child abuse prevention.

From a research perspective, one of the significant advantages of using an infant simulator is that it can allow researchers to experimentally test different conditions that would be impossible with real infants for both practical and ethical reasons. This is precisely what van Anders and her colleagues did. To determine what caregiving conditions would lead to increased versus decreased T levels, they randomly assigned a sample of men to either a neutral control condition (in which men were not exposed to any infant stimuli whatsoever) or to one of three other experimental conditions.

(1) In the "Baby Cries" condition, the men were simply exposed to recordings of infants crying, but with no way to actually respond to the cries. (Since they were not given a RealCare Baby®, there was no opportunity to engage in caregiving.)
(2) In the "True Baby" condition, men were given a fully-functional RealCare Baby®. This made it possible to respond to the infant cries and also provided an opportunity for nurturant caregiving (i.e., if the men

were appropriately responsive to the doll, they could effectively soothe the "baby").

(3) Finally, men assigned to the "False Baby" condition were provided with a RealCare Baby® that had a missing sensor. This meant that, although the men had the opportunity to offer caregiving, these efforts were bound to be *ineffective* at actually calming the baby. Without the crucial sensor, the baby's cries were simply following their preprogrammed schedule rather than responding to the external stimuli provided by the role-playing "fathers." So, this last group was put in the undoubtedly frustrating position of trying to calm a baby (expecting to be able to do so), but to no avail.

Van Anders and her colleagues found that T levels of the men significantly *decreased* when babies could be soothed by effective paternal responses (in the "True Baby" condition). In contrast, average T levels significantly *increased* on average for men who simply heard the infant cries but without any way to actually respond (i.e., the "Baby Cries" condition) and when fathers could respond but only with ineffective attempts to calm the baby (in the "False Baby" condition). These findings suggest that T levels decrease in response to infant stimuli in the context of fathers' nurturant parenting behaviors—especially when those behaviors are *effective*. In other words, T is related not simply to one's *status* as a father, but to the amount of paternal care and, even more important, the degree to which a father's interactions with his child are effectively responsive to the infant's needs, the true reward being a soothed baby.[e]

Taken as a whole, these findings suggest that T is important for the overall story of how young men do—or do not—become good-enough fathers. Given the typical gradual declines in baseline T with age, the young fathers that we have studied can be expected, as a group, to have higher T than their adult father counterparts. This helps explain why some young fathers continue to engage in risky behavior that ultimately interferes with their functioning as fathers.[10] However, this research also sheds some light on the "better-than-expected" fathers in our studies, such as Charles

---

e. One other strength of this experiment was that the researchers statistically controlled for a few other key variables that can affect T levels, including amount of exercise reported by the men in the sample, age, body mass index (BMI), nicotine use, time of testing (since T levels vary over the course of the day), and previous experience with infants. The fact that T levels significantly varied across the different experimental conditions in the study after controlling for these possible confounding variables increases our confidence that it was the different caregiving contexts that actually led to the observed changes in T levels.

(introduced in Chapter 4) and Darnel. The fact that the downregulation of T reinforces engaged fathering helps explain how dramatic turnarounds in fathering behavior occur among these young men. We did not measure changes in T levels, but we would venture to guess that we'd see decreases in fathers like Charles and Darnel over time, helping to set the stage for increased paternal bonding and the development of a paternal identity. No doubt, there are multiple factors contributing to how men like Jed, Tyrone, and Charles are able to beat the odds and do as well as they are doing, but the downregulation of T—both facilitating and in response to father-bonding—appears to be an important piece of the puzzle.

THE ROLE OF OXYTOCIN IN FATHER BONDING

In Chapter 3, we introduced oxytocin as the "love hormone" that functions as a naturally occurring chemical agent, vital to both couples bonding and parent–child bonding. We highlighted how a genetic marker for oxytocin production helps explain individual variation in both maternal and paternal behavior. And we noted that the release of oxytocin helps explain why parents stay engaged in parenting; namely, it feels good. Readers may be familiar with the neurotransmitter dopamine, which activates the pleasure center in our brains and figures prominently in the initial rush we feel when we do some of the things we love to do, like eating chocolate or having an orgasm. Oxytocin plays a more subtle but more important role in how we become attached and crave proximity to those with whom we are attached.[f] Oxytocin levels are associated with heightened feelings of calm, trust, and sociability and decreased feelings of aggression, mistrust, guilt, and anxiety,[22,23] In addition to being involved in pair bonding between romantic partners, oxytocin is released in women during childbirth and lactation and when parents make contact with their children. In fact, the parent–child bonding process begins even before birth, thanks to oxytocin. A significant increase in oxytocin from the first to third trimester of pregnancy predicts the strength of the mother's prenatal emotional bond, and more positive maternal behavior after birth, such as affectionate touch.[22,24]

Although fathers obviously don't lactate, breastfeed, or give birth—events that release oxytocin—it has been documented that fathers tend

---

f. This neuropeptide is secreted by the pituitary gland, but its production is regulated by the hypothalamus, a small but important structure in the mid-brain, which is referred to as the body's "master gland" and is also involved in regulating emotions, motivation, and the autonomic nervous system.[20,21]

to have higher oxytocin levels than nonfathers,[25] and oxytocin levels for *both* fathers and mothers increase significantly from the first few weeks following birth to 6 months postpartum.[g] As with testosterone, oxytocin levels are also associated with specific parental behaviors, as opposed to simply being linked with parental status.

In one of the first studies to examine the link between oxytocin and parental behaviors for both mothers and fathers (which we mentioned briefly in Chapter 3), Ruth Feldman and her colleagues observed mothers and fathers interacting with their 4- to-6-month-old infants during a 15-minute play interaction.[27] For mothers, more affectionate behaviors (as assessed by gaze, positive affect, and touch) were associated with greater increases in oxytocin following the interaction. For fathers, significant increases in oxytocin levels were uniquely associated with positive stimulatory contact with their infants (as assessed by stimulating touch and exploratory play). This same pattern of association between oxytocin levels and affectionate versus stimulatory behaviors has been replicated several times, which increases our confidence that this observed pattern is a reliable finding.

One example of just such a replication was by Ilanit Gordon, Orna Zogoory-Sharon, James Leckman, and Ruth Feldman.[26] Using a free-play procedure to observe parent–child interactions, these researchers studied a sample of 80 cohabitating couples and their first-born infants over the course of the first 6 months of parenthood. When analyzing the parent–child interactions, they found that oxytocin levels were indeed associated with affectionate behaviors for mothers and stimulatory behaviors for fathers. Of note, however, Gordon and her colleagues found that fathers and mothers did not differ in the actual *proportion of time* spent engaging in these different behaviors with their infant. In other words, fathers were just as affectionate with their infants as mothers were (on average), and mothers were equally likely to engage in stimulatory interactions as fathers (on average). Nevertheless, oxytocin concentrations were uniquely linked with affectionate behaviors on the part of mothers and stimulatory contact on the part of the fathers. While this by no means confirms that the differences we observe in the behavior of fathers and mothers are biologically determined, these findings do provide some fodder for that argument and food for thought. It is important to remember that, despite the interesting differences in biological processes between fathers and mothers,

g. The consistently high correlation between fathers' and mothers' oxytocin levels and the comparable increases in those levels corresponding with pregnancy and parenthood suggest that oxytocin does indeed play an important role in biologically reinforcing and "priming" fatherhood, just as it does with mothers.

both fathers and mothers were affectionate *and* stimulating with their children.[h]

Some of the most interesting studies on oxytocin and fathering have examined the effects of intranasal oxytocin administration on fathers' observed interactions with their children. That's right, we are talking about a little oxytocin being sprayed up the nose. In one of the first of these investigations, Fabiënne Naber and several of her colleagues observed a group of Dutch fathers interacting with their children (all between 18 months and 5 years of age) in two different 15-minute play sessions.[28] Before each of the play sessions, fathers were given either an oxytocin nasal spray or a placebo nasal spray. Every father in the sample was observed under both conditions (oxytocin spray and placebo) with a week intervening between the two sessions and with the order of the conditions randomized. Additionally, the researchers used a double-blind procedure so that neither the fathers nor the researchers knew when the placebo or the oxytocin had been administered. The results of the experiment showed that, compared with the placebo, oxytocin led to increased responsiveness and less hostility in the fathers' interactions with their children. Specifically, the researchers observed that, after receiving the boost in oxytocin, fathers provided more optimal support of their child's exploration in the play session, offering structure and guidance in a way that was responsive to the child's needs but that still facilitated the child's autonomy.[i] Additionally, after receiving oxytocin, fathers demonstrated less negativity such as impatience, criticism, and discontent when interacting with their child.[j]

More recent research by Omri Weisman and her colleagues at Bar-Ilan University found that experimental administration of oxytocin also resulted in fathers' increased social engagement with their 5-month-old infants.[31] Interestingly, this set of researchers also assessed the *infants'* oxytocin levels as well as their observed behaviors and found that the boosted oxytocin levels in the fathers was associated with increased oxytocin levels

h. It is possible that oxytocin is linked with whatever parent–child behaviors are perceived as more enjoyable or even "appropriate" for fathers and mothers to display, which tends to be heavily influenced by socialization and gender-role expectations.

i. Elayne MacDonald and several of her colleagues conducted a systematic review of 38 randomized controlled trials on the administration of intranasal oxytocin and found that this results in no reliable, detectable subjective reactions to participants. This suggests that the results of intranasal oxytocin studies with fathers cannot be explained by the subjective experiences of fathers (such as feeling more relaxed or "engaged") as they interact with their infants.[29]

j. Follow-up research found this same pattern of results for autistic children, as well as typically developing children.[30]

in their infants, along with behaviors signaling increased social engagement in response to their fathers.

In sum, the experiments on intranasal oxytocin increase our confidence that oxytocin actually exerts a *causal influence* on paternal behavior and responsiveness (as it does with maternal behavior). These findings suggest that oxytocin plays an important role in priming, supporting, and/or reinforcing paternal involvement, as opposed to simply revealing that involved or responsive fathers have higher baseline levels of oxytocin (although that also appears to be true).[k] Additionally, the finding of the bidirectional relationship between fathers and their children reveals how hormonal and accompanying behavioral changes in the father can, in turn, lead to hormonal and behavioral changes on the part of the child. We can expect that these would then serve to further reinforce paternal engagement and responsiveness, together with accompanying elevations in oxytocin. We can see this as a mutually reinforcing cycle, a positive kind of "domino effect" that makes ongoing engagement and responsiveness in the parent–child dyad more likely.

Similar to testosterone, with oxytocin we see yet another example of a mutually reinforcing process in which the neuroendocrine system is linked with specific parenting behaviors. In this case, changes in oxytocin lead to increases in responsive parenting, which then leads to further increases in oxytocin (both for the parent and the child). One of the leading theories about the role of oxytocin in parenting is that this neuropeptide functions to reinforce responsive care among parents by increasing the experience of reward (through the activation of the dopamine pathways in the brain).[32] Thus, fathers (and mothers) who are more responsive with their children may produce more oxytocin, which enhances the experience of reward (in relation to this responsive parenting), serving to reinforce continued responsiveness. It has also been suggested that oxytocin helps to facilitate positive parent–child interactions by enhancing trust, empathy, and sociability and by decreasing hostile feelings that would clearly get in the way of attuned, responsive parent–child interactions.[28]

The link between oxytocin and father involvement is not only important for understanding the development of good-enough fathers, but it also has important implications for interventions designed to support fathers'

---

k. As mentioned in Chapter 3, variations in oxytocin receptor genes have been found, which translate into individual differences in oxytocin concentrations and, in turn, parental responsiveness. This provides evidence that responsive parents do indeed tend to have higher baseline oxytocin concentrations, and it helps explain individual differences in parental responsiveness.

involvement with their children. It's not just the case that good-enough fathers have more oxytocin (and less T). Rather, fathers' positive involvement and responsiveness helps *activate* a biological process that promotes and reinforces further involvement and responsiveness. This means that intervention efforts that can successfully promote early father bonding may be important and worthwhile, given the way that this involvement can help activate and enhance the physiological mechanisms that support more sustained paternal involvement and responsiveness over time.[33] Additionally, the fact that changes in T and oxytocin occur in tandem gives us a better idea of how dramatic turnarounds are possible with at-risk fathers—like many of the young fathers in our studies—who are unlikely candidates for becoming good enough but who go on to surprise us.

HORMONES AND THE BRAIN

Fluctuations in hormones don't fully explain the biology behind parenting behavior, though. There are other factors, such as the brain, that play an important role. One question that researchers are working to answer is the relationship between hormones, brain activation, and behavior. For example, is brain activation triggering hormonal changes? Are hormones—in concert with brain activation—promoting certain emotions, thoughts, and behaviors of fathers, such as increased motivation to approach and care for the child, increased positive feelings toward the child, or decreased negative affective responses? Or is it the case that certain behaviors on the part of fathers, such as holding, spending time with, and responding to the needs of their infants, trigger hormonal and brain changes? The debate may be somewhat akin to the question about what makes a car go. Is it the ignition to spark plug to the engine to the wheels? Or is it the wheels to the engine to spark plug? Over time, we have designed cars to ignite the spark plug because it's more efficient. However, in the old days, we rolled the wheels to get the process going. The point is that either way can work. When it comes to what makes an automobile move, the "arrow" can go either way.

Indeed, which way the arrow "goes" may indeed vary among different fathers. In other words, perhaps there are some fathers whose brain activation and hormonal changes increase their motivation to be involved in caregiving from the outset and whose continued involvement is then reinforced by the further enhanced reward value of their offspring (this pattern seems to fit with our observations of fathers like Robert and Tyrone). Other fathers may not have the boosted initial motivation to engage in childcare.

But, if they begin to be involved in the direct care of their child, they "entrain" their reward system, which reinforces their continued involvement (a pattern which perhaps helps explain the experiences of fathers like Jed, Steve, and Darnel). Either way, whether it initially follows or precedes the hormone and neural changes that increase the reward value of offspring, it is clear that direct father involvement is a critical part of this process.

One of the most influential models of human behavior, which has been widely applied in both psychology and medicine, is the biopsychosocial model. This model posits that a thorough understanding of human health and functioning (as well as any interventions designed to help individuals) needs to take into account biological, psychological, and social factors. So far, in this section of the book, we have discussed (in this chapter) biological factors related to hormones and paternal behavior, and we have also discussed some important psychological factors, namely father–child bonding, and paternal identity/commitment. In the next chapter, we round out our coverage of key influences in the development of good-enough fathers by talking about the important social context of relationships in which good enough fathers are found.

CHAPTER 20

Fathers Are Found in Relationships

Although all the factors that we have discussed in the first three chapters of this section are important in explaining the development of good-enough fathers—especially those that are able to rise above significant risks—it is important to understand that these influences do not occur in a vacuum, but rather in a relational context. And, in addition to the direct relationship of the father and his child, there are three other relationship "spheres" that are particularly important to the development of fathers. These include the father's relationship with his own father, relationships with parental surrogates and extended family (which often includes his partner's family), and the relationship with the mother of his child, which has already figured prominently it this book. In this chapter, we will discuss each of these important relationship contexts in turn.

WHAT HAPPENED TO DEAR OLD DAD?

In studying young fathers, we have become progressively more optimistic about the potential for many (perhaps even most) of the young men we've met to become good-enough fathers, largely because we've learned that most young men want to be good fathers, at least in the beginning. Obviously, a young man's relationship with his own father is a key component of his own personal development as a father. For many of us, fathers play a psychological role in our lives, because we absorb or "internalize" the relationship we develop with them, drawing upon our experiences with them to inform and guide our own behavior—particularly our parenting behavior. They also play a *symbolic* role, so even if we don't have a tangible relationship with our fathers, we still have an *imagined* relationship. This relationship might feel flat or empty, but still significant, even if its primary impact is to motivate us to be more present and more positively engaged. If a young father's relationship with his father is ongoing—if they still talk and see each other—fathers will continue to play a role, often a supportive role, provided that the father–son relationship is experienced as positive, overall.

For example, Robert has a good relationship with own father, who, when he found out that Sarah was pregnant, stayed calm and counseled Robert on how to focus on both his education and his family. When asked to describe his father during our first interview, Robert told Paul:

> Well, my father, he wasn't strict but he just disciplined a lot. At the same time, I know he loves me. That's one thing I know. I just see him as a loving person. He can joke around a lot; I can joke with him about anything. And it's just, like, we have a real good relationship.

When there is frequent contact, relationships between fathers and sons grow and develop. Young men like Robert who have positive relationships with their fathers sometimes talk with us about how that relationship evolved as they became fathers. For many father and son relationships, the son's transition to fatherhood is a catalyst for growth and maturation. While this process is beneficial overall, it can also be difficult, especially if one or both of them are struggling to adjust their respective roles. When we interviewed Robert a year after Carla was born, he had quite a bit to say about this.

> ROBERT: My dad thinks that he has control over my life, but he doesn't. My mother just accepts the fact that I'm an adult. My father has a hard time doing that. He wants me and Sarah to move back in with him, but I'm not going to. I told him I live in North Chicago and I'm not moving back.
>
> PAUL: Why do you think he wants that?
>
> ROBERT: He still . . . he wants me to come back 'cause he misses me. He wants to try to look out for me but I have to look out for myself. He said he wants to be a father . . . but his fathering times are over. It's my turn.
>
> PAUL: (laughing) So, how do you handle that?
>
> ROBERT: I talk to him. I have to keep talking to him. That's the biggest thing. I have to tell him everything's OK. He tells me how he feels, and I have to tell him how I feel. If I don't, he'll still keep acting like

that. He *does* still act like that, but it's not the same way. It's better. He understands that even though he don't really like that I'm becoming a man, and he still wants me to be his little boy, the fact is I am a man. And I'm not moving back . . . it's not gonna happen.

As revealed in these excerpts, for Robert, the transition to fatherhood forced a renegotiation of roles between Robert and his father, nudging Robert toward greater maturity. His father is having trouble adjusting to his son's growing independence (not quite ready to be the father of an adult). What's important is that they are able to have this conversation. And, despite the challenge of reimaging Robert as a man and a father, his father has continued to be helpful to Robert and Sarah, providing tangible support, giving them money to cover expenses and loaning his car when they need it.

In our studies, there are plenty of young men like Robert who have good relations with their fathers. At the same time, there are just as many, if not more, who never knew their fathers or had bad relationships with them, strained by distance and/or abuse. Our sample of young fathers is replete with examples of young men who were motivated to be precisely the kind of father that their own father was *not*. Tyrone's father gave him up for adoption when he was 9, after his mother left. Jed's father physically and sexually abused his children. Darnel's father disappeared when he was an infant. Steve's father was an alcoholic who sat on the couch, watched TV, and drank. And Carlos' father refused to publicly acknowledge that he *was* his father but would give him money now and then, when they ran into each other in the neighborhood. Frankly, nothing has been more challenging to our optimism about the future of fatherhood than learning about these young fathers' relationships with their own fathers.[a] These stories are disconcerting but also underscore the importance of figuring out what can be done to increase the capacity of fathers to be engaged and to solidify the connection between fathers and their children.

One thing that is disconcerting is that we know how difficult it can be to escape the past. A young man's capacity for fathering behavior is often shaped—both positively or negatively—by his relationship with his own father.[1] This idea that the capacity for fatherhood is transmitted from

---

a. It's important to note that the young men in our studies are not representative of young men in general. As we have discussed previously, many of the young men we recruited would be considered "at risk" or "high risk" because they have already gotten themselves into trouble or dropped out of school. And of course, all of them are, by most standards, having children before they are sufficiently mature.

father to son has received some support from social learning researchers, who package together the concepts of role modeling (e.g., that we identify with those who are closest to us) and attachment theory (e.g., that our internalized models of significant past relationships guide our behavior in current relationships). Social learning theory proposes that our experiences of being parented become integrated into our personalities and behavioral tendencies, so that we habitually say and do things that our parents said and did.

To test this theory, David Kerr and several of his colleagues at the Oregon Social Learning Center conducted a three-generational study in which they recruited and followed the families of 206 nine- and ten-year-old boys and their parents across a full generation.[2] In fact, the study began when Kerr was still a boy. By the time he was hired by the Oregon Social Learning Center to follow up with these families, many of the participants in the study had become fathers. Kerr was able to examine the consistency in fathering behavior across generations, focusing on the concept of "constructive parenting," defined in terms of providing children with an effective and supportive structure and being positively engaged in their everyday lives.

The results of this study indicated that fathers who were more constructive in their parenting were more likely to have sons who were also more constructive as parents. More to the point, constructive parenting in the second generation predicted positive developmental outcomes in the third generation. Not surprisingly, positive or constructive parenting helps explain how healthy development is "transmitted" from one generation to the next.[3] Of course, the reverse is also true. Fathers who are abusive or neglectful often have children who have negative developmental outcomes, and they are also more likely to become abusive or neglectful toward their own children.[4] Documenting these continuities across generations helps us know what puts young men at risk for failing as fathers and helps us focus on how best to diminish these risks.

What is most interesting about Kerr's study, though, is that constructive parenting in one generation accounted for only about 10 to 12 percent of the variance[b] in constructive parenting in the next generation. In

---

b. We provided a brief explanation of variance in Chapter 10 (in a footnote). To use the same analogy that we used there, these findings mean that constructive parenting in the previous generation accounts for a "piece" that is 10 to 12 percent of the whole "pie" that we are trying to predict (i.e., constructive parenting in the next generation). When trying to predict complex phenomena (like the quality of parenting in the next generation), accounting for 10 to 12 percent of the variability in a given outcome by a *single* variable is actually pretty good. At the same time, this finding highlights that 88 to 90 percent of the rest of the constructive parenting "pie" (i.e., quality of parenting

other words, we know that the quality of a young man's relationship with his father is important to his development, but it does not *determine* his outcome as a father. Having a good father certainly helps, but it is not a necessary condition for becoming a good father. This demonstrates what we all probably already know: sons do not always follow in their father's footsteps. Across several intergenerational studies of parent functioning, there are both continuities and discontinuities across the generations.[5] Social learning theory helps to explain the consistencies we observe between fathers and sons, but it fails to explain the discontinuities. Some of the positively engaged fathers in Kerr's sample had sons who grew up to become negatively involved as fathers; other young men became constructive fathers, despite the negative influence of their own fathers.[2]

Indeed, many young fathers with absent or abusive fathers make the point, in their declarations to us, that they would *not* treat their children as they had been treated. Take Tyrone, for example. When we interviewed him 2 years after his son was born, this is what he had to say about his motivation to be a good father.

> TYRONE: [My goal is] being a good father. Not being the type of father *my* father was.
> MIKE: Not the type?
> TYRONE: Yeah, worst father you'll ever have.
> MIKE: Why do you say that, worst father?
> TYRONE: Oh, 'cause, leaving your kids, seven kids. How does someone have seven kids and then leave 'em. Seven kids, you know what I'm saying? Lay up with a lady and have seven kids and then leave her . . . and then giving them all up for adoption. No responsibility at all, none whatsoever. Then want to get back with your son or your kids and stuff like that, be all like, "Oh, I love you and miss you," and all that type of bull crap. Man, where was he at?!

Despite not having a positive relationship with his own father, Tyrone was one of those fathers that did not follow in his own father's footsteps. Indeed, as we have noted, the transition for fatherhood seemed to function as a turning point for him, and he went on to become (based on Sybil's description, his own report, and the quantitative data we collected) one of those good-enough fathers that surprised us.

in the next generation) is accounted for by other variables (other "pieces" of the pie) besides fathers' parenting in the previous generation.

Some fathers have a positive relationship with their own father (like Robert), which helps serve as a positive role model for fatherhood. Other fathers (like Tyrone) are motivated to be good dads by their negative or absent relationships with their own fathers. Some of these men, who lack a positive relationship with their own fathers, discover a positive role model and source of support in extended family members or parental surrogates.

RELATIONSHIPS WITH PARENTAL SURROGATES AND EXTENDED FAMILY

When we designed our interview for expectant fathers many years ago, we threw in a few somewhat potentially awkward questions that turned out to yield some interesting responses. One question went like this: "Becoming a father often forces people to think about what it means to be a man. From your perspective, what do you think it means to be a man?" And the follow-up question to this was "Who helped you learn what it means to be a man?" The intent of these questions was to identify how fathers defined their gender roles and to identify who in their lives helped them define these roles. Robert had a positive relationship with his father who helped with this developmental process, but most of the fathers we've introduced in this book did not. As we mentioned in Chapter 7, when fathers are not available, many young men look to their mothers to teach them what it means to be a man. Whether they are qualified to teach their sons about manhood is something many single mothers spend some time worrying about, often seeking help from the men in their lives.

Awkward as these interview questions may sound to the person doing the asking, many of the young men had asked themselves a similar set of questions, particularly those who do not have readily available male role models. When Mike asked Darnel the first question, for example, it was interesting that he immediately focused on what was most on his mind: becoming a father:

> DARNEL: To become a man ain't to have a kid, 'cause . . . it's like, a thirteen-year-old probably could have a kid, and that don't make him a man. You are only a man if you take care of your responsibilities and act accordingly to being a parent. Then you become a man. Anybody can have a baby. You got to be there for your baby when it needs stuff and when it needs to be loved. You got to know how to show love to your baby. That's the only thing that makes sense to me, really.

MIKE: How did you learn that?

DARNEL: Hmmm . . . I just really, I just sat down and thought about it a lot, you know. Since I been fifteen, I just take time out and, just think about it, like, bein' a parent and what would I do in situations like this and stuff like that. That's basically what I do. I think about it.

MIKE: Has anybody helped you to understand that, what it means to be a man?

DARNEL: Yeah, my friend, I got an older friend, he's about thirty-four, and he got a kid. He just had a kid not too long ago, So basically, we talk a lot 'cause he got a little girl. So basically, I talk to him a lot, we hang out a lot, talk to each other on the phone, and stuff like that. That's basically what we talk about, you know, what makes a man and stuff like that.

MIKE: He's helped you understand that role just by talking to you?

DARNEL: Yeah. When I first met him, you know, I don't really talk to people I don't know. So when I first met him, I didn't really say nothin' to him. But then, we became closer friends, we started hanging out with each other. Stuff like that. I got to know him, got to know his daughter. So, we basically started talkin' about stuff.

This excerpt underscores the role of father surrogates and older peer/ mentor support in the absence of parental support, which can sometimes be meaningful and positive. Did Darnel, who managed a good enough adjustment to parenthood, just get lucky in developing a relationship with someone who seems to have filled the role of a substitute father figure or mentor? We think the answer to that question is yes and no. To this point, the research on resilience—the capacity to overcome hardship—has indicated that some young people's resilience is accounted for by the fact that they have "shining personalities" that tend to invite unsolicited help from others or they have the gumption to ask for the help they need from people who have the capacity to give it. From this perspective, we might say that these people are lucky to encounter people in their lives who are willing and able to provide help, but they also deserve credit for being savvy enough to find the support they need, carefully solicit it, and receive it when it's offered.

Some fathers with negative or absent relationships with their own fathers, like Darnel, are able to garner support and guidance from mentors or father surrogates outside of their own family. For others, relationships with extended family members—including relationships that develop with the girlfriend's parents—function as important sources of support in the development of good enough fathers. This was the case with Jed, the Salt Lake City father who was abused by his own father. In our first interview with Jed, he described his relationship with his girlfriend's parents—especially her father—as playing a very important role in his transition to fatherhood.

> KEITH: How do you get along with Molly's father?
>
> JED: Pretty good. He's a pretty cool guy. We get along and talk about a lot of stuff, like cars and stereos, and stuff like that, but also the baby. He's given me a lot of advice. We get along pretty well. He'll say, "Hey, I'm not going to do this for you, you need to do it yourself, but we're not abandoning you." We've had a lot of talks about what Molly and me are going to do about having a baby and all that.
>
> KEITH: How have Molly's parents been helping you?
>
> JED: Molly's father helped boost my confidence. Both her parents helped me to decide what to do, showed us the options. They haven't pressured us into one decision or the other. They've been supportive. They'd like me to go to college so that I can provide for my family, get a steady career. They'd like me to do that. We've become close and talk a lot about stuff.

Although it is certainly possible for fathers and their partners to still make it as parents—and sometimes even thrive—without the support of extended family, having this additional source of support can make a big difference.[6] For example, having an uncle, aunt, or grandparent available to help watch the child can make it possible to hold down a job or to go back to school, which helps provide for the child (both in the short- and long-term). And, beyond any financial support or additional help with childcare that extended family members might provide, emotional support, encouragement, and advice can be extremely helpful for young fathers and their partners, as was the case for Jed and Molly. Conversely, when there is either the absence of extended family support or, even worse, when there are overtly negative attitudes toward the father by the partner's parent(s) or other influential family members, this can make a father's continued involvement with his child much more difficult to sustain over time.

The importance of relationships with extended family members for young fathers (and their partners) has been demonstrated by several researchers.[6-8] For example, in their review of research on adolescent parents, Lee Savio Beers and Ruth Hollo highlighted how relationships with extended family members can either support or hinder young fathers' involvement and development as parents.[6] Additionally, using data from the Fragile Families Study, Rebecca Ryan and two of her colleagues found that the relationships that a father has with his partner's parents (as well as his own) is particularly important for nonresidential fathers, with higher-quality relationships predicting higher levels of father involvement and increasing involvement over time.[8]

Whereas Jed was able to establish a supportive relationship with Molly's parents, some young fathers and their partners receive extra support from individuals in the community who are not biologically related to either the father or his partner, but who nevertheless clearly function as "family." Tyrone and Sybil, who both grew up in foster care and who had no natural support systems available to them, found a father surrogate and a social support network at church. When Mike asked Tyrone who had helped him understand what it means to be a man, he immediately said, "My pastor!" who was always there to talk and to encourage him through difficult times. Speaking of his pastor, Tyrone said, "He tells me to 'stick it out' and 'do this and do right' and 'don't do that,' providing a lot of good advice." Both Tyrone and Sybil told us that in addition to "just being there" for them, their "church family" had been an important source of tangible support for them, giving them money to help with childcare and books on parenting and relationships.

So far, we have talked about the importance of a father's relationship with his own father, as well as parental surrogates and extended family members (including the partner's parents). But there is another relationship that is obviously even more immediately connected to a father's relationship with his child. That is, of course, the relationship between the father and his partner, the mother of his child. How important is this relationship, when it comes to the development of good-enough fathers? And in what ways is it important?

THE ROLE OF THE FATHER–PARTNER RELATIONSHIP

Although we have mentioned the father's relationship with the mother of his child a few times in this book, there is a lot about this relationship that we have not yet discussed. Our goal in this chapter is to cover this topic in greater detail, highlighting the specific ways in which this relationship is important when it comes to the development of good-enough fathers, based both on our research over the years, as well as the findings of other researchers. We also try to answer the question "So what?" by drawing out the implications of all of this, when it comes to interventions that could help support young fathers and their families.

When we began this research, very few people took the relationship between young mothers and their partners seriously. It was assumed that things wouldn't work out, that the mother would be parenting on her own, relying on her extended family—her mother, her aunt, her older siblings—to help with childcare. Over time, it became increasingly clear that the relationship between mothers and their partners mattered a great deal, that the quality of that relationship was inextricably linked to father involvement. So, if we value the involvement of young fathers in the raising of their children, then the quality of the relationships between young mothers and fathers is indeed a serious matter.

The first question is what role this relationship plays in development of fathers across the transition to parenthood, particularly for those fathers who do not live with and may not be together with their child's mother? To answer this question, it is helpful to recall (as we mentioned in Chapter 4) that a mother's relationship with her infant tends to be more direct, consistent, and intense, whereas the relationship between a father and his infant tends to be more peripheral, mediated through his relationship with the mother, his partner. After all, mothers carry the baby, give birth, and often nurse the newborn. Although family dynamics are more flexible than ever before, mothers still tend to be the primary caregivers, even when fathers are heavily engaged and involved. Given these basic conditions, it should come as no surprise that the status and quality of the father's relationship with the mother, whether good or bad, is an important influence on the father's relationship with his child. And so, the degree to which a father is able to establish and maintain a positive, collaborative co-parenting relationship with his partner is often the *key ingredient* in the fatherhood recipe (i.e., how well that young man functions as a father). We recognize that this is a strong statement. But in our studies of young fathers and their partners, we have found that the quality of the co-parenting relationship was the most important predictor of positive paternal outcomes—especially for those fathers that fared better than expected. And we were certainly not the only ones to make this discovery.[9,10]

This emphasis on the co-parenting relationship might seem like we are oversignifying the power of the mother to make it or break it for the father. Several researchers have described unmarried mothers who act as "gatekeepers," allowing their ex-partner to have access to their children if and when they are pleased with the state of their relationship.[11-13] Of course, this makes sense when the father poses a risk to her safety or the well-being of their children, as we discussed in Part Three, but the idea of gatekeeping is broader than that. The term is used to imply that mothers allow fathers access as a form of leverage or deny access when feeling vengeful, as in "Keep that up and you're not gonna see your baby." Although we have heard some of the pregnant women we work with make threats that reflect such intentions, often in a moment of angry frustration, we rarely see this dynamic play out after the moment has passed. In our experience, even mothers who make that sort of threat rarely follow through. More often than not, they grow up quickly, recognizing both that the baby should not be used as a pawn and that he or she needs a father.[c] That said, we know that young mothers are often plenty annoyed with their ex-partners, who they may regard as unreliable or unhelpful.

Frequently, even annoyed mothers want continued father involvement for the child's sake and therefore tend to leave the "gate" open. Most are able to separate out (in their minds) the father from the romantic partner. Recall (from Chapter 12) Monica's wanting Carlos to stay involved as a father because she felt strongly that their son needed a father, even after she discovered he had another girlfriend and another child across town. Like Monica, we have heard many mothers say "As a partner, he's a dog (or worse), but as a father, he's doing good."

On the other hand, we have worked with plenty of noncustodial fathers who struggle with navigating the shift from romantic partner to co-parent. This may be partly because they aren't sufficiently bonded with the child or haven't developed a strong sense of themselves as fathers. But we think it is often the case that fathers do not have the interpersonal skills to manage their own feelings about the demise of their romantic relationship with their partner. Recall Marcus from Chapter 7, the father from Chicago who had doubts about Diamond's faithfulness and questioned whether her baby was his but never managed to bring that up. To be clear, most young fathers prioritize the needs of their child over their own doubts or discomforts. The problem is that when fathers cannot manage this, it's easier for them to drift away from their child, given that most do not have custody. We estimate that young men, like Marcus, who are unable to "deal with" fatherhood or the interpersonal challenges of romantic uncertainties and disappointments represent about 20 percent of the fathers in our research. These fathers often need more help with the interpersonal part of parenthood than young mothers, who tend to have more interpersonal resources

c. When gatekeeping did occur, there were typically clear and persuasive reasons for limiting or preventing father contact with the child, such as when the father was violent and presented a tangible threat to the mother and/or the child. In the most extreme of these cases, mothers took out restraining orders on the fathers.

to draw upon. That said, some young men, like Darnel, rise to the challenge, and there is much to be learned from a careful consideration of how that happens.

DARNEL AND CLEO (REPRISE)

As readers may recall, after having been put behind bars three times for dealing drugs, Darnel had a "come to Jesus" moment, deciding that he needed to make a significant change in his life if he had any hope of keeping a relationship with his son, Curtis. Although the romantic relationship with his girlfriend Cleo didn't last, Darnel and Cleo were nevertheless able to establish a solid co-parenting relationship together. This, in turn, enabled Darnel to maintain an active, engaged role as father in his son's life. Here is Darnel talking to Mike about his relationship with Cleo when Curtis was 2 years old.[d]

MIKE: How would you describe your relationship with Cleo?
DARNEL: Cleo? I love her, but we can't be together no more 'cause we grew apart while I was locked up. So, basically, we just the best of friends.
MIKE: OK, how has your relationship changed since the baby was born?
DARNEL: It's brought us closer together.
MIKE: How have you gotten closer?
DARNEL: If I ask her for something, she give it to me. If I got a problem, she will sit down and listen to me. She just there for me and my son.
MIKE: Alright. What do you like most about her?
DARNEL: The fact that, um, she's gonna love my son no matter what.
MIKE: What does she like most about you?
DARNEL: I think basically about the fact that I take care of my responsibility as a father of my son and I'm there for the both of them when they need me.
MIKE: What does she like least about you?
DARNEL: The fact that I used to sell drugs and I wasn't there for her when I went to jail.

d. Some of these quotes were also presented in Chapter 4, when we first introduced Darnel. We include them again here to provide the necessary context for the relevant new information in this chapter.

MIKE: How do you think her feelings about you have changed since the baby was born?

DARNEL: We grew apart. The time I spent in jail, we just grew apart. I still care for her, but we just . . . I still love her the same but that time in jail that was missed can't be replaced.

MIKE: What do you think will happen between the two of you?

DARNEL: I don't know. I can't tell what the future holds, but from what is going on now, we probably be the best of friends.

As we described in Chapter 4, when we interviewed Cleo, her story closely aligned with Darnel's. She corroborates Darnel's growth and transformation, and she raves about his positive qualities, noting that he has become a "perfect father" and that he is highly supportive of her and their baby, both emotionally and financially. Yet, consistent with Darnel's report, Cleo tells us that, while she still loves Darnel as a friend and a co-parent, her feelings have indeed changed. She is no longer in love with him and doesn't see them ever getting back together. Nevertheless, like Darnel, Cleo expects that they will remain good friends.

Maintaining a friendly and collaborative co-parenting relationship *after* the demise of a former romantic relationship is no easy feat. Yet, parents like Darnel and Cleo show that it is possible. And their story—along with data that we and other researchers have collected—reveals the importance of the quality of the co-parenting relationship for positive parenting outcomes, as well as the interpersonal skills that enable couples to function effectively as co-parents despite the erosion of any "love connection" that once existed between them.

DO GOOD PARTNERS MAKE GOOD PARENTS?

There are a couple different ways to answer this question. First, there is the question of whether the quality of the relationship between the expectant mother and father predicts positive *relational* outcomes after the baby is born, such as staying together as a couple or being able to establish a positive co-parenting relationship despite no longer being romantically involved. Second, there is the question of whether the quality of the mother–father relationship predicts positive *parenting* outcomes over time, such as higher levels of father engagement and better father–child interactions. To answer both parts of this question, we collected data on the observed interactions of the mothers and fathers as well as the self-reported quality of the parents' relationship with each other, using a questionnaire (the *Quality of Relationship Inventory*, or QRI for short) that focuses on dimensions such as perceived emotional support, depth/intimacy, and conflict. By assessing the quality of the relationship over time, beginning with the prebirth assessment and continuing with the 1-year and 2-year postbirth data collection periods, we were able to examine changes in relationship quality and satisfaction over time. In addition to collecting data on the co-parents' relationship with each other, we also collected data on parenting outcomes, including both negative outcomes (harsh parenting practices, risk for child abuse, and paternal disengagement) and positive outcomes (affirming and nurturing behavior). As previously indicated, we used different methodologies to assess parenting outcomes, including interviews, parenting questionnaires, and observed parent–child interactions during the task where we asked each parent (separately) to help their child put together a puzzle and then read a couple of books to their son or daughter.

The Quality of the Mother–Father Relationship and Relationship Outcomes

One the first questions we addressed was whether the quality of an expectant couple's relationship during pregnancy was an important marker of their ability to remain positively involved—supportive and respectful of each other—across the transition to parenthood. As intuitive as the answer to this question may seem, remember that the reason clinical researchers had not taken seriously the co-parenting relationships between young fathers and mothers is that these relationships were regarded as transient and therefore either irrelevant or too slippery to study or work with. We needed to carefully examine whether our hunch about the importance of these relationships could be supported with data.

When we dug into the data, we found that couples who exhibited higher levels of warmth and lower levels of hostility were more likely to still be co-parenting together when their child was 2 years old, even if they were no longer romantically involved. In contrast, hostile couples were more likely to become disengaged and the fathers disconnected from their children.[14] Similarly, we found that couples who reported higher relationship quality before the baby's birth (less conflict, more support, and more depth) were more likely to remain together as co-parents 2 years following the birth of their child, and they were also less likely to report relationship violence.[14,15] Darnel and Cleo's interpersonal communication with each other at our first prebirth assessment illustrates these findings. When we examined their behavior (which we systematically evaluated using the Structural Analysis of Social Behavior coding scheme we described briefly in the Introduction) both Darnel and Cleo demonstrated a high degree of warmth and very little hostility during the "conflict task" in which we asked them to discuss and resolve a recent disagreement. More specifically, 43 percent of Darnel's behaviors were coded as warm, whereas only 2 percent were coded as hostile (reflecting his defensiveness). The remaining 55 percent of Darnel's behaviors were coded as neutral (neither warm nor hostile), characteristic of assertive or autonomous behavior, such as explaining one's position. For Cleo, 73 percent of her behaviors were coded as warm, and she exhibited no hostility toward Darnel. Compared to the average or standard "profiles" of codes for the couples in our studies, these results indicate notably higher warmth and lower hostility, particularly in the context of this particular task (which involved the same standard instructions, conditions, and duration for all couples).

A more fine-grained analysis of Darnel and Cleo's communication reveals high level of active listening, affirmation, and acceptance and low levels of control or dominance. There was a high level of behaviors that reflect trust and accepting influence of each other, indicating a willingness to take in and consider the other person's perspective. Criticism or blame, which tends to be quite common among the couples in our studies, was completely absent for both Darnel and Cleo. Additionally, the couple displayed a high ratio of warmth relative to hostility, which has been identified in previous research as an important predictor of relationship success.[16]

These findings paint a picture of two partners who, during our prenatal assessment, were able to discuss their differences in a warmly engaged way that managed to avoid the hostile exchanges we commonly observe in young expectant couples. Consistent with the data that emerged from their observed interpersonal behavior with each other, both partners reported a high degree of perceived relationship quality before the baby was born, marked by a high degree of closeness and support, high depth, and low conflict (based on their scores on the QRI).

Darnel and Cleo were off to a good start—at least in terms of their communication with each other—when we first met them. But this was while they were still together as a couple. How were things between them 2 years after their son's birth, after Darnel's time behind bars, and after the romantic relationship ended? Did they demonstrate significant increases in hostility and declines in warmth, as one might expect and as we frequently witnessed among the couples who break up? Two-and-a-half years later, we found that the interpersonal "profile" for Darnel and Cleo remained remarkably consistent and still overwhelmingly positive. Even though they were dealing with significant issues at this time, including how to coordinate their parenting efforts and how to handle Darnel's discomfort with Cleo's new boyfriend, they were considerate and supportive of each other. This is no small achievement for a couple at any age, let alone for two parents who were only 19 and 20 at the time. Both still reported having a close (although nonromantic) relationship with each other. They still had disagreements, but they were able to talk things through.

The Quality of the Mother–Father Relationship and Paternal Outcomes

In addition to finding that the quality of the relationship between expectant fathers and mothers predicts how that relationship looks and feels after the transition to parenthood, we also found that the couples' relationship quality predicted how well fathers functioned as parents. For example, fathers who reported having a higher-quality relationship with their partners during the pregnancy reported less parenting stress, decreased risk for child abuse,[e] and lower levels of physically punitive parenting behaviors 2 years after their children's birth, and this was still true even if (like Darnel) they had broken up.[17] In another one of our studies that focused on African American and Latino couples in Chicago, we found that couples who were expressed more warmth with each other during the pregnancy and reported no violence in their relationship also reported lower rates of physically punitive parenting behaviors and lower child-abuse potential scores when their child was 2.[18] By contrast, a couple's prebirth hostility (when interacting with each other) predicted father-to-child hostility observed during the parent–child play activity.

These findings provide evidence of the potential "spillover" between the co-parenting relationship and the relationship between parents and their children. In general terms, the notion of "spillover" typically refers to the process by which problems in the parents' relationship with each other can beget further problems in the parents' relationship with their child, such as increased parenting stress, as well as negative parent–child interactions. In the previously summarized Chicago study and in others we have conducted, we focus on the *couple's* interactions (i.e., both the father's and mother's interpersonal behavior with each other) as a predictor of the father's parenting behavior rather than just examining the father's separate behavior

---

e. Based on the Child Abuse Potential Inventory (or CAPI for short).

with his partner as a predictor of how he functions as a father. This is a subtle but important distinction. The reason for this is that we see the development of fathers as occurring within the context of his relationship with his partner.

To illustrate this point, when we compared the prebirth interactions of expectant parents and postbirth interactions of young fathers with their children (as well as separate mother–child interactions), we found that hostile control with one's partner was associated with higher levels of hostile control with one's child. Additionally, fathers whose *partners* were more hostile and controlling with them before the child was born were more likely to exhibit higher levels of hostile control with their children at the 2-year postbirth follow-up.[15] In other words, we found that fathers were more likely to treat their children the way that they had been treated by their partners. This highlights the way that a hostile interpersonal climate between partners can spillover into the father–child relationship. It is also consistent with previous research that, compared to mothers, fathers' parenting behavior may be even more strongly influenced by the quality of the relationship with their partners.[19,20]

Generally, these findings indicate that *low levels of interpersonal warmth* and *high hostility* are important targets for intervention. That is, if we can help couples reduce their hostility and maintain (or increase) their warmth with each other—while engaged in managing conflict—the fathers may be able function more effectively as parents. Some of our readers may know (from personal experience) that marital therapists tend to focus on helping couples learn to argue *differently* rather than not argue at all. Thus, learning how to prevent escalating hostility and how to warm up the conversation (even when it entails working through arguments) can prevent destructive interpersonal patterns that predict declines in relationship satisfaction and stability.[16,21]

THE IMPORTANCE OF THE CO-PARENTING RELATIONSHIP: ADDITIONAL EVIDENCE

We are not the only researchers to note the importance of a mother and father's co-parenting relationship in setting the stage for parenting and child development.[22,23] For example, other researchers have found that fathers (and mothers) who demonstrate higher levels of sensitivity and responsiveness toward their spouse are more likely to function as constructive parents, balancing warmth and support with guidance and direction.[24] Others have also found that when relationships between parents are marked by high conflict, fathers and mothers are more likely to engage in harsh parenting behaviors.[25] These particular associations between the mother–father relationship and the parent–child relationships indicate how different parts of the "family system" tend to be interdependent. For example, based on data from the Fragile Families Study, Marcia Carlson and her colleagues found that a cooperative co-parenting relationship—marked by supportiveness, perceived trust, and effective communication—was a powerful predictor of both the frequency of father–child contact as well as the quality of father involvement over the first 5 years after a nonmarital birth.[26] Moreover, Carlson and her fellow researchers identified a few key variables that, perhaps not surprisingly, were negatively associated with father involvement, including the father having another child with another partner, the mother acquiring a new partner, and father violence, substance abuse, and incarceration. Nevertheless, even after taking all these factors into account, the quality of the co-parenting relationship still remained a strong predictor of a father's involvement, defined both terms of whether he saw his child at all and how much time he spent in shared activities. Similar to our own findings, these results suggest that being able to establish and maintain a positive co-parenting relationship may help to mitigate various risk factors—risks that happen to be particularly relevant to young fathers.

WHAT IS A POSITIVE CO-PARENTING RELATIONSHIP?

The idea of co-parenting was first introduced by Philip and Carolyn Cowan, two researchers at the University of California–Berkeley who were among the first to pay attention to the quality of a couple's relationship across the transition to parenthood. If their contribution can be boiled down to a single sentence, they demonstrated that couples who were open to the growth and transformation of themselves and their partners across the transition to parenthood were best able to provide their children with a secure and stable home environment. These researchers, who helped inspire us, were the "grandparents" of this field of research.

James McHale, who worked with the Cowans, elaborated on their work in two important ways. Drawing heavily from family systems theorists, McHale proposed that a father's relationship with his partner is inextricably linked to his relationship with his child and his relationship with his child is linked to his relationship with his partner. Moreover, these links operate on multiple levels of experience. So, how we feel about our partners influences how we behave toward our children, and how we behave toward our children influences how our partners feel about us, which influences how we feel about and behave toward them. More recently (and relevant to our work), McHale applied his co-parenting model to understanding the dynamics of unwed couples who may or may not be in a romantic relationship.[27] The value of McHale's more complex understanding of the co-parenting relationship is that it helps clinicians see multiple ways to help effect positive change when problems arise. For example, when working with a family, clinicians like us might work with a couple to decrease blame and criticism toward each other when engaged in conflict, which can then lead to improvements in each of the parent's interactions with their child. Similarly, helping a father engage more positively with his child can lead to more positive interactions in his co-parenting relationship. The beauty of the family systems approach is that it can help us make strategic decisions about how to engage with a family, knowing that tinkering with one component of the system—a single behavior pattern in the co-parenting or parent–child relationship—will likely affect other components, sometimes facilitating growth.

Building on the work of the Cowans and McHale, Mark Feinberg, at Penn State University, developed a framework for studying (and intervening with) co-parenting relationships that takes into account the larger social context in which families live.[28] Feinberg's model defines co-parenting in terms of how parents work together to provide mutual support, share the tasks and functions of parenthood, and manage family disagreements as they cope with the common and not-so-common stressors of life. Although all these researchers initially focused their attention on married, mostly white and middle-class couples, eventually they all expanded the scope of their interests to include socially and economically disadvantaged couples. Collectively, their work guides much of what will be discussed in upcoming chapters.

Over the years, other researchers have joined the conversation about co-parenting. Some have pointed out that what we mean by a co-parenting relationship might vary somewhat, depending on family, social, and cultural contexts. For example, it is easy to see that couples who live together typically define their respective parental roles differently than couples who live apart. For this reason, most family scholars have come to view the co-parenting relationship as distinct from the marital or the romantic relationship. This distinction is useful because pointing it out can help couples see that some aspects of their co-parenting relationship—such as their commitment to their child, their ability to cooperate, and their willingness to be supportive of each other's well-being—are important to their role *as parents*, regardless of whether they are romantically involved.[29]

Like others, we observed that some young parents were learning how to function as supportive partners but we did not know exactly how this was happening. To make sense of it, we decided to define, operationalize, and measure the particular skills we thought young expectant couples might need to become good-enough co-parents. We recognized that it was important to have an approach that would allow us to assess these skills across social and cultural contexts (e.g., Salt Lake City and Chicago). So, we opted for a fairly abstract definition of what we decided to call *relational competence*, focusing on the broad skills a parent needs to effectively communicate with his or her co-parenting partner in a thoughtful and caring way, regardless of the status of their relationship. We conceptualized a relationally competent father as demonstrating that he can say and do what's necessary to maintain a reasonably cooperative, connected, and cohesive co-parenting relationship with the mother of his child, helping to keep them both focused on the well-being of their child.

CO-PARENTING QUALITY AND PATERNAL OUTCOMES

Based on previous research on important predictors of positive relational functioning among couples, particularly during the transition to parenthood,[30–32] we identified five core relational competencies that we set out to study, to see how these core skills were related to paternal outcomes during the transition to parenthood. These five relational competencies include:

(1) *Empathy*, defined as the ability to consider the perspective of one's partner (including the partner's perspective on the co-parenting relationship itself);
(2) *Acceptance*, defined as the ability and willingness to tolerate one's partner as they are (including characteristics that may alienate others);
(3) *Expression of fondness*, which entails expressing positive feelings toward the partner, such as appreciation, warmth, and affection;
(4) *Cohesion*, which involves cooperation, partnership, and commitment to the co-parenting relationship; and
(5) *Relational growth*, defined as having a growth-oriented mindset toward the co-parenting relationship, seeing the relationship as developing over time, recognizing the need to respond to new challenges, and being willing to make necessary changes to respond to those challenges.

In one of our studies, we focused on a subgroup of fathers (from a larger sample) who were at high risk for poor adjustment to parenthood, based on a compilation of risk factors (young paternal age, school failure, psychological disorder(s), substance abuse, negative family relationships, and having prior children).[33,34] We then conducted several statistical analyses to examine the impact of these risk factors—together with the relational competence scores of both fathers and their partners—on paternal outcomes. We were especially interested in seeing whether fathers' relational competence could potentially offset some of these risk factors and help explain better-than-expected outcomes of some of the young fathers who surprised us.

Our findings revealed that fathers' relational competencies (at both the prebirth and 2-year assessments) were significant predictors of their parenting outcomes in several respects. First, fathers' relational competence scores predicted more positive functioning over the course of the transition to parenthood. More specifically, fathers with higher relationship competencies were less controlling when interacting with their 2-year-olds, reported low rates of punitive parenting, and spent more time taking care of their children (based on their partner's report). Second, father's relational competence at follow-up predicted the quality of his parenting regardless of his level of risk for parenting problems. This is not to suggest that risk factors like substance abuse are not important, because they are. Indeed, we found that a father's risk status (assessed during his partner's pregnancy) predicted his parenting outcome. However, when we included his relational competence scores (assessed when his child was 1), his prenatal risk status no longer predicted his paternal functioning when his child was 2. Taken together, these findings highlight one of the most important takeaways in this chapter, namely that a father's relational competence in his co-parenting relationship may indeed help to offset or compensate for personal problems that might otherwise lead to poor paternal functioning.

These findings suggest that certain core relational skills that can be observed in the co-parenting relationship may translate to how a father behaves with his child. If we examine some relational competencies that we identified, it is easy to see how these could be beneficial to parenting and parenthood. For example, the basic capacity to listen actively is a prerequisite for empathy, and acceptance sets the stage for patience. Although fondness is communicated differently toward a partner than a child, the capacity to express one's warm, loving feeling is important to both relationships.

Although we would not suggest that there is a *perfect* correspondence between the relational skills involved in co-parenting and those involved in parenting, there is some consistency. A father with a stronger set of relational competencies, exhibited in his interactions with the mother of his child, is more likely to be able to draw upon these skills when responding to the challenges (as well as the joys) of parenthood. For example, we would expect that a father who is able to remain empathic and understanding when engaged in disagreement with his partner would be more likely to remain calm and patient when his toddler throws a tantrum or refuses to go to bed. Conversely, we would expect that a father who becomes embroiled in hostile exchanges with his partner when dealing with conflict is more likely to lose his cool and interact in a similarly hostile way with his tantruming child.

Darnel's behavior with Cleo and then with Curtis, his 2-year-old son, illustrates the underlying correspondence between co-parenting and parenting skills. As we previously noted, Darnel's coded interactions with Cleo before Curtis was born revealed a high degree of warmth, very little hostility, very low levels of control with his partner, and an absence of criticism or other negative interaction patterns that we commonly observe with couples. We now fast forward about two-and-a-half years when we had the opportunity to observe (and SASB code) Darnel's interactions with his son Curtis while they engaged in the standard puzzle and book activity that we described earlier.[f]

When we examined the codes assigned to Darnel's behavior during the play activity with his son, we found a remarkably high degree of similarity in his interpersonal profiles across these two contexts. As was the case with his interactions with Cleo, Darnel's father–child interactions were characterized by a high degree of warmth (including positive affirmation, praise, and encouragement toward Curtis), a complete absence of hostile codes (no criticism or blame), and a healthy dose of warm structuring and guidance. At first pass, this may come as no surprise, but it's an important connection for two reasons. First, for a long time it was taken for granted that young at-risk fathers like Darnel were not interpersonally skilled and not likely to stick around to parent their children. Although we are pleased that Darnel can help us illustrate what good-enough fathering looks like, it is important to remember that we selected him to be included in this book because he is representative of a group of young men who have been largely overlooked. Second, this correspondence between co-parenting and parenting skills was important to us because—as you may recall—we

f. Of note, these father–child interactions were coded independently from Darnel's and Cleo's interactions collected at our prenatal assessment and by different coders who were unaware of the codes assigned previously. This provides a system of checks and balances to make sure that the codes assigned are as objective as possible and not influenced by expectations generated from our previously collected data.

set out to find good targets for helping young expectant fathers get ready for fatherhood. So, if young men can develop their skills in the context of their co-parenting relationship, then perhaps they will become good co-parenting partners and good-enough parents, even if (or when) the romance ends.

To help readers have a clearer sense of what coded fathering behavior looks like in real life, we include below a brief play-by-play summary of Darnel's interactions with Curtis during the puzzle activity. Since we can't include actual footage of the video (we wish we could), we figured this was the next best thing.

Curtis watched with anticipation as Darnel pulled a puzzle out of the box, looked at him and said: "What's this? It looks like Elmo to me. Does it look like Elmo to you? How about you and me see if we can figure out how to put this puzzle together?"

Darnel was not overly demonstrative or directive as some parents can be when talking to their children on camera. His tone was soft and casual but lilted upward, encouraging his son to participate. He seemed genuinely interested in Curtis's opinion about whether or not this puzzle piece had Elmo on it. Then he dumped the Elmo puzzle pieces out onto the table, picked up one piece, which he showed Curtis, and said: "OK, you see this piece with Elmo on it? You slide it in right there," pointing to the spot where it belonged and making a sliding motion with his hand.

He pulled it back out and handed it to Curtis, who did exactly what Darnel suggested. When he fit the piece into the right spot, Darnel clapped and said, "That's good! You did it!"

He then moved to the next piece, as Curtis looked on with a big, bright-eyed smile, absorbing his success. Darnel continued to instruct: "Now put this one right there. . . . Just push it right in," followed by an approving "HEY!"

When they were done, Darnel picked up the puzzle said, "And there's Big Bird next to Elmo . . . but who is that?" and then waited for his son who took a moment—thinking deeply—and said (somewhat incomprehensively), "Cookie Monster!"

Darnel responded, saying, "That's right! Cookie Monster!" and then, "OK, we are done with that one! Voila!"

Darnel kept this conversation—mostly a monologue—going with Curtis throughout the entire play activity, which lasted for about 20 minutes. He asked him questions and clapped when he responded, and Darnel congratulated him when he finished a puzzle. Curtis was totally into it. He was focused on the task, responding to Darnel's questions with sounds that were not quite words yet. Curtis clapped his hands whenever Darnel clapped.

We see quite a few fathers who are not so skilled at engaging their children. Some are overbearing, putting the entire puzzle together themselves. Some take their child's hand and force them to put the pieces together. Some let their child do it entirely on their own, not realizing that no 2-year-old could put these puzzles together without some help. And some are preoccupied by their cell phones. While there is nothing unusual about Darnel's interaction with Curtis, it is nonetheless remarkable to watch. Darnel provides a mix of structuring, guiding, affirming, and inquiring behavior that is exactly right for keeping Curtis engaged and entertained. They seemed in sync.

Notably, our research on high-risk fathers indicated that some of these young men (like Darnel) were relationally competent right from the get go, at our first assessment before the baby was born. And they continued to maintain their relational competence throughout the transition to parenthood. For this group of fathers, their relationship skills predicted both (a) a more positive co-parenting relationship after the baby was born (and up to the follow-up assessment when their child was 2) and (b) more positive paternal outcomes. As previously noted, these relationship skills also served as a buffer against some personal problems and helped account for their better-than-expected outcomes.

For other fathers, we observed an interesting process of relational skill *development* during the transition to parenthood. Tracking these young men and their partners over time, we found that those whose *partners* were more interpersonally skilled were also more likely to make a positive transition to parenthood.[34] In particular, mothers with solid relational skills (observed during the pregnancy) tended to have partners who were more positively engaged as fathers 2 years postbirth. Sometimes this was because relationally skilled mothers picked relationally skilled fathers, like Cleo and Darnel. However, some fathers who were not so skilled at first, but who were paired with relationally competent partners, *became* more skilled over time. This suggests that they were learning something from their partners. These fathers, with their improved relational skills, were more likely to be constructively and warmly engaged with their children. As previously suggested, these findings indicate that "spillover" from one relationship onto another can be positive. Indeed, under some circumstances, positive relational skills can be transmitted from one partner to another, perhaps through modeling or the establishment of a secure co-parenting bond, or both.[34-36] Of course, when improvements in the co-parenting relationship occur, the "direction of influence" is not always unidirectional. Young mothers and fathers can learn from each other. The overall point is that, among the young at-risk fathers in our study, improvements in the co-parenting relationship, mediated by the positive influence of a relationally skilled partner, was an important predictor of positive fathering outcomes.

THE IMPORTANCE OF THE CO-PARENTING RELATIONSHIP: PRACTICAL IMPLICATIONS

As indicated in Chapter 7, a positive co-parenting relationship can also be beneficial for mothers. When fathers provide their partners with tangible and emotional support, mothers tend to be less stressed and have more time and positive energy to devote to themselves and their children.[37,38] Our own research has found that significant declines in the quality of the relationship with one's partner over the first year of parenting is associated with higher parenting stress among mothers 2 years postbirth.[17] And previous research has shown that mothers who have stable and supportive relationships with partners are more attuned to their infant's needs and are less likely to engage in negative parenting behaviors.[25,39,40] In contrast, mothers who report serious relationship problems with the father of their baby tend to experience difficulties during the transition to parenthood.[41–43] Other researchers who have focused specifically on adolescent mothers have found that a supportive relationship with the father of their baby is associated with lower levels of depression, compared to mothers with a negative co-parenting relationship.[41,42,44] This finding is especially important, given the extensive evidence that maternal depression can have adverse effects on parenting, parent–child attachment, and overall child development.[45,46] In fact, the research on maternal depression and its effects recently led the US Department of Health and Human Services to begin treating postpartum depression as a public health concern.[g]

When we reflect on the importance of a positive co-parenting relationship, and the core set of interpersonal skills necessary to establish and maintain such a relationship, we think there is room for hope and action. Compared to other important influences in the development of positive, engaged fathers, this one readily lends itself to intervention efforts. More than with any other factor linked with positive father engagement,

---

g. Of note, in the last several years, in keeping with the overall increased attention to fathers and their importance in the family, researchers, as well as the general public, have also begun to recognize the important and significant impact of paternal depression.[47,48]

relational competencies are something that we can *do* something about. They can be taught and directly facilitated, at least to an extent.

Throughout this book, we have focused on understanding the dramatic changes that have occurred in the structure of families over the last 50 years. We have argued that keeping fathers connected to their children is important because their absence destabilizes families and puts children at risk. When it occurs on a massive scale, father absence begins to fray the social fabric for two primary reasons: (a) rootless, disconnected men are particularly prone to engage in dangerous, maladaptive, and harmful behaviors and (b) children with disengaged fathers are at greater risk for problems throughout their childhood because of deprivations associated with father absence. So far, we have not spent much time writing about what could or should be done to help young fathers and their families stay connected. This is about to change. In the next and final section of this book, we discuss what can be done to keep children from losing their fathers, keep mothers from losing their partners, and keep fathers from losing their way.

As we note in the next section of this book, we view the provision of co-parenting support, with a focus on helping young fathers and mothers work together, as a key component of supporting young fathers and stabilizing families in this time of rapid social change. In fact, this approach is something that we have already begun to put into practice, with a co-parenting-based intervention that has demonstrated some initial success. But, before we talk about this, we need to first talk about what other programs designed to support fathers and their families have been tried and how those programs have fared.

PART SIX

New Beginnings

CHAPTER 21

Fatherhood Programs

A Short History of Trial and Failure

When Sigmund Freud was asked about the secret to a happy life he quipped, "Love and work, work and love, that's all there is." Is it that simple? In many respects, much of what we have been writing about leads us to the same conclusion. For most fathers, their capacity for connection to their family can be boiled down to their capacity to work and love. Freud's two-word synopsis of the meaning of life succinctly describes what adheres young fathers to their families. If fathers can positively connect with their partners and meaningfully contribute to raising their children, they are more likely to stick around and become relatively stable, constructive members of society. Freud recognized that work and love are connected, not just serving different functions but also representing different aspects of our human nature. It also seems likely that he was not just referring to passionate romantic love. Love pertains to our children, parents, and siblings, and for some of us, it might even extend to ex-partners, whom we may not like very much.

FATHERS AND WORK

Work is on the minds of most young fathers, and so we've found that asking about work is a good place to begin our interview. Their hopes about what sort of job they'd like is a good ice-breaker and an indicator of their maturity, their hopefulness, their investment in themselves, and their assessment of the opportunities available to them. Many of the young men are working in low-paying service jobs but have high hopes for the future, like owning a business or becoming a police officer or playing for the NBA, which seems unlikely but is certainly typical of adolescent dreams and aspirations. When Mike first asked Darnel about the sort of work he'd like to be doing—before he went to jail—his response indicates that he'd spent some time thinking about this.

> DARNEL: Eventually, what I really want to do is become a heating and air conditioning repairman. That's what I really want to do. I like fixing stuff. Stuff like that.
>
> MIKE: What do you see as the advantages of that kind of work?
>
> DARNEL: Just something I want to do. Maybe I can start my own repair company for heating and air conditioning. I just like fixing things, fixing anything. I'm either going to try to be in the heating and air conditioning business or repair cars. But I don't really like getting greasy and stuff.
>
> MIKE: You want to fix things but stay clean?
>
> DARNEL: Right. I'd like to have a business of my own, a heating and air conditioning business.
>
> MIKE: OK. What's your idea of success?
>
> DARNEL: I guess having a house that my kid can live in. A car for my kid to get around in, food for my kid to eat, clothes on their back. That's my idea of success. As long as I can take care of my family, that's all I want to do.
>
> MIKE: Do you see yourself as someone who has the opportunity for success?
>
> DARNEL: Uhmmm not really. I don't know, 'cause . . . see people . . . certain people might not like you because of the way . . . They see one thing about me, like I don't like wearing suits. So when you own your own business, you might have to get a loan and wear a suit and all that. And I don't like wearing suits, and they might take that and hold that against me, or whatever. I don't know. Really, I see myself . . . maybe I could be successful but it will be hard. It's going to be hard to become successful but I think I could do it.

Later in the interview when Mike asked Darnel about what sort of program would have been helpful for him or helpful for other young men getting ready for fatherhood, he considered the question for a very long time before responding.

DARNEL: Basically, you know, if I can get this job in heating and AC, that's basically the only thing that's holding me back. I don't really like programs, but I think they should have job programs for fathers. Basically, something to teach them a trade, where they'll find a good job. Something like that. That's basically the only program I think that they should have.

Darnel's dream seems modest and reasonable, but his uncertainty about whether he can attain that dream is sadly realistic, given that he is a young African American in a hypersegregated city with no training and no connections. Indeed, one of the striking differences between fathers in Salt Lake City and fathers in Chicago is that, in Salt Lake City, reasonable aspirations are more attainable. It's not unusual for young fathers in Salt Lake to eventually find work building houses in Park City or operating forklifts in the copper mine across the Salt Lake valley. Decent jobs are easier to find because the economy is stronger, and there are readily available networks—made up of family, church friends, and neighbors—working to provide opportunities.

In Chapter 7, we introduced William Julius Wilson, who wrote *The Truly Disadvantaged*. In this book (and in later books), Wilson made an explicit link between our jobs problem (that there are not enough good jobs for unskilled men) and the fatherhood problem (that there are not enough marriageable men, leading to men being less connected to their families). As we discussed in Chapter 7, like Moynihan before him, Wilson was sounding the alarms and making waves in academic institutions and think tanks. At the time, Wilson was arguing that when decent paying jobs for unskilled workers disappear from the American landscape, our assumptions about traditional marital roles are undermined; people stop getting married and families become less stable. If men cannot occupy their expected familial roles, women will no longer see much point in marrying them. Without a decent job to keep them focused, busy, and useful, they may be more trouble than they're worth. Wilson also suggested that if men—particularly African American men—could find decent jobs where they could earn a respectable living, they would become more marriageable and women would presumably be more likely to marry them.

Wilson's books focused most squarely on African American families—he was thinking about men like Darnel—but his theory about work and marriage could easily be applied to other racial or ethnic groups, some of which are now following the same pattern of family formation evident in African American communities. In the years that followed the publication of Wilson's book, the link between young male underemployment and paternal disengagement on the one hand and single motherhood and welfare reliance on the other hand became more prevalent and more entrenched. Reactively, there was a growing conviction among some politicians that welfare was the culprit, effectively relieving absent fathers of their responsibilities. Scholars like Charles Murray[1] and Robert Rector[2] took Wilson's ideas about "marriageable men" in a different direction. They proposed that if absent fathers were heavily penalized for not paying their child support, they would (a) be less likely to have children out of wedlock, and (b) they would be more motivated to make the money they needed to support their children.

So, in 1988, when Congress passed the Family Support Act (FSA), they tied welfare laws, child support enforcement laws, and employment programs together in a way that was designed to discourage welfare dependency among single mothers, encourage marriage, and enforce payment of child support in ways that would discourage out-of-wedlock parenthood. Child support (for those who don't know) is the amount of money that the government orders a noncustodial parent to pay a custodial parent to support their child or children. The formula for determining how much should be paid varies from state to state but typically it's about 17 percent of the noncustodial parent's salary for one child and then an additional percentage for other children, up to a certain proportion of the total income—usually about 40 percent. The formula can get complicated, but this simplified description is intended to give you the gist of it (for the sake of making sense of this section).

For a long time, a parent was expected to pay the other parent directly, but eventually the payments were brokered through the office of Child Support Enforcement (CSE), which is part of the government. Importantly, CSE took a cut because the government expected to be paid back for whatever it had paid to support the custodial parent and the children. For disadvantaged families, this would typically include the reimbursement of welfare payments made to the mother and a portion of the Medicaid payment to the hospital to cover childbirth expenses. This often adds up to a substantial amount of money, well beyond the capacity of most noncustodial fathers.

Just how much of the child support payment could be held back by the government and how much would be passed onto the custodial parent varies from state to state. In 1988, when the FSA was enacted, one of the problems that the legislature was trying to fix was that many noncustodial parents did not make their child support payments. One feature of this new law was that it allowed states to garnish a man's wages to pay for child support that was owed, including what was owed to the government for the support it had provided to his children and their mother. It was intended to be a "tough-love" kind of law to reform "deadbeat dads" as well as reduce the tax burden of welfare and Medicaid. And—this point is especially important—it also prevented custodial and noncustodial parents from working out their own system for sharing the costs of raising their children, which is commonly called "informal child support." The advantages and disadvantages of informal child support are complicated. Sometimes these informal arrangements mean the custodial parent gets less but sometimes it means she (or he) gets more. But when the exchange is not handled by CSE, the government does not receive its "payback" because it is cut out of the deal.

The FSA also funded the first study designed to test the hypothesis that Wilson and others had proposed: If we help absent or disengaging fathers get jobs, they will re-engage with their families and do their "fair share."[3,4] This study, which was called Parents' Fair Share (PFS), was run out of a research shop/think tank in New York City called MDRC (which stands for Manpower Demonstration Research Corporation). MDRC has produced a great deal of high-quality research in the areas of fatherhood and employment. For the PFS study, the MDRC researchers recruited fathers and divided them into two groups: a treatment group that received job support, including training, job placement, and subsidized paychecks, and a control group that received no such services. They hired local providers to deliver this array of services to the treatment group and followed both groups of men over 3 years, gathering data about sustained employment, increased earnings, and child support payments.

To make a long story short, MDRC found that, contrary to expectations, the men in their control group—the group that did *not* participate in the PFS program—were actually doing a little *better* in terms of their earnings and their child support payments than men in the treatment group. These researchers also found that although fathers in the treatment group were paying more for child support than they were before the study, they were also paying less in informal support to help their children and their children's mother. These results were disappointing, but it would be unfair to knock either MDRC or the federal government for this failed experiment to help fathers by providing jobs and training. After all, no one had ever tried conducting a study that was specifically designed to help disengaged, disadvantaged fathers by providing job support. It was a first step.

MDRC wrote a report on the process of administering the PFS project in which they reflected upon their dismal results and made recommendations to future researchers who might take up the challenge of trying to help disadvantaged young men get decent jobs that would allow them to engage with, and support, their families.⁵ Essentially, they said working with the young men they had recruited for the study was harder than they had anticipated because these men were so profoundly ill-prepared for the working world and for parenthood. The MDRC report, written in 2001, begins with the following statement:

> Low-income noncustodial fathers are a disadvantaged group. Many live on the edge of poverty and face severe barriers to finding jobs, while those who can find work typically hold low-wage or temporary jobs. . . . Some services, such as peer support, proved to be very important and valuable to the men and became the focal point of the program. Other services, such as skill building, were hard to implement because the providers had little experience working with such a disadvantaged group; it was difficult to find employers willing to hire the men, and the providers were not equipped to deal with the circumstances of men who often were simply trying to make it from one day to the next. Finally, we learned about the challenges of implementing a program like PFS, which involves the partnership of various agencies with different goals, and about the difficulty of recruiting low-income fathers into such a program.[5pvi]

In other words, the designers of PFS were shocked to find out how hard job training can be. The takeaway lesson: helping fathers (particularly low-income, disadvantaged fathers) find jobs and fulfill their financial responsibilities to their children was not as simple as it seemed.

Around the same time that the PFS project was wrapping up, a fatherhood "movement" was just getting started.[6–8] This movement, which had support from both liberals and conservatives, was oriented toward both affirming the role of men in families and acknowledging that fathers needed to become more responsible for their families. Eventually, this movement led to the development of programs designed to help men become more effective fathers. Some credit Vice President Dan Quayle's critique of the *Murphy Brown* television series as the spark that initiated this movement. *Murphy Brown* featured Candice Bergen as a professionally successful, hard-edged single woman who chooses to have a baby on her own, without a husband or a father. In its essence, the Quayle critique was that the show diminished the importance of fathers and amounted to an assault on the traditional two-parent family because Murphy Brown's decision to raise a baby on her own was treated (by the show) as perfectly acceptable. This was scandalous at the time and galvanized some men to "stand up" for the rights and roles of men in society. There were rallies across the country of "promise keepers" whose loose agenda was to literally stand up and cheer for traditional fatherhood roles and to encourage fathers to fulfill those roles. In 1997, Wade Horn launched the National Fatherhood Initiative and published a paper describing the "Responsible Fatherhood Movement."[9] Over the next few years, along with other fatherhood advocates, Horn created a more concrete agenda for helping fathers take more responsibility for their children.

While the responsible fatherhood movement had its origins in conservatism, Vice President Al Gore, a liberal, picked up the torch and began advocating for fatherhood responsibility too. At this phase of our national debate about how to solve the fatherhood problem, politicians on both sides of the aisle were adopting a "get tough" approach to child support enforcement and welfare reform, hoping to force men to own up to their responsibilities.[10] The angst about absent fathers and single mothers on welfare led to the passage of the Personal Responsibility and Work Opportunity Reconciliation Act (PRWORA), widely known as welfare reform. This law further strengthened child support enforcement but also incentivized fathers to play a more active role in the lives of their children. The law authorized funding for employment programs—open to both men and women—that were specifically designed to "end welfare as we know it."[11] The idea, which was sound in principle, was to help people on welfare find jobs. Following the passage of welfare reform in 1996, Clinton also signed the Deadbeat Parents Punishment Act (yes, that was its official name) in 1998, which stiffened the penalties for not paying child support, without adjustments for a father's ability to pay. During the signing ceremony, President Clinton explained the reasoning behind this law:

> One of the main reasons single mothers go on welfare is that fathers have failed to meet their responsibilities to the children. . . . We have waged an unprecedented campaign to make deadbeat parents live up to their obligations. Thanks to tougher laws, more sophisticated tracking, [and] powerful new collection tools, we've increased child support collections by 68 percent in the last 5 years. Almost a million-and-a-half more children are getting child support today. The Deadbeat Parents Punishment Act of 1998 deals with child support evaders in the most serious cases. From now on, if you flee across state lines and refuse to pay child support, you may be charged with a Federal offense, a felony offense, and may land in jail for up to two years. One way or the other, people who don't support their children will pay.

Clinton was trying to hold fathers accountable by preventing them from cheating their children and the government, but the law he enacted failed to take into account the fact that many fathers don't pay child support (especially formal child support) because they don't have the money. The problem with this law was that, for some fathers, it essentially criminalized poverty.

After George W. Bush won the presidency in 2000, Wade Horn was hired to lead the efforts by the Administration of Children and Families (ACF) to promote responsible fatherhood with a new round of programs for fathers. Congress approved funds—about 50 to 75 million dollars a year—to support these programs. Many of these programs were not exclusively focused on job training or child support payments. Even those that were funded through the CSE office combined job support services with educational support, like GED classes and parenting education, helping fathers understand their role in their child's development. There was a lot of fatherhood excitement in the air, particularly for helping nonresidential fathers reconnect or stay connected. Twenty years and about one billion dollars later, there is little evidence that these programs had much of an impact on any of the criteria by which the federal government was defining "responsible fatherhood," including job stability, increased earnings, or more child support payments.[12-14] Why was there so little impact despite all the money and enthusiasm? It is difficult to know with much certainty because there was remarkably little emphasis on data collection for determining outcomes or impacts.[15,16] What we do know is that these programs had a very difficult time finding, recruiting, or keeping fathers—particularly nonresidential fathers—engaged in their programs.[17-19]

With respect to the issue of work, there are two fundamental structural problems with ACF's approach to helping fathers find and keep jobs. The first is that ACF has tended to fund programs that lack both the expertise and the infrastructure required to provide unskilled men with the sort of training and support they needed to access and keep *good* jobs that could pull them out of poverty. Most of the ACF Responsible Fatherhood money went to small agencies with expertise in fatherhood education *or* to faith-based organizations with expertise supporting the moral rectitude of fathers *or* to CSE agencies with expertise in enforcing child support payment. There was little expertise in job training, job placement, or job coaching support among the grantees in 2006, 2011, or 2015.[20] One of ACF's mistakes, which they repeated over the years, is based on the idea that poor fathers just need a little guidance, inspiration, and incentive. On the face of it, it seemed obvious that the way to help fathers find jobs is to help them write resumes, develop their interviewing/self-presentation skills, and to sit down at a computer and help them peruse job openings and submit applications. If the economy is reasonably healthy, there should be enough jobs available for this process to provide quick support for many unemployed fathers.

This assumption is flawed in two respects. First, helping undereducated young men who lack job skills training get dead-end jobs that pay poorly has limited value when it comes to solving the "responsible fatherhood" problem because such fathers will still lack the means to work their way out of poverty. The second problem—flagged in the previously quoted PFS report—is that many young fathers are more "down and out" than Moynihan or Wilson imagined. The challenge of helping these men requires substantial expertise in the development of marketable skills and in preparing workplace managers to ensure that placements will be successful. This is partly because the job market is a moving target, requiring inge- nuity and flexibility to anticipate changes in what employers need. But it is mostly because helping undereducated, low-skilled young fathers achieve success in the working world requires a high level of expertise in the devel- opment of both "soft" and "hard" skills. Trainers must work closely with employers, technical schools, and, in some cases, mental health providers to build a solid foundation for fathers' future success. Unfortunately, ACF did not heed the advice provided in the PFS report that they had paid for. Not surprisingly (given these significant flaws), there is no evidence that any of the dozens of jobs programs for fathers funded by ACF since the PFS project have resulted in higher earnings, more child support payments, or increased involvement in child-rearing among fathers who participated.

The failure of ACF's job programs for fathers is not an indictment of job programs in general. There have been some successful job programs, and the "science" of workforce development and job training has made great strides in identifying how to help underskilled, disadvantaged young people ready themselves for the workforce.[20] For example, the Department of Labor has published several reports on best practices in job training programs, in- cluding a document entitled, "What Works in Job Training."[21] In summary, these reports recommend that workforce development programs should do the following:

(a) Work directly with specific industries to determine their needs and en- sure that would-be employees are trained to fill anticipated jobs;
(b) Use validated tools to evaluate each young person's skills, deficits, interests, and motivators to make an appropriate employer match and determine what training is needed to make that match successful;
(c) Facilitate the development of necessary skills and address deficits that interfere with job performance before, during, and after job placement, to ensure that performance goals are being met;
(d) Help employers develop management skills needed to work effectively with disadvantaged employees; and

(e) Develop training networks that will allow lower-level workers to acquire new skills incrementally, allowing for advancement.

There is an old and overused adage that goes like this: "If you give a man a fish, you feed him for a day. If you teach him to fish, you feed him for a lifetime." Consistent with this adage, the intended goals of job training programs for fathers are to promote independence and provide men the means to support their families. The failed efforts of ACF to develop effective job programs is that they simply lack the expertise to do so. We believe the takeaway message is that when you try to teach a man to fish, it's best to have someone on hand who knows how to fish.

Another flaw in ACF-funded job programs is that ACF set itself up to be an untrustworthy source of support for fathers.[22] Here's the problem: in addition to managing the "responsible fatherhood" programs, ACF oversees both the Temporary Assistance for Needy Families (TANF) program, our current version of welfare, and CSE services, which is responsible for making sure fathers provide financial support for their children and pay the government back for welfare and Medicaid coverage provided to their children and their children's mother. The fact that the ACF manages all these overlapping family-oriented support activities is not a problem in and of itself. In fact, there is probably some efficiency in that arrangement. The problem is that the ACF uses its leverage in ways that undermine its credibility with the disadvantaged populations it is trying to help, sabotaging the potential effectiveness of its programs. To make certain that fathers pay their fair share of childrearing costs, two important rules were established.

Rule 1: A mother cannot enroll in any government assistance program (TANF, Medicaid, etc.) unless she agrees to help the state enroll her child's father in child support, regardless of whether he is helping her out financially and/or otherwise taking care of the kids. From the perspective of CSE, every man who fathers a child outside of marriage[a] needs a child support order. This helps hold him accountable to his children—and the state—even if he and his partner would rather work out an informal arrangement. For example, before an unmarried mother can enroll in the IRS's Earned Income Tax Credit (EITC) program, which is the nation's largest antipoverty program, she must help the state sign up her child's

a. The fact that married parents are not expected to pay child support might seem problematic to unmarried parents who fully support their children without government involvement. That is, the policy assumes the worst from unmarried parents and assumes the best from those who marry.

father for child support by providing his name and address. If she declines to help, she is not eligible for the credit.[b]

Rule 2: A father cannot enroll in a government-funded job program without agreeing to pay his child support through the state, allowing CSE to hold onto some of his earnings to reimburse the state for their support of his children. While this might seem reasonable, it's important to remember that (a) men who show up for jobs programs tend to be dirt poor and (b) the jobs they get usually pay very little. Once these fathers are signed up for child support, they will automatically be docked for some of what they owe to the government for their partner's welfare support, regardless of their poverty status. Many fathers do the math and quickly realize this arrangement offers little for themselves, their partners, or their children. Finally, if a father signs up and is assessed for child support and then fails to pay what is owed, including back payments, he is in jeopardy of going to jail for failure to pay. Fathers who are currently off the "child support grid" would be effectively turning themselves in for a crime they committed retroactively as soon as they are assessed by CSE. Unfortunately, when a father declines the offer for job training or job placement support (with all those strings attached), he perpetuates the stereotype of the "deadbeat dad." The truth is more complicated.

These two rules regarding child support enrollment were designed to prevent families from "double dipping" into the state's coffers (e.g., receiving child support *and* welfare) and to ensure that fathers who earn a healthy paycheck but are skipping out on child support would be held accountable. These laws are the state's way to hedge its bets against the realistic concern that some fathers will shirk their responsibilities and the less realistic concern that couples would collude to get more than their fair share of the state's available support. These rules are intended—at least in part—to protect entitlement programs such as Medicaid, TANF, and EITC, and the effort to keep these programs solvent by protecting against fraud is reasonable. However, these rules make sense only when a father is making a decent wage and not otherwise helping to support his children. Applying these rules to working men who are also impoverished seems to

---

b. As a side note, the EITC program, which might help working fathers boost themselves out of poverty, does not extend to unmarried and noncustodial fathers. Specifically, a noncustodial father who is working and helping to support his children is not eligible for receiving an earned income tax credit even if he earns a "qualifying" salary (e.g., he is poor). A married father earning the same amount and contributing the same amount to his child would be eligible for that earned income tax credit in tandem with his wife.

defeat the purpose of these programs, especially if they are already helping out informally.

The problem—and it's a big one—is that requiring economically disadvantaged fathers to pay the government back for supporting their economically disadvantaged families has the effect of penalizing the poor for trying to pull themselves out of poverty. If fathers are poor and unable to provide enough support for their child, as many young fathers are, then it might make sense for the state to help support their children without asking for the payback. By providing temporary welfare (TANF) and Medicaid to disadvantaged mothers without the demand that impoverished fathers reimburse them, the government could give the whole family a boost by allowing them to use their modest earnings to pay their bills and maybe get out of debt. When families are "doubly poor" in the sense that *both* partners are impoverished, asking them to pay for their own antipoverty programs seems more than a little perverse. Not surprisingly, this set-up scares some impoverished men away from participating in job training services or enrolling in child support.

It's worth recalling Darnel's goal of becoming a heating and air-conditioning repairman, his doubts about how to make that happen, and his suggestion that programs for fathers focus on helping young men learn a trade. As we indicated earlier, Darnel was eventually able to find legitimate work, after a couple stints in jail, but at the age of 21, he was still not heading for the type of stability he had hoped for when we first met him at the age of 18. Although we present Darnel as a father who is doing better than we expected, we know he also represents someone who has been unable to achieve his own modest goals. What would it take to help a young man like Darnel stay out of trouble and work toward the stability he hopes for?

We are not against child support or the enforcement of child support laws. Encouraging fathers to establish paternity and making sure so-called deadbeat fathers pay child support is an important step toward stabilizing families, at least financially. But, if child support enforcement is to be used as a poverty reduction tool for the doubly poor (i.e., when both parents are impoverished), the rules must be applied more judiciously. Garnering the wages of impoverished men making minimum wage to "reimburse" Medicaid for childbirth expenses and to pay back TANF for their partner's "welfare" check strikes many fathers (and mothers) as cold-hearted. In several states, fathers who are delinquent in their child support payments are put in jail, regardless of their ability to pay, creating a "debtor's prison" situation.[23] Such laws can serve to undermine the credibility of a system intended to support families.

Government-sponsored work programs, child support enforcement programs, and antipoverty financial assistance programs each play an important role in addressing the fatherhood problem. Figuring out ways to make these programs work more effectively isn't rocket science. One of the most successful child support enforcement experiments simply divided impoverished men into two groups. In one group, all child support payments went directly to mother and child. In the other group, it was business as usual, meaning that the state held onto some of it (sometimes, much of it). As anticipated, the fathers in the first group were more likely to be working and their children were doing better at follow-up.[24] The lesson? When the government allows fathers (and mothers) to experience the benefit of their earnings (rather than having to pay the state for services provided to their partner), they are more likely to participate in job programs *and* the child support system. Some state governments have adopted this approach, demonstrating that it can work. Theoretically, allowing poor people to work their way out of poverty will diminish the cost of future antipoverty programs because, hopefully, there would be fewer poor people.

Recall Freud's outlook on the meaning of life that we presented at the beginning of this chapter ("Work and love, love and work . . ."). We meet very few young men who would disagree with Freud about the importance of work. Based on our data, most young men believe having a job that earns a decent wage is vital to their role as fathers. Changing the odds against disadvantaged young men, like Darnel, is a monumental task, requiring fundamental improvements to our educational, criminal justice, and mental health treatment systems. We are not about to suggest how to accomplish all that because doing so would require another book. But we do have a modest suggestion that is within our reach: end government programs and policies that deter disadvantaged men from making use of available services—especially job training programs—and invest in job programs and policies that have been shown to be effective. Like Darnel, most young fathers hope for work that will allow them to support their children and provide them with a sense of purpose. That hope is a tremendous resource, and we should not let it go to waste. And what about love? How do we help young fathers with that part of Freud's prescription for a good life?

FATHERS AND LOVE

Evolutionary theorists have suggested that love is an adaptation that helps to ensure that children will be protected and cared for by their parents.[25]

We fall in love with our children because they need us, and we fall in love with our partners because we need them to help us with the kids.[26] Because human infants take so long to grow up, human parents need some motivating factor to stay invested in the hard work of child-rearing over the long haul. Love helps us endure, and it ensures that the next generation survives. Some may think that talking about love in such functional terms saps it of its magical nature. We think the idea that our survival as a species depends on our capacity to love *deepens* rather than diminishes its significance. Love is a powerfully compelling emotional state of enduring affection for others who we need and who need us, despite everything that happens to drive us apart. Moreover, love often feels like life depends on its outcome, as if we cannot live without the ones we love. In fact, we cannot, at least from an evolutionary perspective. Sure, life goes on when we lose the ones we love, but if we, as a species, were to lose our capacity to love, we'd be screwed. It's an unimaginable proposition because love is so fundamentally part of who we are.

There are claims that our current notions of romantic love are a modern, Western phenomenon, but there is also evidence that romance is not new or distinctively Western. In *The Song of Songs*, which was written sometime around the 5th century BCE, a young woman tells her lover that his kisses are sweeter than wine. And he, in turn, describes the taste of her tongue as like milk and honey, and her fragrance like an orchard of pomegranates. Remarkably, this obscure section of the Old Testament captures the passion of young love with a poignancy that could lend itself to a chart-topping hit single (sung, perhaps, by Taylor Swift). Even more tantalizing than the Song of Songs, the Kamasutra, which is popularly known as India's ancient book of erotica, could be aptly described as an instruction manual for those seeking love. Written in the 3rd century BCE, its chapters provide useful tips on how to make oneself attractive and alluring to a potential partner, how to effectively propose to a would-be spouse or paramour, and, yes, how to keep that romance alive with some interesting tricks.

So, we could argue that, as a species, we have long been preoccupied with the thrill of romantic love. Of course, romantic love is often the spark that leads to the creation of a family, sometimes sooner than expected. And hopefully, as romantic love matures, its flame continues to burn bright, providing both the lovers and their children with the warmth of a secure bond. The problem is that romantic love doesn't always last (or maybe wasn't there to begin with). In these cases, co-parenting partners— former lovers or whatever they might be—must pick up the pieces of their relationship and figure out how to put things back together in a way that might still work. We believe in the power and the value of romantic love, but we also believe that becoming overly focused on romantic love and/or promoting marriage will not address the problem of disengaged fathers. Perhaps, our obsession with romantic love has prevented us from appreciating other forms of love that might be equally important. And so, in this chapter, we will focus on a different type of love. It's the sort of love we need to maintain a reasonable relationship with our child's other parent for the long haul of parenting, regardless of the nature of that relationship. Most readers may feel puzzled here. Is that love? We maintain that because its function is to support a child, it qualifies.

In the musical *The Fiddler on the Roof*, the main character is Tevye, a middle-aged Jewish dairyman in 19th-century Russia with two problems. First, he is a Jew living in anti-Semitic Czarist Russia. And second, he has five daughters, three of whom are reaching adulthood. There is a poignant scene when Tevye is agonizing over the fact that one of his daughters, Chava, has fallen in love with Fyedka, a Russian soldier in a military brigade that recently attacked his village. Despite this, Fyedka is not anti-Semitic and wants to marry Tevye's daughter, whom he loves. When Tevye refuses to grant his permission for them to marry, they run off together. Tevye is dismayed that his daughter could fall for a man like this and defy his authority, but he is also awestruck by the mystery of love. Given that his own marriage was arranged by a matchmaker, who probably cared very little about romance and love, Tevye, still puzzling over his daughter's elopement, turns to his wife, Golde, and asks (perhaps for the first time), "Do you love me?" To which she responds, "Do I *what*!?"

The question surprises Golde, who initially brushes Tevye off as a fool for even asking. But Tevye persists. So, Golde considers the question and points out that she takes care of Tevye, takes care of their children, looks after the house, even milks the cow. Not satisfied with this response, Tevye asks again. At this point, Golde seems to become more interested in the question. She reflects, more to herself than to Tevye, that they have suffered through some hard times and yet still stay together; they argue but still share their bed. She wonders out loud, "If that's not love, what is?" Tevye persists, wanting a direct answer. When she finally says yes, perhaps she does love Tevye, he responds that perhaps he loves her too.

It is hard to believe that Tevye and Golde have raised five daughters without ever considering the issue of love. But in their world, love was about creating and maintaining a family and the hard work of caring for others. Golde defines herself and her love in terms of who she is (Tevye's wife) and what she does (takes care of Tevye and their children). Golde's definition of love is not particularly romantic but, because it holds their family together, she "supposes" that it counts as love. Is that sufficiently meaningful? For Tevye, Golde's love is meaningful enough, and he's satisfied.

Tevye and Golde live in another world, but there are lessons to be learned from their conversation. Golde considers the question of love in purely practical, action-oriented terms. Golde's definition will likely be unsatisfying for those of us who want more from our relationships. But that's not the point. We think Golde's practical definition of love could be useful for co-parenting couples in 21st-century America who are struggling with the paradox of love: that the demands and disappointments of romantic love can, at times, undermine or even destroy the possibility of a kind of love between co-parents that is more functional. For us, Golde's response to Tevye raises two fundamental questions: Can young co-parenting couples learn to love and commit to each other? And, if their romantic love evaporates, can they find contentment with a more functional, practical sort of love?

CAN WE TEACH LOVE?

The sharp rise of divorce in the 1970s and 1980s led to growing concerns that people were losing the capacity to create loving relationships that would endure. This led some scholars and politicians to ask, "Can we help convince young expectant couples that marriage is a good idea?" Determined to find out the answer to this question, in 2001, the Administration for Children and Families (ACF) started funding marriage promotion programs designed to provide relationship education and encourage people—particularly lower income people of color—to get married and stay married. Even skeptics like us, who questioned the fundamental premise of pushing marriage, couldn't help but be interested in whether such an approach could work. Is it possible to talk people into getting married? Would those marriages last?

In 2002, ACF hired Mathematica, another research institute in New York City, to design and implement a large multisite study testing the plausibility of marriage promotion. The goal of this study—called Building Strong Families (or BSF)—was to implement programs in eight communities intended to help unmarried parents develop the skills they needed to resolve whatever doubts they had about their relationship and get married. ACF and Mathematica adapted curricula co-opted from marital therapy, developed by top-notch clinical researchers, such as John and Julie Gottman. Over 5,000 couples were recruited, data were collected from both mothers and fathers prior to randomization, programs were administered to half the couples (with the remaining couples serving as the control group), and then more data were collected 15 and 36 months later. Whether the couples in the treatment group got married was the most fundamental measure of program success, but they also included assessments of relationship quality, parenting behavior, and child development.[27]

The results of BSF were disappointing.[28] In their final report to ACF, Mathematica summarized the outcomes as follows: no effect on the quality of couples' relationships, no impact on the decision to stay together or get married, no effect on co-parenting, and small negative effects on some aspects of father involvement. Some of the more specific findings, illustrated in Figure 21.1, showed that the control group—those couples who received no services—seemed to do *better* than those in the intervention program. These findings flummoxed the proponents of marriage promotion who had to grapple with the question of what went wrong. In their write-up, the BSF researchers suggest the possibility that, for those couples who had strained relationships at the outset, the intervention may have highlighted their relationship problems, helping them realize they were not meant to be together and clinching the decision to break up. This seems

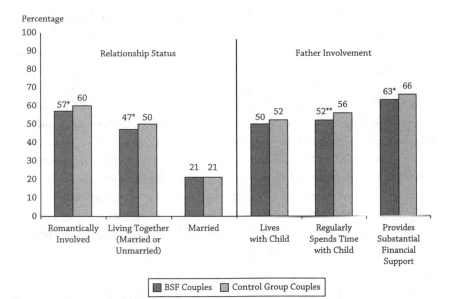

Figure 21.1 Impact of Building Strong Families on relationship status and father involvement at 36 months
From: Wood RG, Moore Q, Clarkwest A, Killewald A, Monahan S. *The Long-Term Effects of Building Strong Families: A Relationship Skills Education Program for Unmarried Parents*, OPRE Report No. 2012-28A, Washington, DC: Office of Planning, Research and Evaluation, Administration for Children and Families, U.S. Department of Health and Human Services; 2012.

plausible for a relatively small subset of young couples, probably less than 10 percent. But we don't think it fully explains why the BSF study failed.

In our estimation, the biggest problem with BSF was that only 55 percent of couples recruited to participate in relationship education classes showed up *even once*. And, among those who did show up, *less than half* completed the full program. For this reason, the BSF was a failed experiment because the researchers weren't able to do what they set out to do. When researchers are unable to implement a program as intended, it is difficult to know whether it might otherwise have worked. If the BSF researchers were laboratory scientists working with germs in petri dishes, they would have just tossed the whole thing away and started over. This happens all the time. But mistakes aren't that easy to fix when we conduct large-scale social experiments in real-world settings. In the BSF study, the researchers were left to make the most of what happened by critically evaluating what did not work.[c]

Why did so few couples show up at all, let alone return to complete the program? Forgive us as we briefly delve into the mundane business of program design. We do so because we think the logistics of how to work effectively with young parents are extraordinarily important, with "make it or break it" consequences. Based on our experiences, we believe the BSF program developers made a logistical mistake when they decided to exclusively use a *group* format to deliver their marriage promotion program to a disadvantaged population. From our perspective, the expectation that young, economically disadvantaged parents could participate in group meetings each week for several weeks or months is a recipe for failure. Although some researchers (not funded by ACF) have had more success with the group format than the BSF researchers,[d] we have found that young disadvantaged couples exercise little control over their work (and school) schedules. This makes coordinating regular meetings with other couples almost impossible. It's no wonder that many couples in the BSF study didn't show up even once. In our own intervention work with young couples, which we describe in the next chapter, we work with one couple at a time. Even so, we have found that it can be challenging to schedule meetings with just *one*

---

c. It would be unfair to not mention that in Oklahoma the BSF program did have some positive effects for African American families. Participants in the Oklahoma City program reported more positive feelings about their relationships at the 15-month follow-up and more family stability at the 36-month follow-up.

d. Most notably, Cowan et al.[29] used a group approach with disadvantaged adult couples (most of whom were married) and reported good rates of recruitment and retention. We discuss the Cowan's approach in the following section.

set of young parents. But there may have been another problem with the BSF study.

Although it's difficult to know, it also seems possible that BSF's emphasis on marriage dissuaded some couples from participating because one or both partners did not want to be pressured to do something that they weren't ready to do. Many young expectant parents are often unsure about whether they want to be together and are struggling with the fundamentals of being in a relationship. Marriage promotion may have hit the wrong notes, by raising their expectations and unnecessarily setting them up for disappointment. This is not to suggest that premarital counseling is a bad idea. For people who are *wanting* to get married, it is a very good idea because marriage is difficult, and premarital counseling can help couples prepare themselves for the inevitable struggles. There are some excellent premarital counseling programs—like PREP[e]—for couples who are looking to get married and want to strengthen their relationship skills.[30] However, when marriage is still just a possibility, premarital counseling might be a mismatch and a bit uncomfortable. How would most young men deal with the discomfort of being in premarital counseling with a partner that he is not quite ready to marry? Find an excuse to skip it perhaps? Frontloading the issue of marriage may elicit feelings of being judged or trapped.

Finally, the BSF programs may have been too generic. Because the needs of young couples are tremendously diverse, programs that can be tailored to address each couple's goals might be more successful in engaging and retaining couples than one that teaches a broad set of skills to a group. Obviously, young couples with serious relationship problems and very few resources will need more time and attention than couples who have significant strengths and plenty of family support. The BSF study was set up so that all couples in a group received the same "dose" of the same program. This one-size-fits-all approach may well have contributed to the program's lack of success.

That said, let's not throw the baby out with the bathwater. It's important to note that there are some effective approaches to stabilizing families, even some that use a group approach. However, such programs have tended to focus on relationship skills, without pushing marriage. For example, Phil and Carolyn Cowan (mentioned earlier) and their colleagues developed a co-parenting support program called Supporting Father Involvement (SFI), designed to help economically disadvantaged couples develop their

---

e. PREP is an evidence-based premarital counseling program that is usually delivered in a group workshop format and run by trained facilitators of varying backgrounds and training (including professional counselors, clergy, and volunteers).

relationship skills through clinician-led group discussions and activities.[31] Over a period of several years, they were able to demonstrate that couples randomized into their program were not only more likely to work well together as parents; they were also more likely to report improvement in their children's social and emotional health.[29] Impressively, these results lend support to the proposition made in Chapter 20 that the skills needed to maintain a positive co-parenting relationship are quite relevant to the skills needed to support child development; when parents are able to listen and provide support to each other, they are also better able to attend to the needs of their children.[32,33]

Shortly after ACF launched the BSF study, they funded the Supporting Healthy Marriage Study (or SHM).[34] Like BSF, SHM was a large multisite study, designed to test relationship education programs intended to "support more stable and more nurturing home environments." The SHM study recruited about 6,300 *married* couples in eight cities scattered across the country. Most of these couples had at least one child and most had low-income jobs. Since couples were already married—many for several years—the goal was to improve the quality of their marriages and keep them married, rather than encourage them to get married. Like BSF, the SHM study randomly assigned half the couples they recruited to marriage/relationship education groups and half the couples to a control group. The average age of the participants in SHM was 34, which was older than those in the BSF study.

SHM researchers followed up with couples assigned to both the relationship education group and the control group to assess how they were doing at 18 months and 36 months after entering the program. The results from these follow-up assessments were mixed. Compared to couples in the control group who received no marriage support, couples in the SHM treatment group reported feeling more satisfied with their relationship and also reported "less antagonistic and hostile behaviors" in their marriage than control group couples. However, intervention group couples were not more likely to stay together than couples in the control group. At the end of the study, about 18.5 percent of couples in both the marriage promotion group and the control group were no longer married. Findings also indicated that the relationship education programs had little effect on co-parenting, parenting, or child well-being.

From our perspective, the most puzzling thing about the SHM study is that it focused on 30-something married parents. The findings that relationship education helps married couples who are doing alright to begin with and not seeking treatment is not something to get terribly excited about. Indeed, the decision to focus on married couples is difficult to understand.

There is an old joke about a guy who loses his car keys at night and is desperately looking around a lamppost but not finding them. A passerby sees him and tries to help, eventually asking where he thinks he dropped the keys. The man says, "Way over there in the bushes!" Confused, the passerby asks, "Why are you looking here by the lamp post?" to which the man replies, "Because I couldn't see anything over there in bushes. The light is over here!" Providing relationship education to married couples who are not seeking help is not a bad thing to do, but it won't help us understand unmarried couples who are struggling with the more fundamental problem of raising their children without much institutional support.[f]

Whether the effort to promote marriage has been a failure and should be scrapped has become the subject of some debate in the research literature. In 2012, Mathew Johnson, a marriage researcher at Binghamton University, wrote a paper outlining the problems with ACF's approach to marriage promotion.[35] He targets some methodological problems with both BSF and SHM that clearly undermined those efforts. But his most vehement critique takes aim at ACF's approach to distributing hundreds of millions of dollars to community-based agencies for the purposes of rolling out marriage programs that have not been tested and are likely ineffective (based on the findings of BSF and SHM). His biggest beef is that ACF doesn't seem particularly concerned with finding out whether these programs work, as they have set aside very little money for evaluating these programs. Ultimately, Johnson concludes that ACF's commitment to the ideology of marriage promotion trumped its commitment to pursuit of knowledge and evidence-based practice, and we agree.

Is this fair? We found that it gets even messier. For example, ACF funded a review of the scholarly research on co-parenting programs for disadvantaged couples. To their credit, funding this review was a positive thing to do. However, the review—conducted by Mathematica—revealed another layer of problems at ACF.[36–38] Mathematica rated the quality of the co-parenting programs they had located in their search as high, moderate, or low, based on widely accepted standards for methodological rigor, such as randomization and attrition. Many of these programs were "unrated," which is worse than having "low-quality evidence" because it meant that program administrators had not collected any data to see whether their program worked. Programs in the unrated category had not been evaluated *at all*, not even poorly evaluated. The upshot of Mathematica's review? From our

---

f. What do we mean by institutional support? Marriage is certainly one form of institutional support but so are antipoverty programs, like TANF, and health entitlements, like programs that ensure access to prenatal care.

perspective, it's that ACF is an agency that keeps shooting itself in the foot, year after year, wasting lots of money. One consequence of this is that we are still a long way from knowing how to stabilize fragile families.

It should be noted that, following Johnson's critique, several marriage and family researchers came to the defense of marriage and relationship promotion programs. Alan Hawkins, the BYU professor we mentioned earlier, together with a full cast of marriage research heavyweights, responded to Johnson's critique by declaring that there are still reasons to be optimistic about the marriage and relationship education initiative spearheaded by ACF.[39] Hawkins and his colleagues point out that Johnson overlooked some of the positive findings that had emerged from the ACF-funded studies and, more broadly, from other relationship researchers.[40] For example, an Oklahoma study, which evaluated a program called Family Expectations, reported that couples who participated were more likely to feel happy and supported and were less conflictual in their relationship. Hawkins also pointed out that we are still in the beginning stages of addressing the phenomenon of marriage decline, and he highlighted the fact that knowing how to help families will take time.

We think that *both* Hawkins and Johnson are right. Hawkins is right to note that developing effective interventions is challenging and requires time and patience.[41] We may still be in the early stages of knowing how to use educators and counselors to strengthen the fragile bond between fathers and their families. Yet, some progress has been made, and—to their credit—Hawkins and others have pushed ACF to raise the research bar for their grantees.[g] But Johnson is right that ACF has bungled a golden opportunity to support meaningful, high-quality research on how to help young families stick together, regardless of marital status. It would be hard for anyone to deny that ACF's mostly haphazard and unscientific approach has been wasteful, yielding findings that are inconclusive at best. ACF has

---

g. There have been some recent findings supporting the potential value of marriage and relationship education. In 2018, Mathematica reported on an ACF-funded study called the Parents and Children Together (PACT, for short), which randomly assigned low-income couples to either relationship education classes or a control group. These researchers found that couples in the relationship education classes reported small but statistically significant better relationship outcomes than couples in the control group, which appears to be an improvement over the SHM study. However, it is worth noting that the PACT evaluation focused on outcomes only (not before and after changes in relationship functioning), and the positive outcomes were largely driven by couples who were married and in their 30s and who reported high levels of relationship commitment and satisfaction at the outset. While these findings should not be dismissed out of hand, there remain many unanswered questions about how to help couples who are most in need of help.

invested more than a billion dollars over the years in agencies that lacked the appropriate clinical expertise to develop or implement couples-focused programs or the research "know how" to conduct complex studies intended to test the effectiveness of these programs.

We do not want to be overly critical of ACF because, after all, they are the only federal agency whose mission is to support the development of programs for young fathers and for young couples. However, we cannot help but hold ACF's feet to the fire precisely *because* they are the only federal agency whose mission is to support research on family stability and father functioning. If the field depends on ACF's money to get a grip on how to manage this sea change in family structure (involving changing social norms and beliefs about marriage and family), then taxpayers and politicians should insist that ACF fund solid research. Imagine if the National Institutes of Health (NIH) were issuing grants to cancer treatment programs that did not require their staff to be trained in cancer treatment or know how to conduct research.

What do we mean by solid research? There is a well-developed and relatively straightforward scientific process to follow when testing fatherhood- or relationship-based programs. While it is logistically difficult to do this type of research, it's not difficult to come up with a plan for collecting data that will allow us to know if a program works. The gold standard for testing whether a new program hits its target is the randomized clinical trial with a control group. In the context of couples counseling, this would involve randomly assigning couples to participate in either program X or a control group. Typically, the control group would get "treatment as usual," which often amounts to nothing. Data would need to be collected from the couples in both program X and the control group in exactly the same fashion at the same points in time. This process would allow the researcher to determine if there are any positive changes among the couples who participated in program X compared to the couples in the control group. If there are differences, then we can be reasonably sure that program participation facilitated that change. If not, as is often the case, we go back to the drawing board and tinker with our program, our research design, or both.

While it's important to not be too dogmatic about how to test the effectiveness of programs, science invokes the right to insist on a systematic design, careful measurements, and critical analysis. The takeaway message from the marriage promotion debate is that we need to be much more strategic about when and how we try to help fathers stay connected with their families. Despite the general failure of the ACF programs to produce meaningful findings, there are some positive signs that helping parents develop co-parenting skills can be an effective approach to stabilizing families and promoting child well-being, whether the parents are together or not. There are a handful of researchers who have demonstrated that it is possible to help families—including unstable families—co-parent more effectively. Moreover, some of these researchers have demonstrated that effectively teaching young men and women to become supportive co-parents can have a positive impact on their parenting skills and even child development. To us, it's just plain common sense that government funding should be redirected to develop, extend, and test those strategies that are showing the most promise.

MARRIAGE COUNSELING, DIVORCE EDUCATION, AND BEYOND

In thinking about better strategies to help fathers stay connected, it might be helpful to back up a bit and consider what can be learned from marriage counseling. In the 1970s, couples who were unhappily married and thinking about divorce started asking for help. The demand for marriage counselors increased dramatically, and marriage counseling became a growth industry.[h] Marriage therapy researchers got busy developing and testing different models for helping distressed couples, with some notable successes.[42]

What does marriage counseling look like? Marriage counselors typically start by helping couples clarify their relationship goals and what they hope to achieve in therapy, an inquiry that can be remarkably enlightening. Sometimes a husband is shocked to find out that his partner wants to end the marriage, and sometimes the wife is shocked to find her partner wants to save it. If a couple indicates that they want to improve their relationship—maybe even stay married—most counselors will teach relationship skills based on which aspects of the relationship are underdeveloped. If a husband cannot stop talking and interrupts his partner whenever she tries to speak, teaching him some simple listening skills can work wonders for their relationship. And if a wife is uncomfortable talking about her feelings and her partner feels lonely and frustrated by the lack of intimacy in their relationship, helping them talk about this can help move things forward, sometimes toward a greater appreciation for their different styles. One of the most important discoveries made by marital therapists came from Neil

h. The Bureau of Labor Statistics projects a 22 percent increase in job openings for marriage and family therapists over the next 10 years, which means that demand for marriage counselors is greater than for most other jobs, including other mental health professionals and even computer programmers.

Jacobson, who found that many couples that came in wanting their partners to change seemed to benefit from an approach designed to help them accept each other's shortcomings.[43] Jacobson and his colleagues found that helping spouses learn to accept their partners for who they are tends to yield happier outcomes than trying to get either one to change for the sake of accommodating the wishes of the other.[44]

The typical metric for success in marital therapy is that a struggling couple decides to stay married and work things out. A less romantic version of success might involve deciding to end an unhappy marriage and figuring out how to minimize the pain and damage of breaking up. When marital therapy does not "save" the relationship, there is still much that can be done to help couples end their relationship without becoming destructive. Over time, some marriage counselors began providing divorce (and predivorce) counseling. The idea that therapy might help couples manage the tail end of their romantic relationship and establish a reasonably civil postromantic co-parenting relationship emerged in the early 1980s when divorce rates spiked. Research documenting the negative effects of divorce on child development began to appear in journals and popular magazines. One of the most compelling findings was that the level of discord between divorcing parents was one of the strongest predictors of adjustment problems in their children.[45,46] By contrast, ending a marriage with some element of civility could make a big difference for the long-term well-being of children, who are always the innocent bystanders in a highly contentious divorce.

The impetus for predivorce counseling emerged from the courthouse, where family court judges were spending more and more of their time overseeing the break-up of families. Some of these judges began working with marriage and family therapists to mitigate the negative impact of divorce by teaching parents about the psychological impact of their bad behavior and providing tools for managing the difficult process of co-parenting postdivorce. Eventually, programs and models began to take shape. Clearly, divorcing parents needed help developing a clear co-parenting plan and an agreed-upon process for making adjustments to that plan when it wasn't working.[47] They also needed help learning to either diffuse conflicts or, most importantly, to at least avoid putting their kids in the middle of their differences.

In 1986, the Johnson County Family Court in Kansas was the first in the United States to mandate that all divorcing couples receive some instruction on how to keep the peace during and after their divorce. By 1998, there were nearly 1,500 divorce education classes being offered in 46 states. The idea of predivorce and postmarriage classes was so appealing to divorce judges that they just took it upon themselves to require that parents participate.

Eventually, local and state lawmakers took notice and, by 2010, 25 states had passed laws mandating that all divorcing parents take these classes.[48] Some of these programs are brief and somewhat generic, providing classroom instruction to groups of divorcing couples. Some are online classes that are also instructional in nature but more private and convenient. And some are more intense one-on-one sessions with counselors trained to help divorcing couples work out co-parenting plans.[49,50]

The quick proliferation of these programs far outpaced the research that was needed to demonstrate their efficacy. However, by 2010, a handful of studies had been completed. In 2011, Tamara Fackrell, a divorce lawyer in Utah, got together with Alan Hawkins (the family studies professor at BYU we mentioned earlier) and conducted a meta-analysis of all the reasonably well-designed studies of these relationship-focused programs for divorcing couples.[51] Across the 19 studies they found, couples who participated in divorce education programs were about 40 percent more likely to manage their conflicts reasonably well and function adequately as co-parents compared to couples who received no relationship education. Although Fackrell acknowledges that some of the studies they reviewed are not exemplars of scientific rigor, they nonetheless concluded that, all in all, divorce education programs worked much of the time.

The brilliance of court-mandated divorce education is that it forces parents to work together to come up with some reasonable plan to provide for their children's financial and emotional security if they want their divorce to be final. That is a significant amount of leverage to work with. Even parents who hate each other will often work *together* to end their marriage. The problem is that divorce education is required only for those families appearing in divorce court (approximately 800,000 each year). For unmarried couples who split up, divorce education is not required because they are not getting divorced. There is no mechanism in place for offering help or insisting that they get help with managing their conflicts. Nonetheless, it seems that there is much to be learned from this approach that might be relevant for all co-parenting couples. The pure focus of these programs on helping ex-partners get along for the sake of the kids seems applicable to unmarried couples too. Could we use this practical approach to stabilize nonconventional family structures?

In this section, we have discussed marriage counseling and divorce education, despite our primary interest in couples who are not getting married or divorced. Why are we diving into this literature? Because there has been little research on how to help young unwed couples, we are trying to extrapolate what might work based on what has been helpful both for distressed married couples who hope to salvage their relationship and for divorcing couples who hope to maintain some sort of reconfigured co-parenting relationship. The wisdom we've gleaned from past research is that when working with unstable couples, some fundamental communication skills (and rules) can help them provide a better environment for their children. Yet, it's not so easy to achieve even the modest goals of helping unhappy partners express their feelings more respectfully, listen to each other more openly, and work together more pragmatically for the sake of their children's well-being, *no matter how they feel about their romantic relationship.*

SO, WHERE DO WE GO FROM HERE?

Despite our frustration with ACF's approach to addressing family instability and supporting the development of evidence-based programs for young parents, we want to note that there has been some solid research demonstrating that prevention-oriented co-parenting programs can work. As previously indicated, Phil and Carolyn Cowan and their colleagues have had good success working with low-income adult couples using their SFI model. Similarly, Mark Feinberg and his colleagues developed the Family Foundations (FF) program, which has demonstrated similarly impressive results helping married adult couples improve their communication skills, their relationship satisfaction, and their children's social and behavioral outcomes. Although both these programs focused on parents who were older, more stable, and more likely to be married than the couples featured in this book, the SFI and FF findings are encouraging because their research designs were solid and their effects were strong. How did they manage this? We suspect that these successes can be attributed, at least in part, to the fact that both teams have been studying co-parenting for many years and have an appreciation for the complexities involved in helping families communicate more effectively. This includes having well-trained clinicians who keep couples focused on the well-being of their children as their primary relationship goal.

Our own research with young fathers and their partners, along with the research of many others, has demonstrated the vital importance of the co-parenting relationship (even in cases where the romantic relationship didn't last) for both father engagement and positive parent–child interactions. The successes of divorce counseling and relationship education, together with the failures of programs that promote marriage, provide further evidence that an early intervention with fathers and their partners that focuses on improving the co-parenting relationship could be a worthy endeavor to pursue. So, as we describe in the next chapter, that's exactly what we did.

CHAPTER 22

Co-Parenting Support

Prenatal Care and the Window of Opportunity

In 2010, Sarah McLanahan and Irv Garfinkel, along with Ron Mincy and Elisabeth Donahue, wrote a paper summing up the take-away messages from the Fragile Families Study, which they had had been leading for about 20 years.[1] As you may recall, the Fragile Families Study was a mammoth-sized longitudinal study of young disadvantaged couples, most of whom were recruited immediately after delivering their first baby and followed for over 10 years. It was conducted with a great deal of care and rigor, giving rise to treasure trove of data that has supported a generation of family research activity. So, when asked to summarize their results, McLanahan and her colleagues declared that:

> Of all the findings from the Fragile Families Study . . . the one with by far the most critical policy implications is the high level of commitment among unmarried new parents . . . For this reason, services to parents in fragile families should be immediate, intense, and focused on the couple in their role as cooperative parents. Fashioned as a bumper sticker, our recommendation would be "Support the three T's: Treat early, Treat often, and Treat together" (pp. 14–15).

What does this mean? From our perspective, *treating "early"* means during the pregnancy, before the child arrives. The idea that the transition to parenthood is an opportune moment for stabilizing families was first advocated by Philip and Carolyn Cowan, who demonstrated that teaching fathers and mothers to listen to each other more carefully helps them develop a stronger co-parenting bond and prepares them for becoming more present and attuned parents for their children.[2] Part of the reason for this is that fathers and mothers tend to be quite open to accepting guidance and support during this moment in their lives. Under most circumstances, young couples approaching parenthood are struggling with feelings of excitement and apprehension, joy and fear, the desire to connect and the wish to flee.

Despite this ambivalence, most young men are invested in becoming good fathers during their partner's pregnancy, before the challenges of parenthood and co-parenthood are fully realized. It is during this time—a honeymoon of sorts—that more fathers can be convinced to participate in programs intended to support their unborn child. Indeed, during the prenatal period, most of us are open to becoming more loving because we are faced with the prospect of building a family and becoming attached. By the same token, we are also prone to feel overwhelmed by the sudden, and often unanticipated, increase in intimacy and responsibility.

There are at least two good reasons for treating fathers and mothers *together*. First, if fathers are to learn how to communicate more effectively with mothers (and vice versa), logic dictates that they need to be in the same room at the same time. Marital researchers have found that couples benefit from learning how to hear each other's perspectives and how to respond to what they hear, carefully and deliberately.[3,4] The tendency to separate men and women into gender-specific groups—with the idea that it will loosen them up, make them more comfortable, and provide a more supportive environment—tends to reinforce the gender divide. When segregated, women and men tend to complain about or make fun of "the other" which might amuse, but rarely helps. Despite our focus on fathers, we believe there are disadvantages in providing *father-only* services because couple-focused services are more effective. Developing relationship skills requires practical instruction and active practice, with both partners talking to each other, face-to-face.

We are less certain about the suggestion that couples be "*treated often.*" Asking couples to meet too much or too often can backfire because the demands of treatment can become burdensome. As we suggested in Chapter 21, one of the problems with most relationship education programs is that they use "one size fits all" models. The dose of treatment is not tailored to the needs of each couple, which are diverse. Some young parents need help learning to talk with their partners about their feelings, so they don't bottle things up and then blow their stacks. Some young parents need help learning to listen to their partners. And some couples need help learning to support each other and diminish relationship stress. Some would benefit from meeting often for an extended period, while others might do quite well with four or five sessions stretched out over the course of the pregnancy and for the first few months following childbirth. The point is that programs should be tailored to address the particular needs of couples, which requires that we have a system in place for understanding and evaluating those needs.

OUR SHIFT FROM OBSERVING TO SUPPORTING YOUNG FATHERS & THEIR FAMILIES

After studying what can go wrong between fathers and their families for several years, and after documenting how some fathers pull themselves together and grow into parenthood, we began to develop some ideas about how we might help young fathers stay meaningfully connected with their children. Like McLanahan and her colleagues, we thought that the co-parenting relationship seemed like the obvious place to start. If the research indicates that the quality of a father's relationship with his partner is one of the most powerful predictors of his continued support of his child—even if the father and mother break up—then it stands to reason that helping couples maintain a positive, or at least a civil relationship, is the most natural way to promote father engagement.[5] This doesn't mean that other factors aren't important determinants of father involvement. A young man's ability to bond with his child and begin to embrace his role as a father are also vitally important, albeit harder to facilitate. Nor does it mean that we should work to keep couples together. Based on our experience and the research literature, we are convinced that trying to do so can backfire by putting undue pressure on couples.

Nonetheless, we have also become convinced that most young fathers want to "be there" for both their child and their child's mother, including many who are not quite up to the task. So, we used our strategy of asking young pregnant women, along with their partners, if they would like to participate in a study focusing on a new program to help young expectant parents. Unlike our previous work, which was designed simply to observe and understand, this study was about facilitating growth. The program was designed to teach communication skills that we thought were important for building and sustaining a co-parenting relationship. Tim and Alyssa were among the first couples we invited to participate.

Tim and Alyssa

When we met Tim at our Salt Lake City study office, he came across as serious and "buttoned down." He was dressed in a sports shirt and pants that looked pressed, and he wore his hair slicked back in a style that looked retro (like from the 60s). He seemed cautious at first, perhaps a little stand-offish about participating in the Young Parenthood Program. But once he settled in, he relaxed and opened-up to Nick, the graduate student who interviewed him.

Tim had moved to Salt Lake City to live with his father when he was 6 years old, after he and his siblings were taken away from their mother by the State of Idaho. Prior to this move, he barely knew his father, who he described as demanding, judgmental, and unemotional. He explained that you could never know how his father was feeling, except when he got pissed off. Then, you knew. Tim told Nick that suddenly losing his mother, moving to another state, and feeling as though he couldn't measure up to his father's expectations was "confusing," which seems like an under-statement. At first, he tried hard to please his father and earn his approval. When that didn't work, he became rebellious. By the time he reached ad-olescence, he and his father were arguing all the time about what he could and couldn't do, what he would and wouldn't do. Eventually his dad kicked him out of the house.

At first, Tim stayed with friends, doing what he could to make some money and sometimes stealing what he needed from stores. Over the next couple of years, Tim learned to support himself as a petty criminal, mostly stealing cars and selling the parts. He was making enough money to rent a small place of his own and felt proud of his independence.

Tim knew a guy—Victor—who ran an auto parts store in West Salt Lake City. Victor, a Mexican immigrant who spoke broken English with a thick accent, occasionally bought auto parts that Tim had stripped from stolen cars. Victor was always warm and friendly with Tim, who had learned to speak a little Spanish. Victor had been the one to suggest that Tim stop stealing cars before he got in trouble. He didn't outright say that he knew Tim was selling him stolen parts; he just said there are safer ways to make a living. Tim respected Victor's subtle, indirect approach and appreciated Victor's concern, so he asked him if he could work at the shop. Victor said he could use a baby-faced kid who could talk to those gringo customers who couldn't understand his English. And with a handshake, Tim was hired.

A bonus to working at Vic's Auto Parts was that Victor's daughter, Alyssa, was cute and flirtatious. When Tim and Alyssa started dating, they hid their relationship from her father, but it didn't take Victor long to figure things out. Victor told Tim that he was a good kid and he knew he was treating his daughter well. Six months later, when they found out Alyssa was pregnant, Victor took it in stride but wanted them to get married, and they did. Alyssa was just 18 at the time.

Tim had a very tough childhood, but he was a survivor and he learned to take care of himself. He was tremendously resilient, but it was difficult for him to trust others and he came across as guarded and aloof. With time, it became more evident that he lacked some important relationship skills— like empathy and compassion—which were needed to make his relationship with Alyssa work. When Nick asked Tim to pick three words to describe Alyssa, Tim quickly came up with "spoiled, manipulative, and lazy." While it's not unusual for young men to use negative words when describing their girlfriends, it's typically done with a touch of warmth or playfulness. Tim was very serious, and his description of Alyssa came across as judgmental. When Nick asked Tim to explain what he meant, Tim's response revealed quite a bit about himself.

TIM: She argues with me a lot . . . not that she really disagrees with what I say. She wants something one way, but she knows that the way I say it's supposed to be is the *right* way. Eventually, she pretty much always comes to my way of seeing things. That's one of the things I like about the relationship. She is easily influenced. I had to raise myself and had to learn to think for myself. The way I think is usually right. Her dad thinks pretty much along the same lines as I do. Everyone in her family thinks along the same lines as I do.

NICK: What do you mean?

TIM: She's gotten in the habit that she can manipulate and get what she wants, like from her parents, but she doesn't get away with that with me. I've seen her throw temper tantrums when she doesn't get her way. I think if she keeps acting that way, the baby will be like that too.

Alyssa told Stacy that when she and Tim were first dating, they were all loving and nice to each other, but when they started to get more comfortable with each other, their negative sides began to show. And the pregnancy only made things worse. She was frequently in a bad mood and didn't want Tim to touch her or even be near her. She hated that he was trying to control her, change her, improve her.

I don't like how he tells me what to do. "I don't want you to eat this. I don't want you to talk to this person." He wants me to change who I am. I am very rude.

He is asking too much. He is asking me to change the way I eat, says I watch too much TV. He wants me to change too much and I don't want him telling me what to do.

Tim had been nagging Alyssa to exercise and eat healthier during her pregnancy because he was worried about her gaining too much weight. This was something Alyssa's doctor had brought up, explaining that she was at risk for gestational diabetes. In response to Tim's nagging, Alyssa agreed to go to the gym (Tim had bought her a membership) and to eat less junk food, but she never went to the gym and ate what she wanted.

In her interview with Stacy, Alyssa admitted that she would agree with Tim just to get him off her back, but she always did what she felt like doing and she didn't feel like going to the gym. This dynamic is captured by what Andrew Christensen, a marriage therapist and researcher, calls the "demand and withdraw" pattern, wherein one partner tries to control the other, often in a hostile, blaming way, and the other responds by ignoring, dismissing, or reacting defensively.[6] It's not a good dynamic because it sucks the warmth and respect out of relationships.[7]

OUR APPROACH TO INTERVENTION

John Bowlby (introduced in Chapter 2) is credited with the idea that when our "primary attachments" (usually our early relationships with parents) are warm and fundamentally secure, we are better able to build strong relationships with others and cope effectively with the challenges of everyday life. These early attachments serve as templates for later attachments, including relations with intimate partners, and they also play an important role in how we respond to our children's need for love and security. If we feel emotionally stable and secure, we will be able to create a safe, warm, and secure environment for our children. The most interesting thing about these "attachment templates" is that they are both enduring *and* malleable. They shape our expectations and our behavior, but they are open to revision.

Young people whose early relationships were unstable, erratic, and sometimes outright hostile—and who develop insecure attachments as children (like Tim)—certainly carry that baggage with them. But this doesn't mean they are doomed to be bad parents. Teaching fathers and mothers to be warm and respectful with each other will help them provide a more stable and secure emotional environment for their children, even if they had little of that in their own early experiences. Theoretically, helping young expectant parents learn to listen to each other will help them develop more trusting, loving relationships with their partners and their children. It's a hopeful premise.

Tim and Alyssa agreed to participate in the Young Parenthood Program (YPP), which we offered through Alyssa's prenatal clinic at the University of Utah. Our approach to working with couples begins with an assessment and feedback session, showing them some of their scores on our measures of relationship quality—based on their own self-reports—and asking them if they would like to move up or down on this or that scale. For example, if a father's responses to our questionnaire on relationship quality indicate that he is sometimes hostile toward his partner or that she is hostile to him, we might ask if he would like to move up or down on that scale. Most fathers would say, "Yes, I would like to fight less" or "Yes, I know I need to control my temper." This approach, borrowed from Miller and Rollnick's motivational interviewing technique,[8] helps young men see the benefits of participating in our program, which we describe to them as "a co-parenting counseling program that helps couples develop their communication skills, so that they can work together to take care of their baby no matter what happens to their relationship."

We designed the program to be flexible enough to be individually relevant for each couple. This includes couples who are in love and want to be together forever and those who already dislike each other and can barely stand to be in the same room. We are careful to say that we remain neutral about the status of their relationship, which is totally up to them. Our goal is to help them communicate well as co-parents, regardless of their status. We are also careful to set ground rules for our sessions, emphasizing physical and emotional safety, asking couples to allow the counselor to act as coach and referee. This means following his or her direction when a "foul" or "time-out" is called.

When we begin working with a couple, we typically ask each partner to identify some personal and relationship strengths and weaknesses (i.e., ways that each of them contributes to positive and negative patterns in their interactions as a couple), so we can develop a set of goals to work on together during our sessions. The approach is designed to develop a clear focus for the intervention and to introduce the idea of cooperative goal-setting. During these early sessions, we emphasize that their relationship with each other is an important part of their child's "emotional home base," regardless of whether they end up living together or remain in a romantic relationship. Most couples have no trouble grasping the idea that how they treat each other will impact how their son or daughter experiences the world, as many young parents know what it's like to grow up with adversarial parents. We also make it explicit that the goal of the program is *not* to keep couples together as romantic partners, but rather to help them work together as co-parents. We believe that this statement is often received with silent relief by one or both partners, who are having their doubts about the relationship. It also helps shift the focus away from making the couple happy and toward helping them learning how to function as a "co-parenting team."

We have a menu of specific skills that couples can choose to work on with the help of their "coach" so that we can tailor the program to meet the needs of each couple. At the same time, there are limits to how flexible we can be. For example, we are clear about maintaining a tight focus on their relationship. We acknowledge the importance of other issues—like unstable housing or substance abuse—but we find ways to bring the primary focus back to the relationship, usually encouraging them to work together to seek additional support, giving them a referral to our contact at the housing authority or a neighborhood 12-step program. But without a good assessment process and a relatively full understanding of each couple, tailoring the process would not be possible.

When Tim and Alyssa came in for their first YPP meeting, there was little warmth between them. Like many contentious couples, both Alyssa and Tim hoped that Sofia, their counselor, would see the problems in their relationship from *their* perspective and that Sofia would focus on changing the *other* partner. Tim was willing to give YPP a try but seemed doubtful about Sofia, their counselor. Sofia is a middle-aged social worker who can be challenging and firm but also warm and inviting. This combination helps put most couples at ease, but Tim got stuck on the challenging part of Sofia's personality. The initial problem was that Sofia did not readily endorse Tim's perspective on what was wrong with their relationship. Alyssa admitted that she could be rude, brash, and moody, but she also said she didn't like being told by *anyone* what to do and would walk out of the relationship if Tim didn't stop trying to control her. She said this like she was daring him to do it, throwing down the gauntlet. Sofia's neutrality irked Tim. After all, even Alyssa's parents were on his side and wanted Alyssa to change how she behaved. When we begin working with a young couple who we know to be in a tough spot, like Tim and Alyssa, we try to keep the discussion constructive and positive so that they leave their first session feeling better about themselves and their relationship than when they came in. Unfortunately, this is not always possible.

Tim did not want to return for their next session. Sofia called to discuss the problem, anticipating that he felt unheard because she had not jumped to his side of the conflict. She explained that she understood and appreciated his perspective, but that she would not be able to help them with their relationship if she took sides. She said she wanted Tim to give the program a chance but also wanted him to know that she wasn't going to take his side or Alyssa's. Staying neutral was the only way she knew how to help them work on their differences. Tim appreciated Sofia's effort to reach out and her direct explanation. He said he understood where she was coming from and agreed to give it another try. The need to persuade young fathers to stick with the program is not at all unusual for us; we have become comfortable with "selling" the program by explaining exactly why we do what we do.

That demand-withdraw dynamic between Tim and Alyssa quickly emerged in their sessions with Sofia. Tim would say something like: "You said you were going to start going to the gym, but you didn't go last week or the week before!" Alyssa would respond to Tim's critical opinions by either refusing the demand, "You are not my coach and I don't want a coach!" or shutting him down by saying, "Not gonna discuss that. Next topic." Tim would continue to blame and shame: "You agree to do things and then you don't do them, so what am I supposed to do?" and Alyssa would get more hostile, "Hmmm, how about you shut the fuck up about the fucking gym!"

Sofia was privately shocked by the things that Alyssa said to Tim, but she was not thrown off balance by their conflict. Rather, she told them that this conflict gave them the perfect opportunity to work on their relationship goals of being able to "solve problems" and "fight less." She then introduced them to the "reflective listening" activity which is about building listening skills. It is an activity that most couples enjoy because the results are immediate. Sofia started with Alyssa, because she thought Tim did not understand Alyssa's feelings about being pregnant or how it felt when he criticized and tried to control her. This activity involves three steps:

(1) One partner speaks as the other listens carefully; any response by the other partner is strictly forbidden.
(2) After the first partner is done talking, the other partner repeats what he or she heard verbatim or summarizes it without any interpretation, asking, "Did I get that right?"
(3) If the listener did not get it right—which is typically the case—the first person simply repeats or rephrases what he or she said again until the message is accurately received.

At the end of this exchange, the first partner is usually eager to have their turn at talking. The point of this exercise is to help couples hear each other differently, particularly when engaging in common disagreements in which they assume they already know what the other person is going to say and already understand the intent behind what's being said. Slowing the communication process down gives the speaker the opportunity to feel heard, and it gives the listener the opportunity to understand.

During this listening activity, Sofia also asked both Tim and Alyssa to express their feelings *without* putting the other person down, to speak from the heart about how they felt rather than focus on what the other person was doing wrong. From the beginning of her work with Tim and Alyssa, Sofia's goal was to warm things up between them, or at least try to reduce their hostility. She didn't try to alter their personalities or even their individual perceptions of the problem, focusing instead on the more modest goal of helping them communicate more effectively. With Sofia's help, Alyssa said she was feeling badly about her body and scared about how "ornery" she was all the time. When Tim started in on how much better Alyssa would feel if she just listened to him, Sofia interrupted him.

Tim's lack of skill in knowing how to connect in a warm way made sense to Sofia, given his bleak history. Knowing about Tim's past helped Sofia to look beyond his tendency to judge and control Alyssa and instead appeal to his desire for a warmer connection. Over time, Sofia earned enough credibility with Tim to point out that sometimes he could come across in ways that worked against his wishes. In this moment, Sofia told Tim she agreed that exercise and healthy eating are important but she didn't think nagging Alyssa's was going to help.

When Tim started to defend his position, she interrupted again, saying she knew that Tim's concern came from the heart; she knew he wanted Alyssa and their baby to be healthy. Then, Sofia asked Tim whether he thought his tendency to get controlling was worse when he was feeling anxious or insecure about something in the moment. Tim paused, taken aback. Then he smiled, looking impressed by the question.

Drawing a deep breath, he said that, yes, he was trying to be helpful but knew that what he was doing was not working. And yes, he did feel insecure because it felt like Alyssa could just end the relationship at any minute all the time. And yes, he was always trying to get things under control, trying to get Alyssa under control, which was just plain stupid. Sofia commended him for being so open. Tim added that all his efforts were having the opposite effect; it just made Alyssa angry and made him feel even more like disaster was about to strike.

Later, when Sofia encouraged them to share their feelings about becoming parents, Tim said he worried about not knowing how to be a loving parent because he never felt much love from his parents. Alyssa responded warmly to this revelation, saying she felt sad about how much Tim's childhood sucked, but she knew that Tim would become a wonderful father. Although Tim and Alyssa were initially uncomfortable with these communication activities, they admitted the exercises helped them understand each other more, both commenting that they were surprised by what came out when Sofia forced them to "speak from their hearts."

Sofia's efforts to get Tim and Alyssa to practice new behaviors was based on the simple principle that effective learning requires deliberate and repeated action. Like an orchestra, couples need a conductor forcing them to practice and sometimes interrupting to make sure they get each part right. This principle draws from the work of Albert Bandura and other social learning theorists, who underscore that when we change our perceptions of interpersonal events (sometimes with the help of a therapist) we tend to respond differently. And, when we change our response—our behavior— we tend to shift our perceptions further. So, the key to couples therapy is to help couples experience their relationship differently, largely through getting them to learn, practice, and implement new patterns of perceptions and interpersonal behaviors. To her credit, Sofia was able to orchestrate some positive moments for Tim and Alyssa. The goal was not to keep them together—Sofia was doubtful about that—but rather to help them become a little more reflective and compassionate.

Tim still lapsed into controlling and judgmental behavior and Alyssa still responded with angry defiance, but both became more sensitive to how their partner felt, more aware of how they came across and better able to repair the damage after such offenses. Their ability to work through these moments was significant, given their tendency to become emotionally cut-off and distant. When these old patterns did re-emerge, the new interpersonal skills that Tim and Alyssa had learned helped them manage and navigate their conflicts more effectively. It helped prevent them from getting stuck in that "demand-withdraw" pattern again and again.

At the end of each YPP session, we ask counselors to fill out a rating scale, describing each couples' level of warmth and hostility, their distress, and their engagement in the therapy process. We also ask each expectant mother and father to complete a similar scale, so that we can track changes in the therapeutic process from multiple perspectives. Based on everyone's report, Tim and Alyssa made steady progress over the course of their eleven sessions with Sofia, reporting more warmth, less conflict, and less distress. Three months after the birth of their daughter, they moved out of Alyssa's parents' house and into their own apartment. Tim was no longer working for Alyssa's dad because he found a better paying job working as a mechanic's assistant. He was hoping to get his certification and start his own shop in a year or two. He was working long hours, trying to stay on top of all the bills. Adulthood had come fast and furious; he was struggling with the responsibilities but also feeling good about handling them.

Because Tim and Alyssa were part of a study designed to test whether YPP helped couples adjust to parenthood, we collected a lot of data from them before and after their child was born. Typically, we examine data for the whole group, comparing those who were randomly selected (and invited) to participate in YPP with those who became part of a control group. In addition to this group-based analysis, this research data can also be useful when trying to determine program effects on an individual couple. The primary question being asked here, of course, is: "Did it help?" Prior to their first session with Sofia, we asked Tim and Alyssa to discuss a recent disagreement, which we videotaped and coded. In that meeting, they launched headlong into their dispute about Alyssa saying she would go to the gym and then not going. Using our coding system designed to quantify the quality of couples' relationships, Tim was coded as being quite controlling with a strong undertone of disapproval. Not surprisingly, Alyssa was coded as engaging in high rates of sulky and walling-off behavior; a combination of "leave me alone" and "screw you." There was little warmth between them.

Six months after their daughter, Christina, was born, their relationship still seemed prickly, but they were managing it much better. We asked Tim and Alyssa to do another communication activity, exactly like the one prior. Using the same interpersonal coding scheme to evaluate their interaction, we found that Tim was less controlling and blaming and significantly warmer toward Alyssa than during the first interaction task 10 months earlier. Alyssa was also less hostile and a little warmer, but also more controlling toward Tim.

Tim and Alyssa were coming to the realization that, although they still loved each other, they did not much *like* each other. When Christina was about 1 year old, they broke up. Alyssa moved back to her parents and Tim moved to a studio apartment nearby. Alyssa enrolled in some college classes and got a job, relying on her younger sister and mother to take care of Christina when she was unavailable and Tim had to work. She and Tim worked out an informal shared custody/child support arrangement, so that he took care of Christina three or four days every week, and both helped pay for what she needed. This break-up did not surprise anyone, but it hit Tim hard because he so badly wanted to create the happy family he never had. About six months after the breakup, when Nick asked Tim what he hoped for in his relationship with Alyssa, he paused and responded "I guess there is part of me that holds out some hope for us, but I don't really think we'll get back together. She is such a mystery to me. I don't understand her at all."

Shortly after they broke up and Tim moved out, he reconnected with his father, who sometimes helped take care of Christina. Eventually, Tim moved back into his father's house to save money and to give Christina more space to play. During our final interview with Tim, when Christina was 2 years old, we met at Tim's father's house. Christina was there too, and she chatted away throughout the interview, vying with Nick (the interviewer) for her father's attention, saying "Daddy, daddy, daddy!" Tim was remarkably patient and warm with Christina throughout the interview, responding to her chattering intermittently, with a quick but genuine acknowledgement of whatever she wanted to share with him. "When she raised a crayon in the air and said "Mine, mine, mine!" Tim said "Yes honey, that is yours, at least for now," which seemed to satisfy her. When Christina started drawing on the table, he redirected her, "Only draw on the paper so your grandfather doesn't get upset," with a gentle, comfortable tone.

As partners, Tim and Alyssa were still struggling with the fact they had such divergent personalities and perspectives, but they were learning to live and let live. For example, Tim expressed his concern that Alyssa's rough manners would rub off on Christina, but he didn't go on a tirade. He paused and said, "She can still be pretty rude, but she's grown up a lot too." When we asked how Alyssa was doing as a mother, he started out on a somewhat critical note saying, "I wish she'd put away her phone and play with Christina. And stick with routines more, like for us to have the same bedtime routine so it's less confusing for Christina going back and forth." But he ended more positively, saying "I guess when I think about it, Alyssa is doing pretty good as a mother. She's working hard to take care of herself and our daughter." And when we asked Alyssa how she thought Tim was doing as a father, she gave him high marks: "He's more of a dad than I am a mom. He's really good with her and she is crazy about him."

Tim and Alyssa seemed simultaneously more distant and more compassionate with each other. Both still had an edge, but those edges were softer. From our perspective, Tim and Alyssa represent a "good enough" transition to parenthood, which we regard as a success. Although we try hard to not make predictions about whether any given couple is going to "make it," Tim and Alyssa were an unlikely pair. With the support of Sofia, they were able to hang in there long enough to figure out how to function as co-parents and break-up without much acrimony. Are they still a family? We think so. Interestingly, after the break-up, they both became more connected with their own parents, who played an important role in their reformatted family. They also reported being happier than when they were married and living under the same roof. Despite the absence of a fairy tale ending, they were still working together to raise their daughter, who seemed to be doing well. Is it love? Practically speaking, it might be.

Alberto and Marcella

Alberto was 16 years old when he agreed to participate in our Young Parenthood Program study. We recruited him through the South Main Street Clinic in Salt Lake City, where his girlfriend, Marcella, was getting her prenatal care. Whereas Tim needed help softening up, Alberto needed help applying the brakes. Like many 16-year-olds, Alberto was all about having fun, being where the action is, and playing the field. Young as he was, he seemed even younger and completely unprepared for parenthood. Alberto met Marcella in math class after their teacher reassigned him to sit next to her because he was being disruptive. Marcella was a quiet, well-behaved student and perhaps the teacher thought Marcella would have a positive, calming influence on Alberto. Instead, he started hitting on her almost immediately. Her initial response was "Leave me alone. I don't know you!" Over the course of the next few weeks, he passed her notes, begging her to go out with him, and when he got no response, he asked mutual friends to plead his case. Then, after she finally agreed to go out, agreed to be his girlfriend, and started to like him, she found out he had cheated on her with two other girls. She confronted him, he confessed, and she was devastated. She broke it off with Alberto, but a couple months later, he came back and asked for another chance. She was still hurt, but she liked him, and she believed in second chances. A few months later, they showed up together at the South Main Street Clinic.

When we first interviewed Alberto, he was friendly but had little to say in response to almost all our standard questions. Alberto represents a type of young man we have not featured in this book: the inarticulate type. When Eric asked him how he felt about Marcella, he was genuinely stumped by the question.

ALBERTO: Umm. Feelings?
ERIC: Yes, what sort of feelings do you have for her? When you think about her, what do you feel?
ALBERTO: (long pause) Well . . . I care about her.
ERIC: How so?
ALBERTO: (long pause)
ERIC: How do you know you care about her?

ALBERTO: Hmmm . . . Well, I . . . when she feels bad about something, I want to be with her and try to help out.

And later, when Eric asked how Alberto felt about becoming a father:

ALBERTO: Never really thought about it.
ERIC: If you thought about it now, what sort of feelings do you have?
ALBERTO: I just see us having our own apartment and me making sure the baby has everything he needs.
ERIC: How does that feel to you?
ALBERTO: I don't know really.

Unlike many of the fathers we selected for this book, Alberto did not have the language skills to formulate detailed answers to these simple but heavily-loaded questions. This is not uncommon among 16-year-old boys. Many of the young men we encounter are not well practiced at looking inward, taking stock of what's there, and conveying it to others with words. When we ask young expectant fathers how they are feeling about becoming a father, some can be incredibly thoughtful and expressive and some freeze and stumble. It is often the case that they are answering this question for the first time. Some seem thunderstruck by the magnitude of what is being asked. Some—like Albert—do not have the skills to express what they feel (or even know how they feel). If the interview goes well, the young expectant father enjoys the opportunity to have a long conversation with someone who is interested in their thoughts and feelings. Many young expectant fathers seem pleased with their responses, as if hearing themselves talk about becoming a father helps them feel it more fully.

The contrast between Tim, who was articulate and controlling, and Alberto, who needed help opening up and reigning himself in, illustrate how important it can be to tailor the counseling process to meet the specific needs of each couple. Tim needed help learning to listen to Alyssa; Alberto needed help learning to identify his feelings, to manage his behavior, and to communicate more effectively with Marcella.

Knowing a couple's strengths is important because we often call upon those strengths during difficult moments in the treatment process. Tim was smart and self-reliant (and took pride in those qualities). So, when conflicts between him and Alyssa emerged, Sofia could ask him to step back and assess the problem and think about what he might tell himself if he was the therapist in the room. This approach would not work with Alberto, who needed more structure and support. Knowing a couple's limits helps a counselor know which therapy activities might be too challenging and which might help them develop specific skills they don't yet have but are capable of developing. Generally, we try to set couples up to feel they've taken an important step in their relationship, and we don't want them to stumble and fall.

At first, Alberto seemed profoundly uncomfortable with talking, which made it difficult for Lisa, his counselor, to avoid having one-on-one conversations with Marcella. Our reflective listening activity or our "I-statement" activity (i.e., saying "I feel . . . " or "I think . . . " rather than "You . . . " in order to reduce blaming and defensiveness) would not be a good place to start with this couple, because the conversation would be unlikely to gain traction with Alberto and might be frustrating for them both.

Some young men get tongue-tied in the presence of their partners, either because they think that saying too much will get themselves in trouble or because they are happy to let their girlfriends do all the talking. For this reason, some counselors think it's best to work with young mothers and fathers separately, each in their own groups. We think the opposite. Our goal is to help partners get comfortable with opening up and sharing more with each other. We want them to become curious about what's going on in their partner's head rather than make assumptions about what he or she is thinking or feeling. When one partner gets stumped or clams up, we might ask the other what she thinks her partner is thinking or feeling, which can lighten the mood and highlight the difficulty of knowing the internal experience of someone we think we know well.

Compared to Tim and Alyssa, Alberto and Marcella got along very well. They didn't fight much; and, when they did, they would go their separate ways until it blew over. As a rule, we don't try to stir up conflicts just for the sake of having something to talk about. Nevertheless, conflicts naturally emerge and provide grist for the "therapeutic mill." Talking about real conflicts in real time gives couples the opportunities for on-the-spot learning. Once a couple feels that their counselor will help them talk about hot topics constructively, they will typically bring up their concerns, be willing to listen to each other, and exhibit greater willingness to cooperate and compromise.

The first time that Lisa got the opportunity to play that role with Alberto and Marcella was after Alberto was arrested at a party and put in juvenile detention for a couple of days, causing him to miss the ultrasound appointment with Marcella. When they came to their next session, Marcella was still angry with him, and he was visibly upset with himself, having a hard time knowing what to say. He focused on how it was unfair that he was taken to detention when others at the party were not arrested. His primary focus was on the cops and the injustice he had suffered, which was missing the point.

> LISA: Even though you did not plan for this to happen and it may have been unfair, you did something that got in the way of you making it to the ultrasound. I can see that you are upset about that, and Marcella is upset too. This is a hard moment. Underneath all that upset is the fact that you both want to be there for each other, to share in this process of becoming parents.

Alberto just sat in silence, looking down and remorseful.

> LISA: On the downside, you made a mistake and got in trouble. On the upside, you have this opportunity to take responsibility and learn. And the good thing is that you care; you are here with Marcella right now, trying to figure this out. I can tell you are thinking hard about your priorities, deciding what matters most to you. We cannot keep the cops from being jerks, but you can avoid trouble with the cops. That's the important thing to focus on. So, the next time there is a party, I am confident you will think about what could go wrong . . . and how to avoid trouble. I am not trying to beat you over the head because you made a mistake. Mistakes are good learning experiences.

Sometimes it is challenging for counselors to avoid talking too much when working with young men (and women) who don't say much. It's important to not say so much that your words begin to lose their meaning and sound like "blah, blah, blah." In this case, what Lisa said seemed to work. There was a long pause . . . and then Alberto turned to Marcella and said:

> ALBERTO: I messed up and I'm sorry. I really wanted to be there.
> MARCELLA: I know and I'm not mad anymore. [Smiling at him] Just don't do it again.

Motivated by wanting Marcella to feel better about him, Alberto takes responsibility and apologizes. It's a good moment, a therapeutic moment. He tacitly admits that his choices have consequences that affect others and shows some glimmering awareness that, in the future, he will need to weigh his choices and decide what matters most. Warm, loving moments cannot always be so successfully orchestrated. For Tim and Alyssa, the goal was to create more understanding and better communication. Sofia helped

Tim use his intelligence and his self-control to learn how to be more emotionally aware of himself and Alyssa. She helped him think his way through conflicts. In so doing, Sofia anticipates that this emotional "know how" will help him with the baby, when she arrives. In contrast, Lisa used Alberto's emotional connection with Marcella to help him develop the ability to think things through and make more deliberate decisions. In all cases, we use the couple's relationship with each other and their investment in their yet-to-be-born baby as a source of motivation for change.

The idea that relationships are effective catalysts for change is borrowed from couples and family therapy researchers who have demonstrated that, if you shift the dynamic between two partners from adversarial to collaborative, this will often lead to individual changes in how they feel about each other, how they feel about themselves, and how they approach and manage their other relationships. If a young man learns to respond to his partner's distress with compassion and support, she will probably feel differently about him and their relationship. And she will likely feel stronger and better equipped to deal with whatever challenges she might face, like finding a job or diapering a rambunctious toddler.

At the outset, Lisa decided to help facilitate conversations between Alberto and Marcella that could help Alberto learn to identify his feelings and talk about his experiences, particularly his experience of Marcella and his feelings about becoming a father. How do we do this? For younger couples who are not particularly conversational, we use worksheets to select non-threatening topics to discuss or we focus on helping them discuss their personal and relationship goals, identified during their first or second session. But even this can be challenging for many young fathers. For example, Alberto said that one of his goals was to "settle down." If Lisa were to ask, "What do you mean by 'settle down'?" Alberto might quickly reach a dead-end when trying to explain, saying, "I don't know . . . I mean just settling down." It can be better to ask more specific questions that allow him to be concrete: "OK . . . so what would your life *look like* if you were more settled?" or to ask Marcella to help out by asking "What do you think Alberto means by settling down?"

Similarly, when couples are having an argument, it can be helpful to ask for concrete details about the sequence of events *before* asking about feelings. For example, the question: "So, what happened?" usually leads to a brief description of activities and events, like "I went out and she got mad, so we broke up." This can give the counselor some traction, allowing her to follow up with a more reflective line of inquiry: "How did you feel when that happened?" and then "How are you feeling about that right now?"

We know that some—maybe most—young men are uncomfortable with counseling for various reasons. Sometimes, it's because they don't know what to expect, or because they don't know what is expected from them, or (in some cases) because they have embraced traditional gender-role expectations that men don't talk about their problems or emotions. We approach this discomfort by explaining why we do what we do. For example, we routinely explain why we so frequently ask what they are feeling. For example, we might say something like this: "As you become more aware of your feelings—your inner self—you gain more self-control and become a better communicator, and that will make you a better partner and a better parent. I can almost guarantee that one day soon you will be asking your son to use his words to tell you what he is feeling or what he wants. That's all we're doing here."

Young men like Alberto need help shifting their attention from everything that is happening "out there" to the internal world of thoughts and feelings, so they can develop a more emotionally aware and self-directed version of themselves. Explanations of the therapeutic process often facilitate the pace of change and growth, but it's not quite that simple. Part of Alberto was much more interested in having fun than exploring his "inner self." This isn't atypical. Many adolescent males relish the feeling being untethered, without responsibilities, open to new adventures. Relationships are not necessarily barriers to this sort of freedom and autonomy, but sometimes that's how it feels. One of the greatest challenges for adolescents—and for some adults—is to negotiate the balance between autonomy and connection, between "what I do for, or by, myself" and "what I do for, or with, others."

Marcella believed Alberto's friends were nothing but bad news and she worried that when he was with his friends, he would get into trouble or cheat on her again. In reality, the problem was with Alberto; it was not really his friends that were getting him in trouble. He got a thrill from doing what he wasn't supposed to do. Lisa understood the dilemma facing this couple because we see it all the time. Without some space of his own, Alberto would feel trapped and would rebel. Without some restraint, Alberto would probably get himself in trouble, as Marcella feared. So the therapeutic task was to help Alberto share his feelings about wanting some freedom (to spend time with his friends) *and* help him demonstrate that he understood—deeply understood—that if he got into trouble, it would seriously affect Marcella and their baby.

Lisa helped Alberto work out what he could do to reassure Marcella (communicate with her when he was out with friends) and helped him plan out what he could do to take care of his relationships when he was out (recognize that when things got really exciting, it might be time to go home). The process of thinking through the decisions he makes—considering the options and consequences—diminished Alberto's sense of boundless freedom (a loss). But as he developed new self-management skills, he began to feel more competent. He also became more attuned to the reality of his circumstances. He was about to become a father, and learning to discuss plans with Marcella helped them both feel more like they were already beginning to function as co-parents. An important component of this process involved listening to Marcella's feelings about his plans and sometimes accepting Marcella's influence (e.g., not going out with his friends quite so much). This sort of experience helped to lay the foundation for Alberto's identity as a father and a partner.

Two-and-a-half years later, Alberto and Marcella had a 2-year-old son and a 1-year-old daughter and were living in the basement of Marcella's mother's house. Alberto had dropped out of high school the previous year and was working at a Jiffy Lube. At his last interview, he was feeling good about himself and his life. Marcella stuck with school, graduated at the top of her class, and she was thinking about college. In the meantime, she was working at a call center, responding to angry customers all day.

Alberto had become more communicative, more comfortable with his internal experience. He had a deeper understanding of himself and was able to reflect upon the experience of his son. He described an incident when he was with his daughter and some friends when they were pulled over by the police. He was not driving, but the driver was arrested for a DUI, and Alberto was arrested for possession of alcohol—because there was a six-pack in the car—and for endangerment of a child, which was a felony. At the police station, he was told that they would take his baby away from him. That didn't happen, but the threat had an impact. Reflecting on this experience, he realized that he had to make a choice: He could hang with his friends or he could take care of his children. And that was the end of his drinking and partying.

ERIC: Tell me about your family situation.
ALBERTO: We got our own place now, so it's just me and the two babies and Marcella.
ERIC: How's that going?
ALBERTO: It's alright but it's hard work. Kids are always running around, there's always a diaper to change, a bottle to make, somebody's always crying about something. There's always something new, never the same thing. So it's fun, exciting.
ERIC: Can you give me an example of how it is fun or exciting?

ALBERTO: Like we took him swimming for the first time this summer and he loved it so much. I didn't think he would, but he did. There is never nothing to do, always something to do. Sometimes he wants to clean, sometimes he plays baseball. Sometimes he wants to box, he likes boxing. Sometimes he runs around without his diaper on. He's pretty easy-going. He's feeding himself, learns everything quick. As long as you just show him what to do, show him "that's how to do it," he does it after a few tries.

ERIC: Good. OK . . . What are three words that describe your feelings about being a parent?

ALBERTO: Patience. You can't always be in a rush with a little kid. You have to slow down, take time. Like showing him how to use the bathroom. You have to be patient and think about when he might want to go.

ERIC: Another word?

ALBERTO: Caring. I care a lot about my kids. I try to go to all their doctor appointments. Never missed a doctor's appointment when Marcella was pregnant. Except one. Always make sure they got what they need and everything.

ERIC: One last word?

ALBERTO: These are hard questions! I love my kids a lot too. I will go to the full extent. I will do whatever I have to do to take care of them. Just gotta keep everything rolling, make sure everything's fine. As long as the kids are fine, taken care of, as long as the house is taken care of, I got nothing to worry about.

ERIC: How has becoming a parent changed you?

ALBERTO: I've changed a lot. I went from partying and hanging out with my friends to taking care of babies. It's so different from what I used to do. I was raising hell and getting into trouble. I've changed a lot, calmed down a lot. I try to take care of them as best I can and to stay on the ball. See, after I got into that trouble, when I was charged with possession of alcohol, that's when I really figured out that it was either my kids or my friends. Going out and hanging with my friends was one thing but taking care of my kids was what needed to be done. I really understood what needed to be done.

One of the interesting things about Alberto is that he was able to redirect his boundless energy away from chasing girls and partying to being a somewhat hyperactive father who takes great pleasure in the exuberance of his son. He figured out how to be a father by channeling all that restless energy into keeping his kids entertained. The change in Alberto's ability to articulate his feelings, learn from his experiences, and reflect upon the nuances of his relationships with his children is impressive. Alberto's transformation could not have been predicted.

NEW SUPPORTS FOR NEW FAMILIES?

As couples are having more trouble staying constructively engaged with each other, the effort to keep them working as co-parents becomes more important and more difficult. Ironically, it's often the case that those who face the most complicated family dynamics are the least likely to have the skills they need to manage their interpersonal challenges. When parents are married and living together, family alliances tend to be more straight-forward and manageable. Under such circumstances, a father and mother are primarily loyal to each other; their commitment to each other helps them protect the integrity of their family. For unmarried couples, family alliances tend to be more complex, more fluid, and more fragile, particularly when they are no longer in a committed romantic relationship. Even when couples are romantically together and committed, they often need help learning to maintain their co-parenting relationship, because the rules and roles are less clearly defined. Fathers like Alberto and Tim may have successfully transitioned to parenthood without the help of a counselor like Lisa or Sofia, but over the years, we have become convinced that many young expectant fathers need the sort of guidance and support that we try to provide through the Young Parenthood Program. Moreover, we think the stakes are too high to leave men like Brian or Jerome or William (from Part 3) to fend for themselves and see if they make it. We developed the Young Parenthood Program precisely because there is a gap in support for these young fathers and their partners.

In filling this gap, we try to set the stage for interpersonal growth in four ways. First, we try to *create a safe, secure environment for couples*. As indicated earlier, safety includes knowing what to expect and what is expected from counseling. A simple, clear explanation for how counseling can help usually increases buy-in. For example, in our program, we tell couples that improving their communication skills will help them provide a more stable family for their child. Safety also means setting some basic ground rules and knowing who's in charge of enforcing the rules. We acknowledge that angry feelings sometimes emerge in couple's counseling, so the counselor's role is to make sure that such feelings are expressed respectfully and in a way that they can be usefully heard. In the first session, we ask both partners to give the counselor the "authority" to interrupt the discussion when doing so is necessary to prevent the conversation from becoming harmful or destructive. Most couples are more than happy to let someone take that role.

Second, we *resist the temptation to solve a couple's problems for them*. When partners are unhappy with their relationship, it is often the case that each partner wants the counselor to "fix" the other. To avoid this impossible task, it's essential to help each partner understand that they are only able to change their *own* behavior, including their own responses to other people's behavior. This is not to say that asking for change—like drinking less and helping more—is unreasonable. But it's usually more helpful to facilitate a conversation in which both partners express their feelings about a problem, and where both partners listen openly to what is being expressed. Sometimes it is the counselor's role to help each partner express his or her feelings of frustration, anger, and sadness about the things they cannot change. Ironically, helping partners understand and empathize with each other will often lead to change without force or coercion.

Third, we *reinforce what is good about each partner and their relationship*. The "positive psychology" movement correctly points out that psychologists often overlook what their clients are doing well and fail to acknowledge the positive motives underlying problematic behaviors. The point is that it's important to call attention to a young person's strengths, to build his or her confidence and motivation. Self-esteem is good because it is the source of generosity and good will. Sometimes, pointing out what a young man does right or how a couple is working well together can help them feel more capable and more motivated to try harder and stick with it. And when the relationship hits a bump in the road, it can be useful to remind couples why they are still there, still talking, still trying to do what's best for their child. That said, we try to avoid lacquering over problems with false affirmations.

Fourth, we *strive to be strategic and realistic about what problems to address*, usually starting out with some agreed-upon goals that can be reasonably addressed with the time we have together. The tools and strategies used by clinicians vary widely, depending on their training and theoretical approach, but the idea that we have tools and the expertise to use these tools is a common element of therapeutic practice. When working with young parents, particularly those who are disadvantaged or have troubled histories, lots of problems may emerge, some of which we cannot reasonably address with the time and tools we have. While we try to be responsive to whatever a couple brings up at the beginning of each session, we also try to focus on what is doable. Some problems—such as drug use or financial problems—cannot be solved in couples counseling, but neither can they be completely ignored or avoided. Therefore, we set parameters around the goals of co-parenting counseling by tactfully keeping the focus on relationship issues.

Is there solid evidence that our approach to co-parenting counseling works? There is some, but more work is needed. For example, in one of our studies we found that compared to couples who were randomized into the control group, couples who participated in YPP demonstrated significant improvement in their relationship skills.[9] And such improvements were associated with significantly better levels of father engagement two years later. So, do we endorse our own program? Yes, but with the caveat that we need more evidence that this approach can effectively help young parents work together to raise their children.

In Chapter 21, we argued that without the institutional supports that accompany marriage, young fathers and mothers are not privy to a process that helps them prepare for parenthood or that offers guidance during difficult moments in their development as families. In this chapter, we have illustrated an approach that is designed to address this need (in the form of co-parenting counseling), highlighting what this approach looks like and what it might accomplish. Yet, without institutional backing, it is nothing more than a nice idea that is unlikely to have a widespread impact on at-risk fathers and their families in need of support. In the next and final chapter, we outline what needs to happen to build a system for institutionalizing such supports for new parents—in general—but, especially for young, unmarried parents.

CHAPTER 23

A Compass and a Map

Helping Young Fathers and Their Families

In this final chapter, we address the question of how to build institutional support systems to help young couples create family stability with or without marriage. Social institutions, such as schools, clubs, churches, neighborhood organizations, and local government, are important because they add structure and provide support for our daily lives. Institutions allow us to live collectively and to collaborate with each other, including people we don't much like but nonetheless depend upon. Indeed, we create these institutions (at least in part) to ensure that our positive human traits, like our willingness to sacrifice personal advantage for the common good (or at least the good of our children), will supersede our tendency toward selfishness.

Generally, when some action is needed to address a pressing social problem, like family dissolution or father disengagement, reformers will make an appeal for new laws or policies to accommodate societal needs, whereas traditionalists will call for moral renewal and individual-level action, imploring the "wayward" members of society to step up and recommit. In this final section, we sidestep the issue of what the current "fatherhood problem" tells us about the character of our nation, refrain from moralistic proclamations, and focus on a fundamentally practical, albeit difficult, solution. Specifically, in this final chapter, we look to the health-care industry for the help that families need because this sector of society, and the institutions it contains, is best situated to support the development of parents and children, particularly those in nontraditional families.

In Part Three, we discussed John Snow and his heroic effort to eradicate cholera in London. The history of medicine is full of heroes who, like Snow, waged slow-going fights against diseases that ravished populations, like polio and smallpox. The vanquishing of diseases makes for good stories, lending an element of drama to the field of public health. However, some public health issues, like pregnancy and childbirth, are not "problems" and do not lend themselves to being eradicated. Despite being a leading cause of death, and perhaps the most dangerous moment in a woman's life, childbirth is necessary for our survival as a species. So, rather than vanquish it, we can only make it safer. Although efforts to make childbirth safe have been going on for thousands of years, relatively little progress was made in the United States until the early 1900s when two women decided to take a serious stab at improving the way childbirth was being handled, institutionally. Very few people know who they are or what they accomplished.

The story begins with Julie Lathrop, a colleague of Jane Addams, who established the discipline of social work and created what we now call "social services." Lathrop's work with Addams and her advocacy for children's rights came to the attention of President Taft, who was under pressure from the suffragettes to appoint a woman to a high-level position in Washington. In 1912, Lathrop became the first woman to run a federal agency when Taft created the Children's Bureau and asked her to figure out what a Children's Bureau is and does. In 1916, Lathrop met Jeannette Rankin, a Montana native who became the first woman elected to Congress, several years *before* women won the right to vote. Like Lathrop, Rankin was part of the progressive movement set on improving the lives of the disadvantaged and marginalized. Together, Rankin and Lathrop wrote and advocated for legislation that would improve services for pregnant women living in rural and poor urban areas. These two women were inspired by advances in maternal and child healthcare in the United Kingdom, which had lowered infant and maternal mortality by employing midwives to provide prenatal care and ensuring the provision of medically assisted childbirth for all women. Midwives—for those who only have a vague sense of what they do—are nurses who have received advanced training in gynecology and obstetrics and are medically qualified to deliver babies. Although midwives had been delivering babies in America since colonial times, it was not until the early 20th century that midwifery became a recognized medical profession in the United States.

At the time, most women in the United States, which was still an agricultural nation, were giving birth at home without the help of a doctor, both

Figure 23.1 Infant mortality rate by year: United States, 1915–1997
From: Centers for Disease Control. Achievements in public health, 1900–1999: healthier mothers and babies. MMR Weekly. 1999;48(38);849–858. https://www.cdc.gov/mmwr/preview/mmwrhtml/mm4838a2.htm.

because there were not enough doctors to attend all births and because poor women could not afford to go to hospitals or pay for doctors to come to them. In the early 1900s, the rate of maternal deaths was almost 800 deaths per 100,000 births, and the rate of infant mortality was about 100 deaths per 1,000 births (as indicated in Figures 23.1 and 23.2). To address

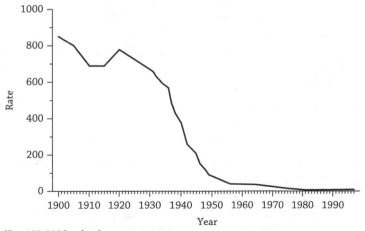

Figure 23.2 Maternal mortality rate by year: United States, 1900–1997
From: Centers for Disease Control. Achievements in public health, 1900–1999: healthier mothers and babies. *MMR Weekly*. 1999;48(38);849–858. https://www.cdc.gov/mmwr/preview/mmwrhtml/mm4838a2.htm.

these two problems, Lathrop and Rankin proposed to develop a network of trained midwives and to build clinics throughout the country, including isolated rural areas with a combination of state and federal funding. First, they had to convince the US Congress that maternal and infant mortality was *their* problem to solve. At the time, the idea that the government would get into the business of healthcare was quite radical, and the law that Lathrop and Rankin wrote failed to pass when first proposed in 1917. Shortly thereafter, Rankin was voted out of office, primarily because her constituents were unhappy that she had opposed Woodrow Wilson's declaration of war against Germany in 1917. When Rankin lost her seat in Congress, she also lost the power to introduce her maternal and child health bill.

Julie Lathrop, determined and politically savvy, did not give up the fight. In 1920, Lathrop persuaded Morris Sheppard, a senator from Texas, and Horace Mann Towner, a congressman from Iowa, to invest some of their political capital in sponsoring the Maternal Child Health Bill which became the Sheppard–Towner Act. After a hard-fought battle, the act passed in 1921 and, in its final form, it funded a pilot program to provide prenatal and birthing services to women in rural and poor urban communities. The act focused on providing services where maternal and infant death rates were highest, within the poorest and most isolated places in our country. A small army of prenatal nurses and midwives were trained and commissioned to provide prenatal care to women in these overlooked communities, with federal and state governments bankrolling the venture. Initially, the project appealed to both progressive and conservative women, who were divided on the issue of the 19th Amendment (which gave women the right to vote in 1920).[1] Saving the lives of mothers and infants is a bipartisan issue, a safe place to meet and agree. But the Sheppard–Towner Act had plenty of adversaries. The primary challenges to the law came from anticommunists, who thought the plan smacked of socialism, and the American Medical Association (AMA), which was concerned about the expansion of nonphysicians into the prenatal care workforce. So, despite its initial (modest) success in reducing maternal and infant death, funding for Lathrop's project was cut and the act was repealed in 1929, largely due to lobbying by the AMA, which didn't want midwives encroaching on their professional territory.

Five years later, the campaign to improve healthcare for mothers and infants was revived during the legislative debates surrounding the Social Security Act. Social Security was part of FDR's response to the devastating effects of the Great Depression and included funding that supported healthcare for pregnant women, young mothers, and infants. Like the Sheppard–Towner Act, Title V of the Social Securities Act was specifically intended to diminish the impact of pervasive poverty on the health of women and children by covering the cost of reproductive care for pregnant women. Over time, Title V services expanded to include healthcare for mothers and their babies for at least a few months after childbirth, when survival was more certain.

Today the rate of maternal death in the United States is 26.4 per 100,000 births and the infant mortality rate is 5.8 per 1.000 births.[2] Most people in the world of maternal and child health would say we could (and should) do better, but as Figures 23.1 and 23.2 indicate, pregnancy and childbirth are far less risky now than they were back then.

Currently, Title V covers most of the costs of healthcare for low-income pregnant women, young mothers, and their babies.[3] In 1966, the US Department of Agriculture (USDA) established a companion program called the Women, Infant, and Child (WIC) program to promote good nutrition for mothers and babies across the transition to parenthood. This program, which distributed milk products to pregnant women, young mothers, and young children, was part of Lyndon Johnson's war on poverty. It used public funds to prevent health problems among the poor by ensuring that poor mothers had the means to have healthy children. The work of Julie Lathrop, Jeannette Rankin, Horace Towner, Morris Sheppard, and the thousands who followed in their footsteps demonstrate that, with persistence, we can address massive public health problems that require a continuous supply of money and effort. But it ain't easy, and it doesn't happen overnight.

OUR PROPOSAL: PRENATAL CARE FOR MEN

In the early 1900s, most women assumed they would not receive medical care during their pregnancy or have a doctor to help with the birth of her child. Within 50 years of the Sheppard–Towner Act, virtually all women in the United States had access to prenatal care and delivered their babies in hospitals under the care of a doctor or midwife, drastically reducing the rate of maternal and infant deaths.[4,5] If we regard father disengagement as a public health issue—a problem that affects the health of mothers, children, and fathers—then it makes sense to do what we can to ensure that men have a good chance to make a healthy transition to fatherhood. Given the dramatic success of making prenatal care universally accessible for women, it seems worth asking: What would make it possible to integrate father health into prenatal care?

Yes, we know that men are not actually pregnant, but we also know—and have hopefully convinced our readers—that the adjustment to parenthood is difficult for many fathers, who can make life difficult for their partners and reduce the chances of success for their children. To be clear, we are not suggesting that the healthcare industry do away with medical or mental health services that cater to the specific needs of women by throwing the doors open and inviting men to participate in all prenatal visits. Like most people, we believe that pregnant women and expectant fathers have separate medical and psychological needs that often require separate types of services. However, we also believe that some health issues (including mental health) are distinctively familial and best addressed by working with men and women together. We are hopeful that, as gender roles become more fluid and gender equity becomes more normative, the rationale for automatically segregating men and women becomes more difficult to justify.

We are not the first to propose integrating fathers into maternal and child healthcare. In 2010, Michael Lu, who was then an ob-gyn professor at UCLA, wrote a paper entitled "Where Is the F in MCH?" that challenged the field of maternal and child healthcare to integrate fathers into maternal child healthcare.[6] In the 10 years since that paper was published, little progress has been made on father-inclusive maternal and child health. Only a small handful of researchers and clinicians have responded to the challenge proposed by Michael Lu.[7]

There are several good reasons for targeting prenatal care for father inclusion. First, as we noted in Chapter 22, the prenatal period, characteristically a time of hopefulness and anxiety, provides a window of opportunity for enlisting couples in a co-parenting program. It is during this period that expectant men and women tend to be most open to receiving help, particularly from those involved in the delivery of their baby. Going to the doctor for prenatal care isn't something they *have* to do; it's something they *want* to do. Second, it's easier and more effective to administer mental health and relationship-focused interventions early, before problems become more complicated and entrenched. Third, expectant fathers tend to be highly motivated to become good fathers (and partners) even when the pregnancy was unexpected and/or their relationship with their partner is rocky. And fourth, prenatal care providers are well positioned to refer young fathers and mothers for psychological or counseling services because of their unique role in the lives of young expectant couples. If psychological services are integrated into the prenatal care settings, men might be more willing to attend, particularly if they see their attendance as relevant to the health of their children.

Granted, there are many questions that need to be answered before such a radical transformation in how we approach prenatal care could gain any traction in our current healthcare system. For example: Is it possible to convince prenatal providers to offer services to young expectant fathers? And what would need to happen before couple-focused co-parenting support could become part of what prenatal clinics offered, as they do with Lamaze classes?

We would begin to address these questions by noting that there are a relatively small number of ways that a new approach to medical practice becomes part of what medical providers actually do on a routine basis. One path to becoming an accepted clinical practice is to be endorsed by a professional organization, such the American College of Obstetricians and Gynecologists (ACOG), as a clinical guideline or recommended practice. A second way to gain credibility is to be reviewed and positively rated by the US Prevention Services Task Force (PSTF) as an effective strategy for preventing an important health problem. The PSTF is paneled by experts across the country but run by the Centers for Disease Control and Prevention (CDC) and is responsible for making recommendations to health providers on the basis of careful scientific reviews. A third path for a new practice to gain support and become institutionalized is for the US Congress to pass a law requiring that a new service be provided, with promises of money attached to support at least some of what it's going to cost. There are times that a healthcare concern becomes so politically charged that state and federal legislatures are moved to pass laws requiring access to services before those other more conventional, evidence-based methods have been completed. In most cases, changes require both political and scientific backing. For example, the passage of the Maternal and Child Healthcare Act was inspired by new evidence, coming out of the United Kingdom, about how to decrease maternal and infant death rates. But it was the political fortitude of Julie Lathrop and her allies that led to the institutionalization of universal prenatal care in the United States.

There are more recent examples of new practices being adopted by prenatal care institutions that might help us think strategically about how to help make prenatal medicine more inclusive. The campaign to promote screening for postpartum depression (PPD) is a good case study of how this process can unfold, even ahead of the scientific evidence. We know that PPD is a serious, debilitating type of depression that is distinct from what is commonly called the "baby blues."[8,9] The baby blues is a period of mild depression and physical exhaustion associated with dramatic shifts in the production of hormones after childbirth. While the baby blues typically resolves itself within a matter of days, postpartum depression lingers and deepens. This illness poses a serious threat to the health of mothers because it can lead to immobilizing depression, frequently accompanied by suicidal thoughts and behavior. It can also be disruptive to the development of the mother–child bond, with negative consequences for the child. When it goes untreated, it can be a big problem.

PPD is not a new phenomenon or a recent discovery. It was first described by Hippocrates, the father of medicine, but very few people understood it or knew what to do about it until relatively recently. In 1968, the first epidemiological study of PPD was completed, estimating that about 10 percent of women experience some form of PPD.[10] That estimate was replicated in subsequent studies[11] and, in 1994, the American Psychiatric Association officially recognized PPD as a subtype of major depression. This helped increase awareness and generated research on treatment. Throughout the first decade of the 21st century, researchers and medical providers began to examine the value of universal screening to facilitate early identification and treatment of PPD. This idea was heralded by several advocacy groups, often founded and run by women and families affected by the illness.

In 2003, Bobby Rush, a congressman from Illinois made an impassioned speech on the floor of Congress, introducing the Melanie Blocker-Stokes Postpartum Depression Research and Care Act, which mandated screening and treatment for all woman receiving prenatal care. This act was named after a woman in Chicago who committed suicide while suffering from severe PPD. Rush had to reintroduce the act three more times before it was finally passed by the House in 2010. Then it languished in the Senate, never seeing the light of day until it was folded into the Affordable Care Act (ACA; aka "Obamacare") in 2014, which included funding for PPD screening and research on the effectiveness of treatments. Because of the ACA, insurance companies are now required to cover the cost of screening and treatment for PPD, a notable political achievement with significant health consequences.

Parallel to this legislative process unfolding in Congress, researchers and clinicians were working on how to best implement PPD screening and treatment. In 2015, the ACOG adopted a set of clinical guidelines for screening. And, in 2016, the PSTF made screening for PPD a recommended preventative practice. Despite these major accomplishments, most advocates for PPD treatment would probably say there is still a long way to go before PPD screening and treatment become a routine part of perinatal healthcare. Although significant progress has been made, most women are never screened during their pregnancy for risk factors, and the illness remains a serious problem. Part of the reason for this is that the effectiveness of treatment for PPD has been slow to accumulate, giving clinicians a reason to take a "wait and see" approach before buying into the idea that all their patients should be screened.

PPD screening and treatment will only become integrated into mainstream perinatal care if the research can convincingly demonstrate the effectiveness of these practices. Without more scientific evidence supporting the medical value of PPD screening and treatment for maternal and child health, the political and institutional efforts to change medical practice will stall. That said, the political push for change in medical practice should not be underemphasized. The story of how John Snow finally convinced city leaders to shut down the water pump that was polluting London's water supply with cholera is one example of how political doggedness was no less important than the evidence. This was also true for Julie Lathrop at the Children's Bureau, who struggled to establish a more inclusive system for women in need of prenatal care, and for Bobby Rush, whose legislative leadership helped put the issue of PPD in the public spotlight and promote the effort to improve treatment and research.

What does all this mean for pushing ahead on a completely out-of-the-box idea like providing prenatal care to fathers? Clearly, there is a great deal of work to be done before such a change would entertain serious consideration in mainstay institutions, like ACOG or PSTF, but we are not starting from scratch. The problem of father disengagement and family instability is widely recognized. And several researchers have found that when fathers are more involved and supportive across the transition to parenthood, their partners are more likely to have healthy pregnancies and their children are more likely to have healthy childhoods.[12,13] Moreover, there is some evidence—albeit still thin and in need of further support—that programs explicitly designed to help parents work together can indeed keep fathers constructively engaged with their children and prevent or reduce violence between partners.[14-16] Nonetheless, there are four significant obstacles that would need to be addressed before fathers could become truly integrated into prenatal care settings.

OBSTACLE ONE: PRENATAL PROVIDERS REGARD FATHERS AS OUTSIDE THE SCOPE OF THEIR PRACTICE

When depression screenings were first introduced to perinatal care providers, there were legitimate concerns about who would be responsible for administering the screenings, how that process would be paid for, and how we could ensure that women determined to need treatment would have access to services. Perinatal providers—obstetricians and nurse midwives—who are not trained to provide mental health services or support had questions about how they would manage to accurately identify and respond to a psychiatric problem they knew was lurking in the shadows. However, with some training and ongoing support from mental health providers, many ob-gyns and midwives have learned to address their patient's initial distress (by demonstrating compassionate understanding) while remaining focused on the practical steps necessary to ensure their health and their child's health. The point here is that medical providers can be convinced to expand their roles, if (a) doing so is in the best interests of their patients, (b) their expanded role will be covered by insurance, and (c) there is a support system in place to help them learn how to manage the challenge.

Yet, even the most open-minded obstetricians and midwives might be resistant to providing fathers with services because doing so would require a paradigm shift in how they think about their practice and, perhaps, a significant transformation in how they think about themselves as professionals. Currently, most prenatal care providers will politely acknowledge an expectant father in the waiting room with a nod or even a warm greeting. And some may strive to make fathers feel more welcome by subscribing to a male-oriented magazine or two for them to read in the waiting room. However, very few prenatal providers regard fathers as integral to the efforts of preparing mothers for a healthy birth. Even in the privacy of the exam room, prenatal care providers know that when they ask young expectant mothers about their partners, they may be opening a Pandora's box, leading to the discovery of problems they are not equipped to manage. Many providers choose to keep that lid shut.

In its current form, prenatal care is a decidedly woman-focused branch of medicine, and people who go into obstetrics or midwifery may prefer to keep men in their waiting rooms. To illustrate this point, we did a word search for "father" in the 7th edition of the *Guidelines for Perinatal Care*, co-published by the American Academy of Pediatricians and the ACOG. This imposing book is 577 pages and approximately 240,000 words long (not including references). The word "father" appears eight times in this edition. More to the point, the privacy of the relationship between prenatal care provider and pregnant woman (and young mother) is regarded as sacred and not to be tampered with. The idea of engaging fathers more fully may feel like a threat to that sacred relationship, even if clear lines were drawn to protect everyone's confidentiality. So, what would it take to convince prenatal providers that it's worth their while to more fully engage with young fathers and offer them services that are relevant to their own health and the health of their partners? First and foremost, healthcare providers who have been trained in the era of evidence-based medicine would need compelling data that offering mental health services or co-parenting counseling to fathers and young expectant couples has a direct (or indirect) impact on the health of expectant mothers and their infants.

To this point, the research evidence is growing but incomplete. On the one hand, we know that the quality of a couple's relationship during the pregnancy is one determinant of maternal well-being across the transition to parenthood, linked to healthy births and child well-being. There is plenty of evidence that when young mothers and fathers support each other, everyone in the family is happier and healthier, including the children.[17,18] On the other hand, the intervention research on how to help distressed couples learn to get along better is still in its infancy and is not yet sufficiently convincing. As indicated in Chapter 22, there is some evidence that programs like the Young Parenthood Program and the Family Foundations Program are effective in (a) improving the quality of couples' relations across the transition to parenthood; (b) keeping fathers engaged and constructively involved in child-rearing, and (c) reducing the risk of intimate partner violence between co-parenting partners. This research marks an important step in building a case for supporting the development of fathers and young couples, but it may not be enough to persuade prenatal care providers to throw open their doors to fathers. The jury is still out on whether co-parenting support programs can have a positive effect on birth outcomes or the immediate health or mental health of new mothers (e.g., reducing the risk for perinatal depression, preterm birth, or low birth weight among infants). Conducting research designed to obtain this sort of hard evidence is quite possible but requires more rigorous tests of co-parenting programs for expectant couples, currently not on the agenda in any federal agency.[a]

Even if the evidence were there, we would still need to address other concerns likely to emerge among prenatal providers. The first question that prenatal providers ask when someone (like us) asks if they'd consider offering services to the *partners* of their clients is this: "Who is going to provide that service?" pointing out that every minute they give to a father is a minute they have taken away from a pregnant woman, emphasizing that *she* is their primary responsibility. Point well-taken. And besides, they may add, "We're not family therapists!" These obstacles could be addressed by hiring psychologists or social workers who have the expertise to teach

---

a. The best way to accomplish this task is for the Administration for Children and Families (ACF) to stop doing what has not worked year after year for the past 15 years and get more serious about funding research on father inclusive co-parenting programs.

co-parenting skills and work with young men and the problems they commonly bring to the table. Of course, obtaining that expertise is also a work in progress. Outside the small world of co-parenting counseling researchers and fatherhood program developers, there are not many clinicians with training to provide these services, at least not yet.

We also know that some prenatal care providers will be concerned that inviting fathers to participate in prenatal care could be uncomfortable for some women who do not have a partner, either because he has already disengaged or because she does not want to have contact with him. This underscores the importance of inquiring about the nature of the pregnant woman's relationship with the father of her child *before* asking her to invite him to come in. We know that some prenatal providers believe that if the father of the child is uninvolved, questions about engaging him could be like throwing salt on open wounds. In our experience, asking young pregnant women about their partners is like asking about the elephant in the room. No matter what the circumstances, he exists and it makes sense to acknowledge that someone else was involved in this pregnancy. Putting that relationship on the table for discussion, if done sensitively, often comes as a relief, even when the circumstances aren't good. If he is truly uninvolved, it does not make sense to move on to a discussion about how to get him in for an appointment. That said, it's important to remember that many young relationships can change about as quickly as the weather. A young father might be gone today and back tomorrow. A young woman may hate her partner at the beginning of the week and love him again by the weekend. We don't mean to poke fun at the mercurial nature of these relationships; it is simply the reality of young love under stressful circumstances. If a young woman reports that the father of her child is not going to be involved, it may be appropriate to leave the door open and ask if it's OK to revisit the issue next month. She may change her mind.

OBSTACLE TWO: THE LACK OF EXPERTISE IN HELPING YOUNG FATHERS PREPARE FOR PARENTHOOD

Currently, if clinics and hospital systems were to expand their prenatal services to include fathers and wanted to hire mental health providers to implement co-parenting counseling and mental health services for expectant fathers, they would have a hard time filling those positions. From a skeptic's perspective, these services don't exist—or the clinicians to provide them—because the demand is not there. Although it's true that expectant fathers and mothers are not asking for these services, we are optimistic that if services were to be integrated into prenatal settings, as we describe in the following discussion, a demand for such services would develop. Though we'd like to point out that no one knew they needed an iPhone until Steve Jobs built one, we recognize that co-parenting counseling is not quite as cool as the iPhone. Nonetheless, if hospitals and clinics were motivated to expand the scope of their prenatal services to include fathers, mental health providers could be trained to meet that need without much trouble. In the world of mental health training, new models and modes of therapy are always being developed and disseminated, primarily through continuing education seminars and certification programs. Among the various obstacles to overcome, training providers to deliver services would be the easiest to address. Most well-trained master's level clinicians who are comfortable working with couples could be easily trained to administer a model like the Young Parenthood Program.

That said, there is a shortage of mental health providers who understand the trials and tribulations of young, unmarried, economically disadvantaged fathers. Most marital counselors are white middle-class married women and men with little personal or professional experience working with couples like those included in this book. It's not that these white middle-class clinicians couldn't do the job; being white middle-class clinicians ourselves, we'd like to think they (we) could do so with some degree of competence and success. But there is good evidence that people who seek health and mental health services sometimes feel more comfortable when working with clinicians who are demographically like themselves. Given the unfortunate reality of our divided world, people often (understandably) prefer to be treated by clinicians who come from similar backgrounds. As such, we believe the diversification of the mental health workforce is extremely important, as this allows for more choice. If we are to build a workforce of clinicians qualified to work with expectant fathers and their families, we need to do a better job of recruiting and supporting students from diverse communities to become counselors, social workers, and psychologists, so that they could occupy this developing professional niche.

OBSTACLE THREE: THERE IS NO CLEAR WAY TO PAY FOR FATHER-INCLUSIVE SERVICES

Perhaps the most difficult obstacle to address before fathers could be integrated into prenatal care settings is figuring out how to get family-focused or father-inclusive services paid for by the public and private insurance industries. Most co-parenting counseling and fatherhood programs—including ours—have been funded by grants. Typically, when those grants end, so does the program they fund. At best, grant-funded programs offer short-term, stop-gap solutions to long-term problems. Grant funding is great for demonstrating that a new solution to a problem works, but even the most effective programs will have a very limited impact if the service does not get covered by insurance.

Whereas hospital administrators might see the expansion of prenatal care to include fathers as a new market that could usher in new revenue, insurance companies might balk, recognizing the potential costs. There is little doubt that convincing prenatal (and perinatal) providers to include fathers in their practice will be contingent upon insurance companies covering the cost of expanded services. Ultimately, if we are to help fathers and mothers manage the interpersonal complexities of family life in the 21st century, we must make it easier for clinicians to work directly with fathers by convincing insurance companies to pay for services. Additionally, ob-gyns or family practice providers would need to know that any expansion of their services will be paid for by new revenue.[b] For this reason, the first step in institutionalizing father-inclusive prenatal care is to convince the insurance industry that they *must* cover the cost of prenatal services for fathers, including co-parenting counseling services.

Until recently, most people with a mental illness (regardless of their diagnosis) did not have access to adequate mental health services, because most insurance companies did not cover treatment for mental illness. For obvious financial reasons, insurance companies did not want to recognize mental illness as a medically necessary concern. Of course, the lack of coverage for mental illness disincentivized healthcare providers, like ob-gyns, from hiring mental health providers to work with their patients. Twenty years ago, an ob-gyn healthcare administrator might have known that some of the patients in his or her clinic would benefit from mental health services, but he or she also would have known that there was no financial mechanism for providing such services. If healthcare administrators were to provide such services, the clinic would have to eat the costs, which may have been financially untenable. This situation forced healthcare providers to make uncomfortable choices. On the one hand, it seemed pointless to

b. The best place to start this revolution in how prenatal care is provided to families would be in clinics run by family practice physicians, trained to provide prenatal care, deliver babies, and provide pediatric care. Family practice doctors are the last true generalists in medicine and—as their name suggests—they are already receptive to the idea of father-inclusive care.

ask their patients about problems they could not treat because there was no coverage. On the other hand, it seemed wrong to ignore problems that so obviously needed treatment and were quite treatable. Eventually, this medical–ethical–financial conundrum became a political issue because the mental health advocates, who were arguing that insurance companies were being discriminatory, gained the support of some influential politicians.^c Slowly but surely, a series of state and federal laws were passed that forced insurance companies to cover the treatment of mental illness and substance use disorders on par with physical illnesses. As things currently stand, if young a man or woman is diagnosed with a mental illness and has insurance coverage, he or she is entitled—theoretically at least—to receive appropriate mental health services. This change in the rule, referred to as mental health parity, was a major victory with significant implications for the healthcare industry. Once mental health parity was in place, healthcare providers could begin to integrate mental health services into their practice, knowing they could recoup the costs.

Convincing insurance companies that they must pay for mental health services for young expectant parents necessarily involves providing either the expectant mother or father with a diagnosis that qualifies them for counseling services. This is not terribly difficult because psychiatry has provided us with widely applicable diagnoses like "adjustment disorder," which is likely to apply to almost anyone who is expecting a child, provided there is some difficulty with the adjustment to parenthood causing symptoms of depression, anxiety, or disturbance in behavior. Consider Jerome (from Chapter 9) who was arrested for hitting Ebony when she was pregnant. Jerome did not have an obvious psychiatric diagnosis, like substance use disorder or depression, but he could have been easily diagnosed with "adjustment disorder with a disturbance in conduct," qualifying him for mental health services under most plans, assuming he was covered. Moreover, if we wanted to provide services to Jerome and Ebony through our Young Parenthood Program, we could bill their insurance company for

c. Mental illness had always been the "stepchild" of the healthcare industry, but in the 1990s, mental healthcare advocates began to talk about the insurance companies' denial of mental health services as discriminatory. Eventually, the disparity in coverage for physical and mental health became a political issue when two senators—Paul Wellstone and Peter Domenici—co-sponsored a bill to make insurance companies accountable for treating mental illness. These two senators agreed on very little but came together because they both had direct experience with family members whose lives were disrupted by costly mental illnesses. Their Mental Health Parity Act, which was signed into law in 2008, wasn't perfect, but it set expectations for services that were more fully realized with the passage of the ACA.

the services provided using the adjustment disorder diagnosis, which is not a stretch. In this way, the problem of paying for services could be solved. We can use the existing systems of coverage—already up and running—to pay for services for young expectant fathers.

One step in the direction of offering co-parenting counseling services to at-risk parents is to establish a system for screening and diagnosing relationship problems so that we could determine who needs such services. The screening and diagnostic process is essential to evidence-based medicine because it allows clinicians to differentiate between types of problems and the severity of those problems, which helps us be more precise in our treatment approach. Such distinctions help facilitate the success of intervention efforts because treatment efficacy is enhanced when we can tailor our approach to meet the particular needs of our patients. There are already some family and marriage "check-up" models that have had promising results with different types of families that could be adapted for young expectant parents.[19,20]

OBSTACLE FOUR: THE FATHERS

Anyone who has spent time with young expectant fathers will know that most are not chomping at the bit for any type of service, particularly mental health services. Historically, young men have been reluctant participants, sometimes obstinate nonparticipants, in medical care. Data collected by the National Center on Health Statistics on healthcare utilization indicates that young men, as a group, are 50 percent less likely to be seen by a primary care doctor.[2] While it's true that young men are healthy in most respects, it is also true that young men between the ages of 18 and 24 report more reckless drug and alcohol use, more unintentional injuries, and more unhealthy sexual behavior (putting themselves and their partners at high risk for sexually transmitted disease) than any other demographic group.[21,22]

The difficulty of engaging fathers in prenatal care is not just that they are reluctant to receive services. We also know that some fathers are deeply ambivalent about their connections, particularly their connections with their partners. Some are doubtful about their readiness for fatherhood, some are too caught up in their own issues to be concerned about others (including their pregnant girlfriends), and some believe they are a bad influence and that things will be better for everyone if they were to just go away. In Chapters 3 and 19, we discussed the biological basis of human connections, emphasizing that fathers' connections with mothers and children are supported by biological processes, built into our DNA. However, we also know that some fathers clearly have problems with that bonding process, as if they have a depleted supply of those "adhesive" chemicals. Indeed, some fathers—unreliable and uncommunicative—seem motivated to keep their distance. In some cases, trying to force a connection might be unwise, even dangerous. However, we know that many such men lack the language or the skills to articulate or make good on their deep longing for a different sort of attachment. Particularly in these cases, facilitating a stronger connection can be beneficial for the father, mother, and child.

This proposed plan presents would-be providers of prenatal services for fathers with a conundrum: those fathers who need help the most (and who need the most help) are often the most reluctant to meet with a counselor to assess their needs and the least likely to accept help when it is offered. Convincing prenatal care providers to invite fathers in for family check-ups would solve only part of the problem. We would still need to persuade young fathers to come in for their "check-ups" and make use of recommended co-parenting services. Just as it will be a challenge to alter the mindset of prenatal care providers, most fathers would have to radically rethink their role in their partner's prenatal care and revise their view of mental health providers. We can imagine a pregnant woman telling her partner that *their* prenatal doctor would like *him* to schedule an appointment for *his* "family check-up." At first pass, many young men would likely mutter "That's not gonna happen" to themselves. However, we think that, with time and encouragement, the request will nag at them. Most of the young men we've met are motivated to do what they can to make sure their baby gets off to a good start. Moreover, based on our experience, we have outlined a few strategies for engaging fathers, even the reluctant ones, into prenatal care services.

1. *Make it routine.* The first step toward including fathers in prenatal care would be to create the expectation among providers that fathers should be actively invited into the process. This does not necessarily mean inviting them into the examination room along with their pregnant partner, but it should involve (a) talking with them about how they are managing the adjustment to parenthood and (b) screening them for concerns they have about the co-parenting relationship and/or personal issues that could get in the way of their functioning as fathers. As suggested earlier, this could be framed as a "father check- up" or a "family check-up." Either way, if the screening process is presented as an opportunity for fathers to self-assess and communicate any concerns, it is likely to yield better information and lead to a stronger patient–provider relationship. Of course, a prenatal clinic would need to establish

its capacity for providing direct services for fathers (or for referring to reliable affiliated services) before requesting that fathers come in for their check-ups.

2. *Ask pregnant women to bring their partners to their next appointment.* If pregnant women are told that including the father in prenatal care is part of the clinic's routine and are asked directly to bring the father of their child to their next appointment for a father check-up, most mothers will gladly comply. This may stretch the credulity of a prenatal provider who is reading this book and operating under the impression that fathers are uninvolved or uninterested. Nonetheless, we have found that some—though certainly not all—fathers are responsive to being asked by their partners to participate in the prenatal care/childbirth process. And those who are reluctant can often be coaxed by their partners, who have a fair amount of leverage at this stage in their relationship. As previously indicated, we think it is important to convey that checking in with the father—even if they are not together as a couple—is routine and not due to a specific concern. If the pregnant woman indicates that she has concerns about her partner, then it is appropriate to find out more and adjust the process accordingly. As previously noted, in some cases including the father is either not possible or not advisable.

3. *Make the process interesting and motivating.* If the "family check-up" is designed to provide young expectant fathers with the opportunity to talk about themselves, their relationships, their hopes and concerns, most will appreciate that experience. We hope that the value of these experiences comes across in the interview excerpts we have included in this book. Recently, we have begun using the "results" of the questionnaires we administer to young fathers (and mothers) to provide them with immediate feedback on their strengths and "areas for growth." This process is designed to help fathers feel proud of what they've accomplished and self-identify what changes they'd like to make. We have found that if the assessment reveals that additional support is indicated and co-parenting counseling is offered, fathers are usually willing to follow through and give counseling a try.

4. *Provide concrete rewards for showing up.* Young pregnant women are routinely rewarded when they show up for their prenatal appointments with baby items such as basinets, diapers, and baby toys to help them get ready for parenthood. We have found that rewarding fathers (with baby paraphernalia or financial incentives) for showing up for their counseling appointments is incentivizing and helps them feel good about contributing to building a "nest" for their child.

5. *Be prepared to deal with the baggage that fathers bring with them.* If we open the door to prenatal care for fathers, we will need to be prepared for whoever walks in and whatever problems they have. We know that, if asked directly, many fathers will report depression, trauma, substance abuse, criminal behavior, and/or intimate partner violence. Some of these problems can be addressed within the context of co-parenting counseling or perhaps referred internally for additional treatment. However, no prenatal clinic can possibly manage all the mental health problems they see and will need to cultivate and maintain a good referral network for their fathers, particularly those with serious psychological concerns.

CONCLUSION: ODYSSEUS AND ATHENA

Some of the stereotypes we collectively hold about fathers go back a long way and are deeply rooted in our psyches. In the 8th century BCE, Homer wrote the *Odyssey*, which is, in essence, about a man who is taking an awfully long time to get back home after a "business" trip. As the story begins, Odysseus is introduced to us as a husband and father who left his wife Penelope and his infant son Telemachus in Ithaca to fight in the Trojan War. After 10 years of fighting, he and the other Greek warriors finally vanquish the Trojans and are headed home. However, due to extenuating circumstances, it takes Odysseus another 10 years to get there. In large part, the problem is that Poseidon, god of the sea, doesn't like Odysseus and sets up obstacle after obstacle, intended to divert him from his return. He is captured by a cyclops, stranded on an island with a sorceress, and tortured by the temptation of false beauty. Fortunately, Athena, the goddess of wisdom, takes pity on Odysseus and helps him scramble his way out of each mishap, eventually delivering him back home to Ithaca.

While he's been away, Penelope has spent day after day, year after year, fending off suitors who want nothing more than to take Odysseus' place beside her. Because he is not entirely sure about the loyalty of his family after such a long absence, Odysseus disguises himself as a beggar when he first arrives home and secretly tests Penelope's devotion. She passes the test and the story ends when Odysseus reveals himself and then defends his place in an all-out battle against a castle full of suitors. Despite being torn apart by his physical and psychological absence, Odysseus triumphs and the family is restored.

Clearly, Odysseus does not represent the typical father. We don't see him driving out in the middle of the night to pick up diapers. He and Penelope don't squabble about whose turn it is to pick up the children from daycare. He doesn't seem terribly concerned about making ends meet and paying the rent at the end of the month. However, the struggles that Odysseus faces on his journey symbolize the struggles that many fathers face. Odysseus is ambivalent about his attachment to his wife and children, questioning their loyalty to him, and, at times, doubting his loyalty to them. On the one hand, he fights against all odds to return to Ithaca, stave off the suitors, and reclaim his position as father and husband. On the other hand, he went away for 20 years and one cannot help but wonder whether he can hack domestic life. He is prone to violence, paranoid about betrayal, and often unable to express his true feelings.

Of course, Homer's epic tale is usually read as a classic hero's journey. But, from our perspective, the *Odyssey* is a story about a father struggling to stay connected with his family, even though most of the book is about Odysseus's trials and tribulations out in the world, apart from his wife and son. Of course, this reflects the reality of many fathers, who leave their wives and children every morning and return in the evening, with the bulk of their day devoted to other things. From our perspective, the most important question about Odysseus—insofar as his story pertains to fatherhood—is how he maintains his commitment and determination to get home. The answer, of course, is that he gets a lot of help; without Athena's interference, there is no way he would have made it back to Ithaca.

Whereas we'd like to believe that Ithaca represents home and fatherhood, it seems quite possible that Penelope might have a different version of this story and a different interpretation of what Ithaca represents. After all, she stayed in Ithaca and managed to raise Telemachus without any help from Odysseus. What is to be made of that? In Chapter 7, we mentioned the work of Sarah Hrdy, who proposed that human beings are "collaborative breeders," meaning that mothers are naturally inclined to weave together a network of "alloparents" (individuals other than biologically related parents who nevertheless function as parental caregivers), including aunts, grandmothers, brothers, and "social fathers" to help them raise their children. Hrdy argues that, given the uncertain role of fathers in child development, cultural institutions have evolved to ensure that children (and mothers) do not get left in the lurch if a father leaves to pursue other interests, including distant wars.

Hrdy tells us that, in some cultures, women go back to live with their mothers when they are pregnant and have young children, so that she learns how to mother and gets help with the child-rearing. And, in some cultures, the mother's brother plays the role of disciplinarian and provider for her children, while their father is more like a companion. Then again, some cultures believe that more than one man can contribute to a woman's pregnancy, so a child can have more than one biological father, making it possible for a mother to enlist several men in providing for her child. It is often the case that our beliefs, right or wrong, reflect our fundamental needs. Hrdy's point in recounting these different cultural family arrangements is that mothers need help raising their children, and society will accommodate that need, one way or another.

We are trying to make a similar point about fathers. Like mothers, fathers must garner the necessary tools for fathering, learning and drawing support from partners, family, and friends who are also parents. We also believe that fathers must learn to rely on institutional support when their natural support systems are unavailable or insufficient. In a world once replete with men's clubs and male-dominated organizations that excluded women, we recognize the risk in suggesting that men need special forms of support or that men are somehow being deprived of the support offered to women. We understand the point that men have guarded their privileged status for many generations and this might make any request for new forms of support suspicious or even galling. We offer two counterpoints to this perspective. First, there are a lot of young fathers who are anything but privileged and badly in need of some assistance. Second, in our society, where we are beginning to achieve gender equity, men are at risk for not knowing how to adjust to the new landscape. Although we value the naturally occurring sources of support for men that are provided in barbershops and on basketball courts and in bars, we caution against the presumption that these types of support will help men adjust to fatherhood. Many young fathers need focused instruction in how to establish enduring bonds with their partner and children. This is not the stuff of locker room talk or barbershop banter.

In these final chapters, we have strongly endorsed the role of prenatal care as a mechanism for providing men with the support they need as they approach fatherhood, a little like Athena's helpful interference in Odysseus's exploits. We conceive of prenatal care as "institutional support" because it is provided to all women as an entitlement by the medical establishment and supported, at least in part, by the government. For fathers, prenatal care could provide a window of opportunity for receiving support because most men already have some level of connection with their partners' prenatal care provider. We believe that drawing men further into prenatal care—particularly if it is packaged as an expectation—is the best option for preparing them for fatherhood. A quick check-up and a modest dose of co-parenting counseling might be enough to prepare most fathers for the challenges of parenthood. And, for those fathers who need more, they will be more likely to go get the additional help they need if their prenatal provider makes the case that their baby needs a healthy father. Moreover, by fully engaging a father in prenatal care, a counselor could establish an ongoing relationship that the father could continue to make use of when new problems emerge or old problems return. Without glamourizing fatherhood, we believe that fathers are worth supporting because they can play important roles in the lives of their children and their co-parenting partners and because society needs them to occupy those roles, contributing to the wellness of their communities.

In this book, we have attempted to faithfully share the stories of a group of young fathers and their partners who graciously shared their stories with us. Along the way, we have heard stories of triumph and defeat, love and heartache, connection and disengagement. We have heard stories of some fathers who were lost, some who were found, and even some who experienced dramatic personal transformation in their journeys to become fathers. It is our sincere hope that these stories inspire others the way that they have inspired us to see fathers as a worthwhile investment. We believe that doing more to help them become the best fathers they can be, and preventing as many fathers as possible from being lost, is a worthwhile endeavor, with potential dividends not only for the fathers themselves, but also for their children, their partners, and for society.

REFERENCES

CHAPTER 1: A TALE OF TWO FATHERS

1. Jessor R. *New perspectives on adolescent risk behavior*. New York, NY: Cambridge University Press; 1998.
2. Bowman PJ. Coping with provider role strain: adaptive cultural resources among black husband-fathers. In: Burlew AKH, Banks WC, McAdoo HP, et al., eds. *African American Psychology: Theory, Research, and Practice*. Thousand Oaks, CA: SAGE; 1992:135–154.
3. Luthar SS. Resilience in development: a synthesis of research across five decades. In: Cicchetti D, Cohen DJ, eds. *Developmental Psychopathology: Vol. 3, Risk, Disorder, and Adaptation*. 2nd ed. Hoboken, NJ: Wiley; 2006:739–795.

CHAPTER 2: THE PROBLEM WITH YOUNG FATHERHOOD

1. Maynard, RA, Hoffman SD. *Kids Having Kids: Economic Costs and Social Consequences of Teen Pregnancy*. Washington, DC: Urban Institute; 2008.
2. Moore MR, Brooks-Gunn J. Adolescent parenthood. In: Bornstein MH, ed. *Handbook of Parenting: Being and Becoming a Parent*. Mahwah, NJ: Erlbaum; 2002:173–214.
3. Blakemore SJ, Choudhury S. Development of the adolescent brain: implications for executive function and social cognition. *Journal of Child Psychology and Psychiatry*. 2006;47(3–4):296–312.
4. Moore DR, Florsheim P. Interpersonal processes and psychopathology among expectant and nonexpectant adolescent couples. *Journal of Consulting and Clinical Psychology*. 2001;69(1):101–113.
5. Martin JA, Hamilton BE, Osterman MJK, Driscoll AK, Drake P. Births: final data for 2016. *National Vital Statistics Reports*. 2018 Jan 1;67(1).
6. Lindberg LD, Maddow-Zimet I. Consequences of sex education on teen and young adult sexual behaviors and outcomes. *Journal of Adolescent Health*. 2012;51(4):332–338.
7. Santelli JS, Lindberg LD, Finer LB, Singh S. Explaining recent declines in adolescent pregnancy in the United States: the contribution of abstinence and improved contraceptive use. *American Journal of Public Health*. 2007;97(1):150–156.
8. Sedgh G, Finer LB, Bankole A, Eilers MA, Singh S. Adolescent pregnancy, birth, and abortion rates across countries: levels and recent trends. *Journal of Adolescent Health*. 2015;56(2):223–230.

9. Kost K, Maddow-Zimet I, Arpaia A. *Pregnancies, Births and Abortions among Adolescents and Young Women in the United States, 2013: National and State Trends by Age, Race and Ethnicity.* Guttmacher Institute: New York, NY; September 2017. https://www.guttmacher.org/report/us-adolescent-pregnancy-trends-2013.

10. Furstenberg FF Jr . The recent transformation of the American family. In: Carlson MJ, England P, eds. *Social Class and Changing Families in an Unequal America.* Stanford, CA: Stanford University Press; 2011:192–220.

11. Reichman NE, Teitler JO, Garfinkel I, McLanahan SS. Fragile families: sample and design. *Children and Youth Services Review.* 2001;23(4-5):303–326.

12. Carlson MJ, Turner KJ. Fathers' involvement and fathers' well-being over children's first five years. Paper presented at: Annual meeting of Population Association of America; Dallas, Texas; September 2010. www.ssc.wiscw.edu/cde/unmarried-fathers/wpcontent/ uploads/2010/09/Carlson_Turner_Sept2010.pdf.

13. Shannon JD, Cabrera NJ, Tamis-Lemonda C, Lamb ME. Who stays and who leaves? father accessibility across children's first 5 years. *Parenting: Science and Practice.* 2009;9(1–2):78–100.

14. Cheadle JE, Amato PR, King V. Patterns of nonresident father contact. *Demography.* 2010;47(1):205–225.

15. Lerman RI. Capabilities and contributions of unwed fathers. *The Future of Children.* 2010;20(2):63–85.

16. Carlson MJ, McLanahan SS. Fathers in fragile families. In: Lamb ME, Lamb ME, eds. *The Role of the Father in Child Development.* Hoboken, NJ: Wiley ; 2010: 241–269.

17. King V, Harris KM, Heard HE. Racial and ethnic diversity in nonresident father involvement. *Journal of Marriage and the Family.* 2004;66(1):1–21.

18. Edin K, Tach L, Mincy R. Claiming fatherhood: race and the dynamics of paternal involvement among unmarried men. *The Annals of the American Academy of Political and Social Science.* 2009;621(1):149–177.

19. Goldberg JS, Carlson MJ. Patterns and predictors of coparenting after unmarried parents part. *Journal of Family Psychology.* 2015;29(3):416–426.

20. Glocker ML, Langleben DD, Ruparel K, Loughead JW, Gur RC, Sachser N. Baby schema in infant faces induces cuteness perception and motivation for caretaking in adults. *Ethology.* 2009;115(3):257–263.

21. Edin, K, Nelson Timothy J. *Doing the Best I Can: Fatherhood in the Inner City.* Los Angeles, CA: University of California Press; 2013.

22. Amato PR, Meyers CE, Emery RE. Changes in nonresident father–child contact from 1976 to 2002. *Family Relations.* 2009;58(1):41–53.

CHAPTER 3: DADS AND CADS: THE SOCIOBIOLOGICAL ROOTS OF FATHERHOOD

1. Fincham FD, May RW. Infidelity in romantic relationships. *Current Opinion in Psychology.* 2017;13:70–74.

2. Trivers R. *Parental Investment and Sexual Selection.* Cambridge, MA: Harvard University Cambridge; 1972.

3. Erickson Warfield M, Hauser-Cram P, Wyngaarden Krauss M, Shonkoff JP, Upshur CC. The effect of early intervention services on maternal well-being. *Early Education and Development.* 2000;11(4):499–517.

4. Bowlby J. *Loss, Sadness and Depression.* New York, NY: Basic Books; 1980. *Attachment and Loss;* vol 3.

5. Waters E, Merrick S, Treboux D, Crowell J, Albersheim L. Attachment security in infancy and early adulthood: a twenty-year longitudinal study. *Child Development*. 2000;71(3):684–689.

6. Bowlby J. Attachment and loss: retrospect and prospect. *American Journal of Orthopsychiatry*. 1982;52(4):664–678.

7. Bretherton I. Fathers in attachment theory and research: a review. *Early Child Development and Care*. 2010;180(1–2):9–23.

8. Grossmann K, Grossmann KE, Kindler H, Zimmermann P. A wider view of attachment and exploration: the influence of mothers and fathers on the development of psychological security from infancy to young adulthood. In: Cassidy J & Shaver PR, eds. *Handbook of Attachment: Theory, Research, and Clinical Applications*. New York, NY: Guilford; 2008:857–879.

9. van Ijzendoorn MH, De Wolff MS. In search of the absent father: meta-analysis of infant–father attachment: a rejoinder to our discussants. *Child Development*. 1997;68(4):604–609.

10. Lucassen N, Tharner A, Van Ijzendoorn MH, et al. The association between paternal sensitivity and infant-father attachment security: a meta-analysis of three decades of research. *Journal of Family Psychology*. 2011;25(6):986–992.

11. Kim S, Boldt LJ, Kochanska G. From parent–child mutuality to security to socialization outcomes: developmental cascade toward positive adaptation in preadolescence. *Attachment & Human Development*. 2015;17(5):472–491.

12. Moullin S, Waldfogel J, Washbrook E. Parent–child attachment as a mechanism of intergenerational (dis)advantage. *Families, Relationships and Societies*. 2018;7(2):265–284.

13. Feldman R, Gordon I, Schneiderman I, Weisman O, Zagoory-Sharon O. Natural variations in maternal and paternal care are associated with systematic changes in oxytocin following parent–infant contact. *Psychoneuroendocrinology*. 2010;35(8):1133–1141.

14. Feldman R, Zagoory-Sharon O, Weisman O, et al. Sensitive parenting is associated with plasma oxytocin and polymorphisms in the OXTR and CD38 genes. *Biological Psychiatry*. 2012;72(3):175–181.

15. Maccoby EE. The gender of child and parent as factors in family dynamics. In: Crouter AC, Booth A, Crouter AC, Booth A, eds. *Children's Influence on Family Dynamics: The Neglected Side of Family Relationships*. Mahwah, NJ: Erlbaum; 2003:191–206.

16. Silverstein LB, Auerbach CF. Are fathers essential? Maybe not. In: Coleman M, Ganong LH, eds. *Points and Counterpoints: Controversial Relationship and Family Issues in the 21st Century: An Anthology*. Los Angeles, CA: Roxbury; 2003:187–191.

17. Brown GL, Mangelsdorf SC, Neff C. Father involvement, paternal sensitivity, and father-child attachment security in the first 3 years. *Journal of Family Psychology*. 2012;26(3):421–430.

18. Coley RL, Lewin-Bizan S, Carrano J. Does early paternal parenting promote low-income children's long-term cognitive skills? *Journal of Family Issues*. 2011;32(11):1522–1542.

19. Tach L, Edin K. The relationship contexts of young disadvantaged men. *The Annals of the American Academy of Political and Social Science*. 2011;635(1):76–94.

20. Bolland JM, Bryant CM, Lian BE, McCallum DM, Vazsonyi AT, Barth JM. Development and risk behavior among African American, Caucasian, and mixed-race adolescents living in high poverty inner-city neighborhoods. *American Journal of Community Psychology*. 2007;40(3-4):230–249.

21. Mincy R, Garfinkel I, Nepomnyaschy L. In-hospital paternity establishment and father involvement in fragile families. *Journal of Marriage and Family*. 2005;67(3):611–626.
22. Webster C, Simpson D, Shildrick T. *Poor Transitions: Social Exclusion and Young Adults*. New York, NY: Policy Press; 2004.
23. Wiatrowski MD, Griswold DB, Roberts MK. Social control theory and delinquency. *American Sociological Review*. 1981;46(5):525–541.
24. Dodge KA, Pettit GS, Bates JE. Socialization mediators of the relation between socioeconomic status and child conduct problems. *Child Development*. 1994;65(2):649–665.
25. Furstenberg FF Jr, Hughes ME. Social capital and successful development among at-risk youth. *Journal of Marriage and the Family*. 1995;57(3):580–592.
26. McLoyd VC. Socioeconomic disadvantage and child development. *American Psychologist*. 1998;53(2):185–204.
27. Furstenberg FF, Weiss CC. Intergenerational transmission of fathering roles in at risk families. *Marriage & Family Review*. 2000;29(2–3):181–201.
28. Conger RD, Belsky J, Capaldi DM. The intergenerational transmission of parenting: closing comments for the special section. *Developmental Psychology*. 2009;45(5):1276–1283.
29. Kerr DC, Capaldi DM, Pears KC, Owen LD. A prospective three generational study of fathers' constructive parenting: influences from family of origin, adolescent adjustment, and offspring temperament. *Developmental Psychology* 2009;45(5):1257–1275.

CHAPTER 6: BIRTH CONTROL ANYONE?

1. Alberts A, Elkind D, Ginsberg S. The personal fable and risk-taking in early adolescence. *Journal of Youth and Adolescence*. 2007;36(1):71–76.
2. Zabin LS, Astone NM, Emerson MR. Do adolescents want babies? The relationship between attitudes and behavior. *Journal of Research on Adolescence*. 1993;3(1):67–86.
3. Frey KA, Navarro SM, Kotelchuck M, Lu MC. The clinical content of preconception care: preconception care for men. *American Journal of Obstetrics and Gynecology*. 2008;199(6):S389–S395.
4. Edin K, Kefalas M. *Promises I Can Keep*. Berkeley, CA: University of California Press; 2005.
5. Guttmacher Institute. Adolescent Sexual and Reproductive Health in the United States. New York, NY: Guttmacher Institute; 2017. https://www.guttmacher.org/fact-sheet/american-teens-sexual-and-reproductive-health.
6. Finer LB, Zolna MR. Declines in unintended pregnancy in the United States, 2008–2011. *New England Journal of Medicine*. 2016;374(9):843–852.
7. Finer LB, Lindberg LD, Desai S. A prospective measure of unintended pregnancy in the United States. *Contraception*. 2018;98(6):522–527.
8. Mosher WD, Jones J, Abma JC. Intended and unintended births in the United States: 1982–2010. *National Health Statistics Report*. 2012;(55):1–28.
9. Gipson JD, Koenig MA, Hindin MJ. The effects of unintended pregnancy on infant, child, and parental health: a review of the literature. *Studies in Family planning*. 2008;39(1):18–38.
10. Brown SS, Eisenberg L. *The Best Intentions: Unintended Pregnancy and the Well-Being of Children and Families*. Washington, DC: National Academies Press; 1995.

11. Kaye K, Suellentrop K, Sloup C. *The Fog Zone: How Misperceptions, Magical Thinking, and Ambivalence Put Young Adults at Risk for Unplanned Pregnancy.* Washington, DC: The National Campaign to Prevent Teen and Unplanned Pregnancy; 2009.

12. Arnett JJ. Risk behavior and family role transitions during the twenties. *Journal of Youth and Adolescence.* 1998;27(3):301–320.

13. Wolfe DA, Jaffe PG, Crooks CV. *Adolescent risk behaviors: Why teens experiment and strategies to keep them safe.* New Haven, CT: Yale University Press; 2006.

14. Blakemore SJ, Choudhury S. Development of the adolescent brain: implications for executive function and social cognition. *Journal of Child Psychology and Psychiatry.* 2006;47(3–4):296–312.

15. McElhaney KB, Allen JP, Stephenson JC, Hare AL. Attachment and autonomy during adolescence. In: Lerner RM, Steinberg L, eds. *Handbook of Adolescent Psychology.* 3rd ed. Vol. 1. Hoboken, NJ: Wiley; 2009:358–403.

16. Erikson EH. *Youth and Crisis.* New York, NY: Norton; 1968.

17. Anderson E. Sex codes and family life among poor inner-city youths. *Annals of the American Academy of Political and Social Science.* 1989;501(1):59–78.

18. Burton LM, Tucker MB. Romantic unions in an era of uncertainty: a post-Moynihan perspective on African American women and marriage. *Annals of the American Academy of Political and Social Science.* 2009;621(1):132–148.

CHAPTER 7: ARE FATHERS NECESSARY?

1. Moynihan DP; US Department of Labor. *The Moynihan Report: The Negro Family: The Case for National Action.* Washington, DC. Government Printing Office; 1965.

2. Rainwater L, Yancey WL, Moynihan DP. *Moynihan Report and the Politics of Controversy: A Trans-Action Social Science and Public Policy Report.* Cambridge, MA: MIT Press, 1967.

3. Murray C. *Losing Ground: American Social Policy, 1950–1980.* New York, NY: Basic Books; 1984.

4. Wilson, WJ. *The Truly Disadvantaged: The Inner City, the Underclass, and Public Policy.* Chicago: University of Chicago; 1987.

5. Wilson WJ. *When Work Disappears.* New York, NY: Knopf; 1996.

6. US Census Bureau. Living arrangements of children under 18 years old: 1960 to present. Historical living arrangements; Table CH-1. https://www.census.gov/data/tables/time-series/demo/families/children.html. Published November 2018.

7. Blankenhorn D. *Fatherless America: Confronting Our Most Urgent Social Problem.* Scranton, PA: HarperCollins; 1995.

8. Pleck JH. Fatherhood and masculinity. In: Lamb ME, ed. *The Role of the Father in Child Development.* 5th ed. Hoboken, NJ: Wiley; 2010:27–57.

9. Silverstein LB, Auerbach CF. Deconstructing the essential father. *American Psychologist.* 1999;54(6):397–407.

10. Amato PR. The impact of family formation change on the cognitive, social, and emotional well-being of the next generation. *The Future of Children.* 2005;15(2):75–96.

11. Lamb ME, Lewis C. The development and significance of father–child relationships in two-parent families. In: Lamb ME, ed. *The Role of the Father in Child Development.* 5th ed. Hoboken, NJ: Wiley; 2010:94–153.

12. McLanahan S, Beck AN. Parental relationships in fragile families. *The Future of Children.* 2010;20(2):17–37.

13. Carlson MJ, Corcoran ME. Family structure and children's behavioral and cognitive outcomes. *Journal of Marriage and Family.* 2001;63(3):779–792.
14. Sigle-Rushton W, McLanahan S. Father absence and child well-being: a critical review. *The future of the family.* 2004;116:120–122.
15. MacDonald K, Parke RD. Parent-child physical play: the effects of sex and age of children and parents. *Sex Roles.* 1986;15(7–8):367–378.
16. Parke RD, Dennis J, Flyr ML, Morris KL, Leidy MS, Schofield TJ. Fathers: cultural and ecological perspectives. *Parenting: An Ecological Perspective.* 2005;2:103–135.
17. Paquette D. Theorizing the father–child relationship: mechanisms and developmental outcomes. *Human Development.* 2004;47(4):193–219.
18. Denham S, Kochanoff AT. Parental contributions to preschoolers' understanding of emotion. *Marriage & Family Review.* 2002;34(3-4):311–343.
19. Eisenberg N, Fabes RA, Murphy BC. Parents' reactions to children's negative emotions: relations to children's social competence and comforting behavior. *Child Development.* 1996;67(5):2227–2247.
20. Lamb ME, Lewis C. The development and significance of father–child relationships in two-parent families. In: Lamb ME, eds. *The role of the father in child development.* Hoboken, NJ: Wiley; 2010:94–153.
21. Cabrera NJ, Fitzgerald HE, Bradley RH, Roggman L. The ecology of father–child relationships: an expanded model. *Journal of Family Theory & Review.* 2014;6(4):336–354.
22. Doucet A. Gender roles and fathering. In: Cabrera NJ, Tamis-Lemonda CS, eds. *Handbook of Father Involvement: Multidisciplinary Perspectives.* 2nd ed. London: Routledge Academic: 2013:297–319.
23. Leidy MS, Schofield TJ, Parke RD. Fathers' contributions to children's social development. In: Cabrera NJ, Tamis-LeMonda CS, eds. *Handbook of father involvement: Multidisciplinary perspectives.* New York, NY: Routledge/Taylor & Francis; 2013:151–167.
24. McHale JP, Rasmussen JL. Coparental and family group-level dynamics during infancy: early family precursors of child and family functioning during preschool. *Development and Psychopathology.* 1998;10(1):39–59.
25. Hrdy SB. *Mothers and Others.* Cambridge, MA: Harvard University Press; 2011.
26. Alio AP, Kornosky JL, Mbah AK, Marty PJ, Salihu HM. The impact of paternal involvement on feto-infant morbidity among whites, blacks and Hispanics. *Maternal and Child Health Journal.* 2010;14(5):735–741.
27. Grych J, Oxtoby C, Lynn M. The effects of interparental conflict on children. In: Fine MA, Fincham FD, eds. *Handbook of Family Theories: A Content-Based Approach.* New York, NY: Routledge/Taylor & Francis; 2013:228–245.
28. Lamb ME. Does shared parenting by separated parents affect the adjustment of young children? *Journal of Child Custody: Research, Issues, and Practices.* 2018;15(1):16–25.
29. Biblarz TJ, Stacey J. How does the gender of parents matter? *Journal of Marriage and Family.* 2010;72(1):3–22.
30. Tasker F. Same-sex parenting and child development: reviewing the contribution of parental gender. *Journal of Marriage and Family.* 2010;72(1):35–40.
31. Owen MT, Caughy MOB, Hurst JR, Amos M, Hasanizadeh N, Mata-Otero A-M. Unique contributions of fathering to emerging self-regulation in low-income ethnic minority preschoolers. *Early Child Development and Care.* 2013;183(3–4):464–482.

32. Tamis-LeMonda CS, Shannon JD, Cabrera NJ, Lamb ME. Fathers and mothers at play with their 2-and 3-year-olds: Contributions to language and cognitive development. *Child Development.* 2004;75(6):1806–1820.

33. Amato PR, Gilbreth JG. Nonresident fathers and children's well-being: a meta-analysis. *Journal of Marriage and the Family.* 1999;61(3):557–573.

34. Brooks-Gunn J, Duncan GJ. The effects of poverty on children. *The Future of Children.* 1997;7(2):55–71.

35. Coley RL, Schindler HS. Biological fathers' contributions to maternal and family functioning. *Parenting: Science and Practice.* 2008;8(4):294–318.

36. Jackson AP, Choi J-K, Franke TM. Poor single mothers with young children: mastery, relations with nonresident fathers, and child outcomes. *Social Work Research.* 2009;33(2):95–106.

37. Knox VW, Bane MJ. Child support and schooling. *Child Support and Child Well-Being.* 1994;31:816–840.

38. Lerman RI. Capabilities and contributions of unwed fathers. *The Future of Children.* 2010;20(2):63–85.

39. Greene AD, Moore KA. Nonresident father involvement and child well-being among young children in families on welfare. *Marriage & Family Review.* 2000;29(2–3):159–180.

40. Koball H, Principe D. Do nonresident fathers who pay child support visit their children more? New federalism: national survey of America's families, Series B, No. B-44. Assessing the new federalism: An Urban Institute program to assess changing social policies. https://files.eric.ed.gov/fulltext/ED464969.pdf. Published March 2002.

41. Nepomnyaschy L. Child support and father-child contact: testing reciprocal pathways. *Demography.* 2007;44(1):93–112.

42. Adamsons K, Johnson SK. An updated and expanded meta-analysis of nonresident fathering and child well-being. *Journal of Family Psychology.* 2013;27(4):589.

43. Conner DB, Knight DK, Cross DR. Mothers' and fathers' scaffolding of their 2-year-olds during problem-solving and literacy interactions. *British Journal of Developmental Psychology.* 1997;15(3):323–338.

44. Baker CE. African American fathers' contributions to children's early academic achievement: evidence from two-parent families from the Early Childhood Longitudinal Study–Birth Cohort. *Early Education and Development.* 2014;25(1):19–35.

45. Cabrera NJ, Fagan J, Wight V, Schadler C. Influence of mother, father, and child risk on parenting and children's cognitive and social behaviors. *Child Development.* 2011;82(6):1985–2005.

46. McKelvey LM, Bokony PA, Swindle TM, Conners-Burrow NA, Schiffman RF, Fitzgerald HE. Father teaching interactions with toddlers at risk: associations with later child academic outcomes. *Family Science.* 2011;2(2):146–155.

47. McBride BA, Schoppe-Sullivan SJ, Ho M-H. The mediating role of fathers' school involvement on student achievement. *Journal of Applied Developmental Psychology.* 2005;26(2):201–216.

48. Pancsofar N, Vernon-Feagans L. Fathers' early contributions to children's language development in families from low-income rural communities. *Early Childhood Research Quarterly.* 2010;25(4):450–463.

49. Rowe ML, Coker D, Pan BA. A comparison of fathers' and mothers' talk to toddlers in low-income families. *Social Development.* 2004;13(2):278–291.

50. Rohner RP, Veneziano RA. The importance of father love: history and contemporary evidence. *Review of General Psychology.* 2001;5(4):382–405.

51. Khaleque A, Rohner RP. Pancultural associations between perceived parental acceptance and psychological adjustment of children and adults: a meta-analytic review of worldwide research. *Journal of Cross-Cultural Psychology.* 2012;43(5):784–800.

52. Young MH, Miller BC, Norton MC, Hill EJ. The effect of parental supportive behaviors on life satisfaction of adolescent offspring. *Journal of Marriage and the Family.* 1995;57(3):813–822.

53. Herzog JM. *Father hunger: Explorations with adults and children.* Mahwah, NJ: Analytic Press; 2001.

54. Child Trends Databank. (2019). *Children in poverty.* Available at: https://www.childtrends.org/?indicators=children-in-poverty.

55. Semega JL, Fontenot KR, Kollar MA. Income and poverty in the United States: 2017. US Census Bureau Current Population Reports P60-259. https://www.census.gov/content/dam/Census/library/publications/2017/demo/P60-259.pdf. Published September 2017.

56. Dickerson A, Popli GK. Persistent poverty and children's cognitive development: evidence from the UK Millennium Cohort Study. *Journal of the Royal Statistical Society: Series A (Statistics in Society).* 2016;179(2):535–558.

57. Lawson GM, Hook CJ, Farah MJ. A meta-analysis of the relationship between socioeconomic status and executive function performance among children. *Developmental science.* 2018;21(2):e12529.

58. Hair NL, Hanson JL, Wolfe BL, Pollak SD. Association of child poverty, brain development, and academic achievement. *JAMA Pediatrics.* 2015;169(9):822–829.

59. Choi JK, Palmer RJ, Pyun HS. Three measures of non-resident fathers' involvement, maternal parenting and child development in low-income single-mother families. *Child & Family Social Work.* 2014;19(3):282–291.

60. Eggebeen DJ, Knoester C. Does fatherhood matter for men? *Journal of Marriage and Family.* 2001;63(2):381–393.

61. Carlson MJ, McLanahan SS, Brooks-Gunn J. Coparenting and nonresident fathers' involvement with young children after a nonmarital birth. *Demography.* 2008;45(2):461–488.

62. Florsheim P, Moore DR. Observing differences between healthy and unhealthy adolescent romantic relationships: Substance abuse and interpersonal process. *Journal of Adolescence.* 2008;31(6):795–814.

63. Mirowsky J, Ross CE. Depression, parenthood, and age at first birth. *Social Science & Medicine.* 2002;54(8):1281–1298.

64. Meadows SO, McLanahan SS, Brooks-Gunn J. Parental depression and anxiety and early childhood behavior problems across family types. *Journal of Marriage and Family.* 2007;69(5):1162–1177.

65. Florsheim P, Ngu LQ. Fatherhood as a Transformative process: unexpected successes among high risk fathers. In: Kowaleski-Jones L, Wolfinger NH, Kowaleski-Jones L, Wolfinger NH, eds. *Fragile Families and the Marriage Agenda.* New York, NY: Springer Science + Business Media; 2006:211–232.

66. Eggebeen DJ, Knoester C, McDaniel B. The implications of fatherhood for men. In: Cabrera NJ, Tamis-LeMonda CS, Cabrera NJ, Tamis-LeMonda CS, eds. *Handbook of Father Involvement: Multidisciplinary Perspectives.* New York, NY: Routledge/Taylor & Francis Group; 2013:338–357.

67. Kravdal Ø, Grundy E, Lyngstad TH, Wiik KA. Family life history and late mid-life mortality in Norway. *Population and Development Review.* 2012;38(2):237–257.
68. Carlson MJ, Turner KJ. Fathers' involvement and fathers' well-being over children's first five years. Fragile Families (Princeton University) Working paper WP 10-10-FF. Published 2010.
69. Settersten Jr RA, Cancel-Tirado D. Fatherhood as a hidden variable in men's development and life courses. *Research in Human Development.* 2010;7(2):83–102.
70. McLanahan SS, Astone NM, Marks NF. The role of mother-only families in reproducing poverty. In: Huston AC, Huston AC, eds. *Children in Poverty: Child Development and Public Policy.* New York, NY: Cambridge University Press; 1994:51–78.
71. Lancaster CA, Gold KJ, Flynn HA, Yoo H, Marcus SM, Davis MM. Risk factors for depressive symptoms during pregnancy: a systematic review. *American Journal of Obstetrics and Gynecology.* 2010;202(1):5–14.
72. Meaney MJ. Maternal care, gene expression, and the transmission of individual differences in stress reactivity across generations. *Annual Review of Neuroscience.* 2001;24(1):1161–1192.
73. Cooper CE, McLanahan SS, Meadows SO, Brooks-Gunn J. Family structure transitions and maternal parenting stress. *Journal of Marriage and Family.* 2009;71(3):558–574.

CHAPTER 8: WHAT GOES WRONG?

1. Mincy RB, Jethwani M, Klempin S. *Failing Our Fathers: Confronting the Crisis of Economically Vulnerable Nonresident Fathers.* New York, NY: Oxford University Press; 2015.
2. Coates EE, Phares V. Predictors of paternal involvement among nonresidential, Black fathers from low-income neighborhoods. *Psychology of Men & Masculinity.* 2014;15(2):138–151.
3. Waller MR. Cooperation, conflict, or disengagement? Coparenting styles and father involvement in fragile families. *Family Process.* 2012;51(3):325–342.
4. McMahon TJ, Rounsaville BJ. Substance abuse and fathering: Some final comments on context and process. *Addiction.* 2002;97(9):1120–1122.

CHAPTER 9: LOVE HURTS

1. Daly M, Wilson M. Evolutionary social psychology and family homicide. *Science.* 1988;242(4878):519–524.
2. Truman JL, Morgan RE. Nonfatal domestic violence, 2003–2012. *Journal of Current Issues in Crime, Law & Law Enforcement.* 2015;8(4):1–21.
3. Smith SG, Basile KC, Gilbert LK, et al. National Intimate Partner and Sexual Violence Survey (NISVS): 2010–2012 state report. Atlanta, GA: Centers for Disease Control; 2017. https://www.cdc.gov/violenceprevention/pdf/NISVS-StateReportBook.pdf.
4. State vs. Jesse Black. Supreme Court of North Carolina, Raleigh. 60 N.C. 266 June, 1864, Decided. https://la.utexas.edu/users/jmciver/357L/60NC266.html.
5. Fulgham vs. State of Alabama. 46 Ala. 143. June term1871. https://flaglerlive.com/wp-content/uploads/Fulghamv.State_.pdf.
6. Jennings WG, Okeem C, Piquero AR, Sellers CS, Theobald D, Farrington DP. Dating and intimate partner violence among young persons ages 15–30: evidence from a systematic review. *Aggression and Violent Behavior.* 2017;33:107–125.

7. Desmarais SL, Reeves KA, Nicholls TL, Telford RP, Fiebert MS. Prevalence of physical violence in intimate relationships, Part 1: rates of male and female victimization. *Partner Abuse.* 2012;3(2):140–169.

8. Desmarais SL, Reeves KA, Nicholls TL, Telford RP, Fiebert MS. Prevalence of physical violence in intimate relationships, Part 2: rates of male and female perpetration. *Partner Abuse.* 2012;3(2):170–198.

9. Simon TR, Miller S, Gorman-Smith D, Orpinas P, Sullivan T. Physical dating violence norms and behavior among sixth-grade students from four U.S. sites. *Journal of Early Adolescence.* 2010;30(3):395–409.

10. Leonard KE, Winters JJ, Kearns-Bodkin JN, Homish GG, Kubiak AJ. Dyadic patterns of intimate partner violence in early marriage. *Psychology of Violence.* 2014;4(4):384–398.

11. Bailey BA, Daugherty RA. Intimate partner violence during pregnancy: incidence and associated health behaviors in a rural population. *Maternal and Child Health Journal.* 2007;11(5):495–503.

12. Gazmararian JA, Lazorick S, Spitz AM, Ballard TJ, Saltzman LE, Marks JS. Prevalence of violence against pregnant women. *JAMA.* 1996;275(24):1915–1920.

13. Allison CJ, Bartholomew K, Mayseless O, Dutton DG. Love as a battlefield: attachment and relationship dynamics in couples identified for male partner violence. *Journal of Family Issues.* 2008;29(1):125–150.

14. Dutton DG, Saunders K, Starzomski A, Bartholomew K. Intimacy-anger and insecure attachment as precursors of abuse in intimate relationships 1. *Journal of Applied Social Psychology.* 1994;24(15):1367–1386.

15. Foran HM, O'Leary KD. Alcohol and intimate partner violence: a meta-analytic review. *Clinical Psychology Review.* 2008;28(7):1222–1234.

16. Johnson MP, Leone JM. The differential effects of intimate terrorism and situational couple violence: findings from the National Violence Against Women Survey. *Journal of Family Issues.* 2005;26(3):322–349.

17. Campbell JC. Health consequences of intimate partner violence. *The Lancet.* 2002;359(9314):1331–1336.

18. Cerulli C, Talbot NL, Tang W, Chaudron LH. Co-occurring intimate partner violence and mental health diagnoses in perinatal women. *Journal of Women's Health.* 2011;20(12):1797–1803.

19. Johnson WL, Giordano PC, Longmore MA, Manning WD. Intimate partner violence and depressive symptoms during adolescence and young adulthood. *Journal of Health and Social Behavior.* 2014;55(1):39–55.

20. Boy A, Salihu HM. Intimate partner violence and birth outcomes: a systematic review. *International Journal of Fertility and Women's Medicine.* 2004;49(4):159–164.

21. Holmes MR. Aggressive behavior of children exposed to intimate partner violence: an examination of maternal mental health, maternal warmth and child maltreatment. *Child Abuse & Neglect.* 2013;37(8):520–530.

22. Renner LM, Boel-Studt S. The relation between intimate partner violence, parenting stress, and child behavior problems. *Journal of Family Violence.* 2013;28(2):201–212.

23. Zarling AL, Taber-Thomas S, Murray A, et al. Internalizing and externalizing symptoms in young children exposed to intimate partner violence: examining intervening processes. *Journal of Family Psychology.* 2013;27(6):945–955.

24. Violence Against Women Act. S-11. 103rd Congr. (1993–1994). https://www.congress.gov/bill/103rd-congress/senate-bill/11.

25. Biden J. 20 years of change: Joe Biden on the Violence Against Women Act. *Time.* September 10, 2014. http://time.com/3319325/joe-biden-violence-against-women/.

26. Maiuro RD, Hagar TS, Lin H-h, Olson N. Are current state standards for domestic violence perpetrator treatment adequately informed by research? A question of questions. *Journal of Aggression, Maltreatment & Trauma.* 2001;5(2):21–44.

27. Bancroft L, Silverman JG, Ritchie D. *The Batterer as Parent: Addressing the Impact of Domestic Violence on Family Dynamics.* Thousand Oaks, CA: SAGE; 2011.

28. Bernstein E. Domestic abusers can reform, studies show. *Wall Street Journal.* September 15, 2014. https://www.wsj.com/articles/domestic-abusers-can-reform-studies-show-1410822557.

29. Karakurt G, Whiting K, Van Esch C, Bolen SD, Calabrese JR. Couples therapy for intimate partner violence: a systematic review and meta-analysis. *Journal of Marital and Family Therapy.* 2016;42(4):567–583.

CHAPTER 10: DROWNING SORROWS

1. Moore TJ, Mattison DR. Adult utilization of psychiatric drugs and differences by sex, age, and race. *JAMA Internal Medicine.* 2017;177(2):274–275.

2. Compton WM, Han B, Jones CM, Blanco C, Hughes A. Marijuana use and use disorders in adults in the USA, 2002–14: analysis of annual cross-sectional surveys. *The Lancet Psychiatry.* 2016;3(10):954–964.

3. Kantor ED, Rehm CD, Haas JS, Chan AT, Giovannucci EL. Trends in prescription drug use among adults in the United States from 1999–2012. *JAMA.* 2015;314(17):1818–1830.

4. Park-Lee E, Lipari RN, Hedden SL, Kroutil L, Porter J. Receipt of services for substance use and mental health issues among adults: results from the 2016 National Survey on Drug Use and Health. NSDUH Data Review. https://www.samhsa.gov/data/sites/default/files/NSDUH-DR-FFR2-2016/NSDUH-DR-FFR2-2016.htm. Published September 2016.

5. Florsheim P, Moore DR. Observing differences between healthy and unhealthy adolescent romantic relationships: substance abuse and interpersonal process. *Journal of Adolescence.* 2008;31(6):795–814.

6. Grant BF, Goldstein RB, Saha TD, et al. Epidemiology of DSM-5 alcohol use disorder: results from the National Epidemiologic Survey on Alcohol and Related Conditions III. *JAMA Psychiatry.* 2015;72(8):757–766.

7. Lipari RN, Van Horn SL. Trends in substance use disorders among adults aged 18 or older. The CBHSQ Report. Rockville, MD: Substance Abuse and Mental Health Services Administration; June 29, 2017. https://www.samhsa.gov/data/sites/default/files/report_2790/ShortReport-2790.html.

8. Bailey JA, Hill KG, Hawkins JD, Catalano RF, Abbott RD. Men's and women's patterns of substance use around pregnancy. *Birth.* 2008;35(1):50–59.

9. Andreas JB, O'Farrell TJ. Longitudinal associations between fathers' heavy drinking patterns and children's psychosocial adjustment. *Journal of Abnormal Child Psychology.* 2007;35(1):1.

10. Kelley ML, Lawrence HR, Milletich RJ, Hollis BF, Henson JM. Modeling risk for child abuse and harsh parenting in families with depressed and substance-abusing parents. *Child Abuse & Neglect.* 2015;43:42–52.

11. Smith VC, Wilson CR. Families affected by parental substance use. *Pediatrics.* 2016;138(2):e20161575.

12. Ammerman RT, Kolko DJ, Kirisci L, Blackson TC, Dawes MA. Child abuse potential in parents with histories of substance use disorder. *Child Abuse & Neglect*. 1999;23(12):1225–1238.

13. Caetano R, Schafer J, Cunradi CB. Alcohol-related intimate partner violence among white, black, and Hispanic couples in the United States. In: Natarajan M, ed. *Domestic Violence: The Five Big Questions*. New York, NY: Routledge; 2017:153–160.

14. Walsh C, MacMillan HL, Jamieson E. The relationship between parental substance abuse and child maltreatment: findings from the Ontario Health Supplement. *Child Abuse & Neglect*. 2003;27(12):1409–1425.

15. Bountress K, Chassin L. Risk for behavior problems in children of parents with substance use disorders. *American Journal of Orthopsychiatry*. 2015;85(3):275–286.

16. Verhulst B, Neale MC, Kendler KS. The heritability of alcohol use disorders: a meta-analysis of twin and adoption studies. *Psychological Medicine*. 2015;45(5):1061–1072.

17. Verweij KJH, Vinkhuyzen AAE, Benyamin B, et al. The genetic aetiology of cannabis use initiation: a meta-analysis of genome-wide association studies and a SNP-based heritability estimation. *Addiction Biology*. 2013;18(5):846–850.

18. Walters GD. The heritability of alcohol abuse and dependence: a meta-analysis of behavior genetic research. *American Journal of Drug and Alcohol Abuse*. 2002;28(3):557–584.

19. Agrawal A, Lynskey MT, Bucholz KK, et al. DSM-5 cannabis use disorder: a phenotypic and genomic perspective. *Drug and Alcohol Dependence*. 2014;134:362–369.

20. Tawa EA, Hall SD, Lohoff FW. Overview of the genetics of alcohol use disorder. *Alcohol and Alcoholism*. 2016;51(5):507–514.

21. Adinoff B. Neurobiologic processes in drug reward and addiction. *Harvard Review of Psychiatry*. 2004;12(6):305–320.

22. Substance Abuse and Mental Health Services Administration. 2015 National Survey on Drug Use and Health. https://www.samhsa.gov/data/sites/default/files/NSDUH-DetTabs-2015/NSDUH-DetTabs-2015/NSDUH-DetTabs-2015.pdf. Published September 8, 2016.

23. Morris C. Legal marijuana sales are expected to hit $10 billion this year. Fortune.com. http://fortune.com/2017/12/06/legal-marijuana-sales-10-billion/. Published December 6, 2017.

24. Kelly TM, Daley DC. Integrated treatment of substance use and psychiatric disorders. *Social Work in Public Health*. 2013;28(3–4):388–406.

25. Substance Abuse and Mental Health Services Administration. Behavioral health barometer: United States, 2013. https://www.samhsa.gov/data/sites/default/files/National_BHBarometer/National_BHBarometer.pdf. Published 2013.

26. Khantzian E. The self-medication hypothesis and attachment theory: pathways for understanding and ameliorating addictive suffering. In Gill R, ed. *Addictions from an Attachment Perspective*. New York, NY: Routledge; 2018:33–57.

CHAPTER 11: BAD SEEDS OR BAD SOIL?

1. Brame R, Bushway SD, Paternoster R, Turner MG. Demographic patterns of cumulative arrest prevalence by ages 18 and 23. *Crime & Delinquency*. 2014;60(3):471–486.

2. Patrick CJ. *Handbook of psychopathy*. 2nd ed. New York, NY: Guilford; 2018.

3. James DJ, Glaze, LE. Mental health problems of prison and jail inmates. Department of Justice, Bureau of Justice Statistics Special Report. https://www.bjs.gov/content/pub/pdf/mhppji.pdf. Revised December 14, 2006.
4. Steadman HJ, Osher FC, Robbins PC, Case B, Samuels S. Prevalence of serious mental illness among jail inmates. *Psychiatric Services.* 2009;60(6):761–765.
5. Glaze LE, & Maruschak, L. M. Parents in prison and their minor children. US Department of Justice, Bureau of Justice Statistics Special Report. https://www.bjs.gov/content/pub/pdf/pptmc.pdf. 2011. Revised March 30, 2010.
6. Wildeman C, Turney K, Yi Y. Paternal incarceration and family functioning: variation across federal, state, and local facilities. *Annals of the American Academy of Political and Social Science.* 2016;665(1):80–97.
7. Turney K. Liminal men: incarceration and relationship dissolution. *Social Problems.* 2015;62(4):499–528.
8. Geller A, Garfinkel I, Cooper CE, Mincy RB. Parental incarceration and child well-being: Implications for urban families. *Social Science Quarterly.* 2009;90(5):1186–1202.
9. Alexander LA, Muñoz MdlFR, Perry DF, Le H-N. The latent symptom structure of the Beck depression inventory: in Latina pregnant women. *Maternal and Child Health Journal.* 2014;18(5):1132–1141.
10. Dyer WJ, Pleck JH, McBride BA. Imprisoned fathers and their family relationships: a 40-year review from a multi-theory view. *Journal of Family Theory & Review.* 2012;4(1):20–47.
11. Schwartz-Soicher O, Geller A, Garfinkel I. The effect of paternal incarceration on material hardship. *Social Service Review.* 2011;85(3):447–473.
12. John A. A timeline of the rise and fall of "tough on crime" drug sentencing. *The Atlantic.* April 22, 2014. https://www.theatlantic.com/politics/archive/2014/04/a-timeline-of-the-rise-and-fall-of-tough-on-crime-drug-sentencing/360983/.
13. Gingrich N, Nolan P. Prison reform: A smart way for states to save money and lives. *Washington Post.* 2011;7.
14. Mauer M, King RS. *Uneven Justice: State Rates of Incarceration by Race and Ethnicity.* Washington, DC: Sentencing Project; 2007.
15. Walker S, Spohn C, DeLone M. *The Color of Justice: Race, Ethnicity, and Crime in America.* Boston, MA: Cengage Learning; 2012.
16. Bishop DM. Juvenile offenders in the adult criminal justice system. *Crime and Justice.* 2000;27:81–167.
17. Bishop DM. The role of race and ethnicity in juvenile justice processing. In: Hawkins DF, Kempf-Leonard K, eds. *Our Children, Their Children: Confronting Racial and Ethnic Differences in American Juvenile Justice.* Chicago, IL: University of Chicago Press; 2005:23–82.
18. Spohn C. Race, crime, and punishment in the twentieth and twenty-first centuries. *Crime and Justice.* 2015;44(1):49–97.
19. Rosich KJ. *Race, Ethnicity, and the Criminal Justice System.* Washington, DC: ASA; 2007.
20. Taylor P, Parker K, Fry R, et al. *King's Dream Remains an Elusive Goal: Many Americans See Racial Disparities.* Washington, DC: Pew Research Center; 2013.
21. Burch T. Skin color and the criminal justice system: beyond black–white disparities in sentencing. *Journal of Empirical Legal Studies.* 2015;12(3):395–420.
22. Kutateladze BL, Andiloro NR, Johnson BD, Spohn CC. Cumulative disadvantage: examining racial and ethnic disparity in prosecution and sentencing. *Criminology.* 2014;52(3):514–551.

23. Johnson BD, King RD. Facial profiling: race, physical appearance, and punishment. *Criminology*. 2017;55(3):520–547.
24. Starr SB, Rehavi MM. Mandatory sentencing and racial disparity: assessing the role of prosecutors and the effects of Booker. *Yale Law Journal*. 2013;123(1):2–80.
25. Wildeman C, Western B. Incarceration in fragile families. *The Future of Children*. 2010;20(2):157–177.
26. Tonry M. Making American sentencing just, humane, and effective. *Crime and Justice*. 2017;46(1):441–504.
27. Nagin DS. Deterrent effects of the certainty and severity of punishment. In: Nagin DS, Cullen FT, Jonson CL, eds. *Deterrence, Choice, and Crime*. New York, NY: Routledge; 2018:167–196.
28. Spohn C, Holleran D. The effect of imprisonment on recidivism rates of felony offenders: A focus on drug offenders. *Criminology*. 2002;40(2):329–358.
29. Latessa EJ, Listwan SL, Koetzle D. *What Works (and Doesn't) in Reducing Recidivism*. New York, NY: Routledge; 2014.
30. Listwan SJ, Sullivan CJ, Agnew R, Cullen FT, Colvin M. The pains of imprisonment revisited: the impact of strain on inmate recidivism. *Justice Quarterly*. 2013;30(1):144–168.
31. Weisburd D, Farrington DP, Gill C. What works in crime prevention and rehabilitation: an assessment of systematic reviews. *Criminology & Public Policy*. 2017;16(2):415–449.
32. Murray J, Janson C-G, Farrington DP. Crime in adult offspring of prisoners: a cross-national comparison of two longitudinal samples. *Criminal Justice and Behavior*. 2007;34(1):133–149.
33. Nagin DS, Cullen FT, Jonson CL. Imprisonment and reoffending. *Crime and Justice*. 2009;38(1):115–200.
34. Durose MR, Cooper AD, Snyder HN. Recidivism of prisoners released in 30 states in 2005: Patterns from 2005 to 2010. Bureau of Justice Statistics Special Report. Washington, DC: US Department of Justice, Office of Justice Programs; April 2014. https://www.bjs.gov/content/pub/pdf/rprts05p0510.pdf.
35. MacKenzie DL, Farrington DP. Preventing future offending of delinquents and offenders: what have we learned from experiments and meta-analyses? *Journal of Experimental Criminology*. 2015;11(4):565–595.
36. Brayford J, Cowe FB, Deering J. *What Else Works? Creative Work with Offenders*. New York, NY: Routledge; 2013.
37. Cullen FT, Gilbert KE. *Reaffirming Rehabilitation*. New York, NY: Routledge; 2012.
38. Veysey B, Christian J, Martinez DJ. *How Offenders Transform Their Lives*. New York, NY: Routledge; 2013.
39. Visher C La Vigne NG, Farrell J. *Illinois Prisoners' Reflections on Returning Home*. Washington, DC: Urban Institute; 2003.
40. Fontaine J, Cramer L, Paddock E. *Encouraging Responsible Parenting among Fathers with Histories of Incarceration*. Washington, DC: Urban Institute; 2017.
41. Hoffmann HC, Byrd AL, Kightlinger AM. Prison programs and services for incarcerated parents and their underage children: results from a national survey of correctional facilities. *Prison Journal*. 2010;90(4):397–416.
42. Loper AB, Tuerk EH. Parenting programs for incarcerated parents: Current research and future directions. *Criminal Justice Policy Review*. 2006;17(4):407–427.
43. Barr R, Morin M, Brito N, Richeda B, Rodriguez J, Shauffer C. Delivering services to incarcerated teen fathers: a pilot intervention to increase the

quality of father–infant interactions during visitation. *Psychological Services.*
2014;11(1):10–21.
44. Eddy JM, Martinez CR Jr, Burraston B. VI. A randomized controlled trial of
a parent management training program for incarcerated parents: proximal
impacts. *Monographs of the Society for Research in Child Development.*
2013;78(3):75–93.

CHAPTER 12: BETRAYAL AND FORGIVENESS

1. Fincham FD, May RW. Infidelity in romantic relationships. *Current Opinion in Psychology.* 2017;13:70–74.
2. McAnulty RD, Brineman JM. Infidelity in dating relationships. *Annual Review of Sex Research.* 2007;18(1):94–114.
3. Guzzo KB. New partners, more kids: multiple-partner fertility in the United States. *Annals of the American Academy of Political and Social Science.* 2014;654(1):66–86.
4. Meyer DR, Cancian M, Cook ST. Multiple-partner fertility: incidence and implications for child support policy. *Social Service Review.* 2005;79(4):577–601.
5. Sinkewicz M, Garfinkel I. Unwed fathers' ability to pay child support: new estimates accounting for multiple-partner fertility. *Demography.* 2009;46(2):247–263.
6. Gordon KC, Baucom DH, Snyder DK. Treating couples recovering from infidelity: an integrative approach. *Journal of Clinical Psychology.* 2005;61(11):1393–1405.
7. Sapolsky RM. *Why Zebras Don't Get Ulcers: The Acclaimed Guide to Stress, Stress-Related Diseases, and Coping.* Rev updated ed. New York, NY: Holt; 2004.

CHAPTER 14: FAMILIES REDEFINED

1. Coontz S. *Marriage, a History: From Obedience to Intimacy or How Love Conquered Marriage.* New York, NY: Viking; 2005.
2. Cherlin AJ. *The Marriage-Go-Round: The State of Marriage and the American Family Today.* New York, NY: Knopf. 2009.
3. Shanley ML, Chasman D. *Just Marriage.* Oxford, England: Oxford University Press; 2004.
4. Amato PR. Research on divorce: continuing trends and new developments. *Journal of Marriage and Family.* 2010;72(3):650–666.
5. DeRose L, Lyons-Amos M, Wilcox W, Huarcaya G. *The Cohabitation Go-Round: Cohabitation and Family Instability across the Globe.* New York, NY: Social Trends Institute. 2017.
6. Gove WR, Hughes M, Style CB. Does marriage have positive effects on the psychological well-being of the individual? *Journal of Health and Social Behavior.* 1983;24(2):122–131.
7. Rosenkrantz Aronson S, Huston AC. The mother–infant relationship in single, cohabiting, and married families: a case for marriage? *Journal of Family Psychology.* 2004;18(1):5–18.
8. Cherlin A. *Marriage, Divorce, Remarriage.* Cambridge, MA: Harvard University Press; 2009.
9. Cherlin AJ. The deinstitutionalization of American marriage. *Journal of Marriage and Family.* 2004;66(4):848–861.
10. Inglehart R, Norris P. *Rising Tide: Gender Equality and Cultural Change around the World.* Cambridge, England: Cambridge University Press; 2003.

11. Scheingold SA. *The Politics of Rights: Lawyers, Public Policy, and Political Change.* Ann Arbor, MI: University of Michigan Press; 2010.
12. Flexner E, Fitzpatrick EF. *Century of Struggle: The Woman's Rights Movement in the United States.* Cambridge, MA: Harvard University Press; 1996.
13. Toossi M. A century of change: the US labor force, 1950–2050. *Monthly Labor Review.* 2002;125(5):15–28.
14. Goldin C. The quiet revolution that transformed women's employment, education, and family. *American Economic Review.* 2006;96(2):1–21.
15. National Center for Education Statistics. Digest of education statistics, Table 104.20. https://nces.ed.gov/programs/digest/d16/tables/dt16_104.20.asp. Published 2016.
16. Association of American Medical Colleges. Enrollment, graduates, and MD-PhD data. https://www.aamc.org/data/facts/enrollmentgraduate/. Published 2019.
17. American Bar Association. American Bar Association law school data: JD total FY class enrollment data, aggregate, fall 2018. https://www.americanbar.org/groups/legal_education/resources/statistics/. Published 2019.
18. Abraham KG, Kearney MS. *Explaining the Decline in the US Employment-to-Population Ratio: A Review of the Evidence.* Washington, DC: National Bureau of Economic Research; 2018.
19. Semyonov M. The social context of women's labor force participation: A comparative analysis. *American Journal of Sociology.* 1980;86(3):534–550.
20. Wang W, Parker K. Record share of Americans have never married. Social & Demographic Trends Project. Washington DC: Pew Research Center; September 24, 2014. https://www.pewsocialtrends.org/2014/09/24/record-share-of-americans-have-never-married/.
21. Edin K, Kefalas M. *Promises I Can Keep.* Berkeley, CA: University of California Press; 2005.
22. Hrdy SB. *Mothers and Others.* Cambridge, MA: Harvard University Press; 2011.
23. Furstenberg FF Jr. The recent transformation of the American family. In: Carlson MJ, England P, eds. *Social Class and Changing Families in an Unequal America.* Stanford, CA: Stanford University Press; 2011:192–220.

CHAPTER 15: DISCOVERING FATHERHOOD

1. Malinowski B. *The Father in Primitive Psychology.* New York, NY: Norton; 1927.
2. McCord J, McCord W, Thurber E. Some effects of paternal absence on male children. *The Journal of Abnormal and Social Psychology.* 1962;64(5):361–369.
3. Parke RD, Sawin DB. The father's role in infancy: a re-evaluation. *Family Coordinator.* 1976;25(4):365–371.
4. Power TG. Sex-typing in infancy: the role of the father. *Infant Mental Health Journal.* 1981;2(4):226–240.
5. Power TG, Parke RD. Patterns of mother and father play with their 8-month-old infant: a multiple analyses approach. *Infant Behavior and Development.* 1983;6(4):453–459.
6. Lamb ME, Pleck JH, Charnov EL, Levine JA. Paternal behavior in humans. *American Zoologist.* 1985;25:883–894.
7. Pleck JH. Paternal involvement. In: Lamb ME, ed. *The Role of the Father in Child Development.* 5th ed. Hoboken, NJ: Wiley; 2010;58–93.
8. Bianchi SM, Robinson JP, Milke MA. *The Changing Rhythms of American Family Life.* New York, NY: Russell Sage Foundation; 2006.

9. Carlson MJ, Magnuson KA. Low-income men and fathers' influences on children. *Annals of the American Academy of Political and Social Sciences.* 2011;635(1):95–116.
10. Pleck EH, Pleck JH. Fatherhood ideals in the United States: historical dimensions. In: Lamb ME, ed. *The Role of the Father in Child Development.* 3rd ed. Hoboken, NJ: Wiley; 1997:33–48.
11. Sarkadi A, Kristiansson R, Oberklaid F, Bremberg S. Fathers' involvement and children's developmental outcomes: a systematic review of longitudinal studies. *Acta Paediatrica.* 2008;97(2):153–158.
12. Coltrane S. *Family Man.* New York, NY: Oxford University Press; 1996.
13. Fagan J, Day R, Lamb ME, Cabrera NJ. Should researchers conceptualize differently the dimensions of parenting for fathers and mothers? *Journal of Family Theory & Review.* 2014;6(4):390–405.
14. McGill BS. Navigating new norms of involved fatherhood: employment, fathering attitudes, and father involvement. *Journal of Family Issues.* 2014;35(8):1089–1106.
15. Doherty WJ, Kouneski EF, Erickson MF. Responsible fathering: an overview and conceptual framework. *Journal of Marriage and the Family.* 1998;60(2):277–292.
16. Marsiglio W, Roy K. *Nurturing Dads: Fatherhood Initiatives beyond the Wallet.* New York, NY: Russell Sage Foundation; 2012.
17. Cabrera NJ, Fitzgerald HE, Bradley RH, Roggman L. The ecology of father–child relationships: an expanded model. *Journal of Family Theory & Review.* 2014;6(4):336–354.

CHAPTER 16: A TALE OF (ANOTHER) TWO FATHERS

1. Lamb ME. *The Role of the Father in Child Development.* 5th ed. Hoboken, NJ: Wiley; 2010.
2. Lamb ME. How do fathers influence children's development? Let me count the ways. In Lamb ME, ed. *The Role of the Father in Child Development.* Hoboken, NJ; 2010:1–26.
3. Winnicott DW. Transitional objects and transitional phenomena: a study of the first not-me possession. *International Journal of Psychoanalysis.* 1953;34:89–97.
4. Winnicott DW. Mirror-role of the mother and family in child development. In: Lomas P, ed. *The Predicament of the Family: A Psycho-Analytical Symposium.* London, England: Hogarth; 1967:26–33.

CHAPTER 17: THE FATHER–CHILD BOND

1. Condon JT. The assessment of antenatal emotional attachment: development of a questionnaire instrument. *British Journal of Medical Psychology.* 1993;66(2):167–183.
2. Condon JT, Corkindale CJ. The assessment of parent-to-infant attachment: development of a self-report questionnaire instrument. *Journal of Reproductive and Infant Psychology.* 1998;16(1):57–76.
3. Habib C, Lancaster S. The transition to fatherhood: identity and bonding in early pregnancy. *Fathering: A Journal of Theory, Research, and Practice about Men as Fathers.* 2006;4(3):235–253.
4. de Cock ESA, Henrichs J, Vreeswijk CMJM, Maas AJBM, Rijk CHAM, van Bakel HJA. Continuous feelings of love? The parental bond from pregnancy to toddlerhood. *Journal of Family Psychology.* 2016;30(1):125–134.

5. Maas AJB, de Cock ES, Vreeswijk CM, Vingerhoets AJ, van Bakel HJ. A longitudinal study on the maternal–fetal relationship and postnatal maternal sensitivity. *Journal of Reproductive and Infant Psychology*. 2016;34(2):110–121.
6. Siddiqui A, Hägglöf B. Does maternal prenatal attachment predict postnatal mother–infant interaction? *Early Human Development*. 2000;59(1):13–25.
7. de Cock ESA, Henrichs J, Klimstra TA, et al. Longitudinal associations between parental bonding, parenting stress, and executive functioning in toddlerhood. *Journal of Child and Family Studies*. 2017;26(6):1723–1733.
8. Bretherton I. Fathers in attachment theory and research: a review. *Early Child Development and Care*. 2010;180(1-2):9–23.
9. Mason ZS, Briggs RD, Silver EJ. Maternal attachment feelings mediate between maternal reports of depression, infant social–emotional development, and parenting stress. *Journal of Reproductive and Infant Psychology*. 2011;29(4):382–394.
10. Blair C, Razza RP. Relating effortful control, executive function, and false belief understanding to emerging math and literacy ability in kindergarten. *Child Development*. 2007;78(2):647–663.
11. Clark CAC, Pritchard VE, Woodward LJ. Preschool executive functioning abilities predict early mathematics achievement. *Developmental Psychology*. 2010;46(5):1176–1191.
12. Roman GD, Ensor R, Hughes C. Does executive function mediate the path from mothers' depressive symptoms to young children's problem behaviors? *Journal of Experimental Child Psychology*. 2016;142:158–170.
13. Sulik MJ, Blair C, Mills-Koonce R, Berry D, Greenberg M. Early parenting and the development of externalizing behavior problems: longitudinal mediation through children's executive function. *Child Development*. 2015;86(5):1588–1603.

CHAPTER 18: REDEFINING THE SELF AS FATHER: DEVELOPING A PATERNAL IDENTITY

1. Stryker S, Serpe RT. Commitment, identity salience, and role behavior: Theory and research example. In: Ickes W, Knowles ES, eds. *Personality, Roles, and Social Behavior*. New York, NY: Springer; 1982:199–218.
2. Sullivan HS. *The Interpersonal Theory of Psychiatry*. New York, NY: Norton ; 1953.
3. Maurer TW, Pleck JH, Rane TR. Parental identity and reflected-appraisals: Measurement and gender dynamics. *Journal of Marriage and Family*. 2001;63(2):309–321.
4. Erikson EH. *Youth and Crisis*. New York, NY: Norton; 1968.
5. Erikson EH. *The Life Cycle Completed*. New York, NY: Norton; 1982.
6. Fletcher G, Kerr P. Love, reality, and illusion in intimate relationships. In: Simpson JA, Campbell L, Simpson JA, Campbell L, eds. *The Oxford Handbook of Close Relationships*. New York, NY: Oxford University Press; 2013:306–320.
7. Beitel AH, Parke RD. Paternal involvement in infancy: the role of maternal and paternal attitudes. *Journal of Family Psychology*. 1998;12(2):268–288.
8. Gaunt R. Biological essentialism, gender ideologies, and role attitudes: what determines parents' involvement in child care. *Sex Roles*. 2006;55(7-8):523–533.
9. Hofferth SL. Race/ethnic differences in father involvement in two-parent families: culture, context, or economy? *Journal of Family Issues*. 2003;24(2):185–216.
10. McGill B. *Navigating New Norms of Involved Fatherhood: Employment, Gender Attitudes, and Father Involvement in American Families*. College Park, MD: University of Maryland Press; 2011.

11. Hawkins AJ, Christiansen SL, Sargent KP, Hill EJ. Rethinking fathers' involvement in child care: a developmental perspective. In: Marsiglio W, ed. *Fatherhood: Contemporary Theory, Research, and Social Policy.* Thousand Oaks, CA: SAGE; 1995:41–56.

12. Marsiglio W. *Fatherhood: Contemporary Theory, Research, and Social Policy.* Thousand Oaks, CA: SAGE; 1995.

13. Bowman PJ. Coping with provider role strain: adaptive cultural resources among black husband-fathers. In: Burlew AKH, Banks WC, McAdoo HP, et al., eds. *African American Psychology: Theory, Research, and Practice.* Thousand Oaks, CA: SAGE; 1992:135–154.

14. Rowley LL, Bowman PJ. Risk, protection, and achievement disparities among African American males: cross-generation theory, research, and comprehensive intervention. *Journal of Negro Education.* 2009;78(3):305–320.

15. Ihinger-Tallman M, Pasley K, Buehler C. Developing a middle-range theory of father involvement postdivorce. *Journal of Family Issues.* 1993;14(4):550–571.

16. Minton C, Pasley K. Fathers' parenting role identity and father involvement: a comparison of nondivorced and divorced, nonresident fathers. *Journal of Family Issues.* 1996;17(1):26–45.

17. Bruce C, Fox GL. Accounting for patterns of father involvement: age of child, father–child coresidence, and father role salience. *Sociological Inquiry.* 1999;69(3):458–476.

18. McBride BA, Rane TR. Role identity, role investments, and paternal involvement: implications for parenting programs for men. *Early Childhood Research Quarterly.* 1997;12(2):173–197.

19. Habib C, Lancaster S. The transition to fatherhood: identity and bonding in early pregnancy. *Fathering: A Journal of Theory, Research, and Practice about Men as Fathers.* 2006;4(3):235–253.

CHAPTER 19: ON BECOMING A DAD: THE BIOLOGY OF GOOD-ENOUGH FATHERING

1. Archer J. Testosterone and human aggression: an evaluation of the challenge hypothesis. *Neuroscience & Biobehavioral Reviews.* 2006;30(3):319–345.

2. Mazur A, Booth A. Testosterone and dominance in men. *Behavioral and Brain Sciences.* 1998;21(3):353–363.

3. Booth A, Dabbs JM Jr. Testosterone and men's marriages. *Social Forces.* 1993;72(2):463–477.

4. Wingfield JC, Hegner RE, Dufty Jr AM, Ball GF. The "challenge hypothesis": theoretical implications for patterns of testosterone secretion, mating systems, and breeding strategies. *The American Naturalist.* 1990;136(6):829–846.

5. Hirschenhauser K, Oliveira RF. Social modulation of androgens in male vertebrates: meta-analyses of the challenge hypothesis. *Animal Behaviour.* 2006;71(2):265–277.

6. Gray PB, Kahlenberg SM, Barrett ES, Lipson SF, Ellison PT. Marriage and fatherhood are associated with lower testosterone in males. *Evolution and Human Behavior.* 2002;23(3):193–201.

7. Gray PB, Yang C-FJ, Pope HG. Fathers have lower salivary testosterone levels than unmarried men and married non-fathers in Beijing, China. *Proceedings of the Royal Society of London B: Biological Sciences.* 2006;273(1584):333–339.

8. Kuzawa CW, Gettler LT, Muller MN, McDade TW, Feranil AB. Fatherhood, pairbonding and testosterone in the Philippines. *Hormones and Behavior.* 2009;56(4):429–435.
9. Alvergne A, Faurie C, Raymond M. Variation in testosterone levels and male reproductive effort: insight from a polygynous human population. *Hormones and Behavior.* 2009;56(5):491–497.
10. Gettler LT, McDade TW, Feranil AB, Kuzawa CW. Longitudinal evidence that fatherhood decreases testosterone in human males. *Proceedings of the National Academy of Sciences.* 2011;108(39):16194–16199.
11. Muller MN, Marlowe FW, Bugumba R, Ellison PT. Testosterone and paternal care in East African foragers and pastoralists. *Proceedings of the Royal Society of London B: Biological Sciences.* 2009;276(1655):347–354.
12. Hunt KE, Hahn TP, Wingfield JC. Endocrine influences on parental care during a short breeding season: testosterone and male parental care in Lapland longspurs (Calcarius lapponicus). *Behavioral Ecology and Sociobiology.* 1999;45(5):360–369.
13. Gray PB, Anderson KG. *Fatherhood: Evolution and Human Paternal Behavior.* Cambridge, MA: Harvard University Press; 2010.
14. Wynne-Edwards KE. Hormonal changes in mammalian fathers. *Hormones and Behavior.* 2001;40(2):139–145.
15. Storey AE, Walsh CJ, Quinton RL, Wynne-Edwards KE. Hormonal correlates of paternal responsiveness in new and expectant fathers. *Evolution and Human Behavior.* 2000;21(2):79–95.
16. Gordon I, Pratt M, Bergunde K, Zagoory-Sharon O, Feldman R. Testosterone, oxytocin, and the development of human parental care. *Hormones and Behavior.* 2017;93:184–192.
17. Fleming AS, Corter C, Stallings J, Steiner M. Testosterone and prolactin are associated with emotional responses to infant cries in new fathers. *Hormones and behavior.* 2002;42(4):399–413.
18. Hermans EJ, Putman P, van Honk J. Testosterone administration reduces empathetic behavior: a facial mimicry study. *Psychoneuroendocrinology.* 2006;31(7):859–866.
19. van Anders SM, Tolman RM, Volling BL. Baby cries and nurturance affect testosterone in men. *Hormones and Behavior.* 2012;61(1):31–36.
20. Holman S, Goy RW. Experiential and hormonal correlates of care-giving in rhesus macaques. In: Pryce CR, ed. *Motherhood in Human and Nonhuman Primates: Biosocial Determinants.* Basel, Switzerland: Karger; 1995:87–93.
21. Neumann ID. Brain oxytocin: A key regulator of emotional and social behaviours in both females and males. *Journal of Neuroendocrinology.* 2008;20(6):858–865.
22. Feldman R, Weller A, Zagoory-Sharon O, Levine A. Evidence for a neuroendocrinological foundation of human affiliation: plasma oxytocin levels across pregnancy and the postpartum period predict mother–infant bonding. *Psychological Science.* 2007;18(11):965–970.
23. Uvnäs-Moberg K. Oxytocin may mediate the benefits of positive social interaction and emotions. *Psychoneuroendocrinology.* 1998;23(8):819–835.
24. Levine A, Zagoory-Sharon O, Feldman R, Weller A. Oxytocin during pregnancy and early postpartum: individual patterns and maternal–fetal attachment. *Peptides.* 2007;28(6):1162–1169.
25. Mascaro JS, Hackett PD, Rilling JK. Differential neural responses to child and sexual stimuli in human fathers and non-fathers and their hormonal correlates. *Psychoneuroendocrinology.* 2014;46:153–163.

[388] *References*

26. Gordon I, Zagoory-Sharon O, Leckman JF, Feldman R. Oxytocin and the development of parenting in humans. *Biological Psychiatry.* 2010;68(4):377–382.
27. Feldman R, Gordon I, Schneiderman I, Weisman O, Zagoory-Sharon O. Natural variations in maternal and paternal care are associated with systematic changes in oxytocin following parent–infant contact. *Psychoneuroendocrinology.* 2010;35(8):1133–1141.
28. Naber F, van IJzendoorn MH, Deschamps P, van Engeland H, Bakermans-Kranenburg MJ. Intranasal oxytocin increases fathers' observed responsiveness during play with their children: a double-blind within-subject experiment. *Psychoneuroendocrinology.* 2010;35(10):1583–1586.
29. MacDonald E, Dadds MR, Brennan JL, Williams K, Levy F, Cauchi AJ. A review of safety, side-effects and subjective reactions to intranasal oxytocin in human research. *Psychoneuroendocrinology.* 2011;36(8):1114–1126.
30. Naber FB, Poslawsky IE, van IJzendoorn MH, Van Engeland H, Bakermans-Kranenburg MJ. Brief report: oxytocin enhances paternal sensitivity to a child with autism: a double-blind within-subject experiment with intranasally administered oxytocin. *Journal of Autism and Developmental Disorders.* 2013;43(1):224–229.
31. Weisman O, Zagoory-Sharon O, Feldman R. Oxytocin administration, salivary testosterone, and father–infant social behavior. *Progress in Neuro-Psychopharmacology and Biological Psychiatry.* 2014;49:47–52.
32. Strathearn L, Fonagy P, Amico J, Montague PR. Adult attachment predicts maternal brain and oxytocin response to infant cues. *Neuropsychopharmacology.* 2009;34(13):2655–2666.
33. Yogman M, Garfield CF, Child CoPAo, Health F. Fathers' roles in the care and development of their children: the role of pediatricians. *Pediatrics.* 2016;138(1):e20161128.

CHAPTER 20: FATHERS ARE FOUND IN RELATIONSHIPS
1. Hawkins AJ, Dollahite DC. *Generative Fathering: Beyond Deficit Perspectives.* Thousand Oaks, CA: SAGE; 1997.
2. Kerr DC, Capaldi DM, Pears KC, Owen LD. A prospective three generational study of fathers' constructive parenting: influences from family of origin, adolescent adjustment, and offspring temperament. *Developmental Psychology.* 2009;45(5):1257–1275.
3. Hofferth SL, Pleck JH, Vesely CK. The transmission of parenting from fathers to sons. *Parenting: Science and Practice.* 2012;12(4):282–305.
4. Pears KC, Capaldi DM. Intergenerational transmission of abuse: a two-generational prospective study of an at-risk sample. *Child Abuse & Neglect.* 2001;25(11):1439–1461.
5. Conger RD, Belsky J, Capaldi DM. The intergenerational transmission of parenting: closing comments for the special section. *Developmental Psychology.* 2009;45(5):1276–1283.
6. Beers LAS, Hollo RE. Approaching the adolescent-headed family: a review of teen parenting. *Current Problems in Pediatric and Adolescent Health Care.* 2009;39(9):216–233.
7. Fagan J, Lee Y. Do coparenting and social support have a greater effect on adolescent fathers than adult fathers? *Family Relations.* 2011;60(3):247–258.

8. Ryan RM, Kalil A, Ziol-Guest KM. Longitudinal patterns of nonresident fathers' involvement: the role of resources and relations. *Journal of Marriage and Family.* 2008;70(4):962–977.

9. Goldberg JS, Carlson MJ. Patterns and predictors of coparenting after unmarried parents part. *Journal of Family Psychology.* 2015;29(3):416–426.

10. Pruett MK, Pruett K, Cowan CP, Cowan PA. Enhancing father involvement in low-income families: a couples group approach to preventive intervention. *Child Development.* 2017;88(2):398–407.

11. Fagan J, Barnett M. The relationship between maternal gatekeeping, paternal competence, mothers' attitudes about the father role, and father involvement. *Journal of Family Issues.* 2003;24(8):1020–1043.

12. Puhlman DJ, Pasley K. Rethinking maternal gatekeeping. *Journal of Family Theory & Review.* 2013;5(3):176–193.

13. Schoppe-Sullivan SJ, Brown GL, Cannon EA, Mangelsdorf SC, Sokolowski MS. Maternal gatekeeping, coparenting quality, and fathering behavior in families with infants. *Journal of Family Psychology.* 2008;22(3):389–398.

14. Moore DR, Florsheim P, Butner J. Interpersonal behavior, psychopathology, and relationship outcomes among adolescent mothers and their partners. *Journal of Clinical Child and Adolescent Psychology.* 2007;36(4):541–556.

15. Florsheim P, Smith A. Expectant adolescent couples' relations and subsequent parenting behavior. *Infant Mental Health Journal.* 2005;26(6):533–548.

16. Gottman JM. *What Predicts Divorce? The Relationship between Marital Processes and Marital Outcomes.* Hillsdale, NJ: Erlbaum; 1994.

17. Florsheim P, Sumida E, McCann C, et al. The transition to parenthood among young African American and Latino couples: relational predictors of risk for parental dysfunction. *Journal of Family Psychology.* 2003;17(1):65–79.

18. Moore DR, Florsheim P. Interpartner conflict and child abuse risk among African American and Latino adolescent parenting couples. *Child Abuse & Neglect.* 2008;32(4):463–475.

19. Belsky J, Putnam S, Crnic K. Coparenting, parenting, and early emotional development. *New Directions for Child and Adolescent Development.* 1996;1996(74):45–55.

20. Parke RD. Fathers and families. In: Bornstein MH, ed. *Handbook of Parenting. Vol. 3: Being and Becoming a Parent.* 2nd ed. Hillsdale, NJ: Erlbaum; 2002:27–73.

21. Gottman JM, Silver N. *The Seven Principles for Making Marriage Work: A Practical Guide from the Country's Foremost Relationship Expert.* New York, NY: Harmony; 2015.

22. Goldberg WA, Easterbrooks MA. Role of marital quality in toddler development. *Developmental Psychology.* 1984;20(3):504–514.

23. Lundy BL. Paternal socio-psychological factors and infant attachment: the mediating role of synchrony in father-infant interactions. *Infant Behavior & Development.* 2002;25(2):221–236.

24. Millings A, Walsh J, Hepper E, O'Brien M. Good partner, good parent: responsiveness mediates the link between romantic attachment and parenting style. *Personality and Social Psychology Bulletin.* 2013;39(2):170–180.

25. Kitzmann KM. Effects of marital conflict on subsequent triadic family interactions and parenting. *Developmental Psychology.* 2000;36(1):3–13.

26. Carlson MJ, McLanahan SS, Brooks-Gunn J. Coparenting and nonresident fathers' involvement with young children after a nonmarital birth. *Demography.* 2008;45(2):461–488.

27. McHale J, Khazan I, Erera P, Rotman T, DeCourcey W, McConnell M. Coparenting in diverse family systems. In: Bornstein MH, ed. *Handbook of Parenting. Vol. 3: Being and Becoming a Parent*. 2nd ed. Hillsdale, NJ: Erlbaum; 2002:75–107.

28. Feinberg ME. The internal structure and ecological context of coparenting: a framework for research and intervention. *Parenting: Science and Practice*. 2003;3(2):95–131.

29. McHale JP. Coparenting and triadic interactions during infancy: the roles of marital distress and child gender. *Developmental psychology*. 1995;31(6):985–996.

30. Alexandrov EO, Cowan PA, Cowan CP. Couple attachment and the quality of marital relationships: method and concept in the validation of the new couple attachment interview and coding system. *Attachment & Human Development*. 2005;7(2):123–152.

31. Cowan CP, Cowan PA. *When Partners Become Parents: The Big Life Change for Couples*. Mahwah, NJ: Erlbaum; 2000.

32. Shapiro AF, Gottman JM, Carrere S. The baby and the marriage: identifying factors that buffer against decline in marital satisfaction after the first baby arrives. *Journal of Family Psychology*. 2000;14(1):59–70.

33. Florsheim P, Ngu LQ. Fatherhood as a Transformative process: unexpected successes among high risk fathers. In: Kowaleski-Jones L, Wolfinger NH, eds. *Fragile Families and the Marriage Agenda*. New York, NY: Springer Science + Business Media; 2006:211–232.

34. Ngu L, Florsheim P. The development of relational competence among young high-risk fathers across the transition to parenthood. *Family Process*. 2011;50(2):184–202.

35. Hatton H, Conger R, Larsen-Rife D, Ontai L. An integrative and developmental perspective for understanding romantic relationship quality during the transition to parenthood. In: Schulz MS, Pruett MK, Kerig PK, Parke RD, eds. *Strengthening Couple Relationships for Optimal Child Development: Lessons from Research and Intervention* Washington, DC: American Psychological Association; 2010:115–129.

36. Martin A, Ryan RM, Brooks-Gunn J. The joint influence of mother and father parenting on child cognitive outcomes at age 5. *Early Childhood Research Quarterly*. 2007;22(4):423–439.

37. Glazier R, Elgar F, Goel V, Holzapfel S. Stress, social support, and emotional distress in a community sample of pregnant women. *Journal of Psychosomatic Obstetrics & Gynecology*. 2004;25(3–4):247–255.

38. Mulsow M, Caldera YM, Pursley M, Reifman A, Huston AC. Multilevel factors influencing maternal stress during the first three years. *Journal of Marriage and Family*. 2002;64(4):944–956.

39. Cox MJ, Paley B, Payne CC, Burchinal M. The transition to parenthood: marital conflict and withdrawal and parent–infant interactions. In: Cox MJ, Brooks-Gunn J, Cox MJ, Brooks-Gunn J, eds. *Conflict and Cohesion in Families: Causes and Consequences*. Mahwah, NJ: Erlbaum; 1999:87–104.

40. Frosch CA, Mangelsdorf SC, McHale JL. Marital behavior and the security of preschooler–parent attachment relationships. *Journal of Family Psychology*. 2000;14(1):144.

41. Cutrona CE, Hessling RM, Bacon PL, Russell DW. Predictors and correlates of continuing involvement with the baby's father among adolescent mothers. *Journal of Family Psychology*. 1998;12(3):369.

42. Gee CB, Rhodes JE. Postpartum transitions in adolescent mothers' romantic and maternal relationships. *Merrill-Palmer Quarterly (1982-)*. 1999:512–532.
43. Nitz K, Ketterlinus RD, Brandt LJ. The role of stress, social support, and family environment in adolescent mothers' parenting. *Journal of Adolescent Research*. 1995;10(3):358–382.
44. East PL, Felice ME. *Adolescent Pregnancy and Parenting: Findings from a Racially Diverse Sample*. Mahwah, NJ: Erlbaum; 1996.
45. Lovejoy MC, Graczyk PA, O'Hare E, Neuman G. Maternal depression and parenting behavior: a meta-analytic review. *Clinical Psychology Review*. 2000;20(5):561–592.
46. Martins C, Gaffan EA. Effects of early maternal depression on patterns of infant–mother attachment: a meta-analytic investigation. *Journal of Child Psychology and Psychiatry and Allied Disciplines*. 2000;41(6):737–746.
47. Wilson S, Durbin CE. Effects of paternal depression on fathers' parenting behaviors: a meta-analytic review. *Clinical Psychology Review*. 2010;30(2):167–180.
48. Quenqua D. Can fathers have postpartum depression? *New York Times*. October 17, 2017.

CHAPTER 21: FATHERHOOD PROGRAMS: A SHORT HISTORY OF TRIAL AND FAILURE

1. Murray C. *Losing Ground*. New York, NY: Basic Books. 1984.
2. Rector RE, Johnson KA, Fagan PF, Noyes LR. Increasing marriage would dramatically reduce child poverty. In: Crane DR, Heaton TB, eds. *Handbook of Families and Poverty*. Thousand Oaks, CA: SAGE; 2009:457–470.
3. Maldonado S. Deadbeat or deadbroke: redefining child support for poor fathers. *UC Davis Law Review*. 2005;39:991–1023.
4. Sorensen E. *Obligating Dads: Helping Low-Income Noncustodial Fathers Do More for Their Children*. Washington, DC: Urban Institute; 1999.
5. Miller C, Knox V. The challenge of helping low-income fathers support their children: final lessons from parents' fair share. New York, NY: Manpower Demonstration Research Corporation; November 2001. https://files.eric.ed.gov/fulltext/ED459354.pdf.
6. Doherty WJ, Kouneski EF, Erickson MF. Responsible fathering: an overview and conceptual framework. *Journal of Marriage and the Family*. 1998;60:277–292.
7. Horn WF. You've come a long way, daddy. *Policy Review*. 1997;84:24–30.
8. Levine JA, Pitt EW. *New Expectations: Community Strategies for Responsible Fatherhood*. New York, NY: Families and Work Institute; 1995.
9. Horn WF, Blankenhorn D, Pearlstein MB. *The Fatherhood Movement: A Call to Action*. Lanham, MD: Lexington Books; 1999.
10. Edelman P. The worst thing Bill Clinton has done. *The Atlantic*. 1997;279:43–51.
11. Goldberg W, Lucas-Thompson R. Effects of maternal and paternal employment. In: Benson JB, Haith MM, eds. *Social and Emotional Development in Infancy and Early Childhood*. Oxford, England: Academic Press; 2009:229–240.
12. Bloom D, Sherwood K. Matching opportunities to obligations: lessons for child support reform from the Parents' Fair Share pilot phase. ED373270. New York, NY: Manpower Demonstration Research Corporation, April 2014. https://files.eric.ed.gov/fulltext/ED373270.pdf.
13. Pearson J, Thoennes N, Price D, Venohr J. OCSE responsible fatherhood programs: early implementation lessons. ED463839. Denver, CO: Center for Policy Research; 2000. https://files.eric.ed.gov/fulltext/ED463839.pdf.

14. Pearson J, Thoennes N, Davis L, Venohr J, Price D, Griffith T. OCSE responsible fatherhood programs: client characteristics and program outcomes. ED463839. Denver, CO: Center for Policy Research; June 2003. https://files.eric.ed.gov/fulltext/ED463839.pdf.

15. Miller DP, Mincy RB. Falling further behind? Child support arrears and fathers' labor force participation. *Social Service Review.* 2012;86(4):604–635.

16. Meyer D, Wood R, Paulsell D, et al. Helping noncustodial parents support their children: early implementation findings from the Child Support Noncustodial Parent Employment Demonstration (CSPED) evaluation. Madison, WI: Institute for Research on Poverty; September 2015. https://www.irp.wisc.edu/wp/wp-content/uploads/2018/06/CSPEDInterImpl2015-Compliant.pdf.

17. Karberg E, Aldoney D, Cabrera N. Fatherhood in America: the context, practice, and gaps in responsible fatherhood programs. In: Mazza C, Perry AR, eds. *Fatherhood in America: Social Work Perspectives on a Changing Society.* Springfield, IL: Charles C Thomas; 2017:302–321.

18. Avellar S, Dion MR, Clarkwest A, et al. Catalog of research: programs for low-income fathers. OPRE Report 2012-09. Washington, DC: Office of Planning, Research, and Evaluation; May 2012. https://www.acf.hhs.gov/sites/default/files/opre/catalog_couples.pdf.

19. Anderson EA, Kohler JK, Letiecq BL. Low-income fathers and "responsible fatherhood" programs: a qualitative investigation of participants' experiences. *Family Relations.* 2002;51(2):148–155.

20. Heinrich CJ, Holzer HJ. Improving education and employment for disadvantaged young men: proven and promising strategies. *Annals of the American Academy of Political and Social Science.* 2011;635(1):163–191.

21. US Department of Labor, US Department of Commerce, US Department of Education, US Department of Health and Human Services. What works in job training: a synthesis of the evidence. https://www.dol.gov/asp/evaluation/jdt/jdt.pdf. Published July 22, 2014.

22. Solomon-Fears C, Tollestrup J. Fatherhood initiatives: connecting fathers to their children. Report No. RL31025. Washington, DC: Congressional Research Service; May 1, 2018. https://fas.org/sgp/crs/misc/RL31025.pdf.

23. Haney L. Incarcerated fatherhood: the entanglements of child support debt and mass imprisonment. *American Journal of Sociology.* 2018;124(1):1–48.

24. Cancian M, Meyer DR, Caspar E. Welfare and child support: complements, not substitutes. *Journal of Policy Analysis and Management.* 2008;27(2):354–375.

25. Daly M, Wilson M. Evolutionary social psychology and family homicide. *Science.* 1988;242(4878):519–524.

26. Fletcher GJO, Simpson JA, Campbell L, Overall NC. Pair-bonding, romantic love, and evolution: the curious case of *Homo sapiens. Perspectives on Psychological Science.* 2015;10(1):20–36.

27. Wood RG, McConnell S, Moore Q, Clarkwest A, Hsueh J. The effects of building strong families: a healthy marriage and relationship skills education program for unmarried parents. *Journal of Policy Analysis and Management.* 2012;31(2):228–252.

28. Wood RG, Moore Q, Clarkwest A, Killewald A. The long-term effects of building strong families: a program for unmarried parents. *Journal of Marriage & Family.* 2014;76(2):446–463.

29. Cowan PA, Cowan CP, Pruett MK, Pruett K, Gillette P. Evaluating a couples group to enhance father involvement in low-income families using a benchmark comparison. *Family Relations*. 2014;63(3):356–370.

30. Stanley SM, Amato PR, Johnson CA, Markman HJ. Premarital education, marital quality, and marital stability: findings from a large, random household survey. *Journal of Family Psychology*. 2006;20(1):117–126.

31. Pruett MK, Pruett K, Cowan CP, Cowan PA. Enhancing father involvement in low-income families: a couples group approach to preventive intervention. *Child Development*. 2017;88(2):398–407.

32. McHale JP, Rasmussen JL. Coparental and family group-level dynamics during infancy: early family precursors of child and family functioning during preschool. *Development and Psychopathology*. 1998;10(1):39–59.

33. Feinberg ME, Kan ML. Establishing family foundations: intervention effects on coparenting, parent/infant well-being, and parent–child relations. *Journal of Family Psychology*. 2008;22(2):253–263.

34. Lundquist E, Hsueh J, Lowenstein AE, et al. A family-strengthening program for low-income families: final impacts from the Supporting Healthy Marriage evaluation. OPRE Report 2014-09A. New York, NY: MDRC; January 2014. https://www.acf.hhs.gov/sites/default/files/opre/shm2013_30_month_impact_reportrev2.pdf.

35. Johnson MD. Healthy marriage initiatives: on the need for empiricism in policy implementation. *American Psychologist*. 2012;67(4):296–308.

36. Office of Planning, Research, and Evaluation. Proven and promising responsible fatherhood and family strengthening initiatives: evidence review, 2010–2013 https://www.acf.hhs.gov/opre/research/project/proven-and-promising-responsible-fatherhood-and-family-strengthening. Published 2011–2012.

37. Bronte-Tinkew J, Horowitz A, Metz A. "What works" in fatherhood programs? Ten lessons from evidence-based practice. Practice Brief. National Responsible Dunwoody, GA: Fatherhood Clearinghouse; 2007. https://www.fatherhood.gov/sites/default/files/files-for-pages/NRFC%20Practice%20Brief_What%20Works_508.pdf.

38. US Government Accountability Office. Healthy Marriage and Responsible Fatherhood Initiative: further progress is needed in developing a risk-based monitoring approach to help HHS improve program oversight. GAO-08-1002. https://www.gao.gov/new.items/d081002.pdf. Published September 2008.

39. Hawkins AJ, Stanley SM, Cowan PA, et al. A more optimistic perspective on government-supported marriage and relationship education programs for lower income couples. *American Psychologist*. 2013;68(2):110–111.

40. Arnold LS, Beelmann A. The effects of relationship education in low-income couples: a meta-analysis of randomized-controlled evaluation studies. *Family Relations*. 2018;68(1):22–38.

41. Hawkins AJ, Erickson SE. Is couple and relationship education effective for lower income participants? A meta-analytic study. *Journal of Family Psychology*. 2015;29(1):59–68.

42. Gurman AS, Fraenkel P. The history of couple therapy: a millennial review. *Family Process*. 2002;41(2):199–260.

43. Hines M. acceptance versus change in behavior therapy: an interview with Neil Jacobson. *The Family Journal*. 1998;6(3):244–251.

44. Jacobson NS, Christensen A, Prince SE, Cordova J, Eldridge K. Integrative behavioral couple therapy: an acceptance-based, promising new treatment for couple discord. *Journal of Consulting and Clinical Psychology.* 2000;68(2):351–355.
45. Amato PR. The consequences of divorce for adults and children: an update. *Društvena istraživanja: časopis za opća društvena pitanja.* 2014;23(1):5–24.
46. Kline M, Johnston JR, Tschann JM. The long shadow of marital conflict: a model of children's postdivorce adjustment. *Journal of Marriage and the Family.* 1991;53(2):297–309.
47. Bloom BL, Hodges WF, Kern MB, McFaddin SC. A preventive intervention program for the newly separated: final evaluations. *American Journal of Orthopsychiatry.* 1985;55(1):9–26.
48. Pollet SL, Lombreglia M. A nationwide survey of mandatory parent education. *Family Court Review.* 2008;46(2):375–394.
49. Ferraro AJ, Malespin T, Oehme K, Bruker M, Opel A. Advancing co-parenting education: toward a foundation for supporting positive post-divorce adjustment. *Child & Adolescent Social Work Journal.* 2016;33(5):407–415.
50. Oehme K, Ferraro AJ, Stern N, Panisch LS, Lucier-Greer M. Trauma-informed co-parenting: how a shift in compulsory divorce education to reflect new brain development research can promote both parents' and children's best interests. University of Hawaii Law Review, 39(37):1–10.
51. Fackrell TA, Hawkins AJ, Kay NM. How effective are court-affiliated divorcing parents education programs? A meta-analytic study. *Family Court Review.* 2011;49(1):107–119.

CHAPTER 22: CO- PARENTING SUPPORT: PRENATAL CARE AND THE WINDOW OF OPPORTUNITY

1. McLanahan S, Garfinkel I, Mincy RB, Donahue E. Introducing the issue. *The Future of Children.* 2010;20(2):3–16.
2. Cowan CP, Cowan PA. Prevention: Intervening with couples at challenging family transition points. In: Balfour A, Morgan M, Vincent C, eds. *How couple relationships shape our world: clinical practice, research, and policy perspectives.* London: Karnac Books; 2012:1–14.
3. Christensen A, Jacobson N. *Acceptance and change in couple therapy: A therapist's guide to transforming relationships.* New York: Norton; 1998.
4. Jacobson NS, Christensen A, Prince SE, Cordova J, Eldridge K. Integrative behavioral couple therapy: an acceptance-based, promising new treatment for couple discord. *Journal of Consulting and Clinical Psychology.* 2000;68(2):351.
5. Cabrera NJ, Fagan J, Farrie D. Why should we encourage unmarried fathers to be prenatally involved? *Journal of Marriage and Family.* 2008;70(5):1118–1121.
6. Eldridge KA, Christensen A. Demand-withdraw communication during couple conflict: A review and analysis. In: Noller P, Feeney JA, eds. *Understanding marriage: Developments in the study of couple interaction.* New York: Cambridge University Press; 2002:289–322.
7. Schrodt P, Witt PL, Shimkowski JR. A meta-analytical review of the demand/withdraw pattern of interaction and its associations with individual, relational, and communicative outcomes. *Communication Monographs.* 2014; 81(1):28–58.
8. Miller WR, Rollnick S. *Motivational interviewing: Helping people change.* Guilford press; 2012.

9. Florsheim P, Burrow-Sánchez JJ, Minami T, McArthur L, Heavin S, Hudak C. Young parenthood program: Supporting positive paternal engagement through coparenting counseling. *American Journal of Public Health.* 2012;102(10):1886–1892.

CHAPTER 23: A COMPASS AND A MAP: HELPING YOUNG FATHERS AND THEIR FAMILIES

1. Moehling CM, Thomasson MA. *Saving babies: the contribution of Sheppard-Towner to the decline in infant mortality in the 1920s.* NBER working paper 17996. http://www.nber.org/papers/w17996.pdf. Published 2012.
2. National Center for Health Statistics. Health, United States, 2016: with chartbook on long-term trends in health. DHHS report no. 2017-1232. https://www.cdc.gov/nchs/data/hus/hus16.pdf. Published May 2017.
3. Health Services and Resource Administration. Title V MCH Block Grant Program national snapshot. https://mchb.tvisdata.hrsa.gov/uploadedfiles/TvisWebReports/Documents/NationalSnapshot.pdf. Published 2018.
4. Devitt N. The transition from home to hospital birth in the United States, 1930–1960. *Birth.* 1977;4(2):47–58.
5. Loudon I. On maternal and infant mortality 1900–1960. *Social History of Medicine.* 1991;4(1):29–73.
6. Lu MC, Jones L, Bond MJ, et al. Where is the F in MCH? Father involvement in African American families. *Ethnicity & Disease.* 2010;20:S2–S49.
7. Garfield CF. Supporting fatherhood before and after it happens. *Pediatrics.* 2015;135(2):e528–e530.
8. Field T. Postpartum depression effects on early interactions, parenting, and safety practices: a review. *Infant Behavior and Development.* 2010;33(1):1–6.
9. Wisner KL, Parry BL, Piontek CM. Postpartum depression. *New England Journal of Medicine.* 2002;347(3):194–199.
10. Pitt B. "Atypical" depression following childbirth. *British Journal of Psychiatry.* 1968;114(516):1325–1335.
11. O'hara MW, McCabe JE. Postpartum depression: current status and future directions. *Annual Review of Clinical Psychology.* 2013;9:379–407.
12. Alio AP, Kornosky JL, Mbah AK, Marty PJ, Salihu HM. The impact of paternal involvement on feto-infant morbidity among whites, blacks and Hispanics. *Maternal and Child Health journal.* 2010;14(5):735–741.
13. Cabrera NJ, Volling BL, Barr R. Fathers are parents, too! Widening the lens on parenting for children's development. *Child Development Perspectives.* 2018;12(3):152–157.
14. Florsheim P, Burrow-Sanchez JJ, Minami T, McArthur L, Heavin S, Hudak C. Young parenthood program: supporting positive paternal engagement through coparenting counseling. *American Journal of Public Health.* 2012;102(10):1886–1892.
15. Feinberg ME, Jones DE, Hostetler ML, Roettger ME, Paul IM, Ehrenthal DB. Couple-focused prevention at the transition to parenthood, a randomized trial: Effects on coparenting, parenting, family violence, and parent and child adjustment. *Prevention Science.* 2016;17(6):751–764.
16. Petch J, Halford WK, Creedy DK, Gamble J. Couple relationship education at the transition to parenthood: a window of opportunity to reach high-risk couples. *Family Process.* 2012;51(4):498–511.

17. Alio AP, Mbah AK, Kornosky JL, Wathington D, Marty PJ, Salihu HM. Assessing the impact of paternal involvement on racial/ethnic disparities in infant mortality rates. *Journal of Community Health*. 2011;36(1):63–68.
18. Grych J, Oxtoby C, Lynn M. The effects of interparental conflict on children. In: Fine MA, Fincham FD, eds. *Handbook of Family Theories: A Content-Based Approach*. New York, NY: Routledge/Taylor & Francis; 2013:228–245.
19. Dishion TJ, Shaw D, Connell A, Gardner F, Weaver C, Wilson M. The family check-up with high-risk indigent families: preventing problem behavior by increasing parents' positive behavior support in early childhood. *Child Development*. 2008;79(5):1395–1414.
20. Cordova JV, Fleming C, Morrill MI, et al. The marriage checkup: a randomized controlled trial of annual relationship health checkups. *Journal of Consulting and Clinical Psychology*. 2014;82(4):592.
21. Substance Abuse and Mental Health Services Administration. Key substance use and mental health indicators in the United States: results from the 2015 National Survey on Drug Use and Health. Publication No. SMA 16-4984, NSDUH Series H-51. https://www.samhsa.gov/data/sites/default/files/NSDUH-FFR1-2015/ NSDUH-FFR1-2015/NSDUH-FFR1-2015.pdf. Published September 2016.
22. Park MJ, Mulye TP, Adams SH, Brindis CD, Irwin Jr CE. The health status of young adults in the United States. *Journal of Adolescent Health*. 2006;39(3):305–317.

INDEX

Figures are indicated by *f* and notes by *na*, *nb*, etc following the page numbers.

For the benefit of digital users, indexed terms that span two pages (e.g., 52–53) may, on occasion, appear on only one of those pages.

Charnov, Eric, 210–12
Cheadle, Jacob, 45–46, 47
Chicago, 8–10, 15–17
child abuse
    associated with substance abuse, 149
    Child Abuse Potential Inventory
        (CAPI), 282ne
    decreased risk for, 282
    generational, 270
    occurring in study participant
        families, 127–28na
    prevention programs, 259
    risk of among study
        participants, 220–21
    suffered by study participants, 74
child development
    attachment process and, 72
    benefits of two-parent families,
        103–9, 118–19
    consequences of intimate partner
        violence (IPV), 142–43
    co-parenting relationships
        and, 283–84
    costs of father absence, 109–18
    early attachment security and, 51
    effect of divorce, 319
    effect of unwed parenthood on, 44–45
    impact of incarcerated fathers, 169
    impact of paternal involvement, 355
    impact of positive father involvement,
        230, 239–41
    impact of substance abuse on
        families, 149
    Lamb–Pleck model of fatherhood
        and, 210–12
    maternal depression and, 291
    necessity of fathers for optimum,
        101–2, 118–19
    physical punishment, 127na, 128
    positive impact of married
        parents, 200–1
    problem of limited resources, 39
    skills needed to support, 313–14
    sociobiological factors of
        parenting, 48–56
    transmitting healthy
        development, 270
children of young parents, limited
    resources for, 39
Children's Bureau, 348, 355

child support
    ACF rules regarding, 304–6
    description of, 298
    enforcement issues, 306
    formal child support, 301–2
    "get tough" approach to
        enforcing, 301–2
    informal child support, 298–99,
        304–6, 334–35
    successful child support
        enforcement, 307
    wage garnishment for child
        support, 298–99
Child Support Enforcement (CSE) office,
    298, 302, 304–5
Choi, Jeong-Kyun, 111–12
Christensen, Andrew, 328
Church of the Latter Day Saints (LDS), 9,
    76–77, 90
Cleo (study participant)
    co-parenting without romantic
        connections, 64–65, 278–79
    impact of paternal relationships, 278
    original view of Darnel, 3–4
    perspective on partner's father-child
        bond, 253
    relationship with partner, 280–82
clinical guidelines, for assessing perinatal
    depression, 353
Clinton, Bill, 172–73, 195, 301–2
coded fathering behavior, 288–89
collaborative breeders, 366
communication. See interpersonal
    communication
communication activity, 12, 334
conflict. See interpersonal conflict
constructive parenting, 270–71
contraception. See sex and birth control
Cooper, Alexia, 178
co-parenting
    benefits of planned pregnancies, 83
    benefits of two-parent families, 103–9
    collaborative approach to, 249–51
    counseling programs for, 329, 345–
        46, 352, 353, 356–62, 363, 364,
        365, 367–68
    definition of positive
        co-parenting, 284–86
    effectiveness of support
        programs, 357

postpartum depression (PPD), 291, 353–55
signs of among nonresident fathers, 114
developmental pathway
  definition of, 30na
  identity development, 91
  increasing speed of development, 42–43
Diamond (study participant)
  psychological cost of unreliable father, 118
  relationship with partner, 115–16
  view of motherhood, 117–18
discrimination, 15–17
divorce
  divorce education, 318–22
  predivorce counseling, 319
  rates, 201
  views toward, 201
Doherty, William, 211–12
Doherty Relationship Institute, 211–12
Doing the Best I Can: Fatherhood in the Inner City (Edin and Nelson), 7nb, 8, 63
domestic violence. *See* intimate partner violence (IPV)
dominance. *See* interpersonal control
Donahue, Elisabeth, 323
dopamine, 261, 264
drug use. *See* substance abuse
Durose, Matthew, 178

Earned Income Tax Credit (EITC) program, 304–5
Ebony (study participant)
  approach of reducing drama and instability, 144–45
  participation in intimate partner violence (IPV), 135–42
economic costs
  of father absence, 110–12
  of young fatherhood, 38
Eddie (study participant)
  as a good enough father, 221–23
  paternal identity of, 249–50
Eddy, J. Mark, 182nc
Edin, Kathryn, 7nb, 8, 63, 205

educational opportunities
  diminished by young fatherhood, 37–38
  support for, 302
Elkins, David, 81
empathy, 258, 264, 286, 287, 327
employment and underemployment
  ACF's job program for fathers, 302–6
  aspirations of young fathers, 295–97
  connection between work and love, 295
  effect of economy on, 297
  effect on fathers, 100
  effect on marriageability of young men, 297–98
  example of Darnel, 296–97
  job programs, 297, 303–4
  loss of blue-collar jobs, 99–100
  Parents' Fair Share (PFS) program, 299–300
  Personal Responsibility and Work Opportunity Reconciliation Act (PRWORA), 301
  racial equity in, 97
  wage garnishment for child support, 298–99, 306
epidemiological approach, 125–26, 194–95, 348
Erikson, Erik, 91
evidence-based practice, 313ne, 315, 321, 353, 356–57, 362
evolutionary theory, Trivers' work on, 48–50
executive functioning, 239–40
extended family, 272–75

Fackrell, Tamara, 320
families
  benefits of two-parent families, 103–9, 118–19
  changes in structure of, 44–46
  declines in stability, 283
  hardship of single parenthood, 115–18
  lesbian, 104–5
  maintaining stability of, 195
  philosophy about maintaining stability of, 195
  stability and marriage, 201

predicting father engagement, 54–56
preventing early parenthood, 72
sense of purpose derived from
    fatherhood, 29
sociobiological roots of
    fatherhood, 48–56
underestimation of, 2–4, 66
father-to-child bond
  benefits derived by fathers, 237–38
  biological reinforcement of, 51–53
  characteristics of strong, 230–31
  connection to paternal
      identity, 251–54
  definition of, 229–30
  example of Jed, 234
  example of Robert, 231–33, 234–35
  example of Steve, 235–36
  example of Tyrone, 233–34, 237
  impact on child development, 51
  quality of, 230
  research addressing, 238–40
Feinberg, Mark, 285, 321
Feldman, Ruth, 40, 262–63
Fine, Lawrence, 84
Fleming, Alison, 258
Fog Zone study, 85–86
forgiveness
  components of, 190
  defined, 189–90
  as process, 189–91
Fox, Greer Litton, 248
Fragile Families Study, 44–45, 111–12,
    114, 169, 274–75, 283–84, 323
Freud, Sigmund, 295, 307
Furstenberg, Frank, 47, 206–7

Garfinkel, Irv, 323
gay and lesbian couples, 10nc, 104–5
Geller, Amanda, 169
gender identity, 208–10
gender roles
  breaking down rigid, 105
  constructed by social
      expectations, 103–4
  defined by fathers, 272
  father-inclusive prenatal care and, 352
  gender-role expectations, 258nb
  gender-role socialization, 249–50
  imposition of, 209–10
  increasing consciousness of, 208

influence on parent-chile
    interactions, 108ng
labor market and, 202–3
transformation of, 211, 212
Gettler, Lee, 257
Gilbreth, Joan, 105–6
Gingrich, Newt, 172–73
Glaze, Lauren, 168–69
Goldberg, Julia, 46–47
"good-enough" fathering
  biology of, 255–66
  changing roles and expectations of
      fathers, 208–18
  characteristics of good and bad
      fathers, 219, 229
  development of, 267–68, 271–72,
      275–76, 286
  Edin and Nelson's message
      on, 7–8nb, 63
  example of Darnel, 273
  example of Eddie, 221–23
  example of James, 219–21
  example of Tim, 335–36
  fatherhood as multifaceted, 223–24
  identifying good enough
      fathers, 219–26
  origin of phrase, 224–26
  paternal identity and, 242–54
  Pleck's views on, 101–2, 119
  redefining the meaning of family,
      199–207
"good-enough" mothering, 225
Gordon, Ilanit, 258nd, 262–63
Gordon, Kristina, 189–91
Gore, Al, 301
Gottman, John, 310–13
Gottman, Julie, 310–13
Grant, Bridget, 148, 152nd
Guttmacher Institute, 84

Habib, Cherine, 251
Hägglöf, Bruno, 238
Handbook of Forgiveness (Gordon,
    Baucom, and Snyder), 189–91
Hawkins, Alan, 246, 316–17, 320
health insurance. See insurance
high-quality parent-child interactions,
    106–9, 210–13, 216–17
Hoffman, Health, 181
Hoffman, Saul, 38, 39

Holleran, David, 176–77
Hollo, Ruth, 274–75
Homer, 365–66
hormones and brain function, 265–66.
    See also oxytocin (love hormone);
    testosterone (T)
Horn, Wade, 300–1, 302
hostility. *See* interpersonal hostility
Hrdy, Sarah, 104*nc*, 205–6, 366–67

identity development, 33, 40, 86–
    87, 91, 243–45. *See also* father
    involvement; gender identity
Important Father Hypothesis, 101–2
individuation, 86–87
infant attachment, 50–56
infant mortality, 348–51, 349*f*
infant-to-parent attachment, 230
infidelity
    effect on long-term relationships, 184
    effort required to overcome, 188–89
    emotional and practical aspects of, 183
    experience of Carlos, 184–88
    forgiveness following, 189–91
    frequency of, 183–84
    as interpersonal trauma, 189–91
    loss of trust due to, 187–88
    predictors of, 187
    sociobiological perspective, 187
informal child support, 298–99
institutional support systems
    importance of institutions in
        society, 347
    role of healthcare industry, 347
insurance
    coverage for including fathers in
        prenatal care, 355–56, 359–62
    effect of Affordable Care Act
        (ACA), 354
internalization, 72–73
interpersonal communication, 277–
    78, 279, 280–83, 286, 290–92,
    320–21, 325
interpersonal conflict, 330–31, 333
interpersonal control, 281, 283, 287, 288
interpersonal growth, 344–46
interpersonal hostility, 10*nc*, 263,
    280–83, 288, 332, 333–34
interpersonal warmth, 12*ne*, 217, 280–82,
    283–84, 286, 288–89, 333–34

intervention programs and services
    advantages of early
        interventions, 323–24
    advantages of treating parents
        together, 324–25, 338
    approach to interventions, 328–46
    benefits of additional for young
        men, 6–7
    Building Strong Families (BSF),
        310–14, 315
    co-parenting counseling programs
        and support, 323–46, 352–53,
        356–65, 367–68
    couples therapy, 333–44
    creating effective, 347–68
    desired by young fathers, 296–97
    divorce education, 318–22
    failure of ACFs approach, 302–6
    Family Foundations (FF) Program,
        321, 357
    father-inclusive prenatal
        care, 351–65
    frequency and depth of
        treatment, 324–25
    issues with program design, 312–14
    job training and job support, 178, 299,
        300, 302, 303–4, 305–6, 307
    Just Beginning program, 181–82
    new supports for new
        families, 344–46
    Parents' Fair Share (PFS) program,
        299–300
    predivorce counseling, 319
    premarital counseling, 313
    relationship education, 87, 310–18,
        321–22, 323–46
    relationship-focused interventions,
        320, 352
    successful child support
        enforcement, 307
    Supporting Father Involvement (SFI),
        313–14, 321
    Supporting Healthy Marriage Study
        (SHM), 314–15
    testing effectiveness of, 317–18
    Young Parenthood Program (YPP),
        329–46, 357
intimate partner violence (IPV)
    associated with substance abuse, 149
    bi-directional, 128*nb*

mixed quantitative and qualitative
approach, 12–13
partner inclusion, 1–2, 34–35
public health approach to, 125–26,
194–95, 348
Quality of Relationship Inventory
(QRI), 279–80
recommendations stemming from,
7–8, 17–18
recruitment strategy, 7–11, 88nd,
269na
scientific process, 317–18
Structural Analysis of Social Behavior
(SASB), 12ne, 288
types of fathers identified, 5, 13
Michelle (study participant)
background information, 77
experience with contraception, 81
perspective on partner's father-child
bond, 236
pressure from partner to abort
pregnancy, 89–90
relationship with parents, 78–79
relationship with partner, 77–78
midwives, 348–50, 351, 355–57
Miller, William R., 329
Mincy, Ron, 323
Minton, Carmelle, 248
Molly (study participant),
encouragement of partner to
reconnect with family, 42
Monica (study participant), experience
of infidelity, 184–88
mothers and motherhood
attunement with child, 224
bonding with child, 230, 261–62
and child development, 238–40
and father involvement, 103–9
physiological investment of,
48–50, 52, 54
play interactions and, 258nb,
262–63, 264
and poverty, 110–12
single mothers (see unwed
parenthood)
Mothers and Others (Hrdy), 104nc, 205–6
motivational interviewing
technique, 329
Moynihan, Daniel Patrick, 97–98, 100–1,
297, 303

Muller, Martin, 256
Murphy Brown (TV show), 300–1
Murray, Charles, 98–99, 100–1, 297–98

Naber, Fabiënne, 263
National Campaign to Prevent Teen and
Unplanned Pregnancy, 85
National Fatherhood Initiative, 300–1
Nelson, Timothy, 7–8nb, 63
neural activation. See brain activation
New Jim Crow: Mass Incarceration in
the Age of Colorblindness, The
(Alexander), 170–71
Nicole (study participant), experience
with criminal behavior, 163–64
Nolan, Patrick, 172–73
nonresident fathers. See also father
disengagement; father
involvement
covering costs of child-raising, 105–7
enrolling in support programs, 302
impact of poverty and, 111–12
paternal identity salience
among, 248
perceived father-child relationship
quality among, 108
quality versus quantity of paternal
involvement, 45–47
role of relationship with partner's
parents, 274–75
signs of depression among, 114
nurturance, 213, 217, 230, 250
Nurturing Dads (Marsiglio and
Roy), 213

Obama, Barack, 118
Obamacare, 354
Odysseus, 365–66
Oregon Social Learning Center, 270
oxytocin (love hormone), 51–52,
72, 261–65

package deal, 63
pair bonding, 255–56
parental ambivalence, 83
parental investment, 48–55
parental surrogates, 272–75
Parent and Children Together (PACT),
316ng
parent-infant attachment, 50–56

Quinton (study participant)
  apprehension about future and
    parenthood, 24–26
  confusion and disappointment
    over relationship with partner,
    28–29, 32–33
  factors leading to failure as a
    father, 33–34
  feelings of defeat over failure as a
    father, 29–30
  frozen by inadequacies, 113–14
  inability to use available
    resources, 31–32
  loss of hope and self-esteem, 37–38
  as overwhelmed and
    demoralized, 35–36
  psychological costs of being
    disengaged, 118

race and ethnicity
  impact of, 15–17
  inequality of law enforcement actions,
    30, 172–74, 174f
racism, 8–9, 15–17, 97, 173–76
Rankin, Jeanette, 348–50, 351
RealCare infant simulator, 259–61
recommendations
  basis for, 7–8
  broader definition of fatherhood, 102
  current government programs and
    policies, 307
  impact of life experiences on, 17–18
  including men in prenatal
    healthcare, 347–68
  parental mental health services, 161
  predicting father engagement, 54–56
  preventing early parenthood,
    42–43, 72
  promotion of positive father-child
    connections, 230
  on question of fathers as
    essential, 119
  relationship education, 87
Rector, Robert, 297–98
reflective listening, 331–32, 338
relational competence, 286–91
relationship education.
    See also co-parenting
  advantages of early
    interventions, 323–24

advantages of treating together,
    324–25, 338
  approach to interventions, 328–46
  example of Alberto and
    Marcella, 336–44
  example of Tim and Alyssa, 326–28,
    329, 330–34
  frequency and depth of
    treatment, 324–25
  integrating with sex education, 87
  new supports for new
    families, 344–46
  programs for, 310–18
  relationships as catalysts for
    change, 340
  shift from observing to supporting
    young fathers, 325
  success of, 321–22
  Young Parenthood Program
    (YPP), 329–30
relationship-focused interventions,
    320, 352
resilience, factors supporting, 35–36
Responsible Fatherhood
    Movement, 300–1
Returning Home study, 178–79
risk factors
  criminal behavior and
    incarceration, 162–82
  infidelity, 183–91
  intimate partner violence
    (IPV), 127–46
  overview of, 123–26
  as predictors of outcomes, 4
  substance abuse, 147–61
risk-taking behavior, reasons
    behind, 86–87
Robert (study participant)
  acceptance of lack of educational
    opportunities, 37–38
  adjustment to fatherhood, 234–35
  effect of partner's pregnancy
    on, 88–89
  on expectations of fathers, 214
  factors leading to success as a
    father, 33–35
  father-to-child bond of, 231–33
  fear of disappointing mother, 88
  love of being a father, 26–28
  offers security to partner, 73

Robert (study participant) (*cont.*)
optimism about future and
parenthood, 21–24
paternal identity of, 243, 248–49
relationship with father, 268–69
view of ideal father, 246–47
Role of the Father in Child Development,
The (Pleck), 101–2
role salience, and parental
identity, 247–48
role satisfaction, and parental
identity, 247–48
role strain, 32, 246, 250–51
Rollnick, Stephen, 329
Ron (study participant)
participation in intimate partner
violence (IPV), 131–34, 135
refusal to take responsibility for
behavior, 145–46, 162–63, 192
rough-and-tumble play, 51–52,
103–4, 118–19
Rox, Carol, 248
Roy, Kevin, 213, 230
Rush, Bobby, 354, 355
Ryan, Rebecca, 274–75

safe base, 50
Salt Lake City, 9–10, 15–17
Samantha (study participant),
participation in intimate partner
violence (IPV), 131–35
same-sex couples, 10*nc*
Sarah (study participant)
conceives second child, 26–27
insecure relationship with parents, 73
perspective on partner's father-child
bond, 232–33
protectiveness of partner, 21
relationship with parents, 73
relationship with partner, 34
support of partner, 28
scaffolding behaviors, and parenting, 107
semi-structured interviews, 11–12
sex and birth control
adolescent recklessness in
developmental context, 86–87
availability of birth control, 85
behavior–intention contradiction, 81
biological forces behind
procreation, 71–72

effect on family structure, 203–4
inconsistent use of, 81–83
options available once
pregnant, 87–88
planned pregnancies, 83–84
rates of unprotected sex, 84, 85
unintended pregnancies, 84
young people's attitudes toward,
80–81, 85–86
sexual opportunists, 48
Sexual Selection and the Descent of Man
(Trivers), 53–54
Shari (study participant)
focus on own adjustment to
parenthood, 31
frustration with partner's
selfishness, 34
lack of resilience, 35–36
relationship with partner,
25–26, 28–29
Shauffer, Carole, 181–82
Sheppard, Morris, 350, 351
Sheppard-Towner Act, 350–51
Siddiqui, Anver, 238
Silverstein, Louis, 53
Simon, Thomas, 130
single mothers. *See* unwed parenthood
Snow, John, 124–25, 193–95, 348, 355
Snyder, Douglas, 189–91
Snyder, Howard, 178
social learning theory, 55–56,
269–71, 333
Social Security Act, 350–51
social services, establishment of
field, 348
societal costs, 38
sociobiological factors
biological forces behind
procreation, 71–73
bonding process, 50–51
differences between individual
fathers, 52–54
father-child attachments, 51–52
gender-based biological parenting
differences, 52
hormones and brain function, 265–66
parental investment, 48–55
parenting behaviors of mothers versus
fathers, 49–50
paternal involvement, 48